高橋 和希

THIS IS MY SCHEDULE FOR THE WEEK:
- MONDAY IS MY DAY OFF.
- ON TUESDAY I LIE AROUND, BUT I THINK ABOUT THE UPCOMING DEVELOPMENTS IN THE STORY. I ALSO START ON THE STORYBOARDS.
- BY WEDNESDAY, THE STORYBOARDS ARE FINISHED AND I DISCUSS THEM WITH MY EDITOR. SOMETIMES I CHANGE THINGS BASED ON MY EDITOR'S SUGGESTIONS.
- ON THURSDAYS I START ON THE PENCILS, AND I WORK WITH MY ASSISTANTS.
- ON FRIDAY, SATURDAY AND SUNDAY I FINISH THE MANGA PAGES.

—KAZUKI TAKAHASHI, 2001

Artist/author Kazuki Takahashi first tried to break into the manga business in 1982, but success eluded him until **Yu-Gi-Oh!** debuted in the Japanese **Weekly Shonen Jump** magazine in 1996. **Yu-Gi-Oh!**'s themes of friendship and fighting, together with Takahashi's weird and wonderful art, soon became enormously successful, spawning a real-world card game, video games, and two anime series. A lifelong gamer, Takahashi enjoys Shogi (Japanese chess), Mahjong, card games, and tabletop RPGs, among other games.

YU-GI-OH!: DUELIST VOL. 19
The SHONEN JUMP Manga Edition

STORY AND ART BY
KAZUKI TAKAHASHI

Translation & English Adaptation/Joe Yamazaki
Touch-up Art & Lettering/Eric Erbes
Design/Andrea Rice
Editor/Jason Thompson

Editor in Chief, Books/Alvin Lu
Editor in Chief, Magazines/Marc Weidenbaum
VP of Publishing Licensing/Rika Inouye
VP of Sales/Gonzalo Ferreyra
Sr. VP of Marketing/Liza Coppola
Publisher/Hyoe Narita

In the original Japanese edition, YU-GI-OH!, YU-GI-OH!: DUELIST and YU-GI-OH!: MILLENNIUM WORLD are known collectively as YU-GI-OH!. The English YU-GI-OH!: DUELIST was originally volumes 8-31 of the Japanese YU-GI-OH!.

Printed in the U.S.A.

Published by VIZ Media, LLC
P.O. Box 77010
San Francisco, CA 94107

SHONEN JUMP Manga Edition
10 9 8 7 6 5 4 3 2
First printing, February 2007
Second printing, February 2008

www.viz.com

PARENTAL ADVISORY
YU-GI-OH!: DUELIST is rated T for Teen and is recommended for ages 13 and up. Contains fantasy violence.
ratings.viz.com

SHONEN JUMP MANGA

Vol. 19
DUEL WITH THE FUTURE

STORY AND ART BY
KAZUKI TAKAHASHI

THE STORY SO FAR...

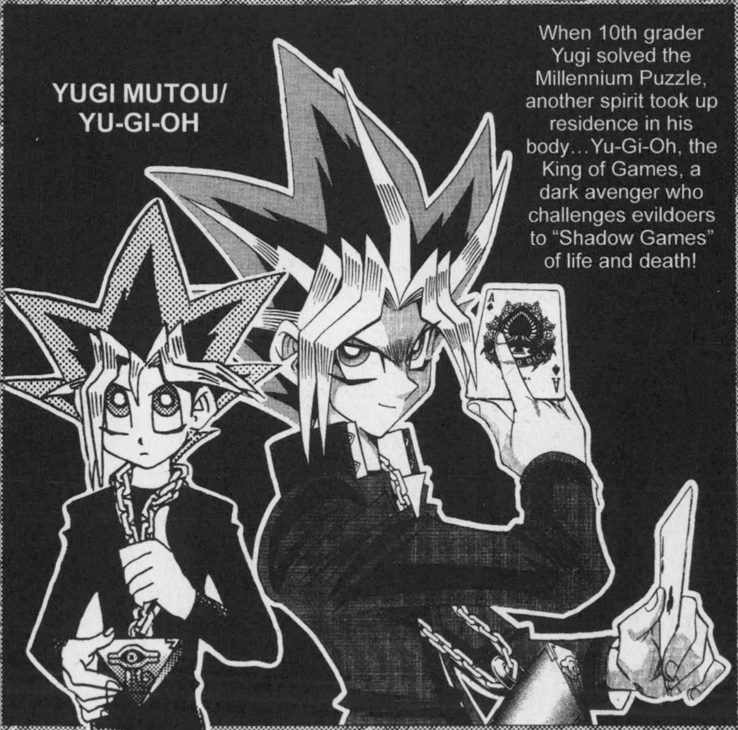
YUGI MUTOU/
YU-GI-OH
When 10th grader Yugi solved the Millennium Puzzle, another spirit took up residence in his body…Yu-Gi-Oh, the King of Games, a dark avenger who challenges evildoers to "Shadow Games" of life and death!

YUGI FACES DEADLY ENEMIES!

Using his gaming skills, Yugi fights ruthless adversaries like Maximillion Pegasus, multimillionaire creator of the collectible card game "Duel Monsters," and Ryo Bakura, whose friendly personality turns evil when he is possessed by the spirit of the Millennium Ring. But Yugi's greatest rival is Seto Kaiba, the world's second-greatest gamer—and the ruthless teenage president of Kaiba Corporation. At first, Kaiba and Yugi are bitter enemies, but after fighting against a common adversary—Pegasus—they come to respect one another. But for all his powers, there is one thing Yu-Gi-Oh cannot do: remember who he is and where he came from.

HIROTO HONDA
ANZU MAZAKI
KATSUYA JONOUCHI
MARIK
ISHIZU ISHTAR
SETO KAIBA

THE TABLET OF THE PHARAOH'S MEMORIES

Then one day, when an Egyptian museum exhibit comes to Japan, Yugi sees an ancient carving of himself as an Egyptian pharaoh! The curator of the exhibit, Ishizu Ishtar, explains that there are seven Millennium Items, which were made to fit into a stone tablet in a hidden shrine in Egypt. According to the legend, when the seven Items are brought together, the pharaoh will regain his memories of his past life.

THE EGYPTIAN GOD CARDS

But Ishizu has a message for Kaiba as well. Ishizu needs Kaiba's help to win back two of three Egyptian God Cards—the rarest cards on Earth—from the clutches of the "Rare Hunters," a criminal syndicate led by the evil Marik, Ishizu's brother. In order to draw out the thieves, Kaiba announces "Battle City," an enormous "Duel Monsters" tournament. As the tournament rages, Yugi, Kaiba and Marik struggle for possession of the God Cards, ending up with one apiece. At last, eight finalists make it to the second stage of the tournament aboard Kaiba's blimp. Yugi's friend Jonouchi somehow manages to survive the second stage, but their friend Mai is not so lucky. Marik defeats her easily, and prepares to blast her into oblivion... until Yugi and Jonouchi intervene!

Yu-Gi-Oh!
DUELiST

Vol. 19

CONTENTS

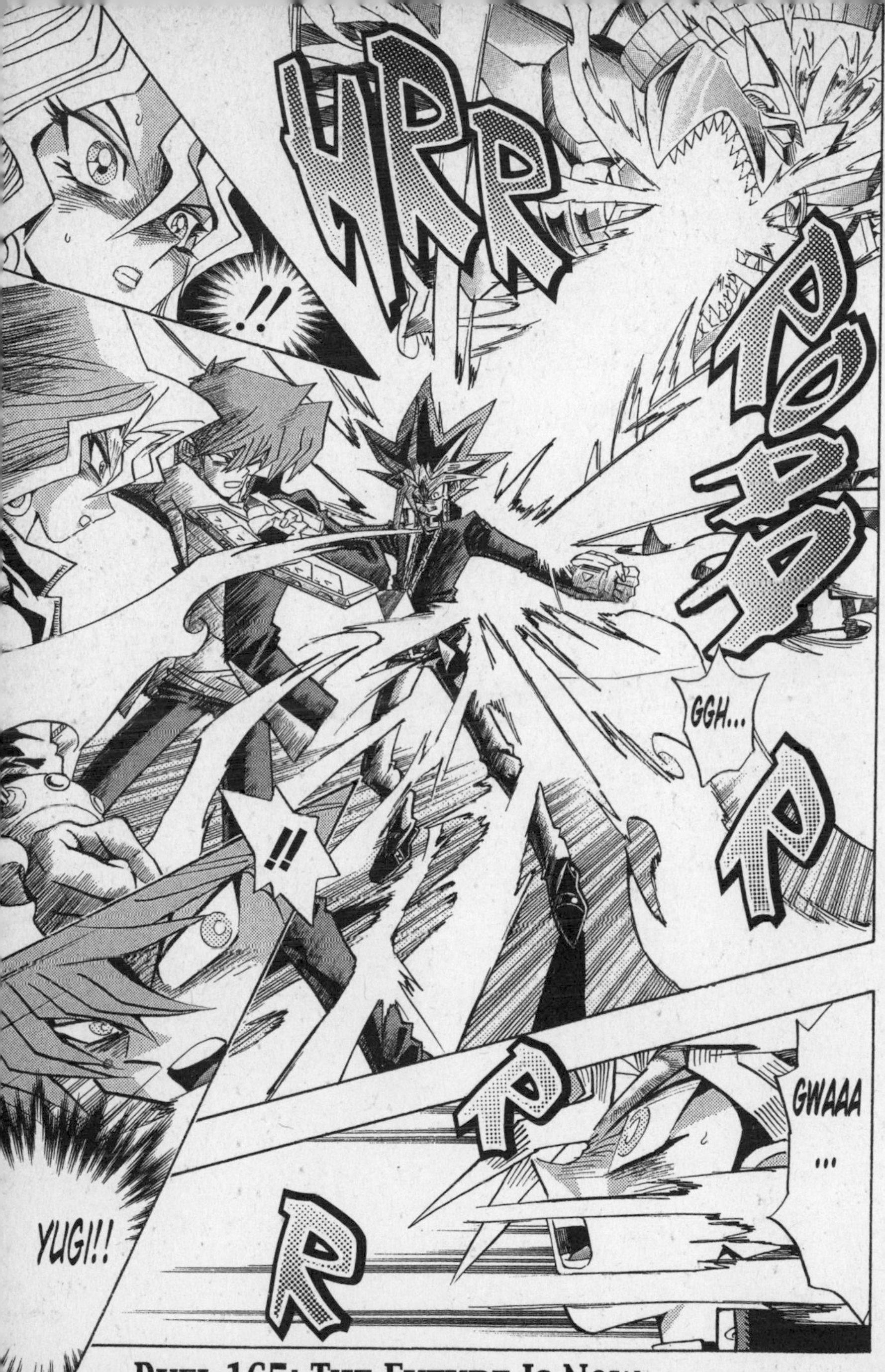
HRRR
ROAAR
!!
GGH...
!!
RR
GWAAA...
YUGI!!

Duel 165: The Future Is Now

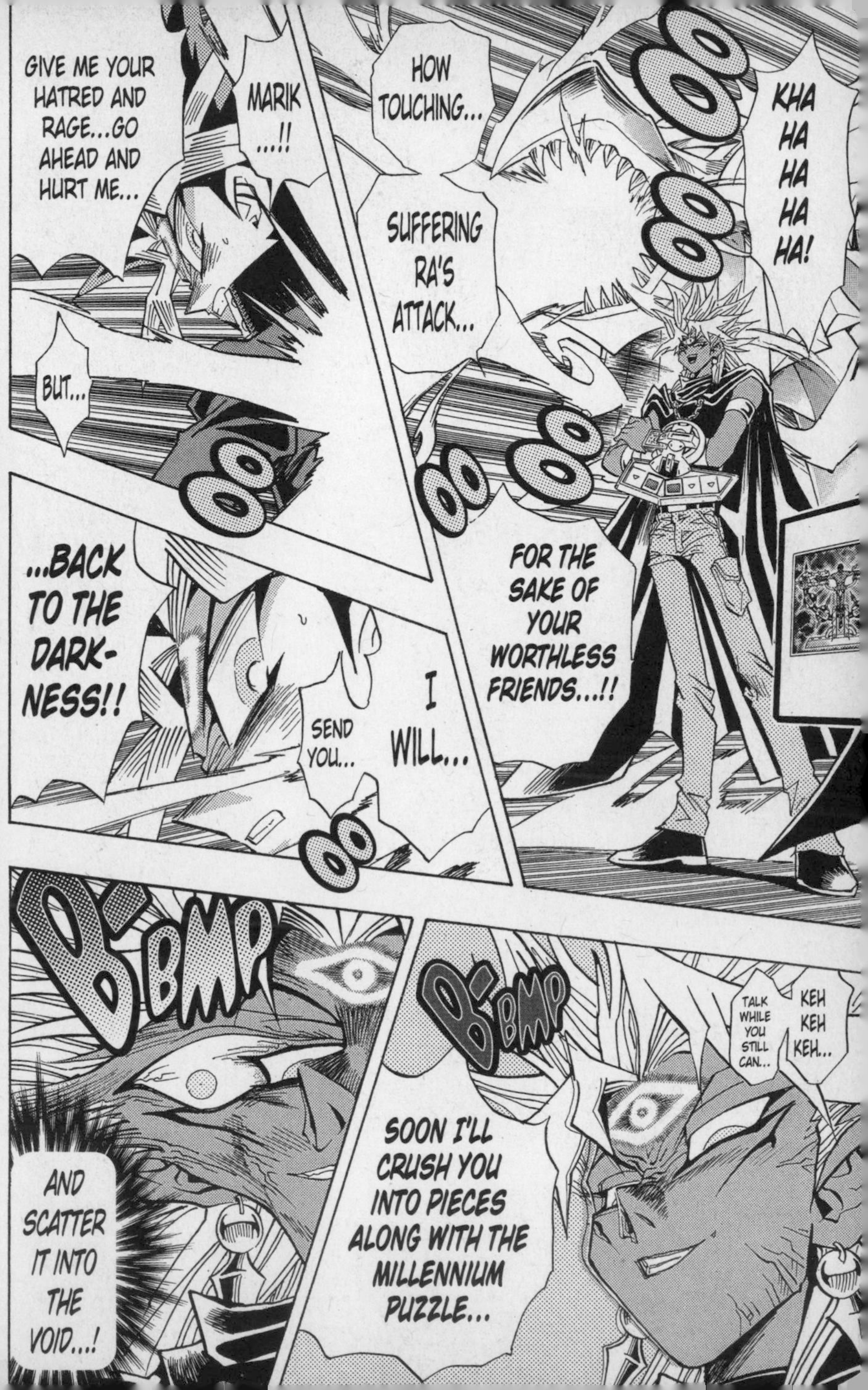
KHA HA HA HA HA!
OOOO
HOW TOUCHING...
SUFFERING RA'S ATTACK...
OOOO
FOR THE SAKE OF YOUR WORTHLESS FRIENDS...!!
GIVE ME YOUR HATRED AND RAGE...GO AHEAD AND HURT ME...
MARIK ...!!
BUT...
OOO
...BACK TO THE DARK-NESS!!
I WILL...
SEND YOU...
OO
KEH KEH KEH...
TALK WHILE YOU STILL CAN...
B'BMP
SOON I'LL CRUSH YOU INTO PIECES ALONG WITH THE MILLENNIUM PUZZLE...
B'BMP
AND SCATTER IT INTO THE VOID...!

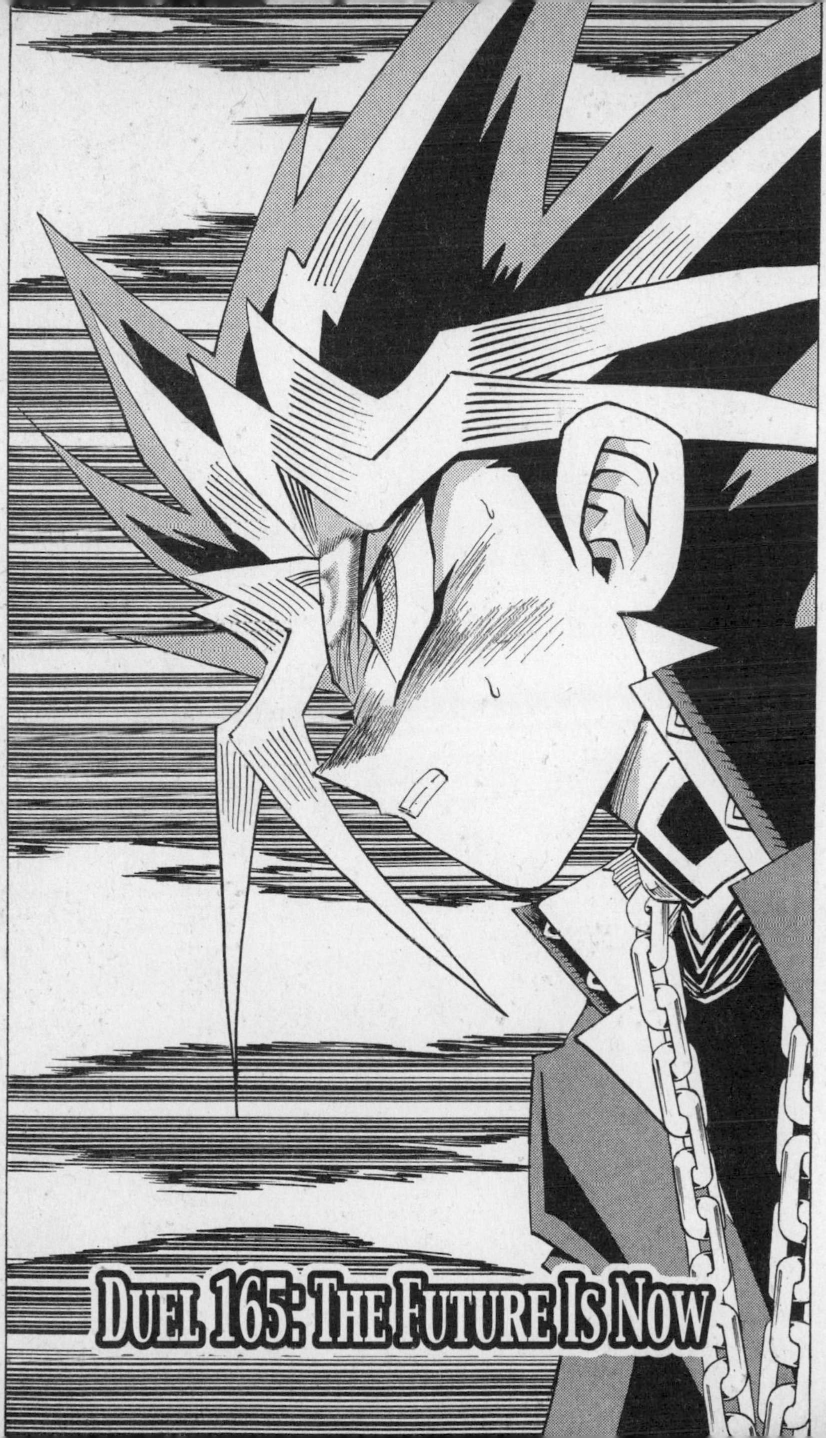
DUEL 165: THE FUTURE IS NOW

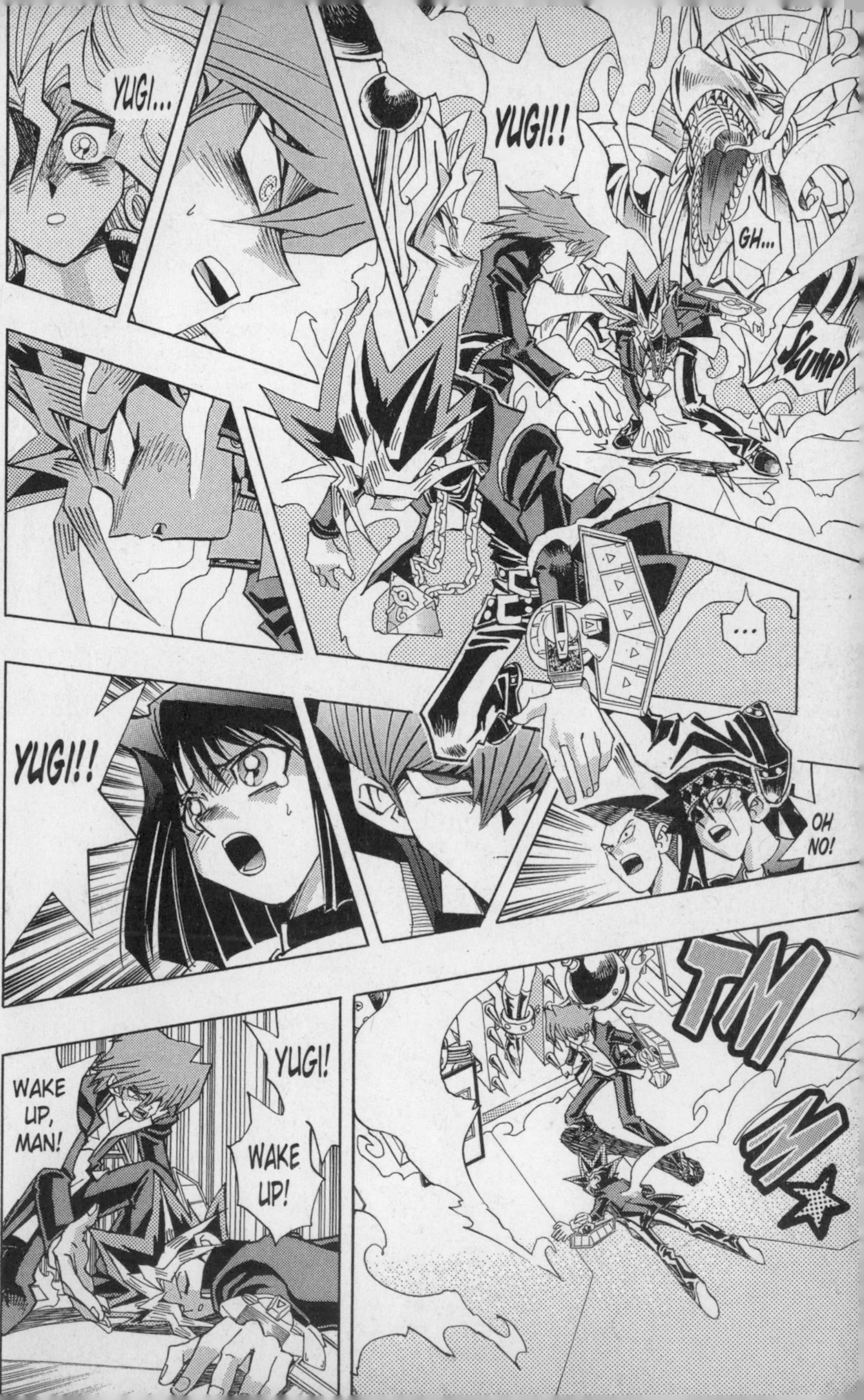
YUGI!!
GH...
SLUMP
YUGI...
...
OH NO!
YUGI!!
TM
M
YUGI!
WAKE UP!
WAKE UP, MAN!

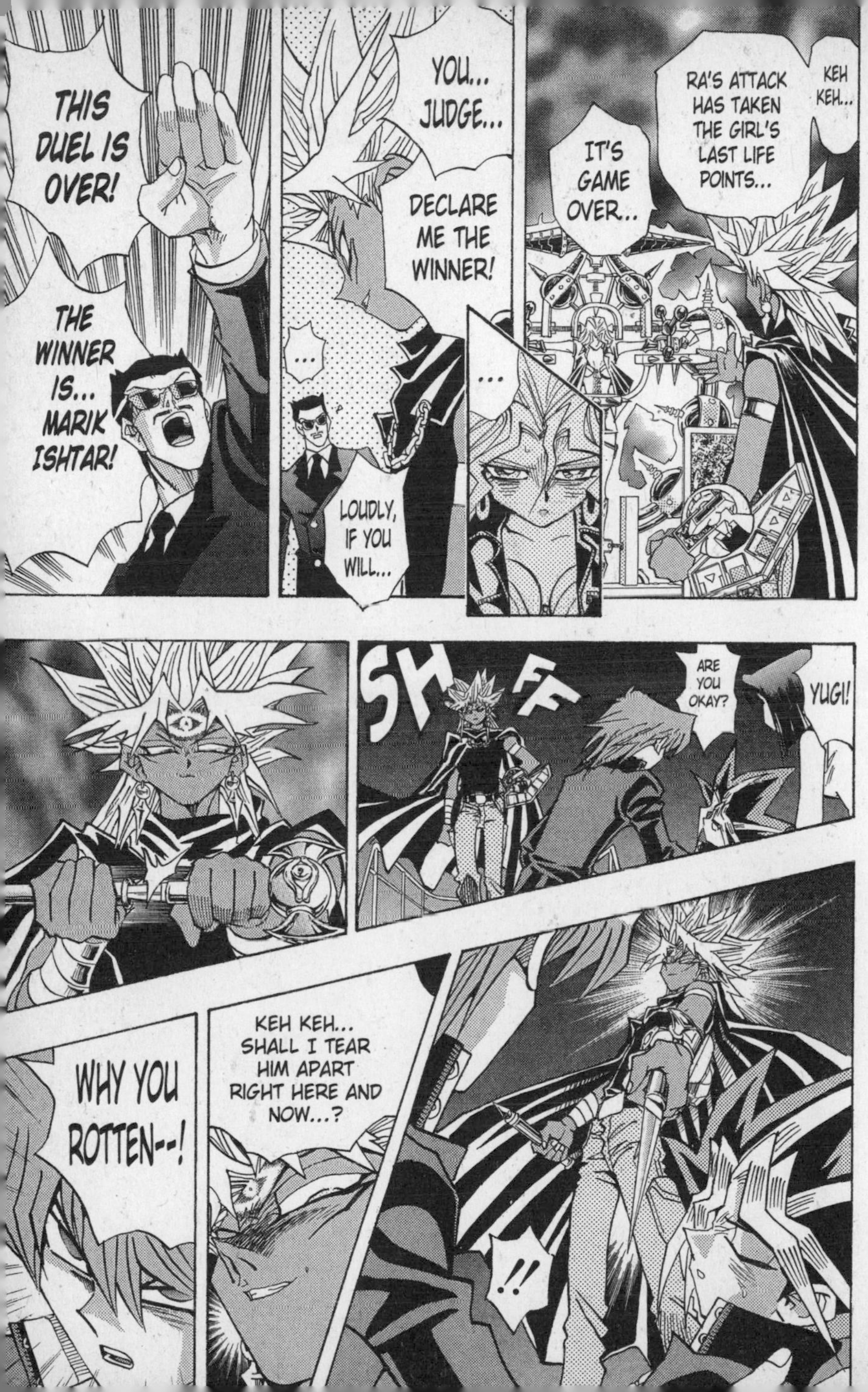
KEH KEH...
RA'S ATTACK HAS TAKEN THE GIRL'S LAST LIFE POINTS...
IT'S GAME OVER...
...
YOU... JUDGE...
DECLARE ME THE WINNER!
...
LOUDLY, IF YOU WILL...
THIS DUEL IS OVER!
THE WINNER IS... MARIK ISHTAR!
YUGI!
ARE YOU OKAY?
SH FF
!!
KEH KEH... SHALL I TEAR HIM APART RIGHT HERE AND NOW...?
WHY YOU ROTTEN--!

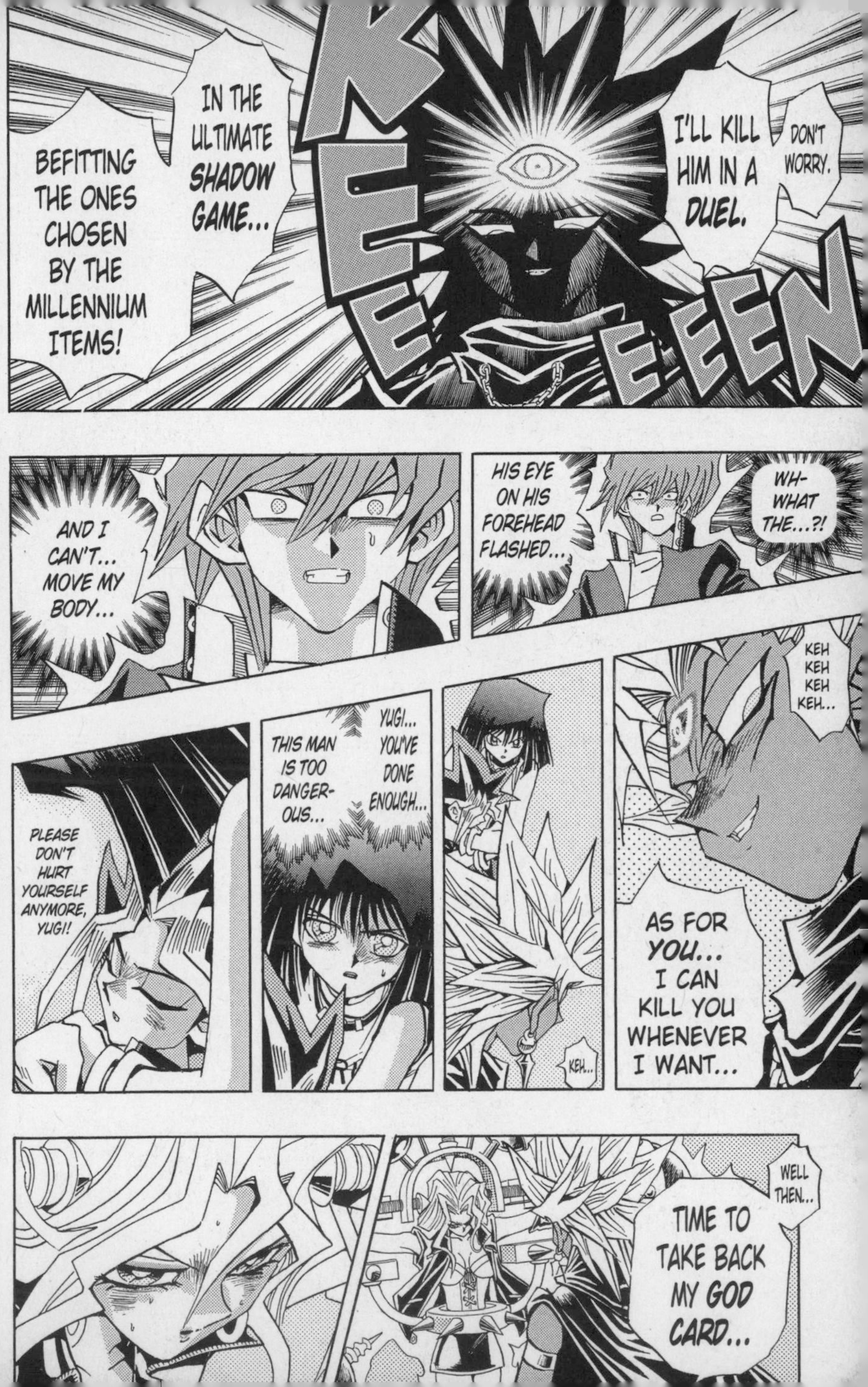
DON'T WORRY.
I'LL KILL HIM IN A DUEL.
KEEEEEN
IN THE ULTIMATE SHADOW GAME...
BEFITTING THE ONES CHOSEN BY THE MILLENNIUM ITEMS!
WH-WHAT THE...?!
HIS EYE ON HIS FOREHEAD FLASHED...
AND I CAN'T... MOVE MY BODY...
KEH KEH KEH KEH...
AS FOR YOU... I CAN KILL YOU WHENEVER I WANT...
KEH...
YUGI... YOU'VE DONE ENOUGH...
THIS MAN IS TOO DANGER-OUS...
PLEASE DON'T HURT YOURSELF ANYMORE, YUGI!
WELL THEN...
TIME TO TAKE BACK MY GOD CARD...

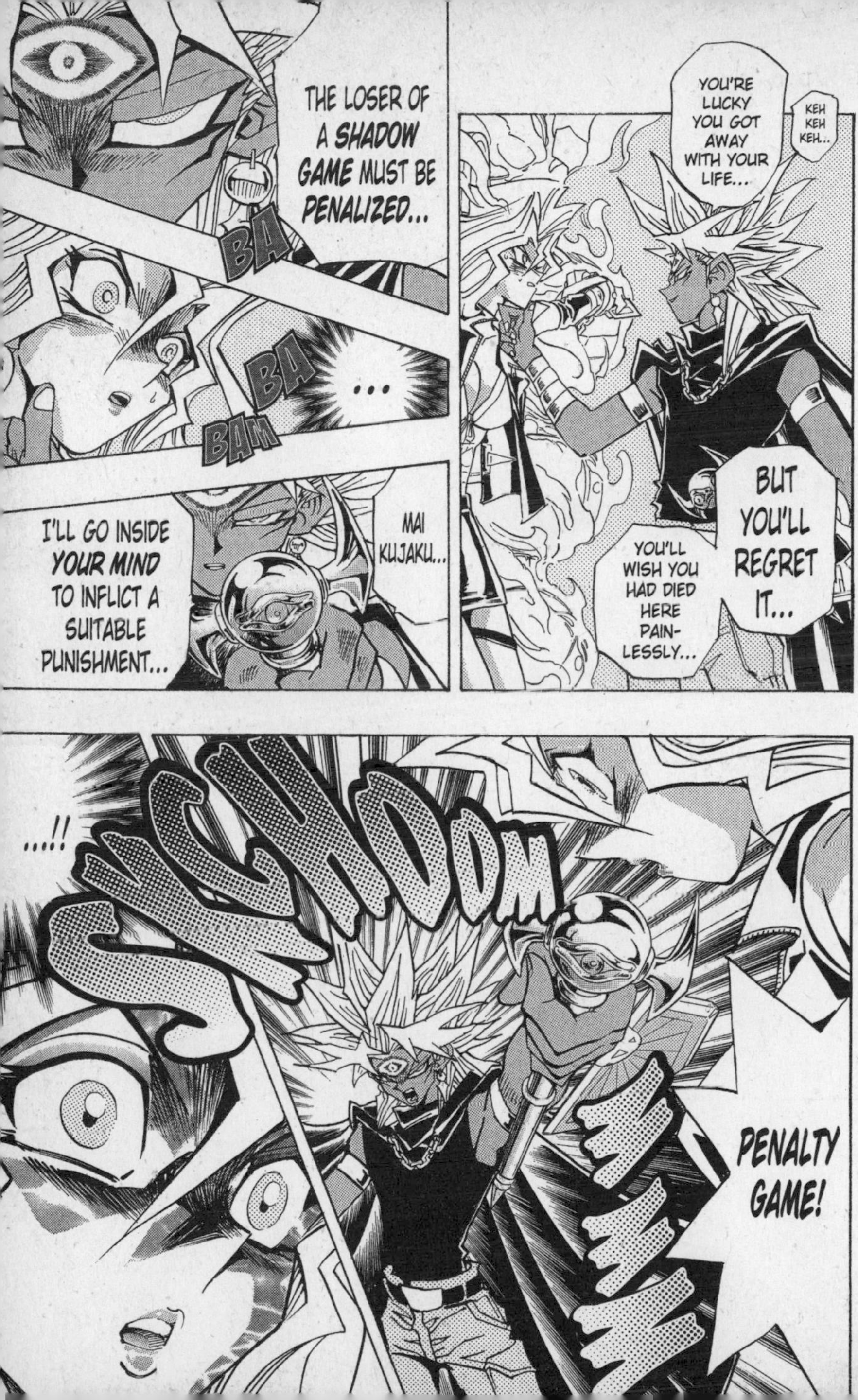
YOU'RE LUCKY YOU GOT AWAY WITH YOUR LIFE...
KEH KEH KEH...
BUT YOU'LL REGRET IT...
YOU'LL WISH YOU HAD DIED HERE PAIN-LESSLY...
THE LOSER OF A SHADOW GAME MUST BE PENALIZED...
BA
BA
BAM
...
MAI KUJAKU...
I'LL GO INSIDE YOUR MIND TO INFLICT A SUITABLE PUNISHMENT...
...!!
SHOOM
PENALTY GAME!

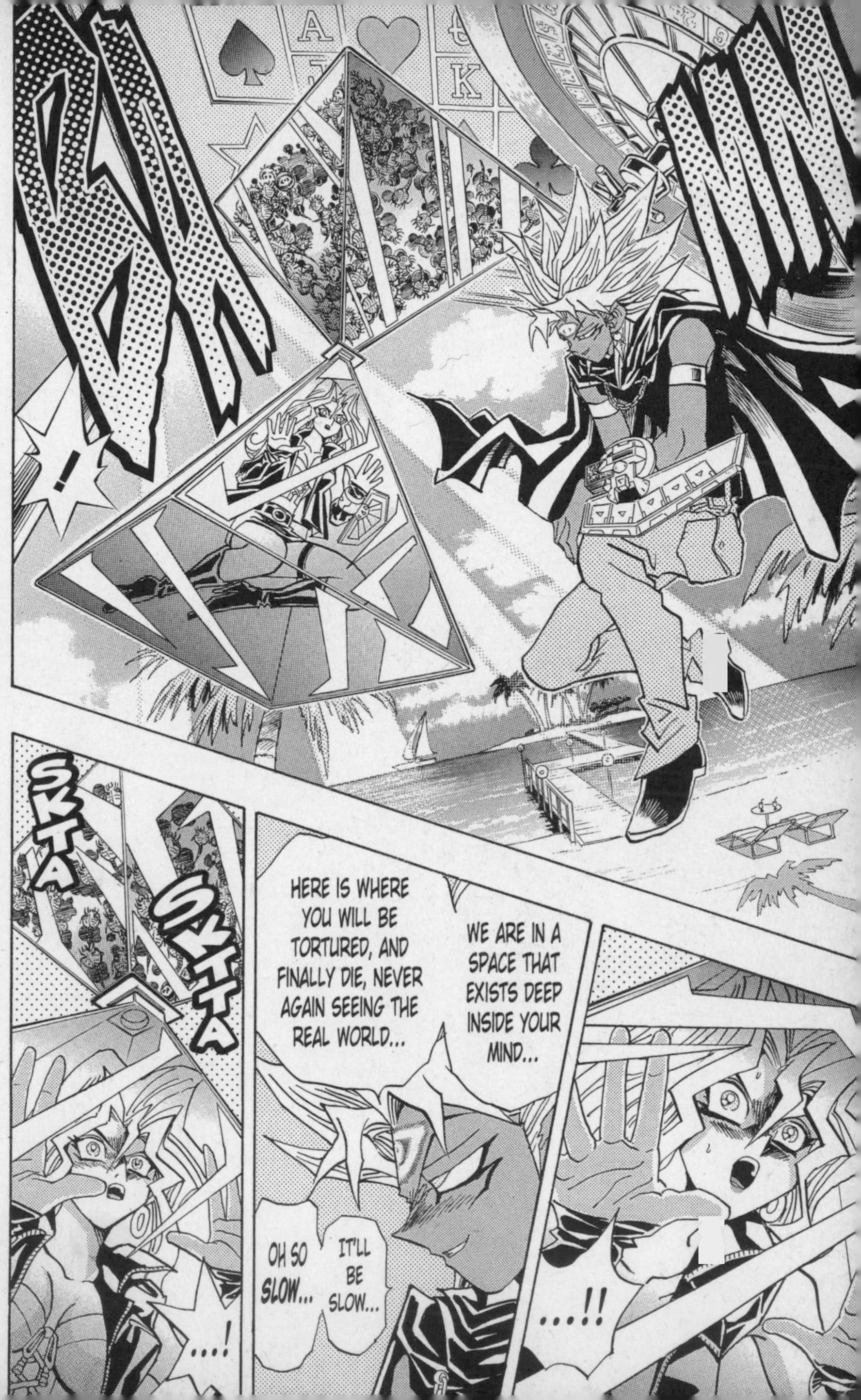
!
...!!
WE ARE IN A SPACE THAT EXISTS DEEP INSIDE YOUR MIND...
HERE IS WHERE YOU WILL BE TORTURED, AND FINALLY DIE, NEVER AGAIN SEEING THE REAL WORLD...
IT'LL BE SLOW...
OH SO SLOW...
SKTTA
SKTA
...!

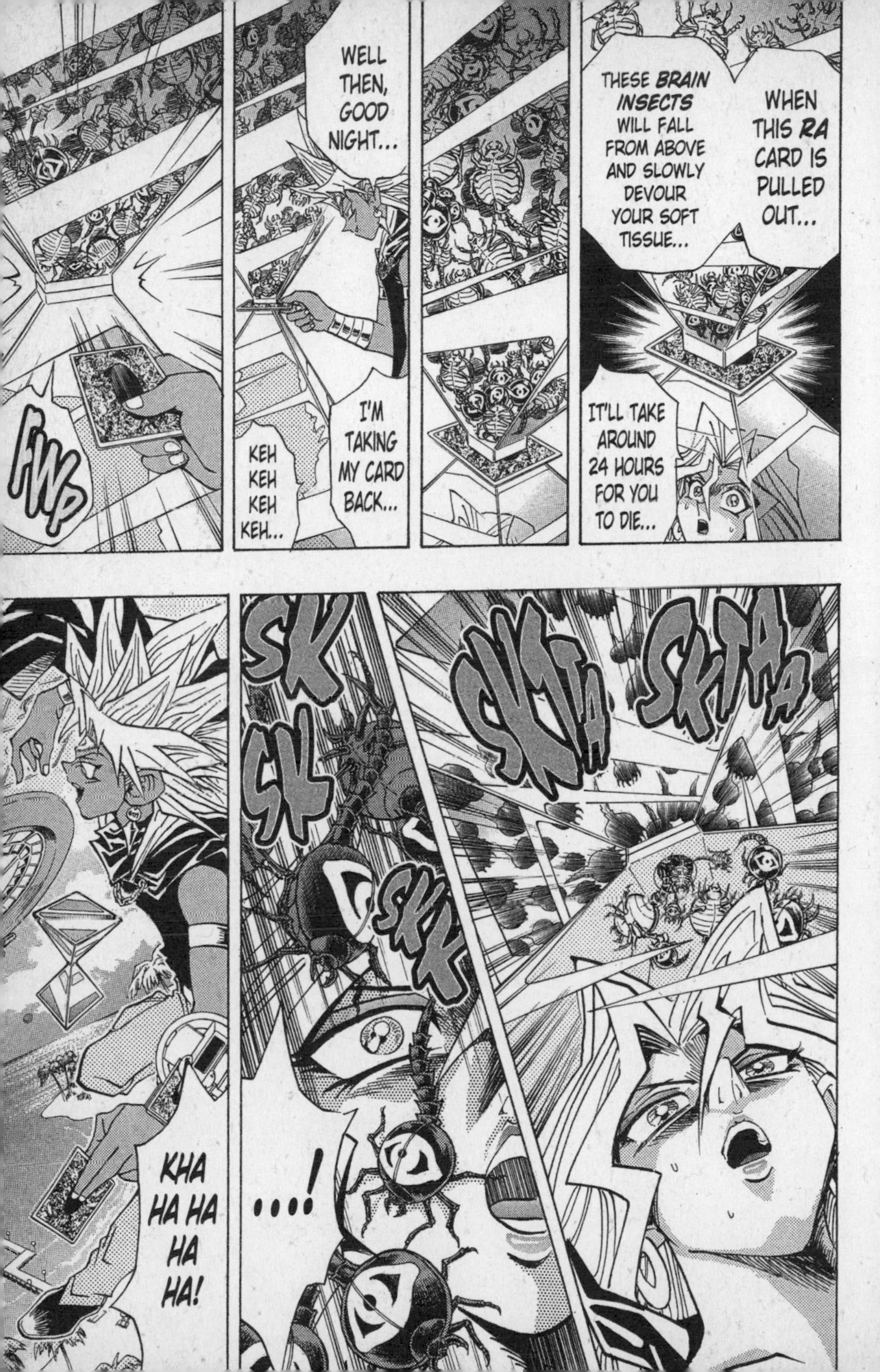
WHEN THIS ***RA*** CARD IS PULLED OUT...
THESE ***BRAIN INSECTS*** WILL FALL FROM ABOVE AND SLOWLY DEVOUR YOUR SOFT TISSUE...
IT'LL TAKE AROUND 24 HOURS FOR YOU TO DIE...
WELL THEN, GOOD NIGHT...
I'M TAKING MY CARD BACK...
KEH KEH KEH KEH...
FWP
SKTA
SKTA
SK
SK
SKK
....!
KHA HA HA HA HA!

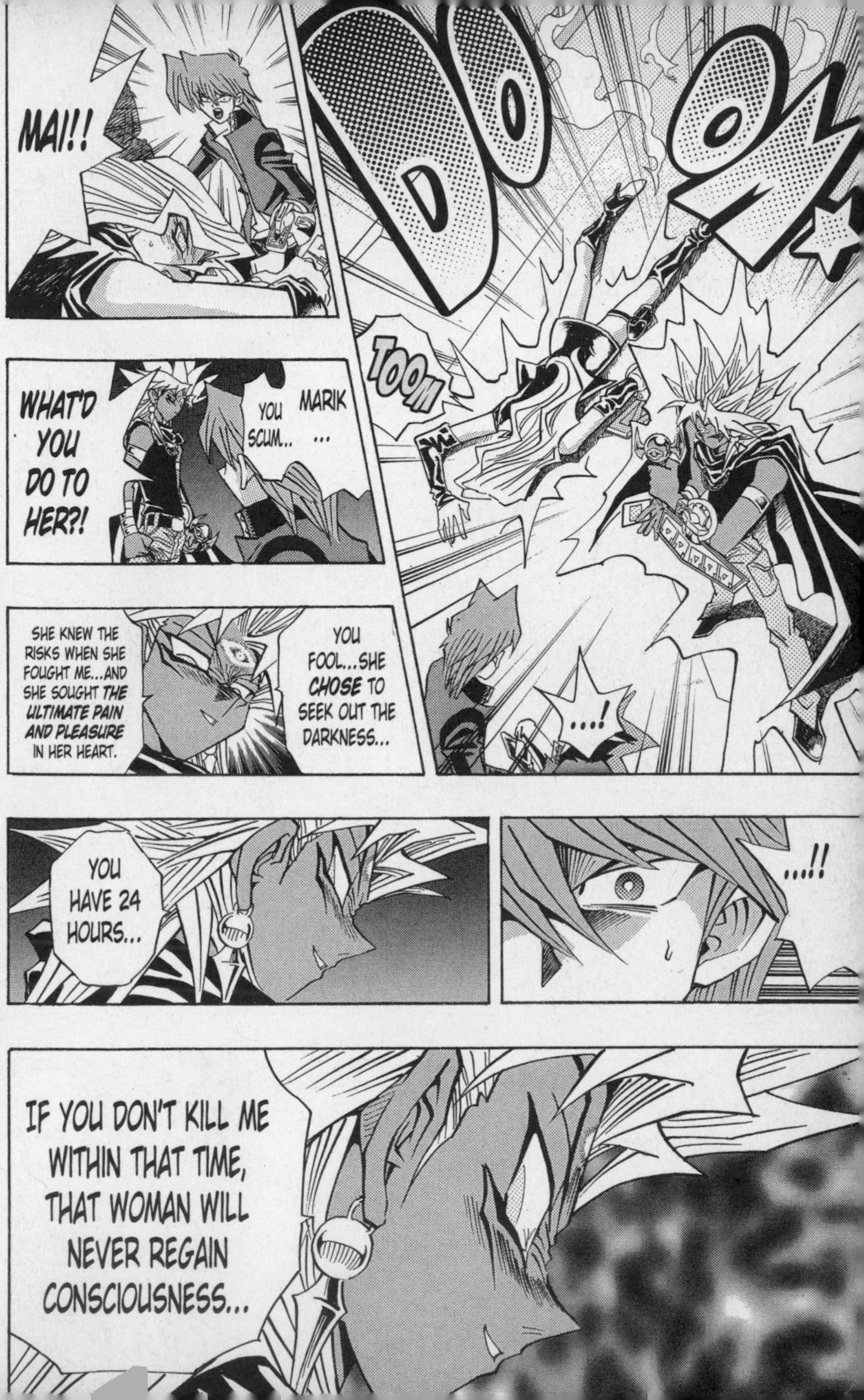
DOOOM
TOOM
...!
MAI!!
MARIK ...
YOU SCUM...
WHAT'D YOU DO TO HER?!
YOU FOOL...SHE CHOSE TO SEEK OUT THE DARKNESS...
SHE KNEW THE RISKS WHEN SHE FOUGHT ME...AND SHE SOUGHT THE ULTIMATE PAIN AND PLEASURE IN HER HEART.
...!!
YOU HAVE 24 HOURS...
IF YOU DON'T KILL ME WITHIN THAT TIME, THAT WOMAN WILL NEVER REGAIN CONSCIOUSNESS...

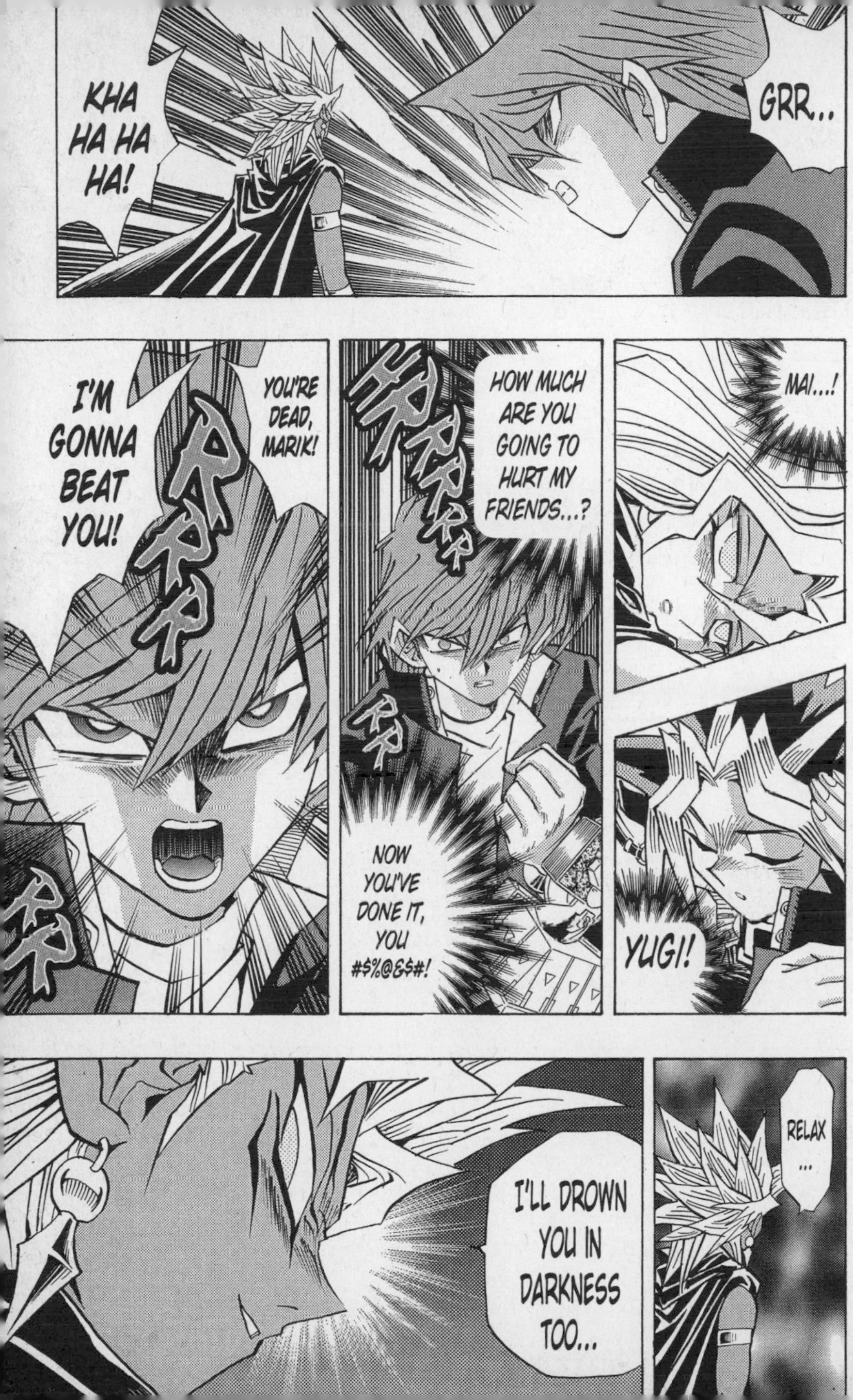
GRR...
KHA HA HA HA!
MAI...!
YUGI!
HRRRRR
HOW MUCH ARE YOU GOING TO HURT MY FRIENDS...?
RR
NOW YOU'VE DONE IT, YOU #$%@&$#!
YOU'RE DEAD, MARIK!
I'M GONNA BEAT YOU!
RRRR
RR
RELAX ...
I'LL DROWN YOU IN DARKNESS TOO...

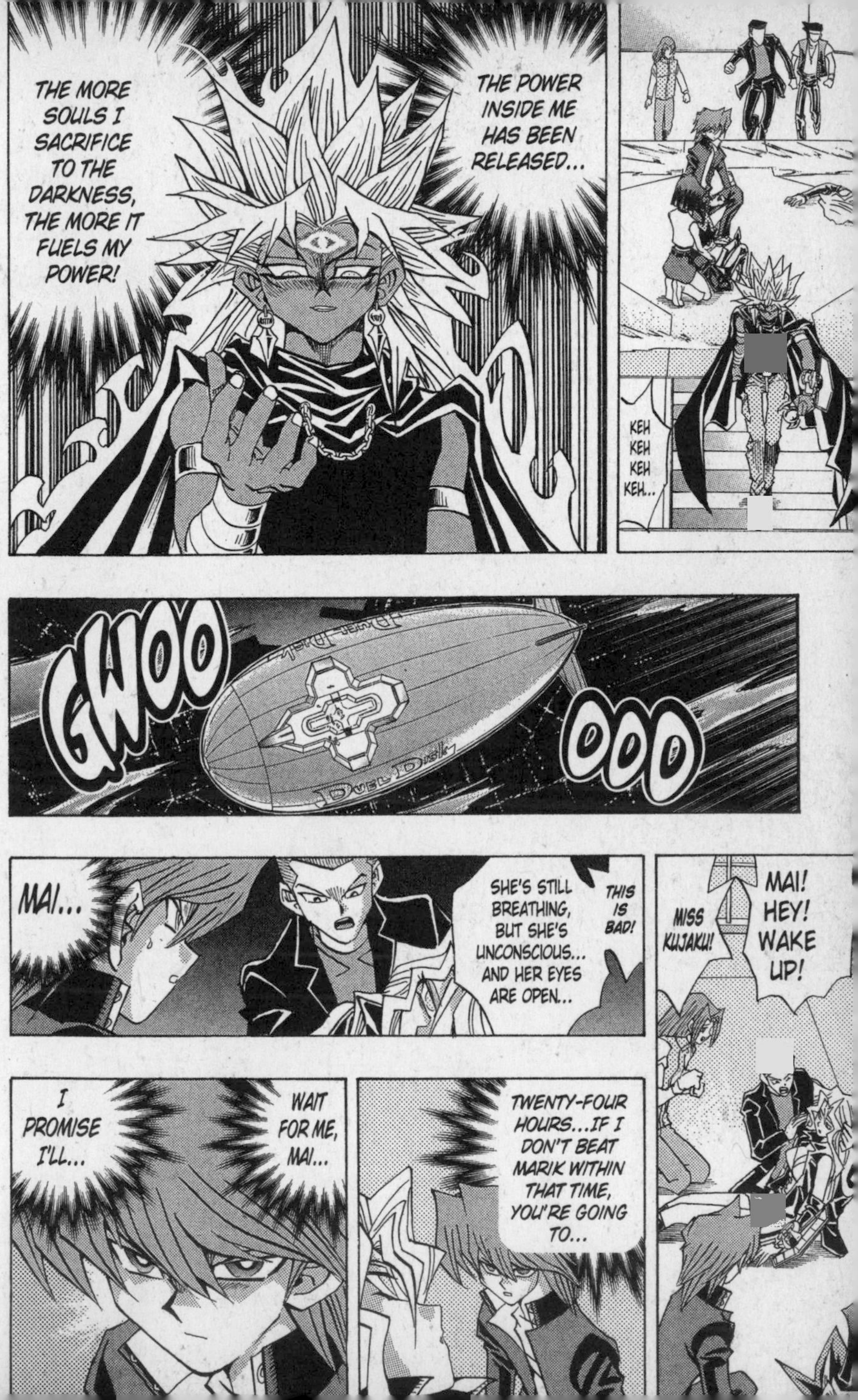
KEH KEH KEH KEH...
THE POWER INSIDE ME HAS BEEN RELEASED...
THE MORE SOULS I SACRIFICE TO THE DARKNESS, THE MORE IT FUELS MY POWER!
GWOOOOO
MAI! HEY! WAKE UP!
MISS KUJAKU!
THIS IS BAD!
SHE'S STILL BREATHING, BUT SHE'S UNCONSCIOUS... AND HER EYES ARE OPEN...
MAI...
TWENTY-FOUR HOURS...IF I DON'T BEAT MARIK WITHIN THAT TIME, YOU'RE GOING TO...
WAIT FOR ME, MAI...
I PROMISE I'LL...

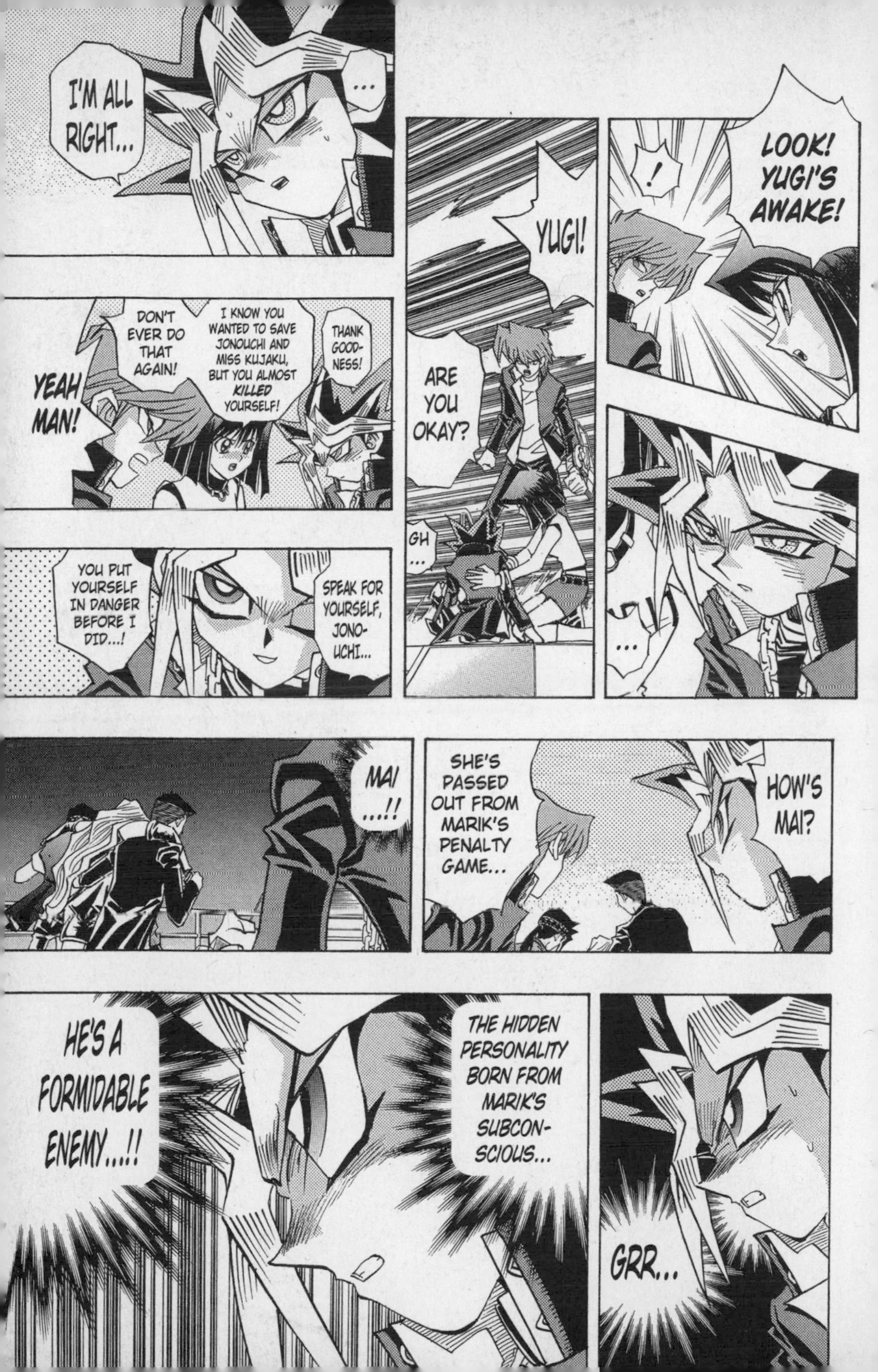
LOOK! YUGI'S AWAKE!
!
YUGI!
ARE YOU OKAY?
GH...
...
I'M ALL RIGHT...
...
THANK GOODNESS!
I KNOW YOU WANTED TO SAVE JONOUCHI AND MISS KUJAKU, BUT YOU ALMOST KILLED YOURSELF!
DON'T EVER DO THAT AGAIN!
YEAH MAN!
SPEAK FOR YOURSELF, JONO-UCHI...
YOU PUT YOURSELF IN DANGER BEFORE I DID...!
HOW'S MAI?
SHE'S PASSED OUT FROM MARIK'S PENALTY GAME...
MAI ...!!
GRR...
THE HIDDEN PERSONALITY BORN FROM MARIK'S SUBCON-SCIOUS...
HE'S A FORMIDABLE ENEMY...!!

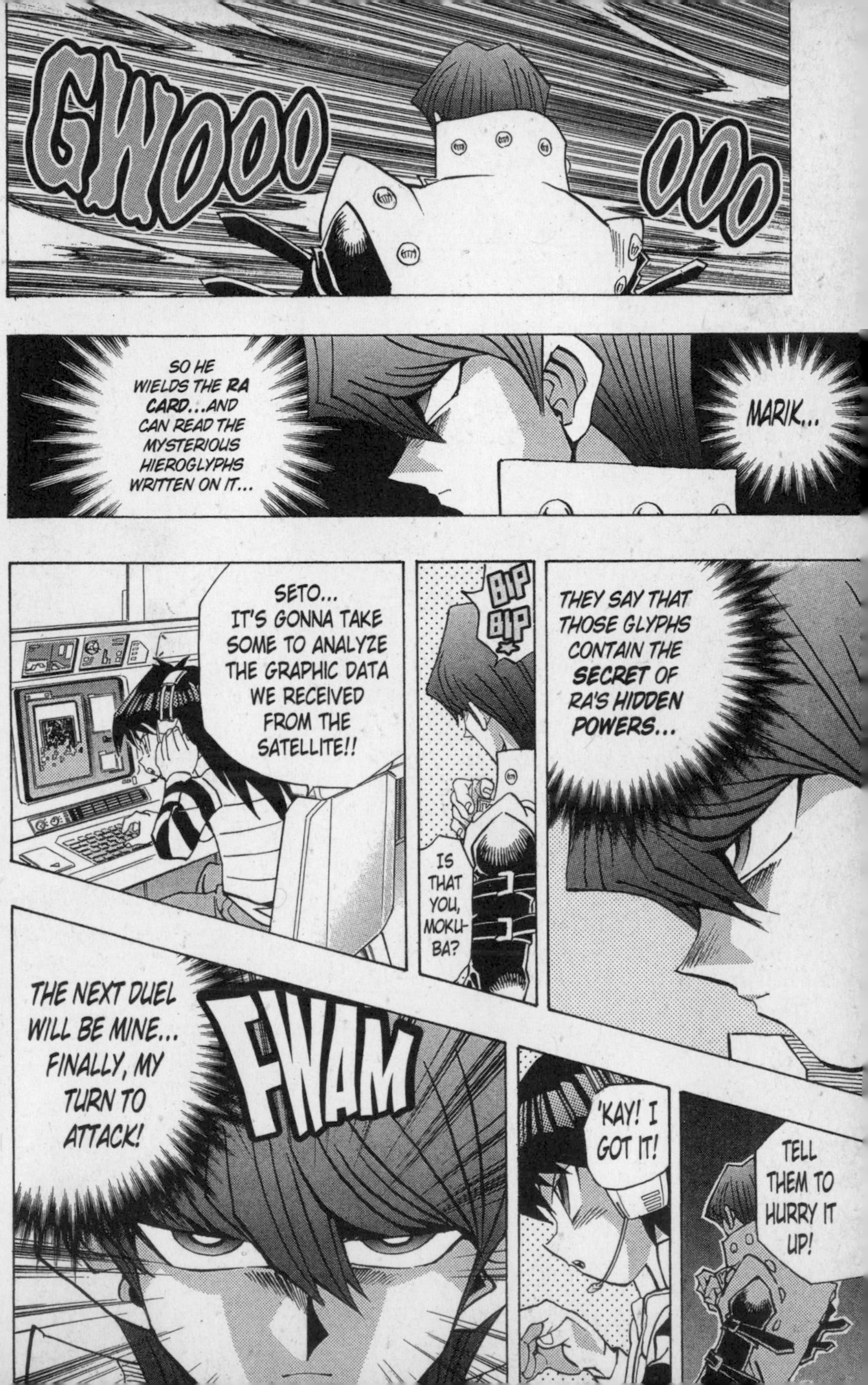
GWOOOOOO
MARIK...
SO HE WIELDS THE RA CARD...AND CAN READ THE MYSTERIOUS HIEROGLYPHS WRITTEN ON IT...
THEY SAY THAT THOSE GLYPHS CONTAIN THE SECRET OF RA'S HIDDEN POWERS...
BIP BIP
IS THAT YOU, MOKU-BA?
SETO... IT'S GONNA TAKE SOME TO ANALYZE THE GRAPHIC DATA WE RECEIVED FROM THE SATELLITE!!
TELL THEM TO HURRY IT UP!
'KAY! I GOT IT!
FWAM
THE NEXT DUEL WILL BE MINE... FINALLY, MY TURN TO ATTACK!

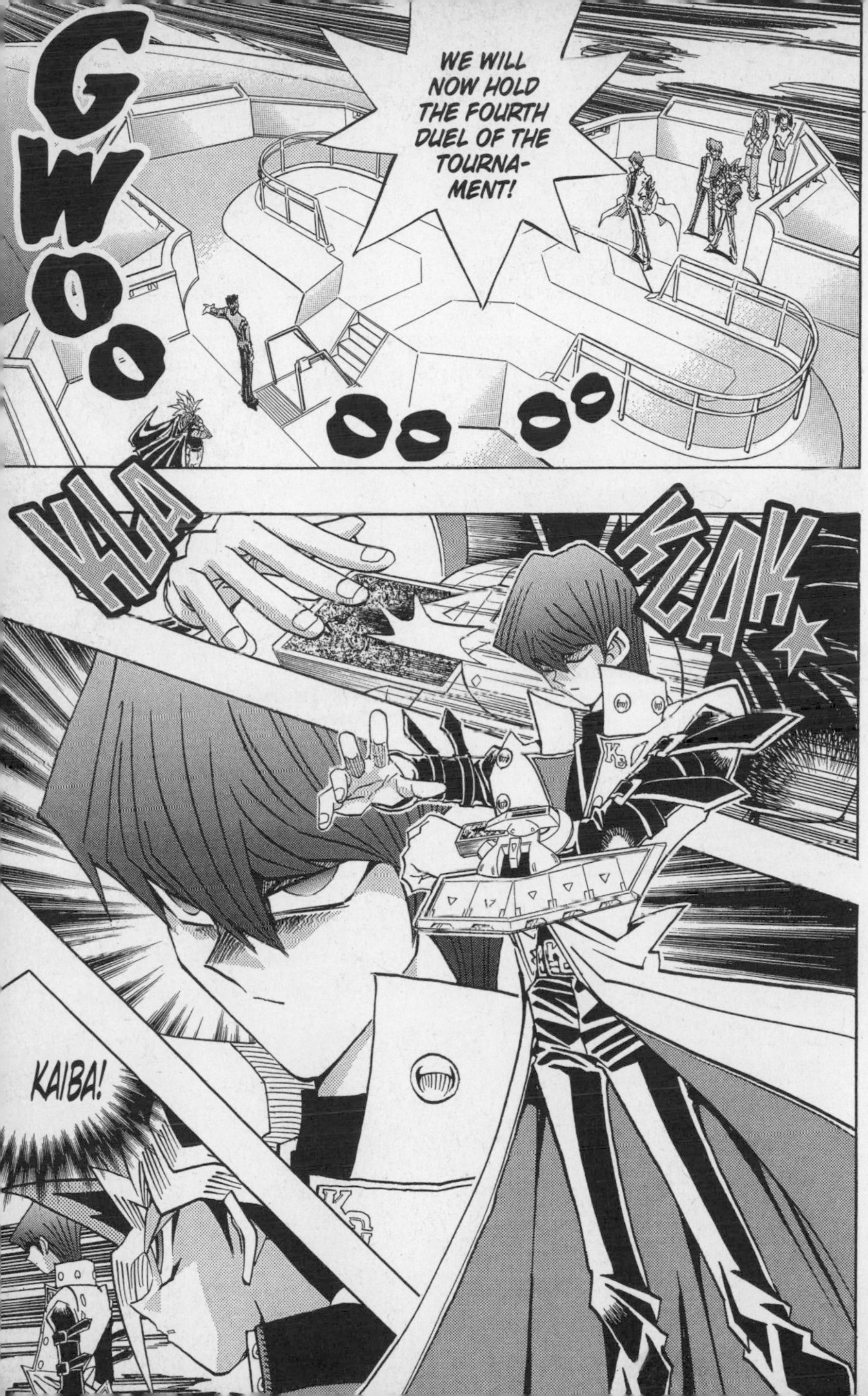
WE WILL NOW HOLD THE FOURTH DUEL OF THE TOURNA-MENT!
GWOOOOOOO
KLAK
KLA
KAIBA!

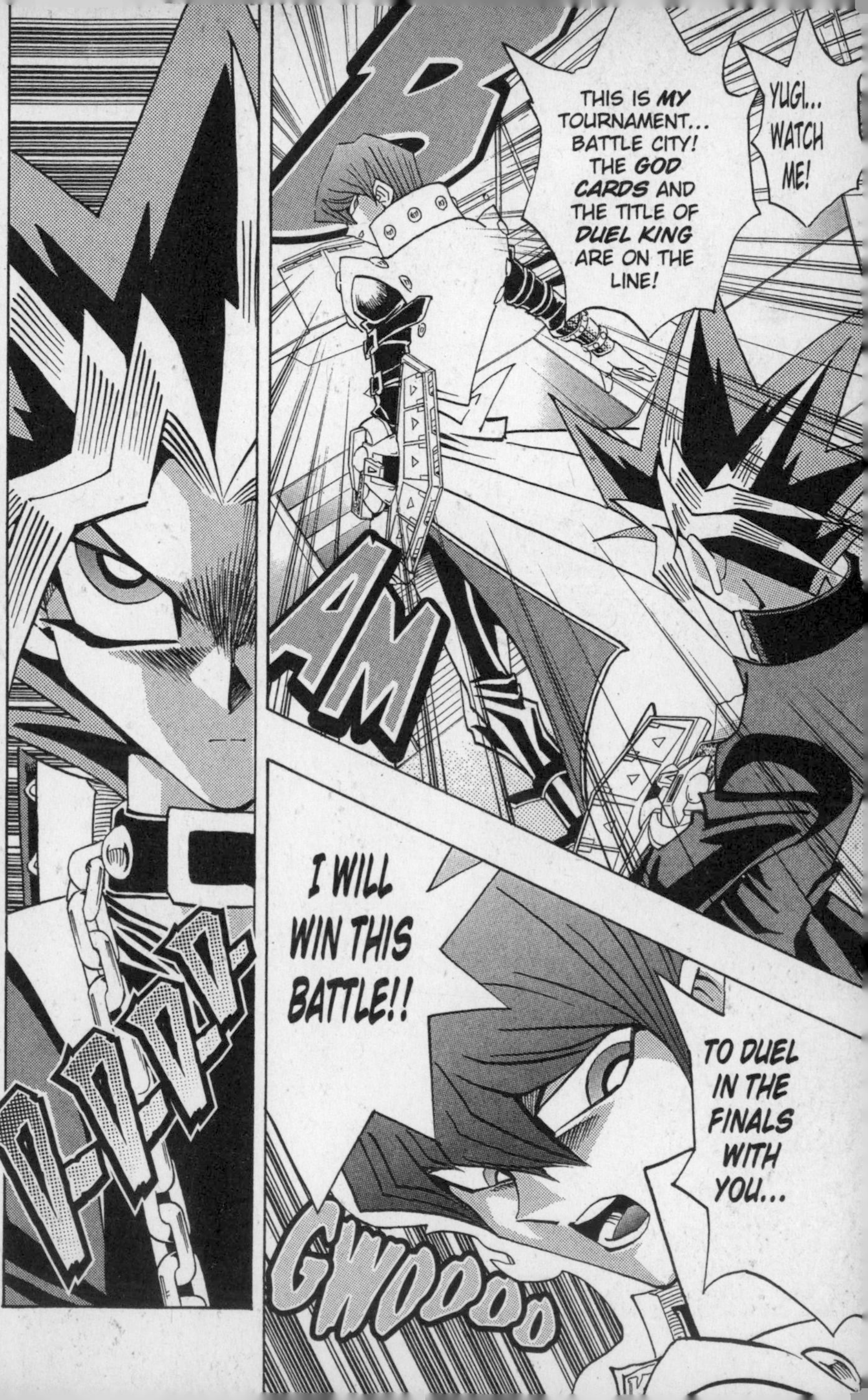
YUGI... WATCH ME!
THIS IS MY TOURNAMENT... BATTLE CITY! THE GOD CARDS AND THE TITLE OF DUEL KING ARE ON THE LINE!
AM
TO DUEL IN THE FINALS WITH YOU...
I WILL WIN THIS BATTLE!!
GWOOOO
D-D-D-D

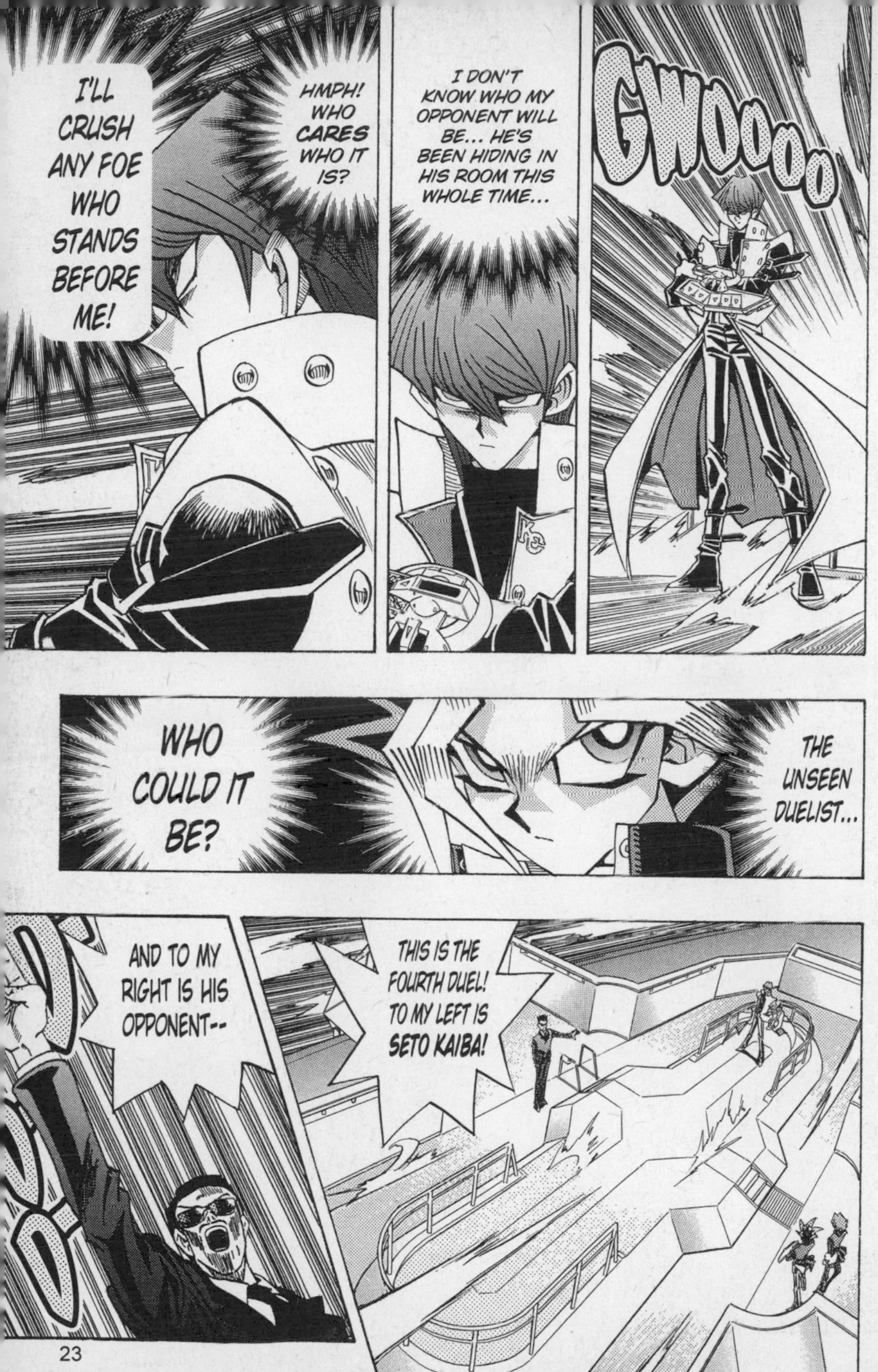
GWOOOOO
I DON'T KNOW WHO MY OPPONENT WILL BE... HE'S BEEN HIDING IN HIS ROOM THIS WHOLE TIME...
HMPH! WHO CARES WHO IT IS?
I'LL CRUSH ANY FOE WHO STANDS BEFORE ME!
THE UNSEEN DUELIST...
WHO COULD IT BE?
THIS IS THE FOURTH DUEL! TO MY LEFT IS SETO KAIBA!
AND TO MY RIGHT IS HIS OPPONENT--

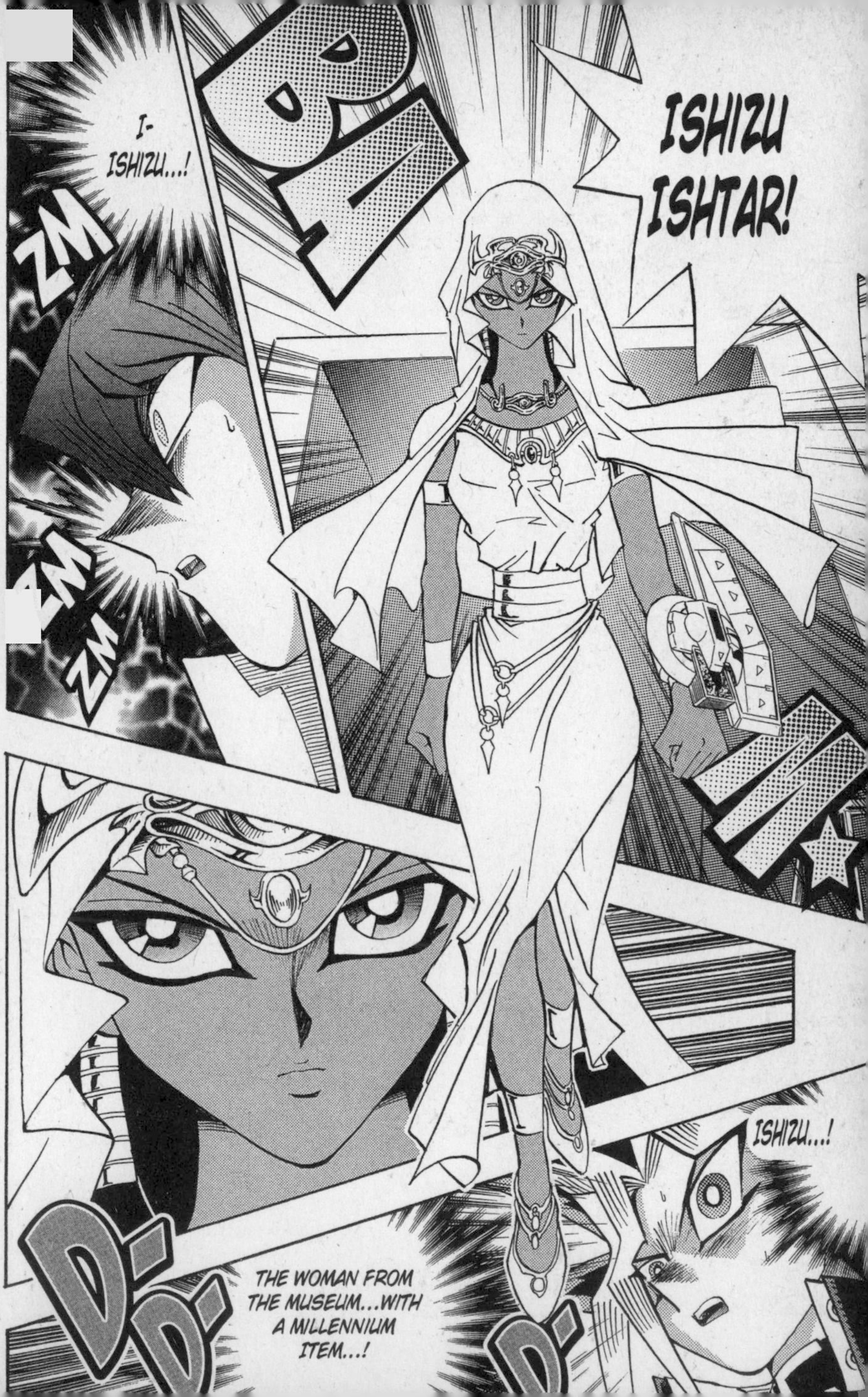
ISHIZU ISHTAR!
I- ISHIZU...!
ZM
ZM ZM
ISHIZU...!
THE WOMAN FROM THE MUSEUM...WITH A MILLENNIUM ITEM...!

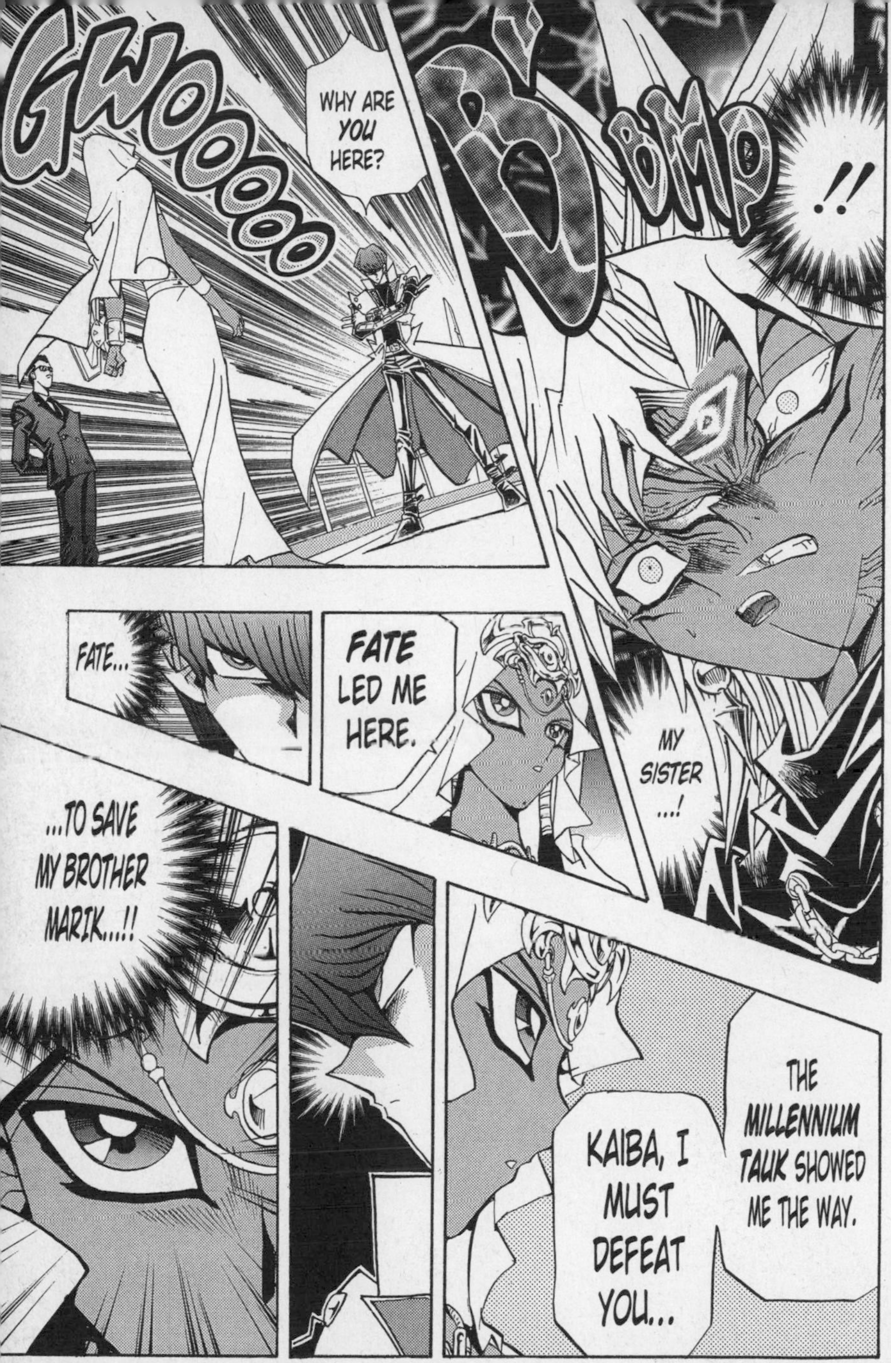
BMP!!
MY SISTER ...!
GWOOOOOO
WHY ARE YOU HERE?
FATE LED ME HERE.
FATE...
THE MILLENNIUM TAUK SHOWED ME THE WAY.
KAIBA, I MUST DEFEAT YOU...
...TO SAVE MY BROTHER MARIK...!!

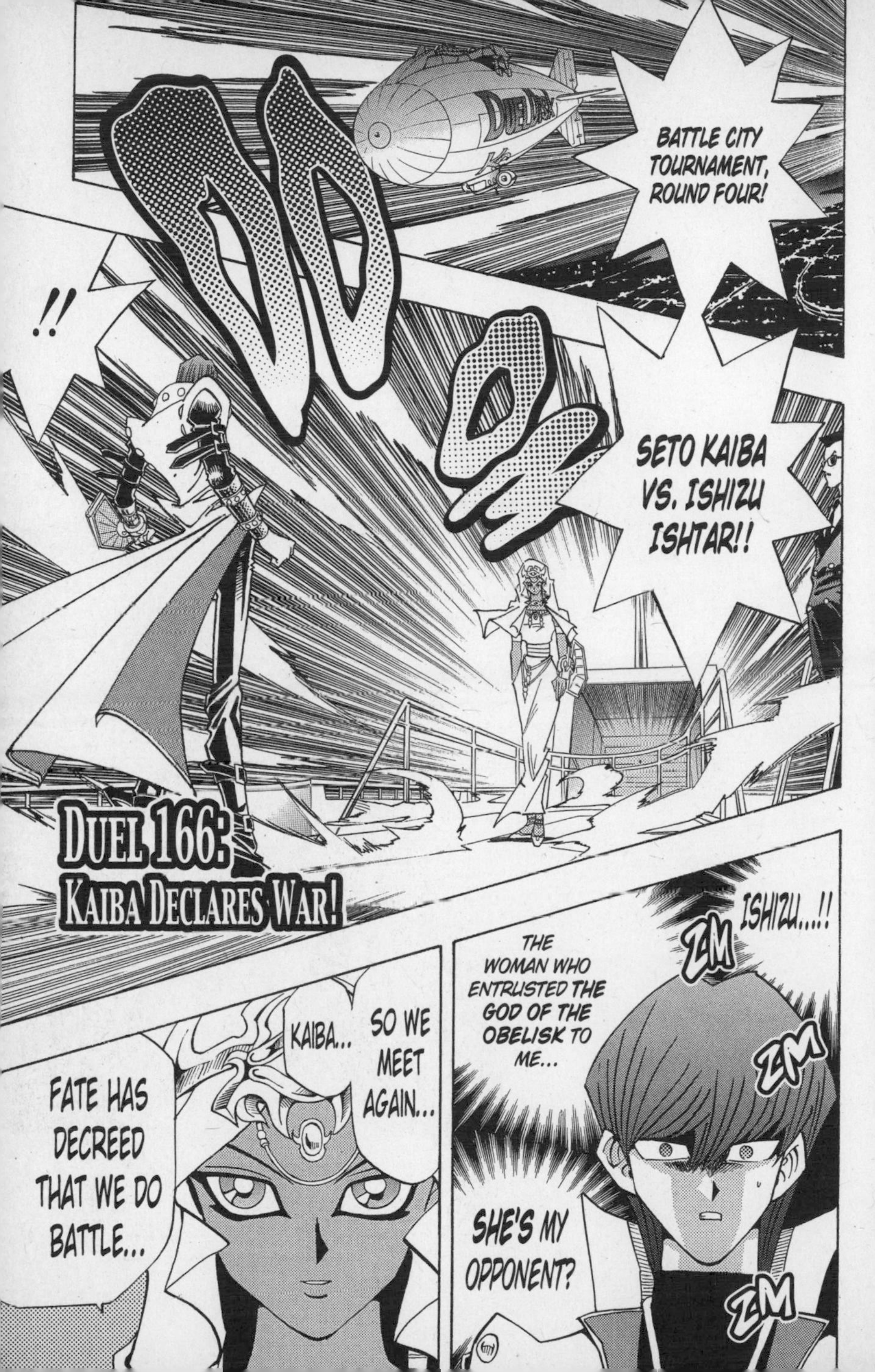
BATTLE CITY TOURNAMENT, ROUND FOUR!
SETO KAIBA VS. ISHIZU ISHTAR!!
!!
DUEL 166: KAIBA DECLARES WAR!
ISHIZU...!!
ZM
THE WOMAN WHO ENTRUSTED THE GOD OF THE OBELISK TO ME...
ZM
SHE'S MY OPPONENT?
ZM
KAIBA...
SO WE MEET AGAIN...
FATE HAS DECREED THAT WE DO BATTLE...

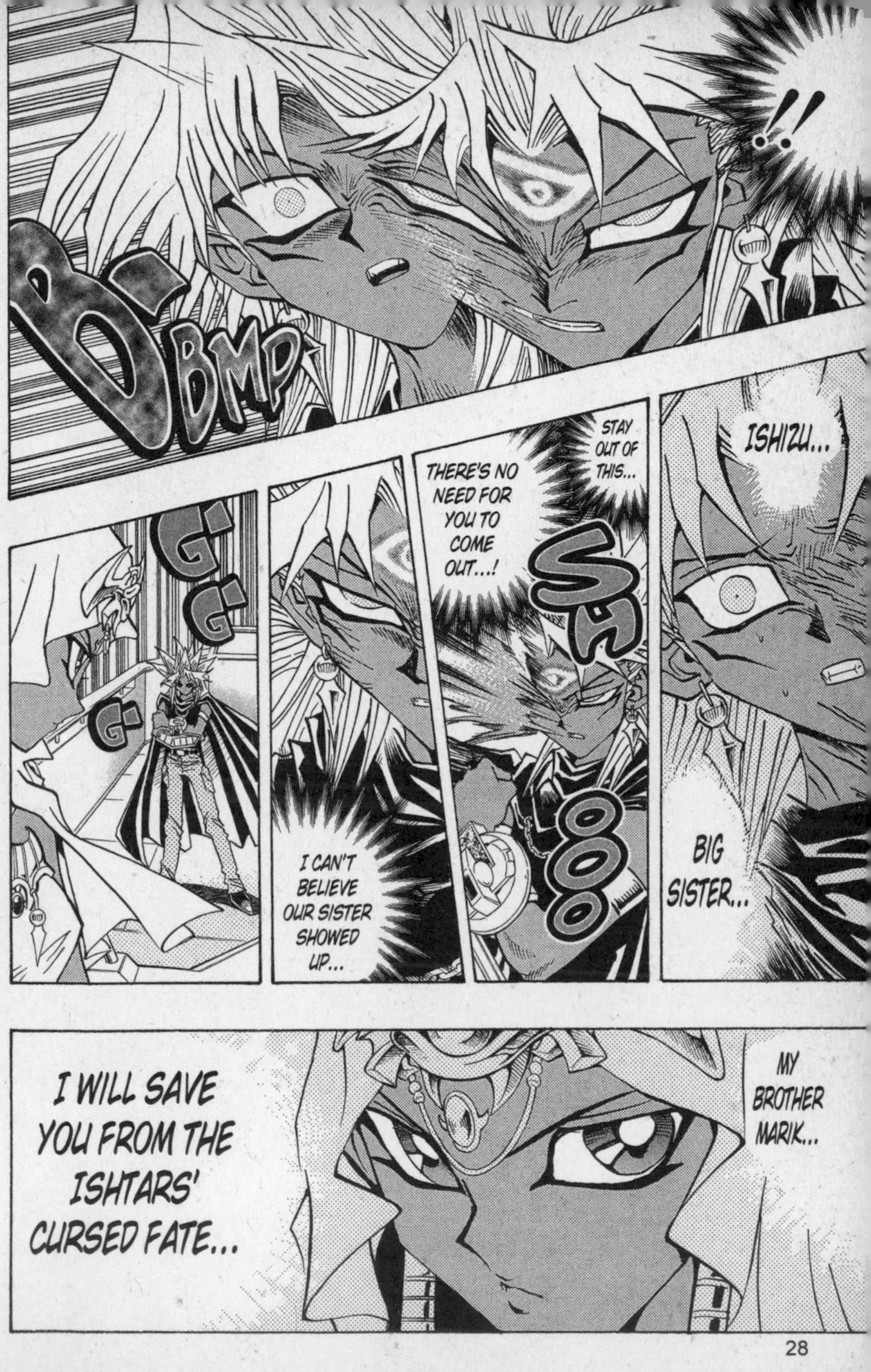
!!
BDMP
ISHIZU...
BIG SISTER...
STAY OUT OF THIS...
THERE'S NO NEED FOR YOU TO COME OUT...!
SHA
OOO
I CAN'T BELIEVE OUR SISTER SHOWED UP...
G
G
G
MY BROTHER MARIK...
I WILL SAVE YOU FROM THE ISHTARS' CURSED FATE...

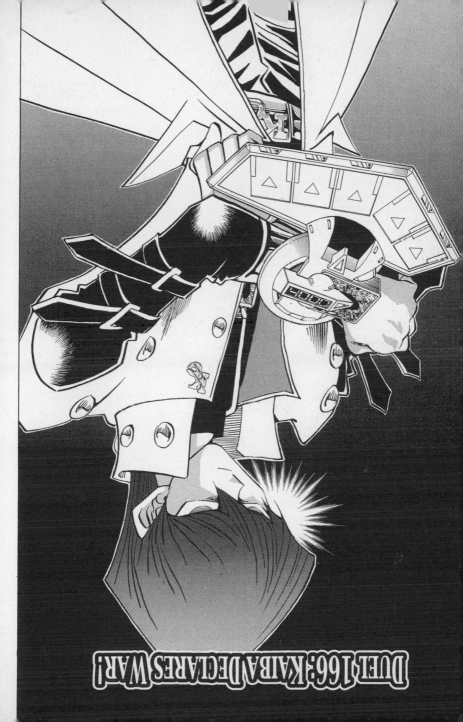

DUEL 166: KAIBA DECLARES WAR!

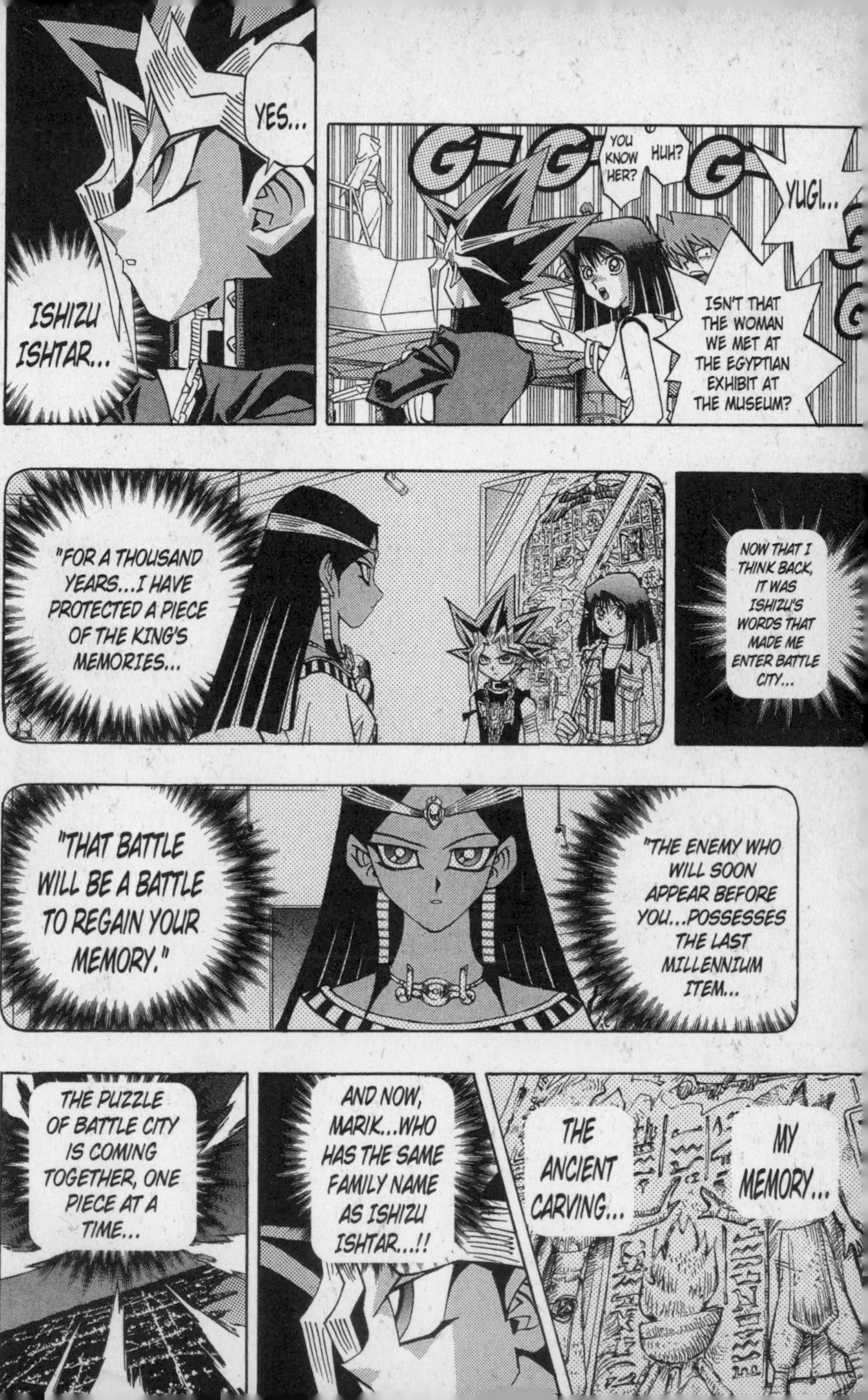
YUGI...
ISN'T THAT THE WOMAN WE MET AT THE EGYPTIAN EXHIBIT AT THE MUSEUM?
HUH?
YOU KNOW HER?
YES...
ISHIZU ISHTAR...
NOW THAT I THINK BACK, IT WAS ISHIZU'S WORDS THAT MADE ME ENTER BATTLE CITY...
"FOR A THOUSAND YEARS...I HAVE PROTECTED A PIECE OF THE KING'S MEMORIES...
"THE ENEMY WHO WILL SOON APPEAR BEFORE YOU...POSSESSES THE LAST MILLENNIUM ITEM...
"THAT BATTLE WILL BE A BATTLE TO REGAIN YOUR MEMORY."
MY MEMORY...
THE ANCIENT CARVING...
AND NOW, MARIK...WHO HAS THE SAME FAMILY NAME AS ISHIZU ISHTAR...!!
THE PUZZLE OF BATTLE CITY IS COMING TOGETHER, ONE PIECE AT A TIME...

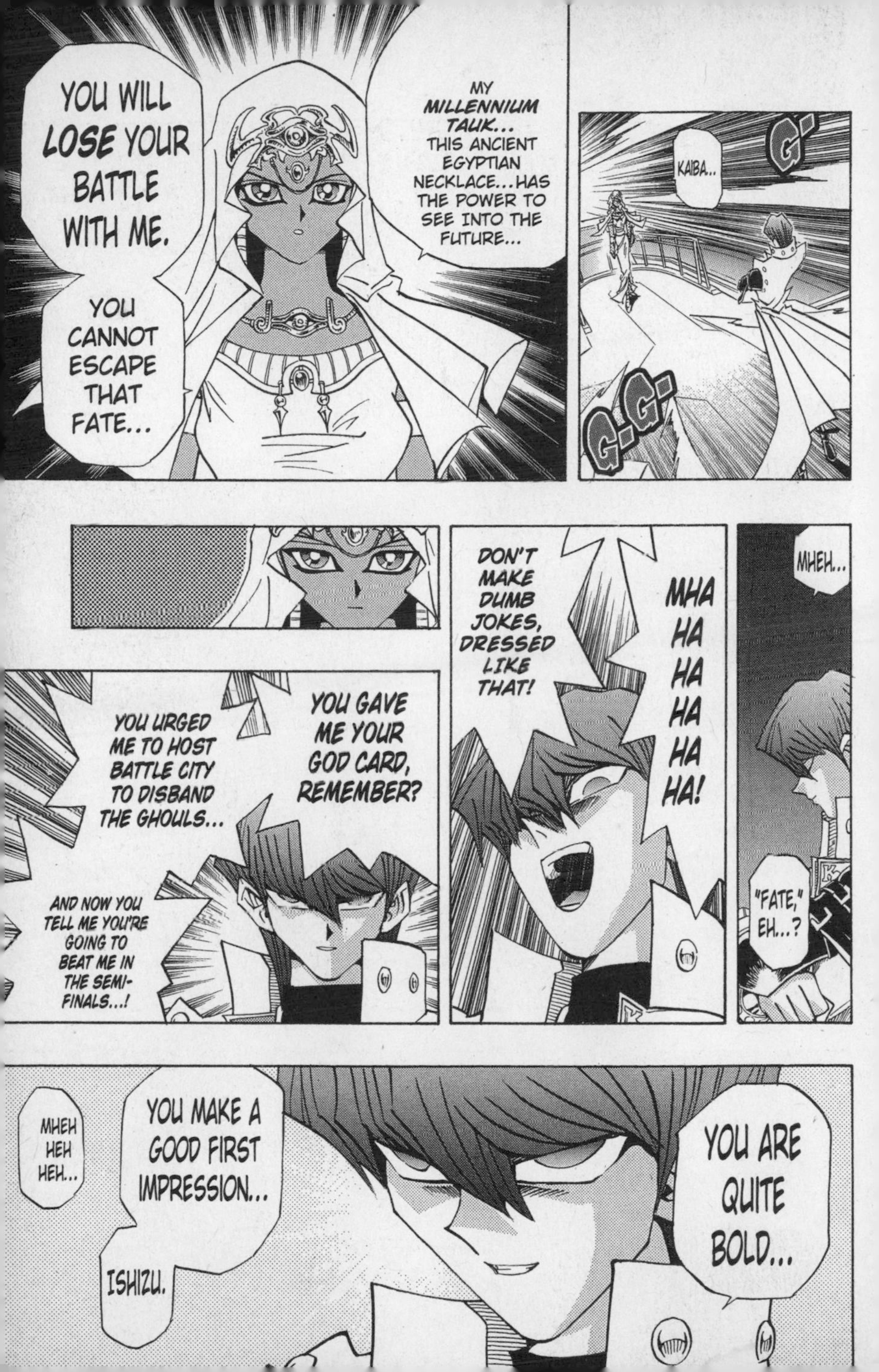
KAIBA...
G'
G-G-
MY MILLENNIUM TAUK... THIS ANCIENT EGYPTIAN NECKLACE...HAS THE POWER TO SEE INTO THE FUTURE...
YOU WILL LOSE YOUR BATTLE WITH ME.
YOU CANNOT ESCAPE THAT FATE...
MHEH...
"FATE," EH...?
MHA HA HA HA HA HA!
DON'T MAKE DUMB JOKES, DRESSED LIKE THAT!
YOU GAVE ME YOUR GOD CARD, REMEMBER?
YOU URGED ME TO HOST BATTLE CITY TO DISBAND THE GHOULS...
AND NOW YOU TELL ME YOU'RE GOING TO BEAT ME IN THE SEMI-FINALS...!
YOU ARE QUITE BOLD...
YOU MAKE A GOOD FIRST IMPRESSION...
ISHIZU.
MHEH HEH HEH...

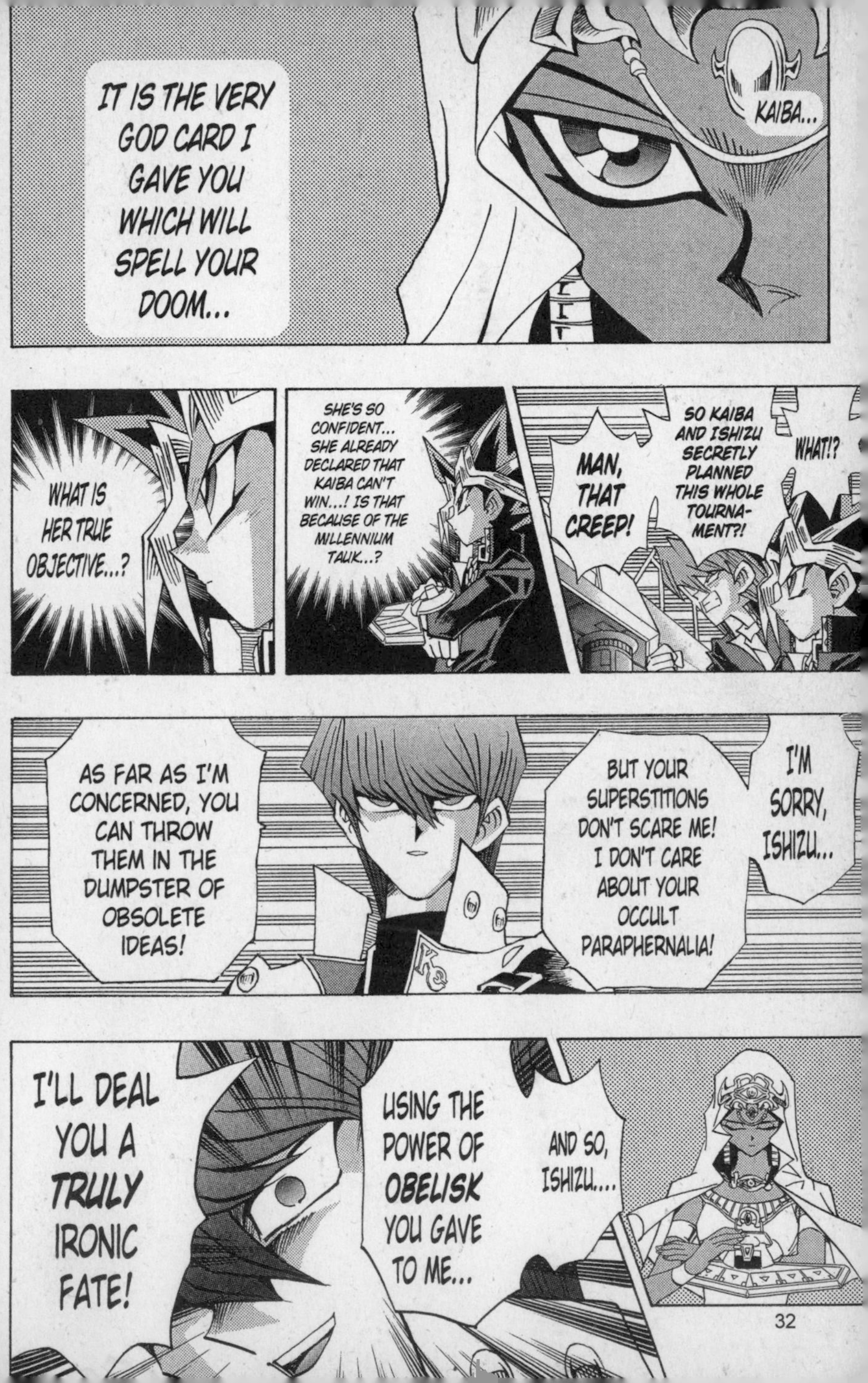
KAIBA...
IT IS THE VERY GOD CARD I GAVE YOU WHICH WILL SPELL YOUR DOOM...
WHAT!?
SO KAIBA AND ISHIZU SECRETLY PLANNED THIS WHOLE TOURNA-MENT?!
MAN, THAT CREEP!
SHE'S SO CONFIDENT... SHE ALREADY DECLARED THAT KAIBA CAN'T WIN...! IS THAT BECAUSE OF THE MILLENNIUM TAUK...?
WHAT IS HER TRUE OBJECTIVE...?
I'M SORRY, ISHIZU...
BUT YOUR SUPERSTITIONS DON'T SCARE ME! I DON'T CARE ABOUT YOUR OCCULT PARAPHERNALIA!
AS FAR AS I'M CONCERNED, YOU CAN THROW THEM IN THE DUMPSTER OF OBSOLETE IDEAS!
AND SO, ISHIZU...
USING THE POWER OF OBELISK YOU GAVE TO ME...
I'LL DEAL YOU A TRULY IRONIC FATE!

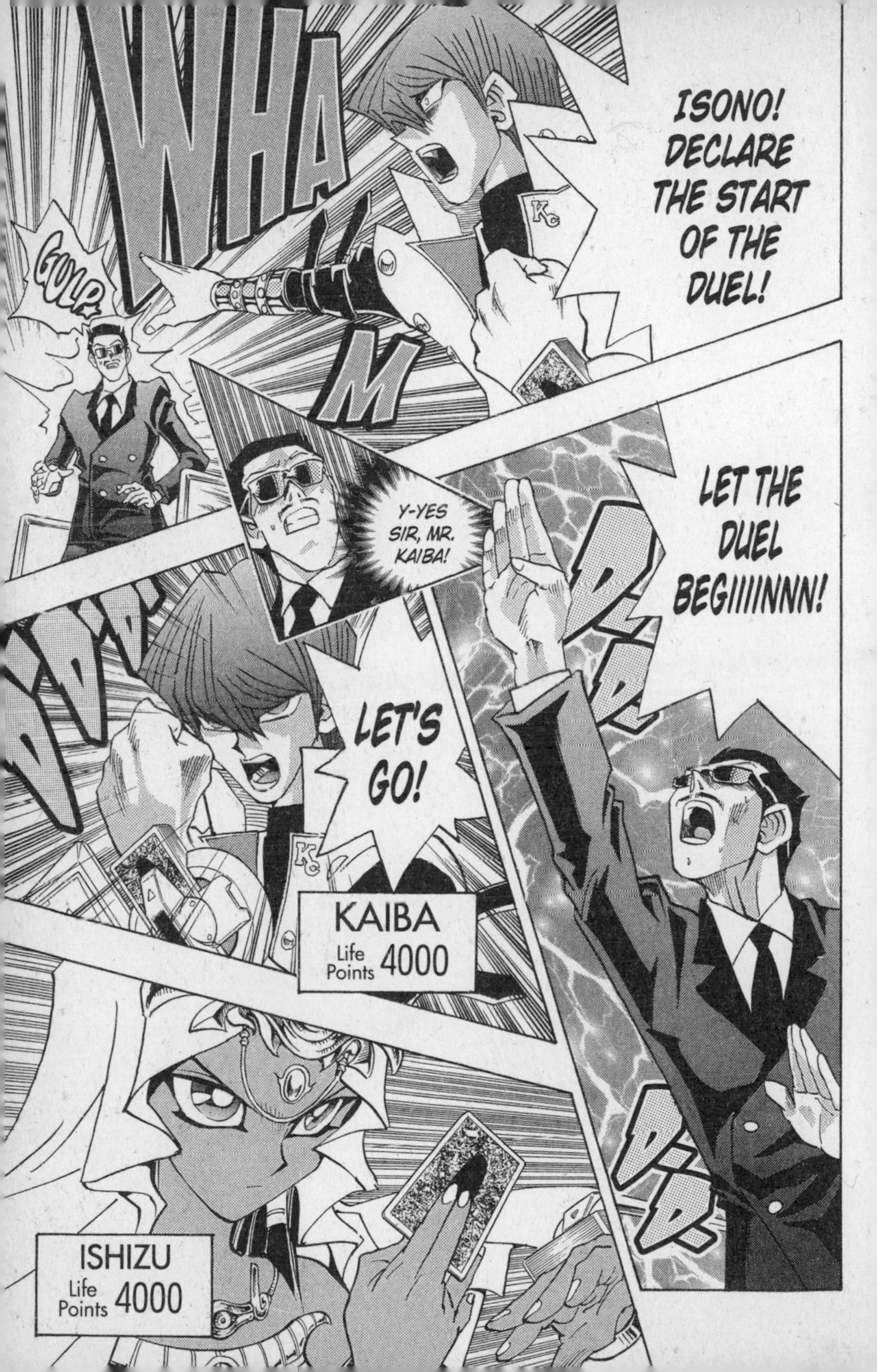
ISONO! DECLARE THE START OF THE DUEL!
WHAM
GULP
Y-YES SIR, MR. KAIBA!
LET THE DUEL BEGIIIINNN!
LET'S GO!
KAIBA Life Points 4000
ISHIZU Life Points 4000

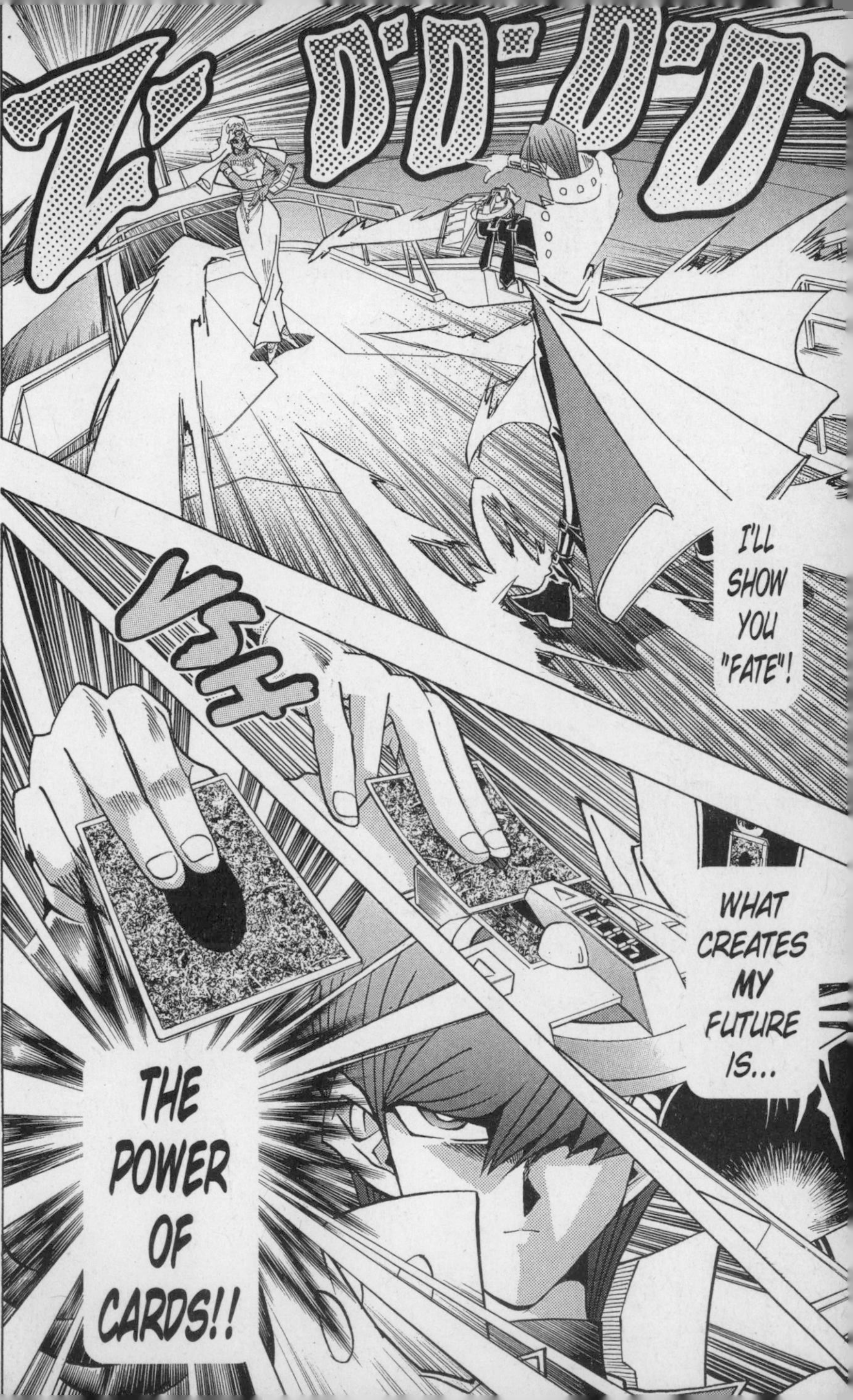
Z- D-D-D-D-
I'LL SHOW YOU "FATE"!
VSH
WHAT CREATES MY FUTURE IS...
THE POWER OF CARDS!!

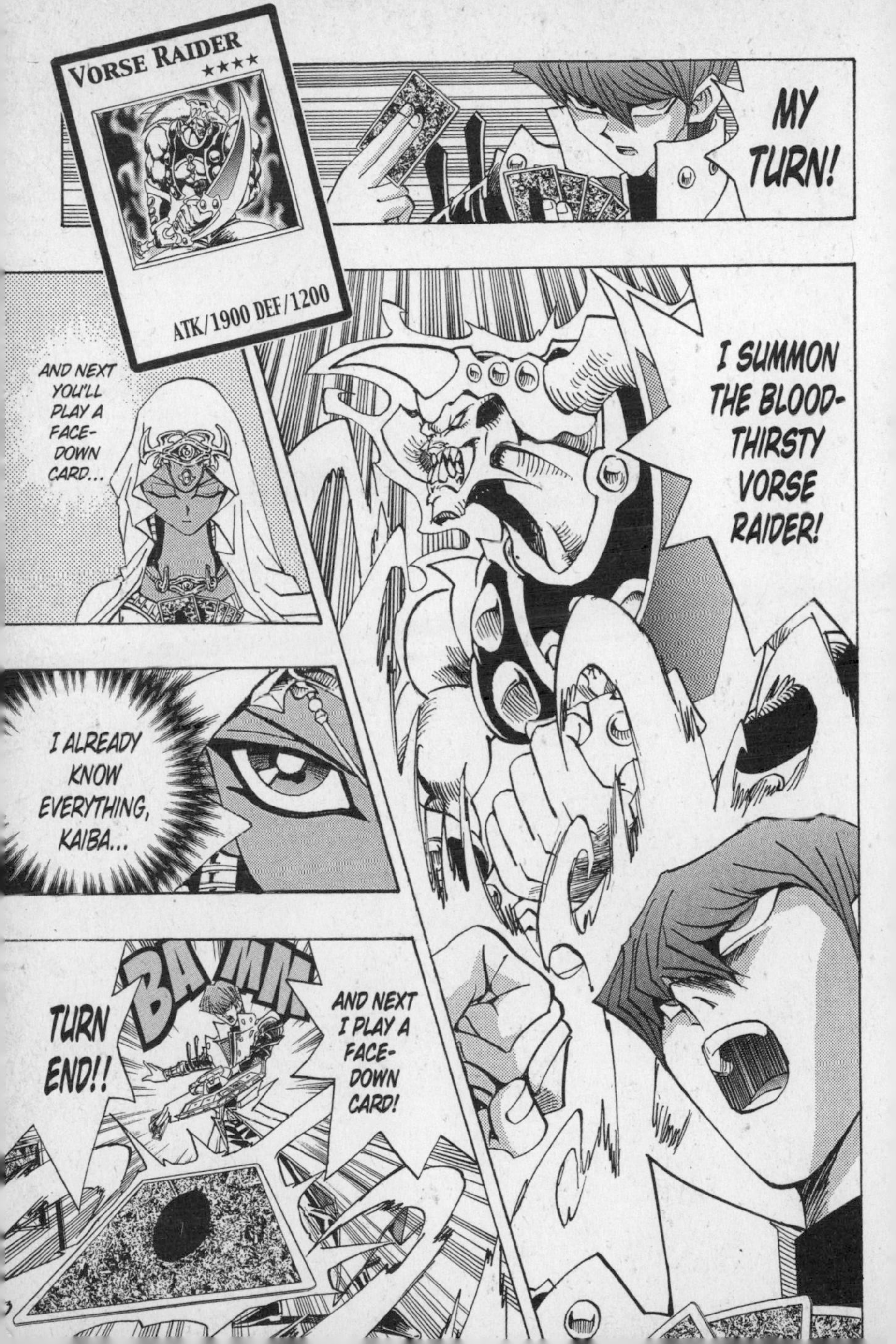
MY TURN!
VORSE RAIDER
★★★★
ATK/1900 DEF/1200
I SUMMON THE BLOOD-THIRSTY VORSE RAIDER!
AND NEXT YOU'LL PLAY A FACE-DOWN CARD...
I ALREADY KNOW EVERYTHING, KAIBA...
AND NEXT I PLAY A FACE-DOWN CARD!
BAMM
TURN END!!

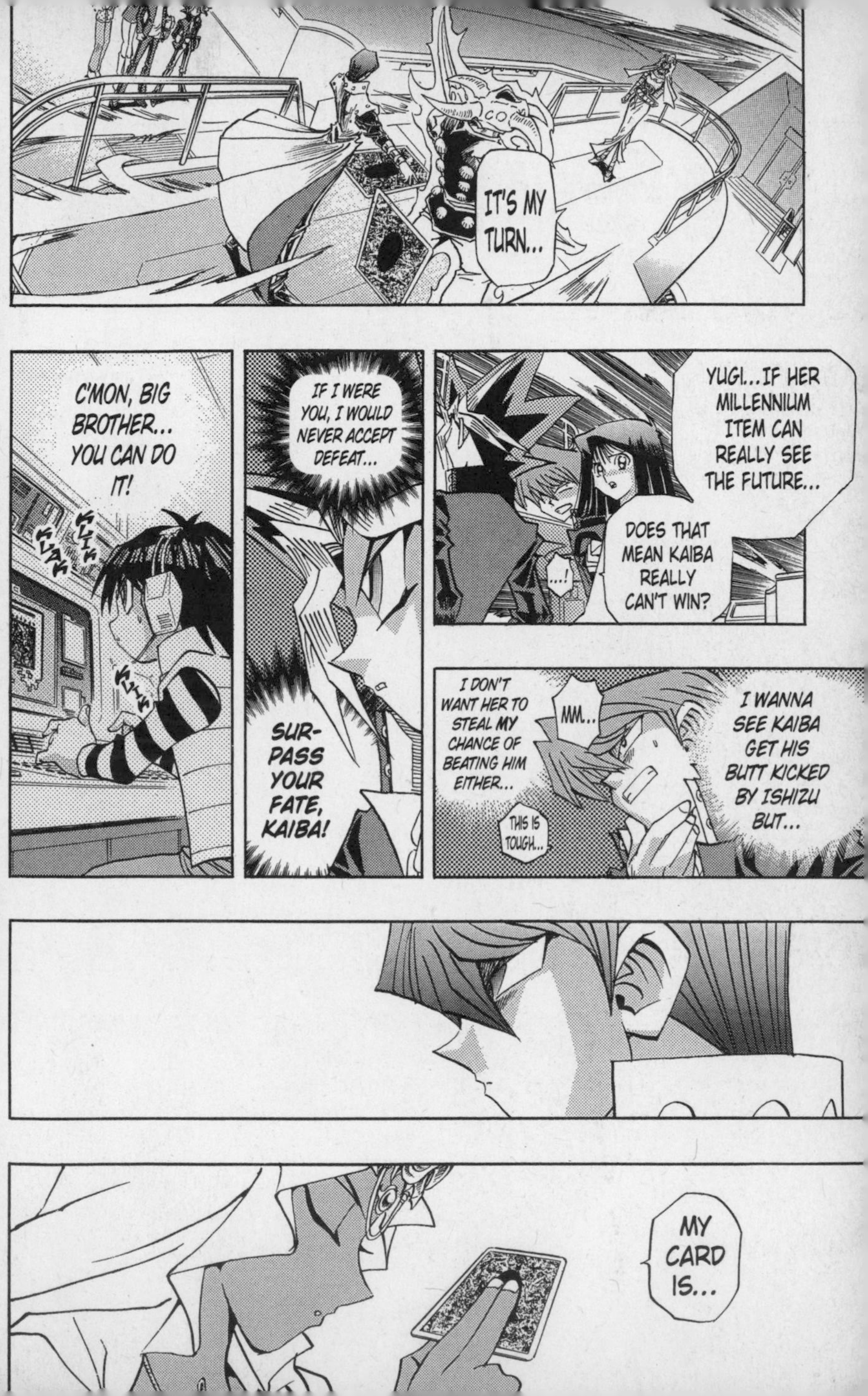
IT'S MY TURN...
YUGI...IF HER MILLENNIUM ITEM CAN REALLY SEE THE FUTURE...
DOES THAT MEAN KAIBA REALLY CAN'T WIN?
...!
I WANNA SEE KAIBA GET HIS BUTT KICKED BY ISHIZU BUT...
MM...
I DON'T WANT HER TO STEAL MY CHANCE OF BEATING HIM EITHER...
THIS IS TOUGH...
IF I WERE YOU, I WOULD NEVER ACCEPT DEFEAT...
SUR-PASS YOUR FATE, KAIBA!
C'MON, BIG BROTHER... YOU CAN DO IT!
MY CARD IS...

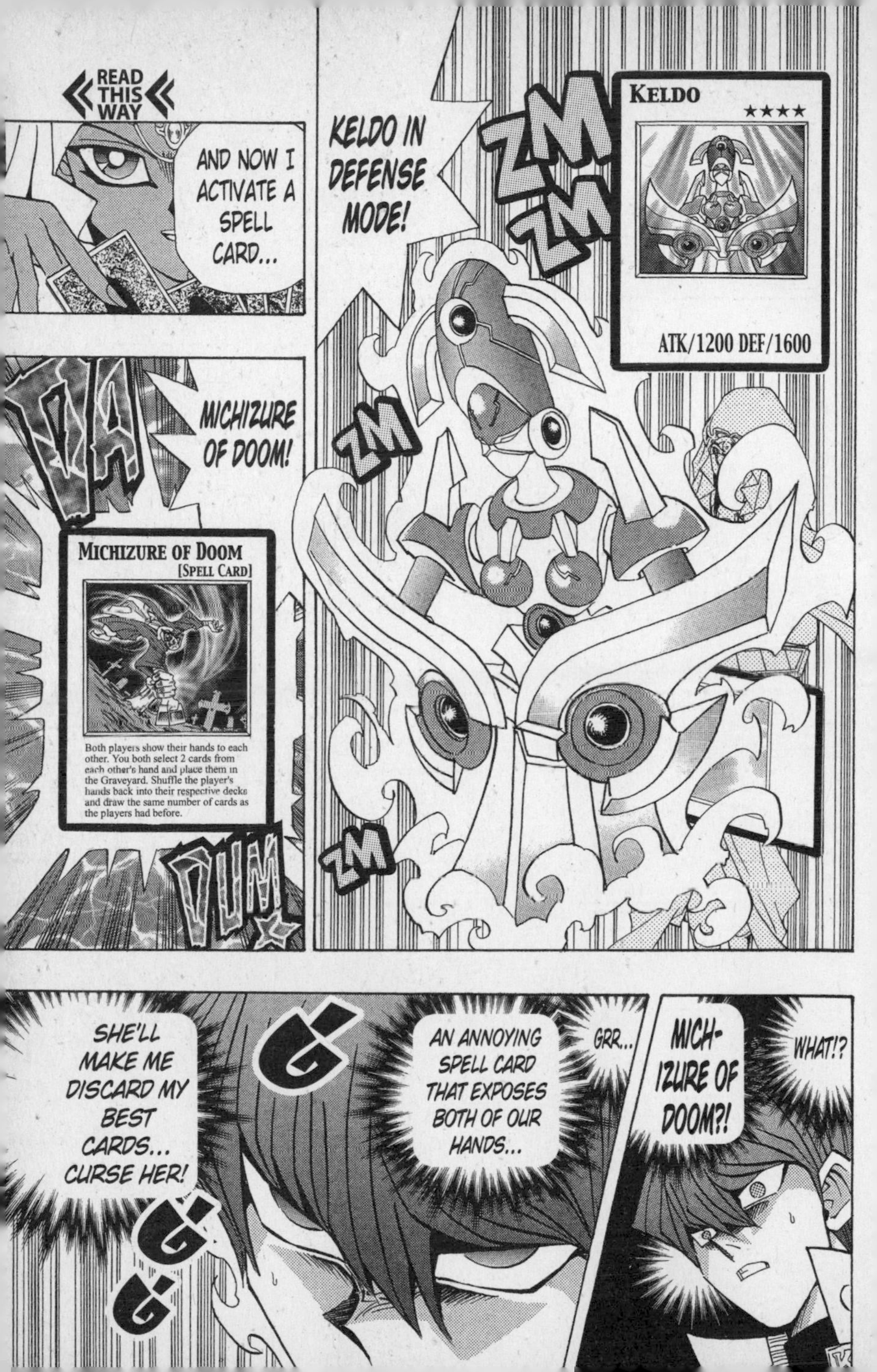
READ THIS WAY
ZM ZM ZM
KELDO IN DEFENSE MODE!
KELDO
★★★★
ATK/1200 DEF/1600
ZM
ZM
AND NOW I ACTIVATE A SPELL CARD...
VA
MICHIZURE OF DOOM!
MICHIZURE OF DOOM
[SPELL CARD]
Both players show their hands to each other. You both select 2 cards from each other's hand and place them in the Graveyard. Shuffle the player's hands back into their respective decks and draw the same number of cards as the players had before.
DUM
WHAT!?
MICH-IZURE OF DOOM?!
GRR...
AN ANNOYING SPELL CARD THAT EXPOSES BOTH OF OUR HANDS...
G
SHE'LL MAKE ME DISCARD MY BEST CARDS... CURSE HER!
G G

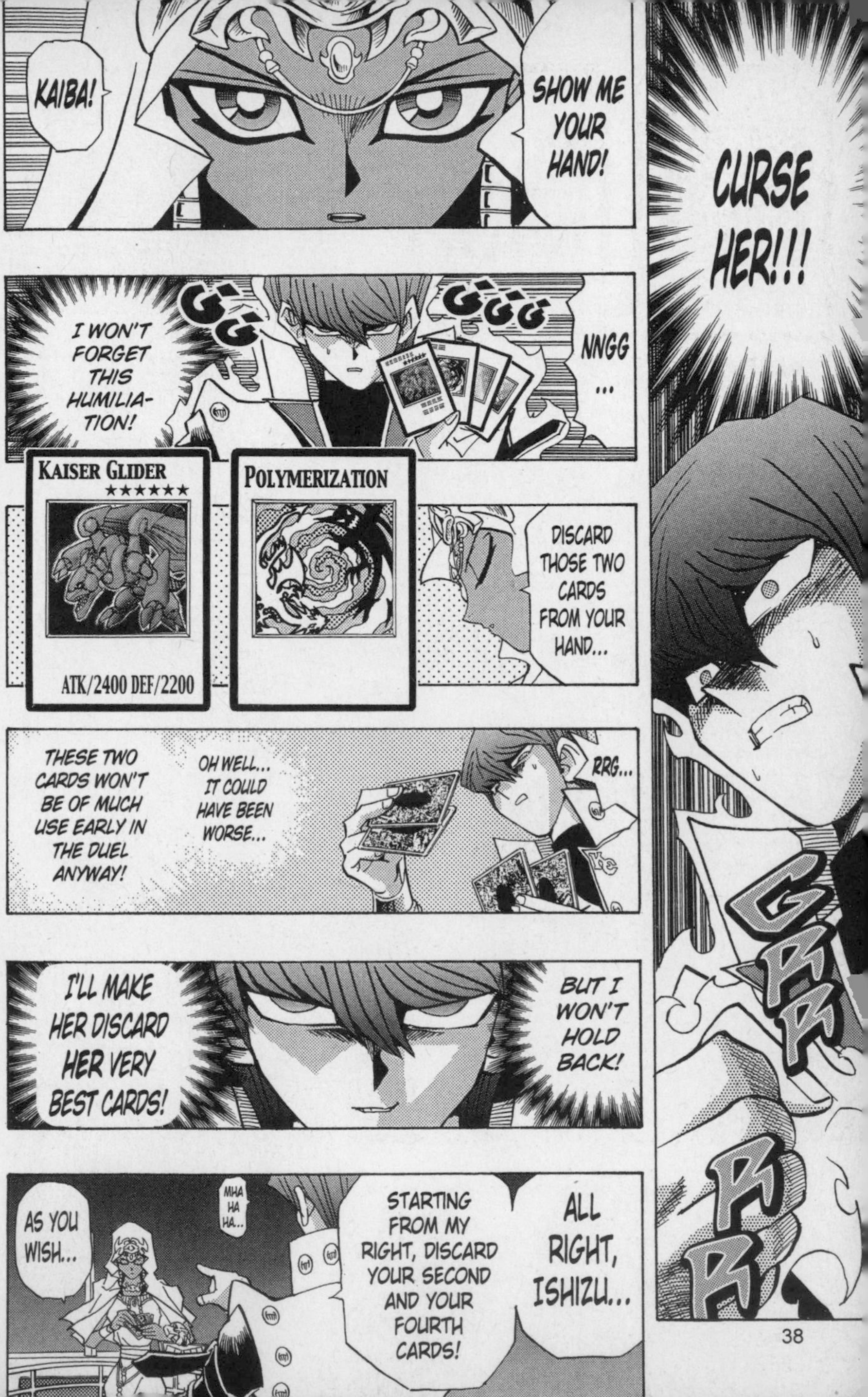
CURSE HER!!!
GRRR
RRR
SHOW ME YOUR HAND!
KAIBA!
NNGG ...
G G G G G
I WON'T FORGET THIS HUMILIA-TION!
DISCARD THOSE TWO CARDS FROM YOUR HAND...
KAISER GLIDER
★★★★★★
ATK/2400 DEF/2200
POLYMERIZATION
RRG...
OH WELL... IT COULD HAVE BEEN WORSE...
THESE TWO CARDS WON'T BE OF MUCH USE EARLY IN THE DUEL ANYWAY!
BUT I WON'T HOLD BACK!
I'LL MAKE HER DISCARD HER VERY BEST CARDS!
ALL RIGHT, ISHIZU...
STARTING FROM MY RIGHT, DISCARD YOUR SECOND AND YOUR FOURTH CARDS!
MHA HA HA...
AS YOU WISH...

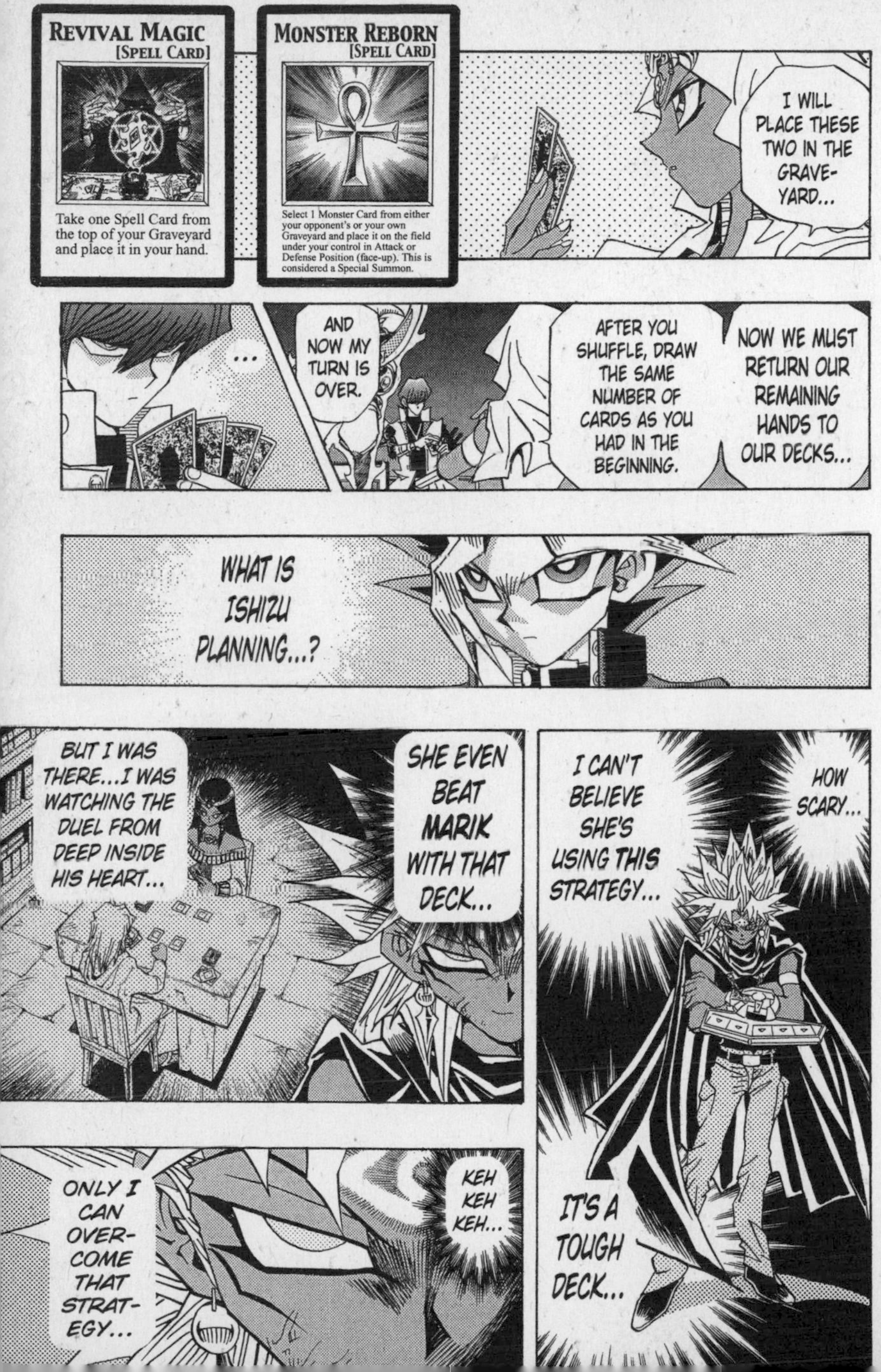
I WILL PLACE THESE TWO IN THE GRAVE-YARD...
REVIVAL MAGIC
[SPELL CARD]
Take one Spell Card from the top of your Graveyard and place it in your hand.
MONSTER REBORN
[SPELL CARD]
Select 1 Monster Card from either your opponent's or your own Graveyard and place it on the field under your control in Attack or Defense Position (face-up). This is considered a Special Summon.
NOW WE MUST RETURN OUR REMAINING HANDS TO OUR DECKS...
AFTER YOU SHUFFLE, DRAW THE SAME NUMBER OF CARDS AS YOU HAD IN THE BEGINNING.
AND NOW MY TURN IS OVER.
...
WHAT IS ISHIZU PLANNING...?
HOW SCARY...
I CAN'T BELIEVE SHE'S USING THIS STRATEGY...
IT'S A TOUGH DECK...
SHE EVEN BEAT MARIK WITH THAT DECK...
BUT I WAS THERE...I WAS WATCHING THE DUEL FROM DEEP INSIDE HIS HEART...
KEH KEH KEH...
ONLY I CAN OVER-COME THAT STRAT-EGY...

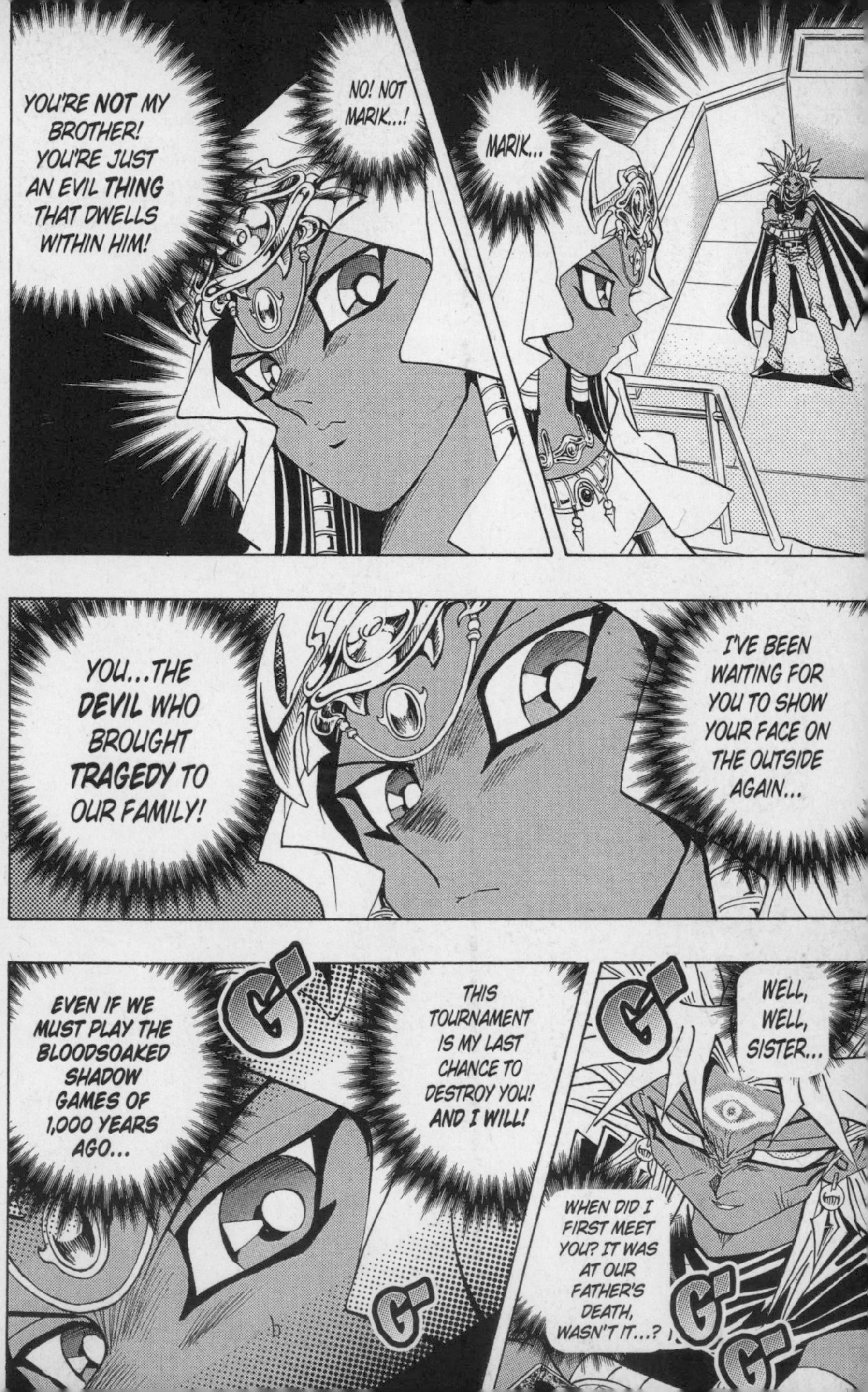
MARIK...
NO! NOT MARIK...!
YOU'RE NOT MY BROTHER! YOU'RE JUST AN EVIL THING THAT DWELLS WITHIN HIM!
I'VE BEEN WAITING FOR YOU TO SHOW YOUR FACE ON THE OUTSIDE AGAIN...
YOU...THE DEVIL WHO BROUGHT TRAGEDY TO OUR FAMILY!
WELL, WELL, SISTER...
G
WHEN DID I FIRST MEET YOU? IT WAS AT OUR FATHER'S DEATH, WASN'T IT...?
G
G
THIS TOURNAMENT IS MY LAST CHANCE TO DESTROY YOU! AND I WILL!
G
EVEN IF WE MUST PLAY THE BLOODSOAKED SHADOW GAMES OF 1,000 YEARS AGO...
G

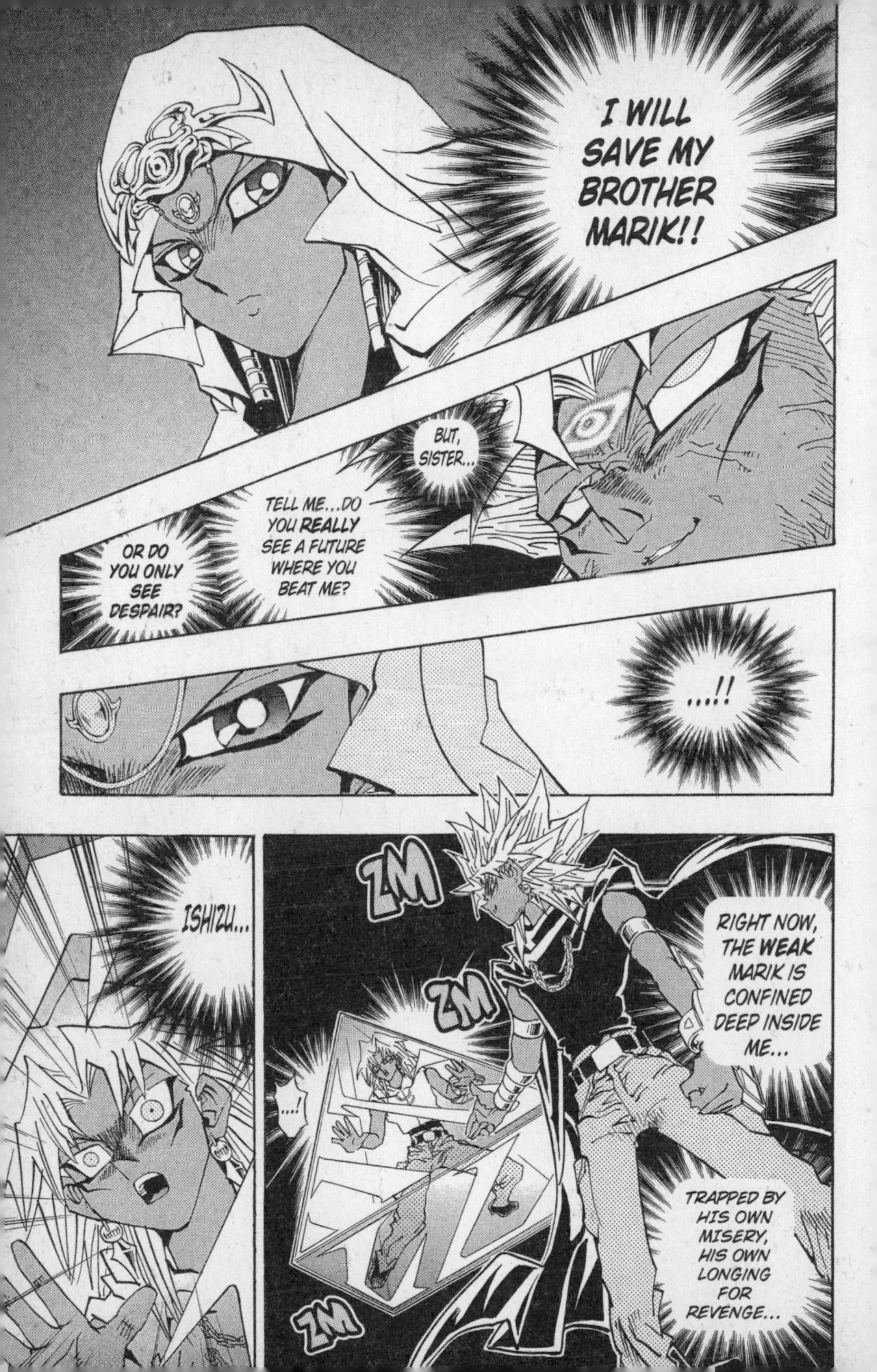
I WILL SAVE MY BROTHER MARIK!!
BUT, SISTER...
TELL ME...DO YOU REALLY SEE A FUTURE WHERE YOU BEAT ME?
OR DO YOU ONLY SEE DESPAIR?
...!!
RIGHT NOW, THE WEAK MARIK IS CONFINED DEEP INSIDE ME...
ZM
ZM
...!
TRAPPED BY HIS OWN MISERY, HIS OWN LONGING FOR REVENGE...
ZM
ISHIZU...

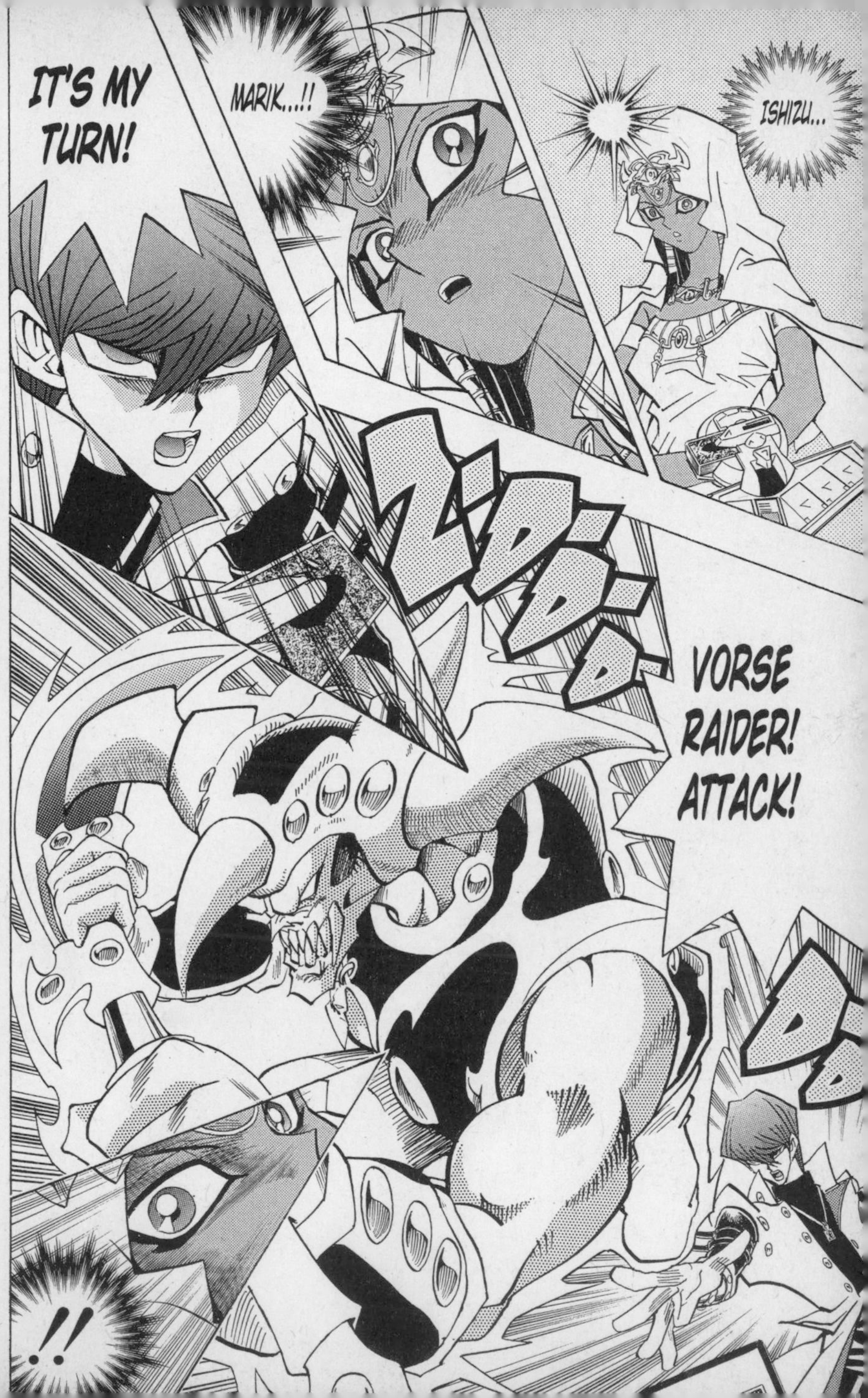
ISHIZU...
MARIK...!!
IT'S MY TURN!
Z'D'D'D'
VORSE RAIDER! ATTACK!
D'D
!!

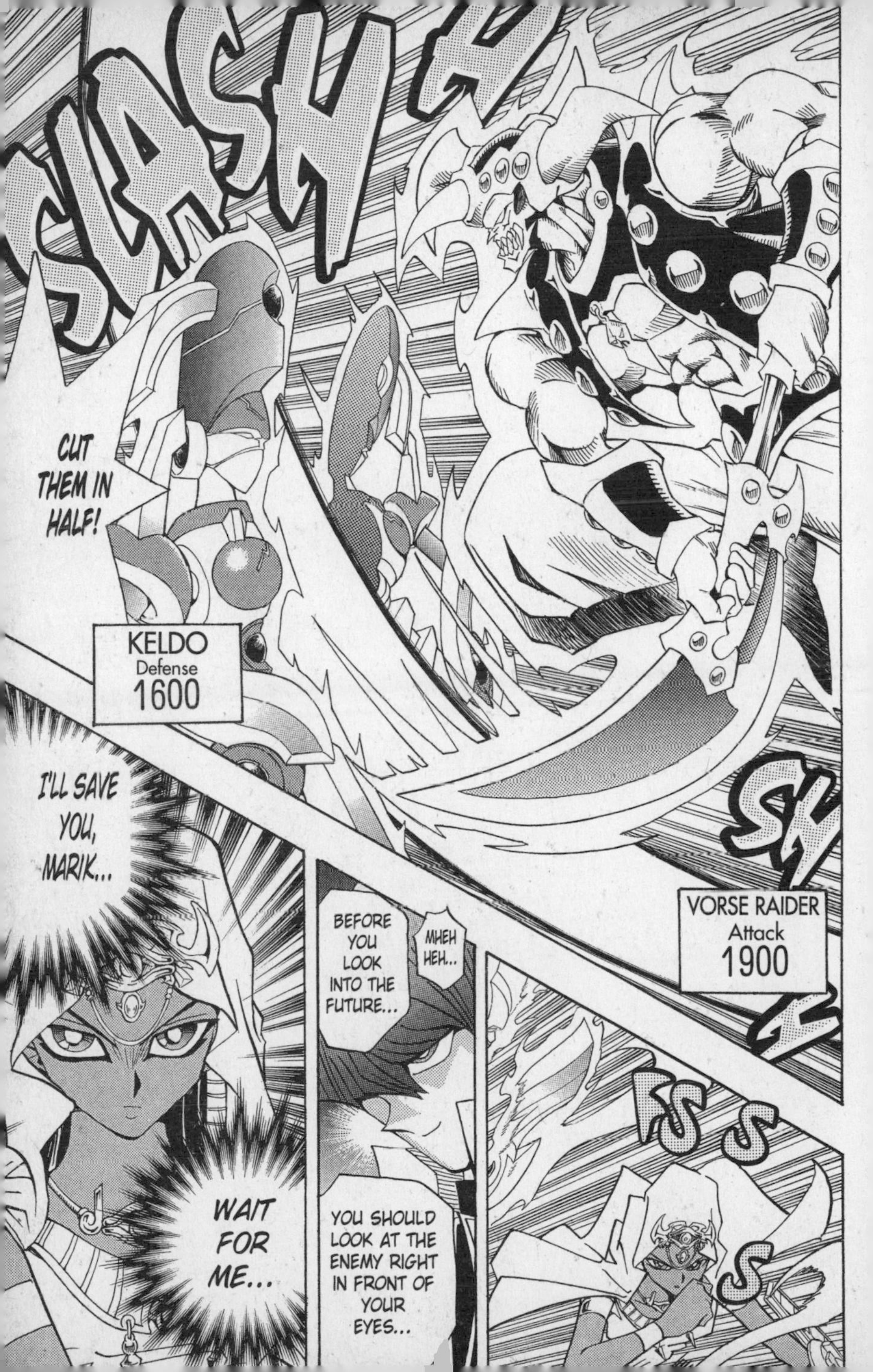
SLASH
CUT THEM IN HALF!
VORSE RAIDER Attack 1900
KELDO Defense 1600
SH
FSS
S
S
MHEH HEH...
BEFORE YOU LOOK INTO THE FUTURE...
YOU SHOULD LOOK AT THE ENEMY RIGHT IN FRONT OF YOUR EYES...
I'LL SAVE YOU, MARIK...
WAIT FOR ME...

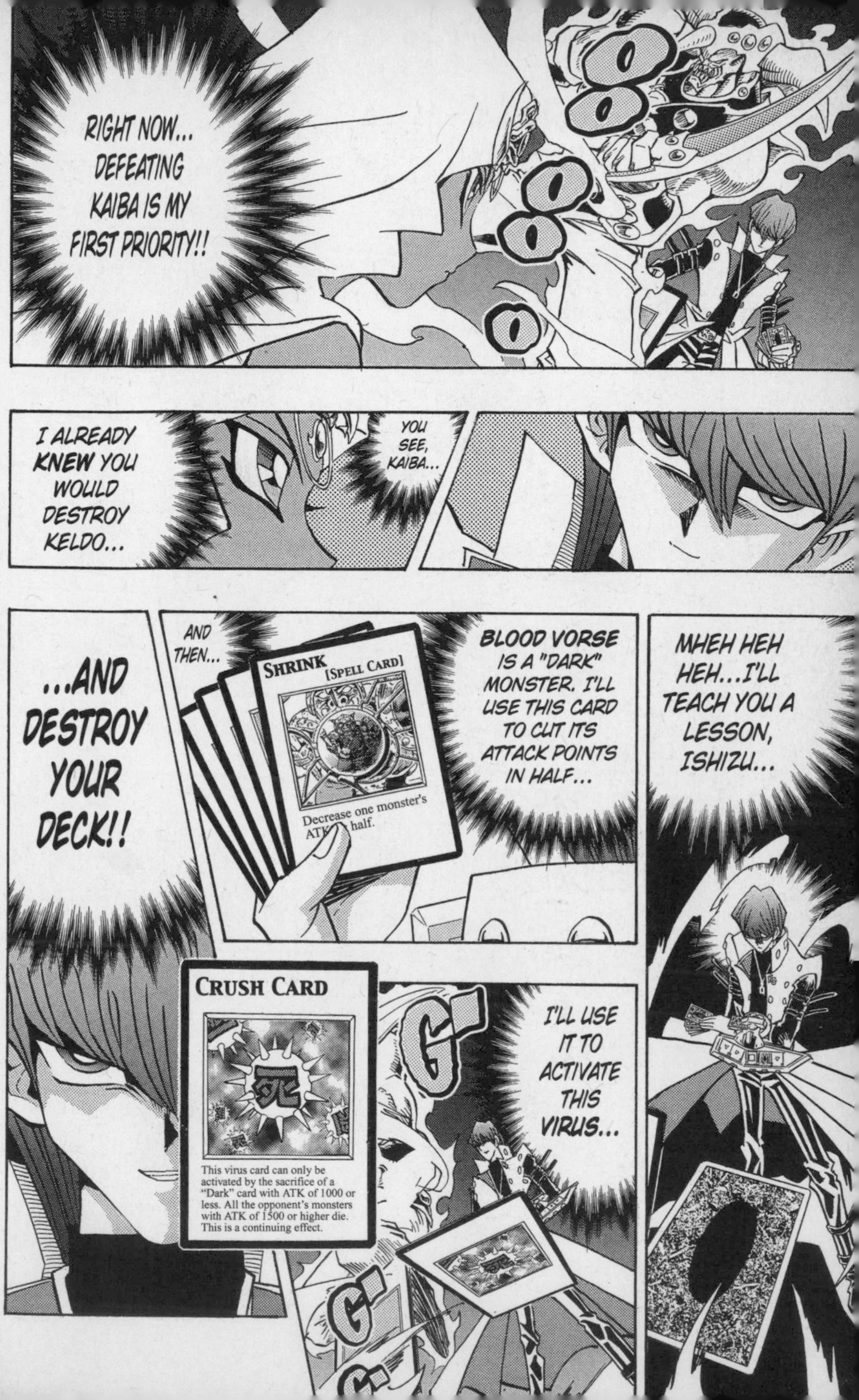
RIGHT NOW... DEFEATING KAIBA IS MY FIRST PRIORITY!!
YOU SEE, KAIBA...
I ALREADY KNEW YOU WOULD DESTROY KELDO...
MHEH HEH HEH...I'LL TEACH YOU A LESSON, ISHIZU...
BLOOD VORSE IS A "DARK" MONSTER. I'LL USE THIS CARD TO CUT ITS ATTACK POINTS IN HALF...
AND THEN...
SHRINK
[SPELL CARD]
Decrease one monster's ATK by half.
I'LL USE IT TO ACTIVATE THIS VIRUS...
G
CRUSH CARD
This virus card can only be activated by the sacrifice of a "Dark" card with ATK of 1000 or less. All the opponent's monsters with ATK of 1500 or higher die. This is a continuing effect.
...AND DESTROY YOUR DECK!!

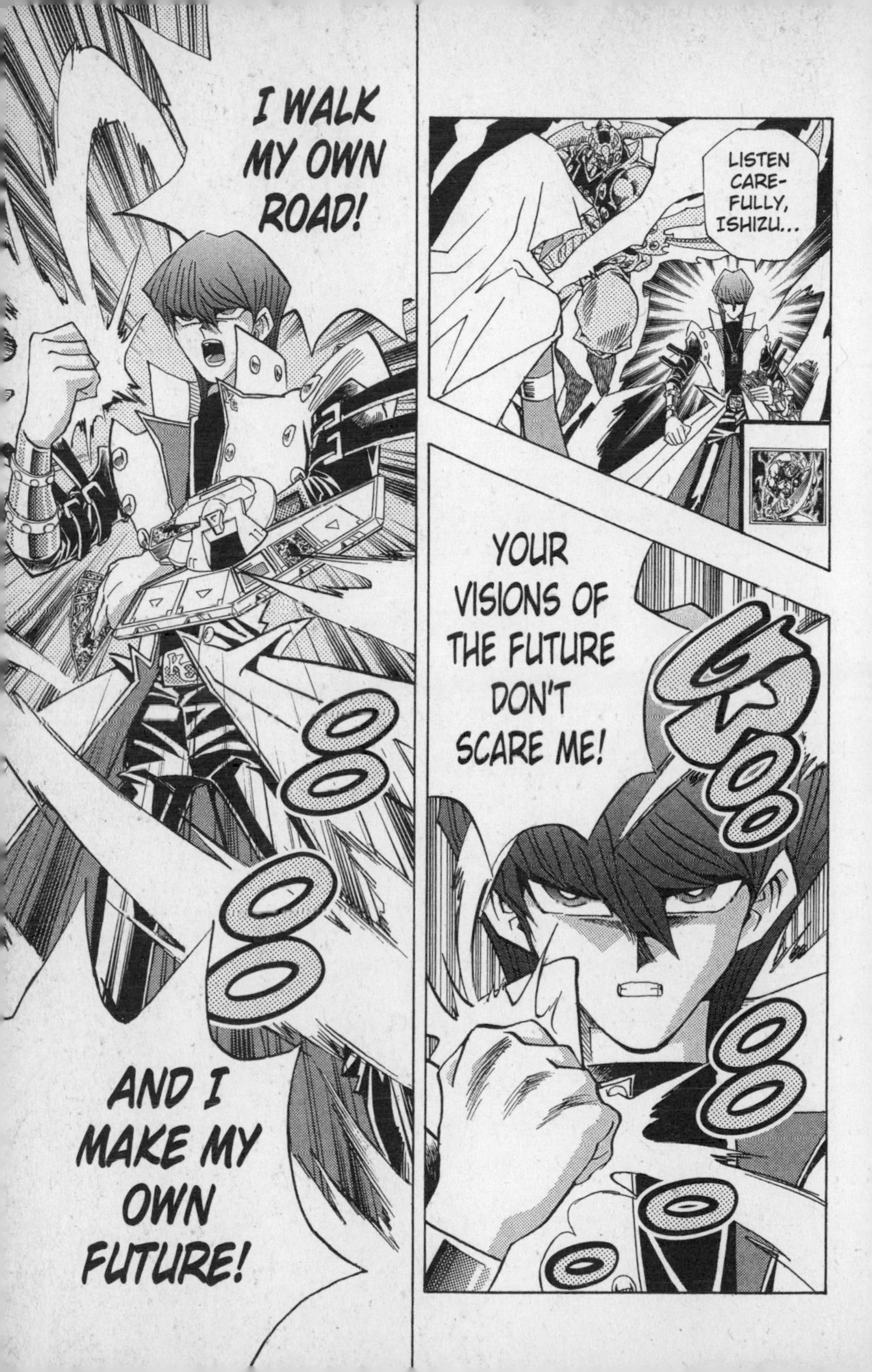
LISTEN CARE-FULLY, ISHIZU...
YOUR VISIONS OF THE FUTURE DON'T SCARE ME!
UOOO
OOO
I WALK MY OWN ROAD!
OO
OO
AND I MAKE MY OWN FUTURE!

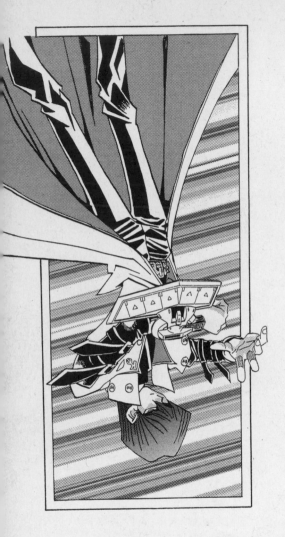

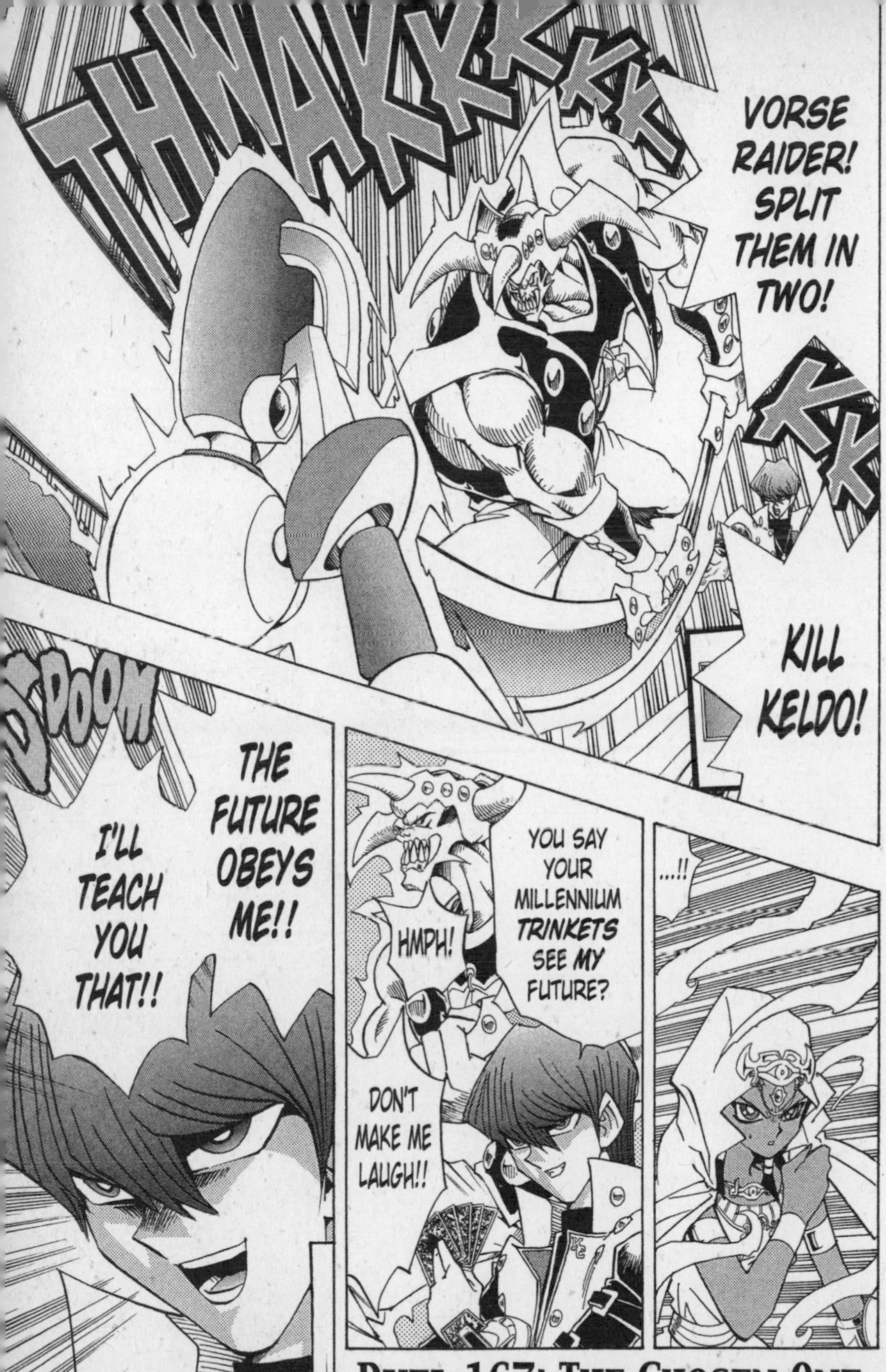
VORSE RAIDER! SPLIT THEM IN TWO!
THWAKKKK
KK
KILL KELDO!
...!!
YOU SAY YOUR MILLENNIUM TRINKETS SEE MY FUTURE?
HMPH!
DON'T MAKE ME LAUGH!!
THE FUTURE OBEYS ME!!
I'LL TEACH YOU THAT!!
SDOOM

DUEL 167: THE CHOSEN ONE

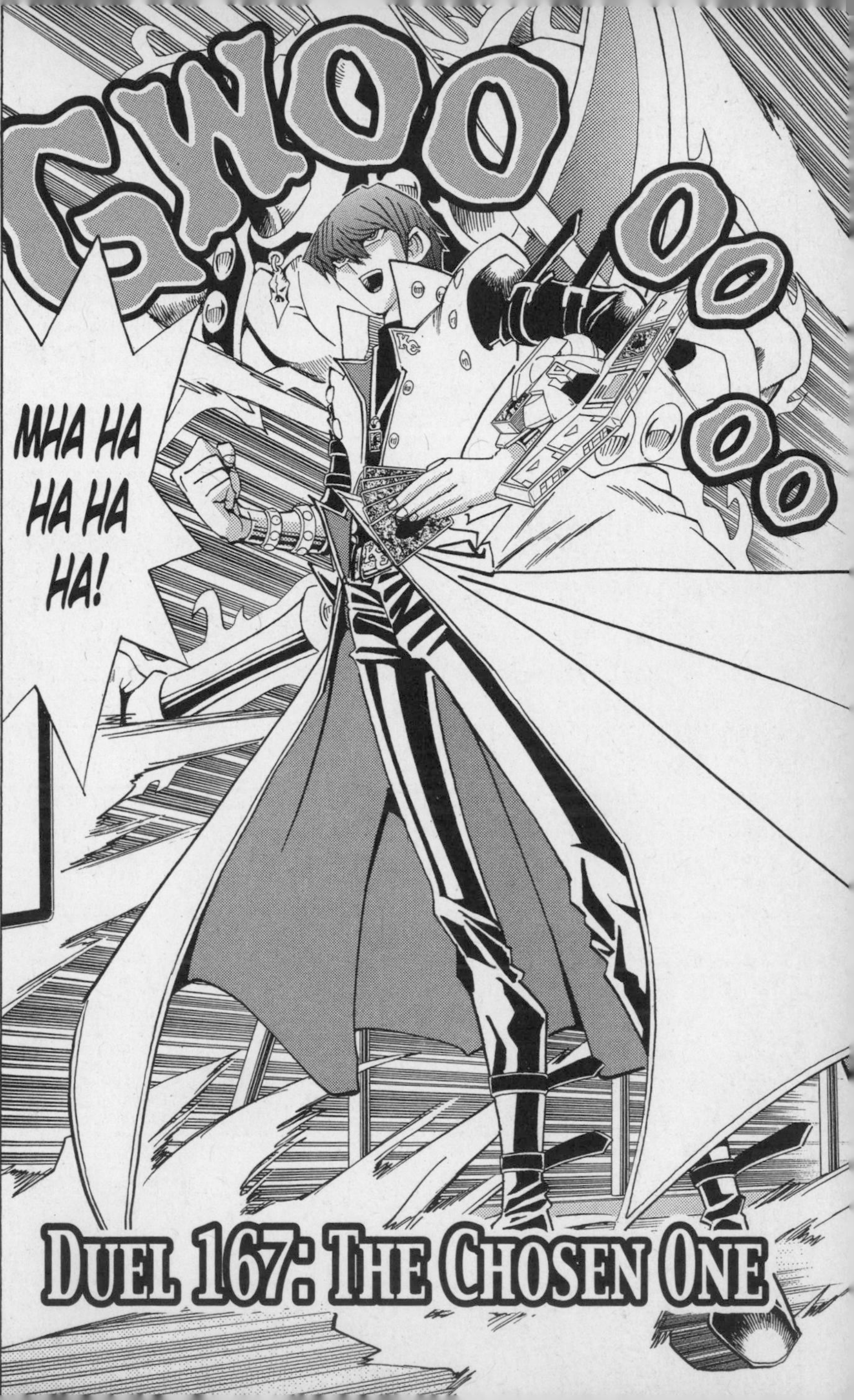
SWOOOOOOO
MHA HA HA HA HA!

Duel 167: The Chosen One

READ THIS WAY

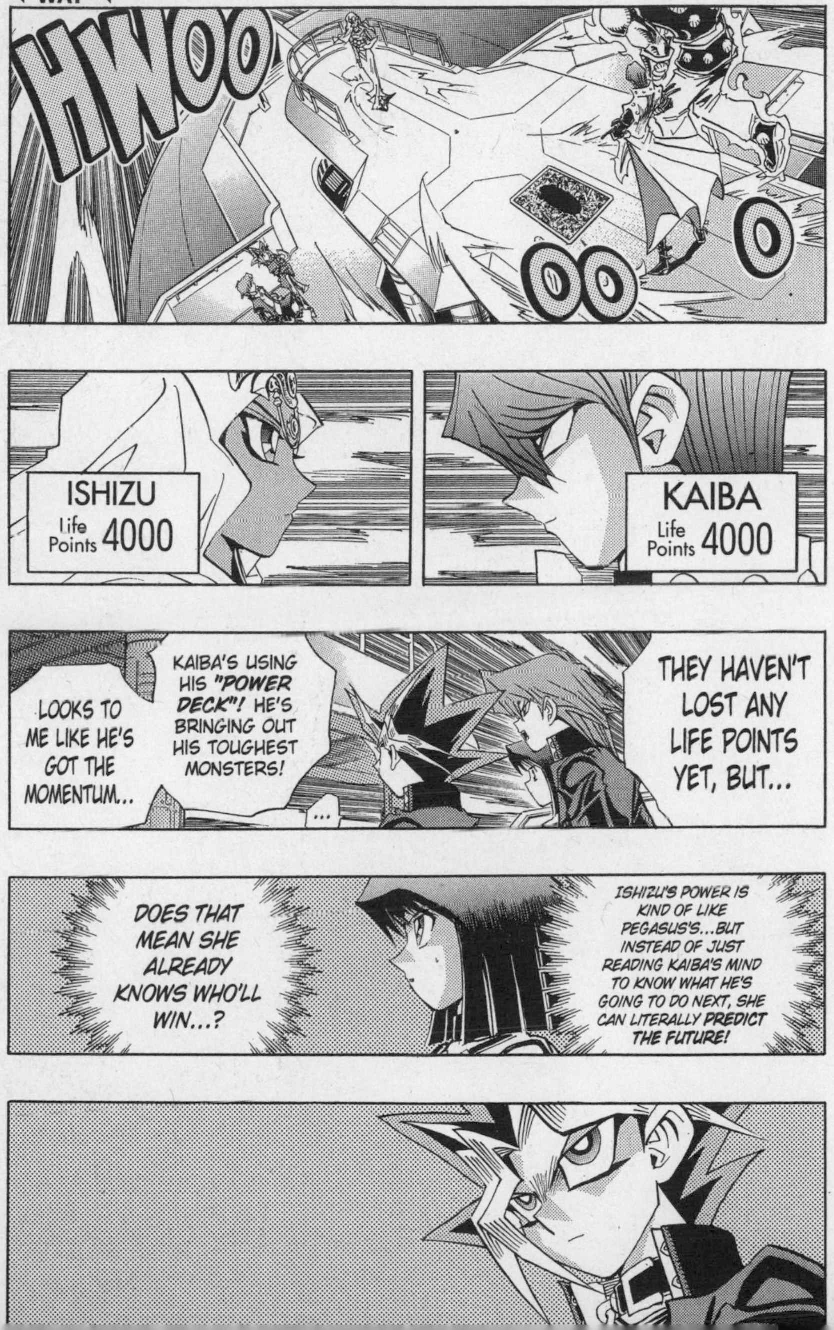
HWOO
KAIBA Life Points 4000
ISHIZU Life Points 4000
THEY HAVEN'T LOST ANY LIFE POINTS YET, BUT...
KAIBA'S USING HIS "POWER DECK"! HE'S BRINGING OUT HIS TOUGHEST MONSTERS!
LOOKS TO ME LIKE HE'S GOT THE MOMENTUM...
...
ISHIZU'S POWER IS KIND OF LIKE PEGASUS'S...BUT INSTEAD OF JUST READING KAIBA'S MIND TO KNOW WHAT HE'S GOING TO DO NEXT, SHE CAN LITERALLY PREDICT THE FUTURE!
DOES THAT MEAN SHE ALREADY KNOWS WHO'LL WIN...?

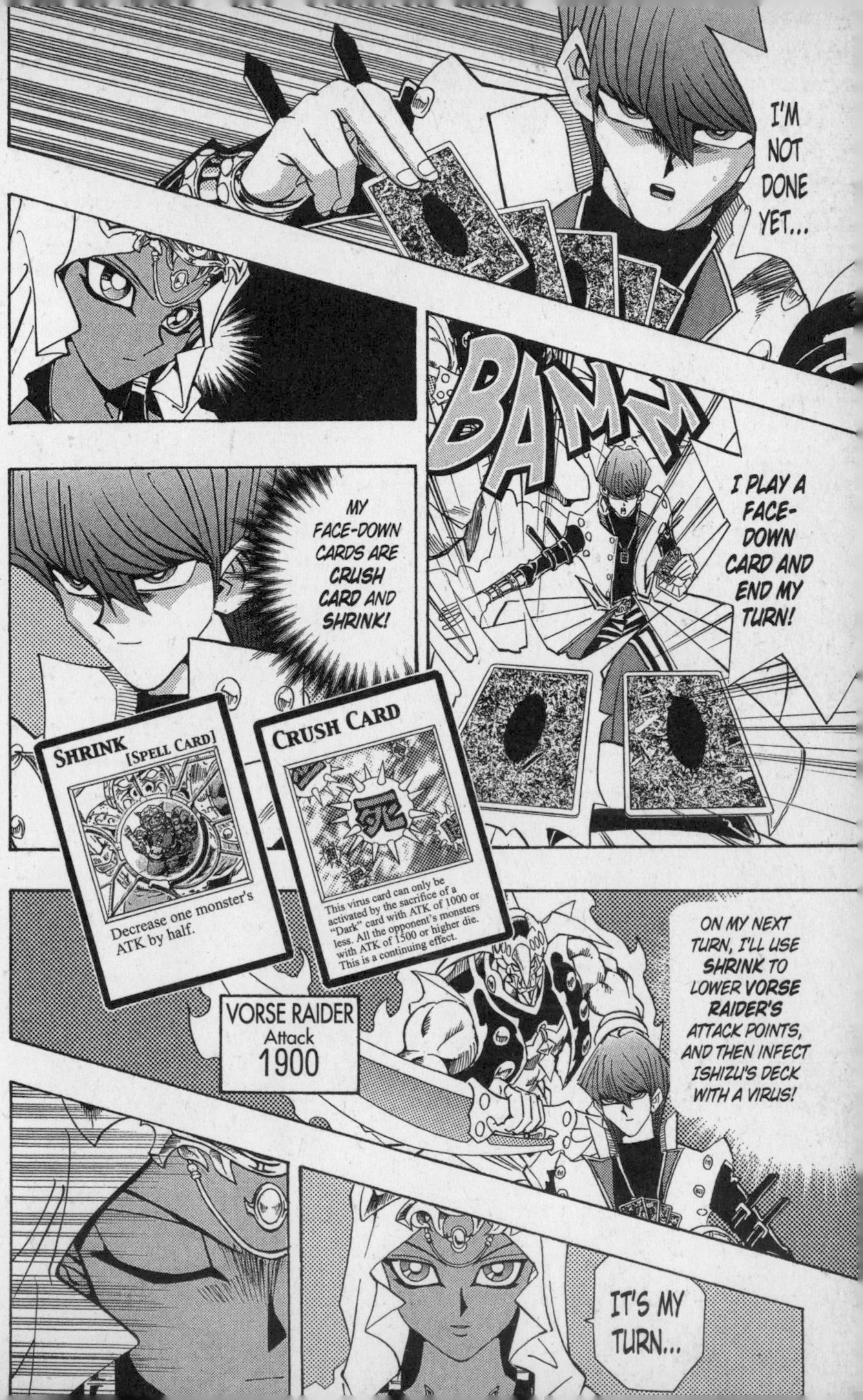
I'M NOT DONE YET...
BAMM
I PLAY A FACE-DOWN CARD AND END MY TURN!
MY FACE-DOWN CARDS ARE CRUSH CARD AND SHRINK!
SHRINK [SPELL CARD]
Decrease one monster's ATK by half.
CRUSH CARD
This virus card can only be activated by the sacrifice of a "Dark" card with ATK of 1000 or less. All the opponent's monsters with ATK of 1500 or higher die. This is a continuing effect.
ON MY NEXT TURN, I'LL USE SHRINK TO LOWER VORSE RAIDER'S ATTACK POINTS, AND THEN INFECT ISHIZU'S DECK WITH A VIRUS!
VORSE RAIDER
Attack
1900
IT'S MY TURN...

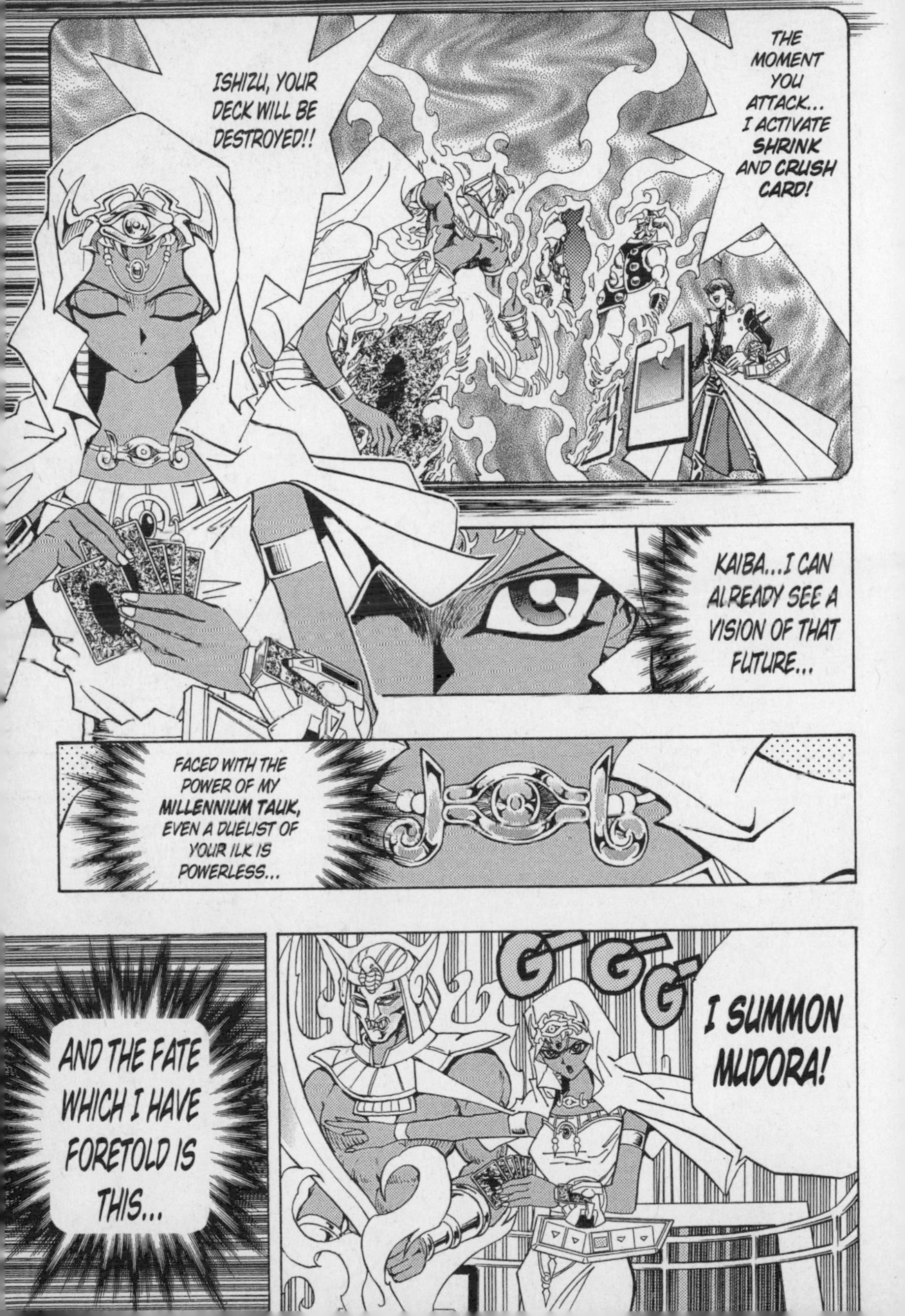
THE MOMENT YOU ATTACK... I ACTIVATE SHRINK AND CRUSH CARD!
ISHIZU, YOUR DECK WILL BE DESTROYED!!
KAIBA...I CAN ALREADY SEE A VISION OF THAT FUTURE...
FACED WITH THE POWER OF MY MILLENNIUM TAUK, EVEN A DUELIST OF YOUR ILK IS POWERLESS...
G-G-G-
I SUMMON MUDORA!
AND THE FATE WHICH I HAVE FORETOLD IS THIS...

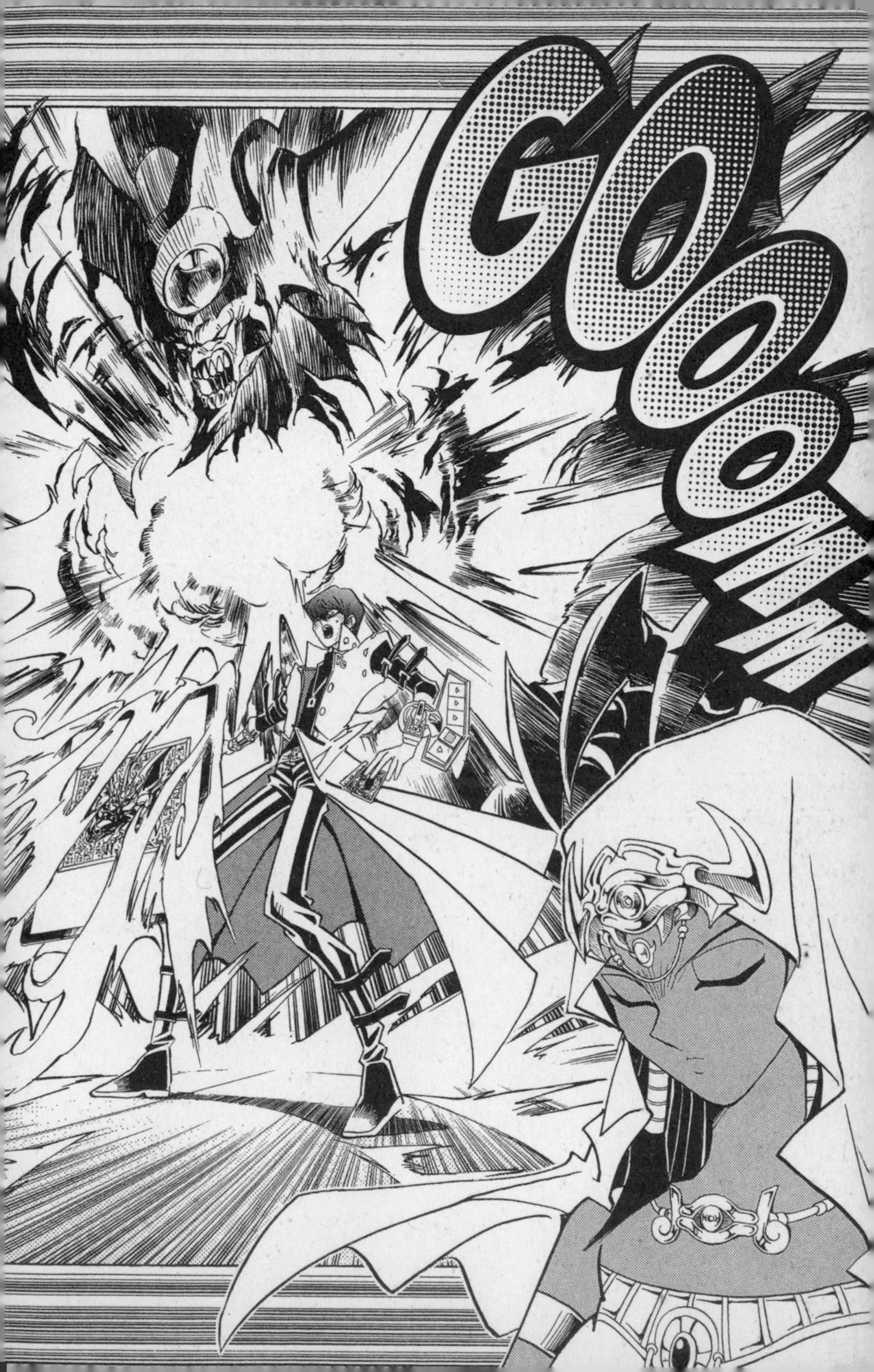
GOOOOMM

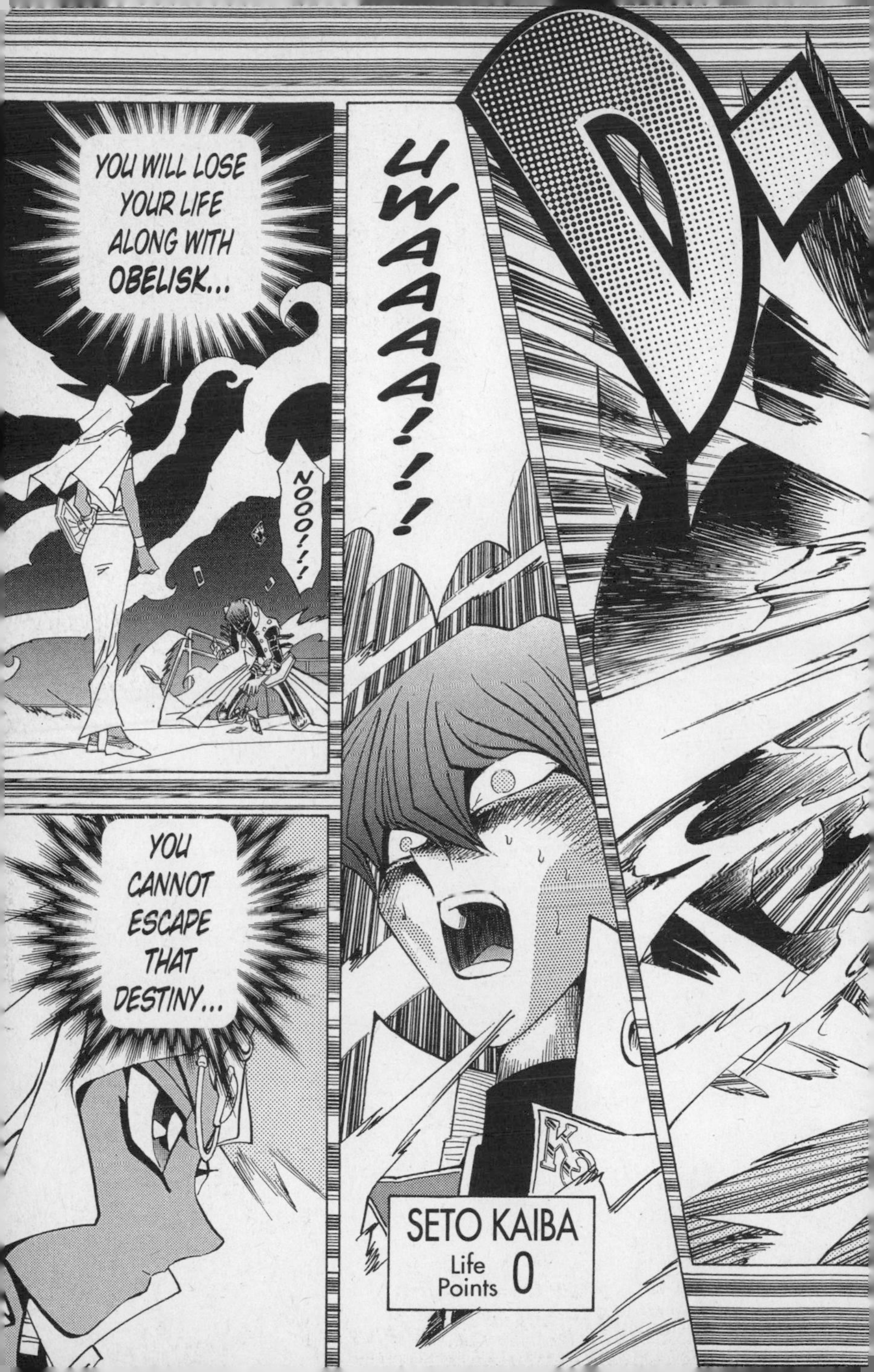
UWAAAAA!!!
SETO KAIBA
Life Points 0
YOU WILL LOSE YOUR LIFE ALONG WITH OBELISK...
NOOO!!!
YOU CANNOT ESCAPE THAT DESTINY...

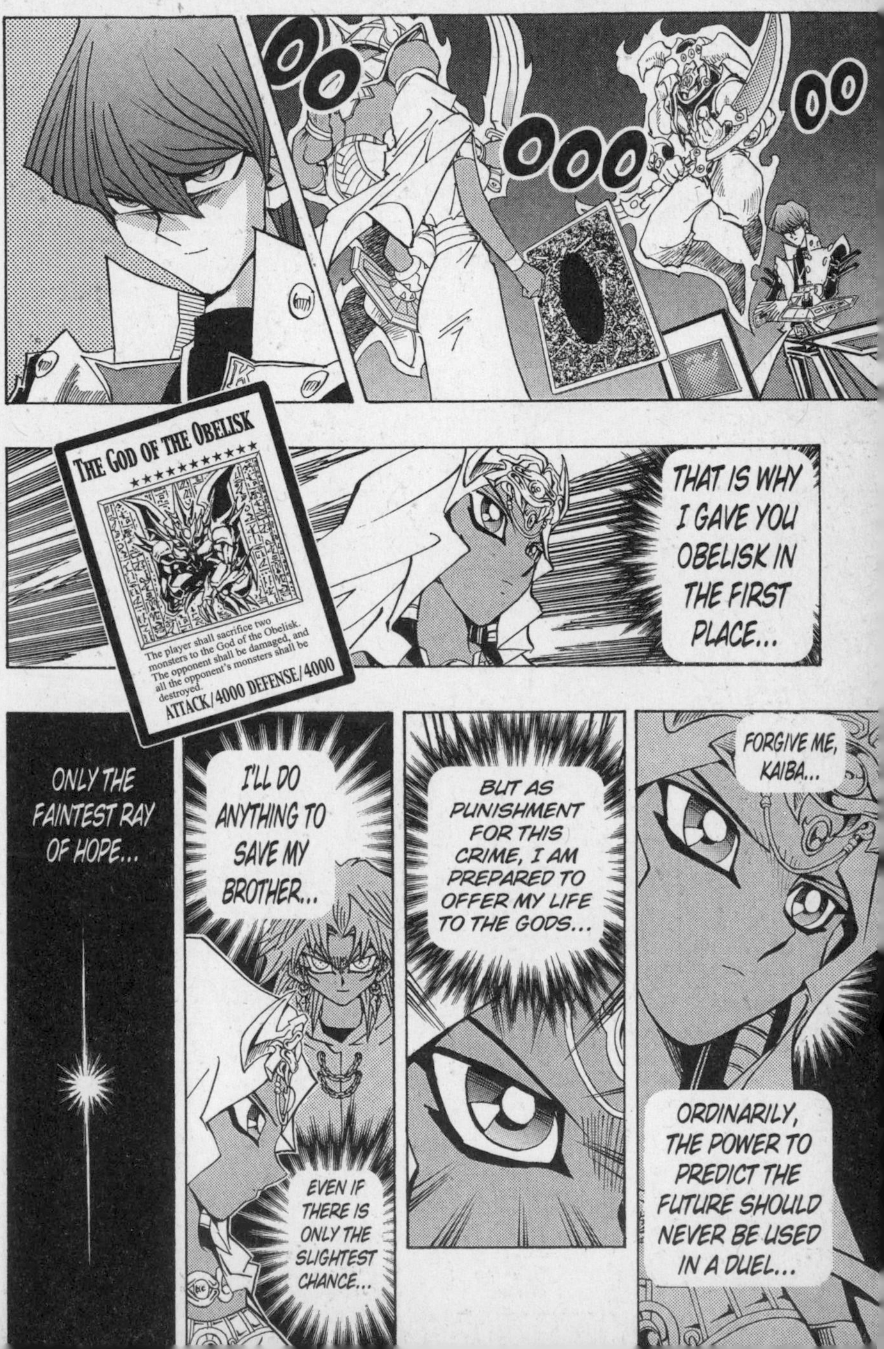
OO
OOO
OO
THAT IS WHY I GAVE YOU OBELISK IN THE FIRST PLACE...
THE GOD OF THE OBELISK
The player shall sacrifice two monsters to the God of the Obelisk. The opponent shall be damaged, and all the opponent's monsters shall be destroyed.
ATTACK/4000 DEFENSE/4000
FORGIVE ME, KAIBA...
ORDINARILY, THE POWER TO PREDICT THE FUTURE SHOULD NEVER BE USED IN A DUEL...
BUT AS PUNISHMENT FOR THIS CRIME, I AM PREPARED TO OFFER MY LIFE TO THE GODS...
I'LL DO ANYTHING TO SAVE MY BROTHER...
EVEN IF THERE IS ONLY THE SLIGHTEST CHANCE...
ONLY THE FAINTEST RAY OF HOPE...

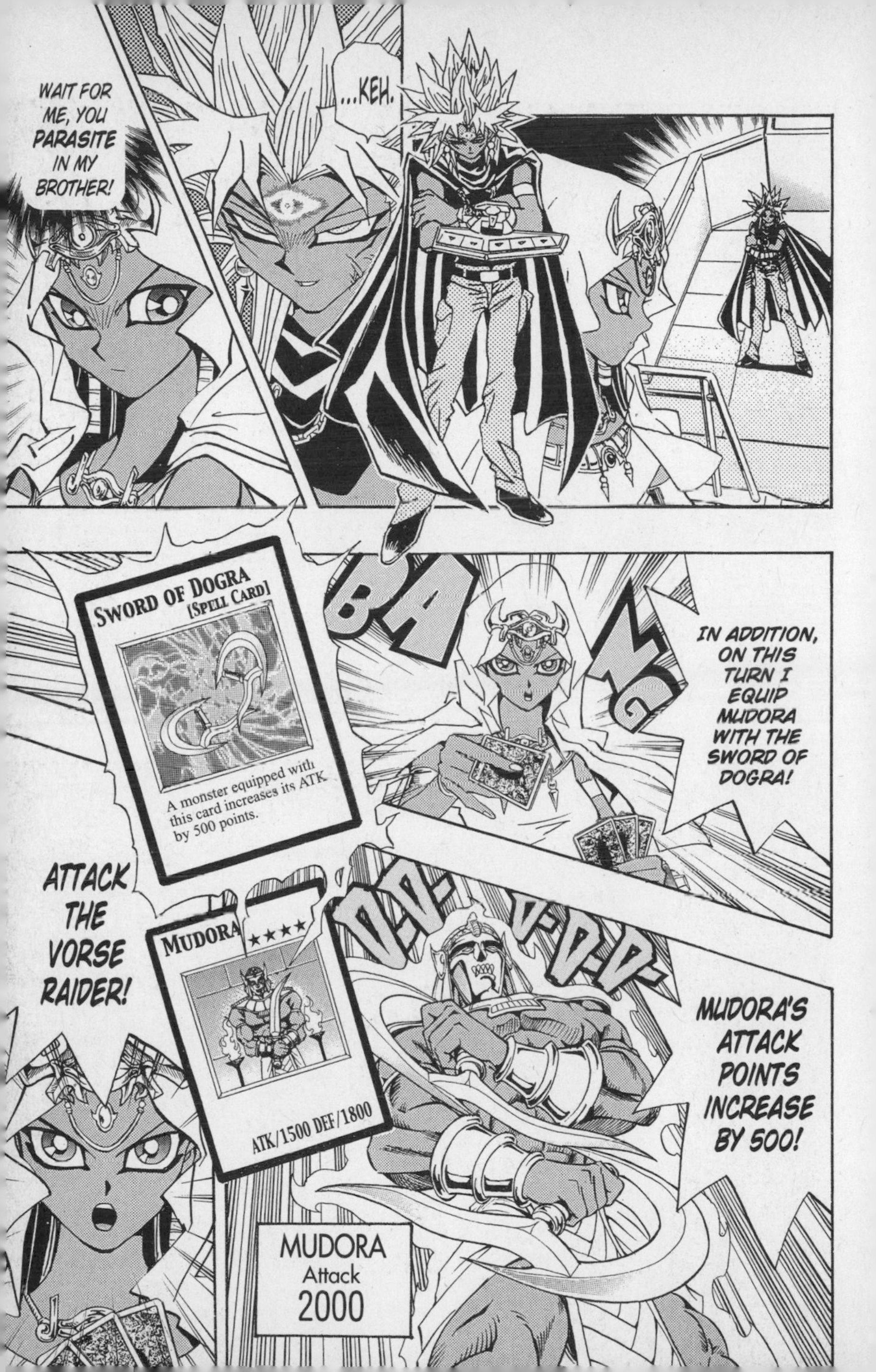
...KEH.
WAIT FOR ME, YOU PARASITE IN MY BROTHER!
IN ADDITION, ON THIS TURN I EQUIP MUDORA WITH THE SWORD OF DOGRA!
BA NG
SWORD OF DOGRA
[SPELL CARD]
A monster equipped with this card increases its ATK by 500 points.
MUDORA'S ATTACK POINTS INCREASE BY 500!
D-D- D-D-D-
ATTACK THE VORSE RAIDER!
MUDORA ★★★★
ATK/1500 DEF/1800
MUDORA
Attack
2000

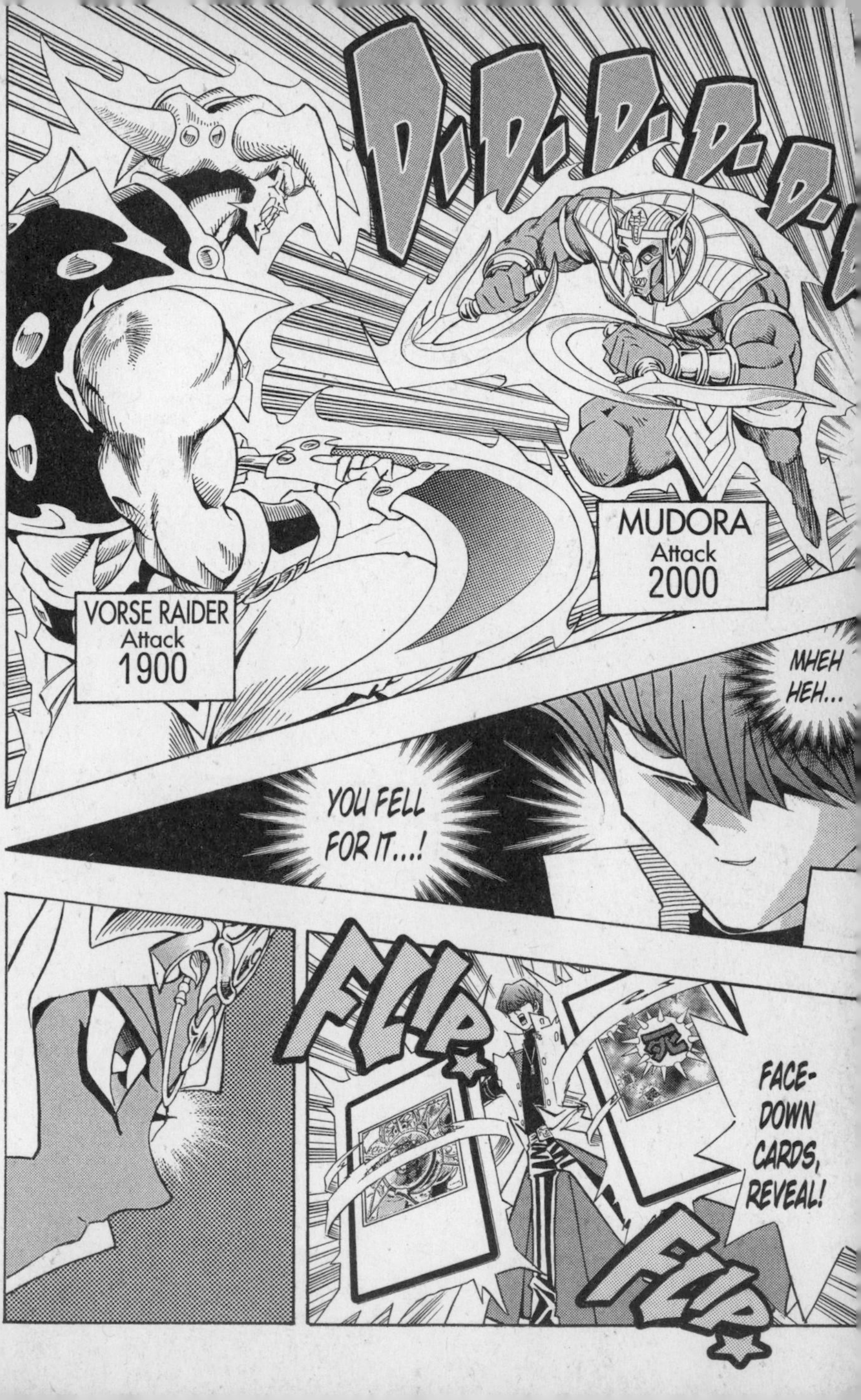
D.D.D.D.D.
MUDORA
Attack
2000
VORSE RAIDER
Attack
1900
MHEH HEH...
YOU FELL FOR IT...!
FACE-DOWN CARDS, REVEAL!
FLIP
FLIP

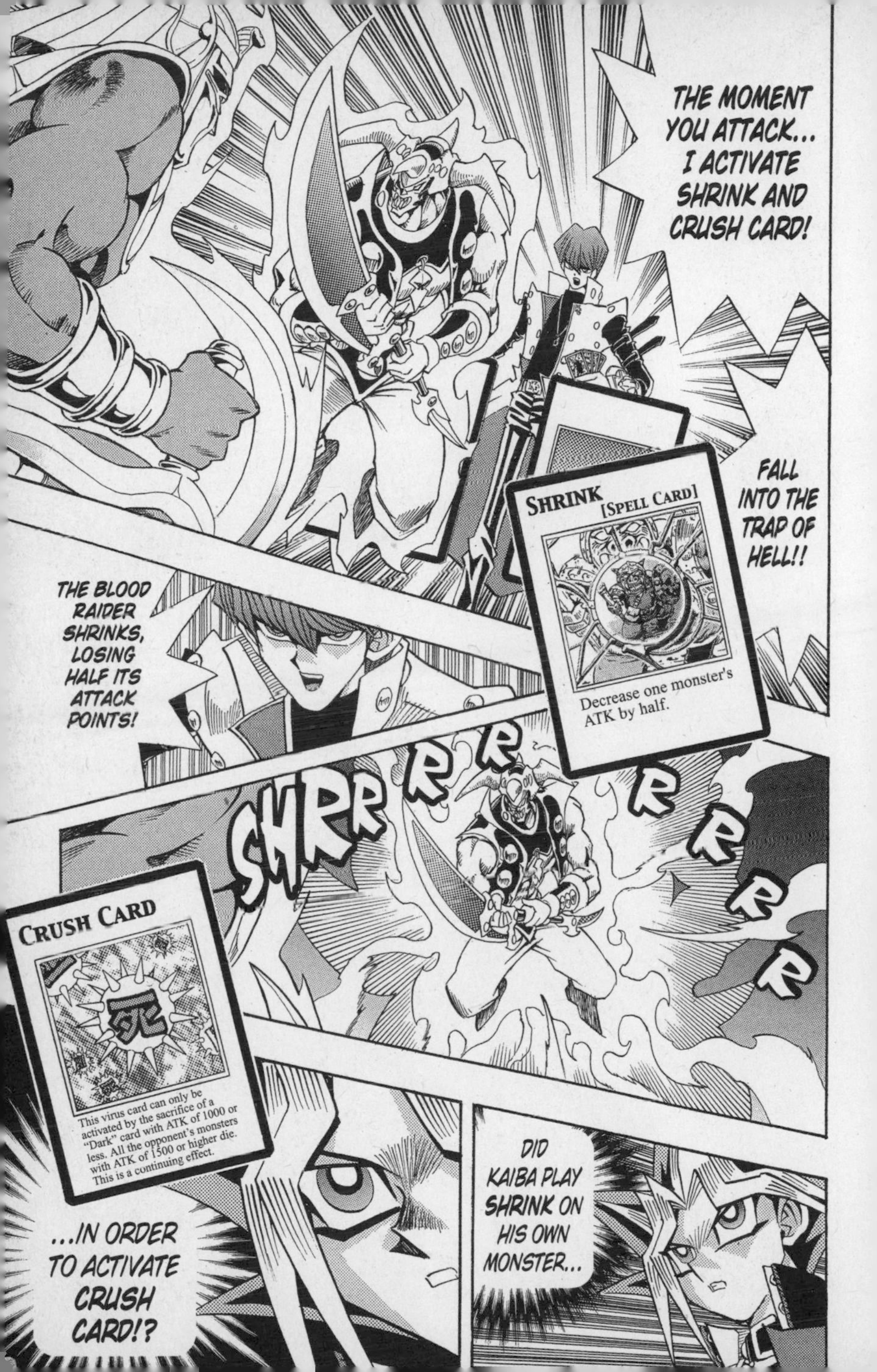
THE MOMENT YOU ATTACK... I ACTIVATE SHRINK AND CRUSH CARD!
FALL INTO THE TRAP OF HELL!!
SHRINK [SPELL CARD]
Decrease one monster's ATK by half.
THE BLOOD RAIDER SHRINKS, LOSING HALF ITS ATTACK POINTS!
SHRR R R R R R R R
CRUSH CARD
This virus card can only be activated by the sacrifice of a "Dark" card with ATK of 1000 or less. All the opponent's monsters with ATK of 1500 or higher die. This is a continuing effect.
DID KAIBA PLAY SHRINK ON HIS OWN MONSTER...
...IN ORDER TO ACTIVATE CRUSH CARD!?

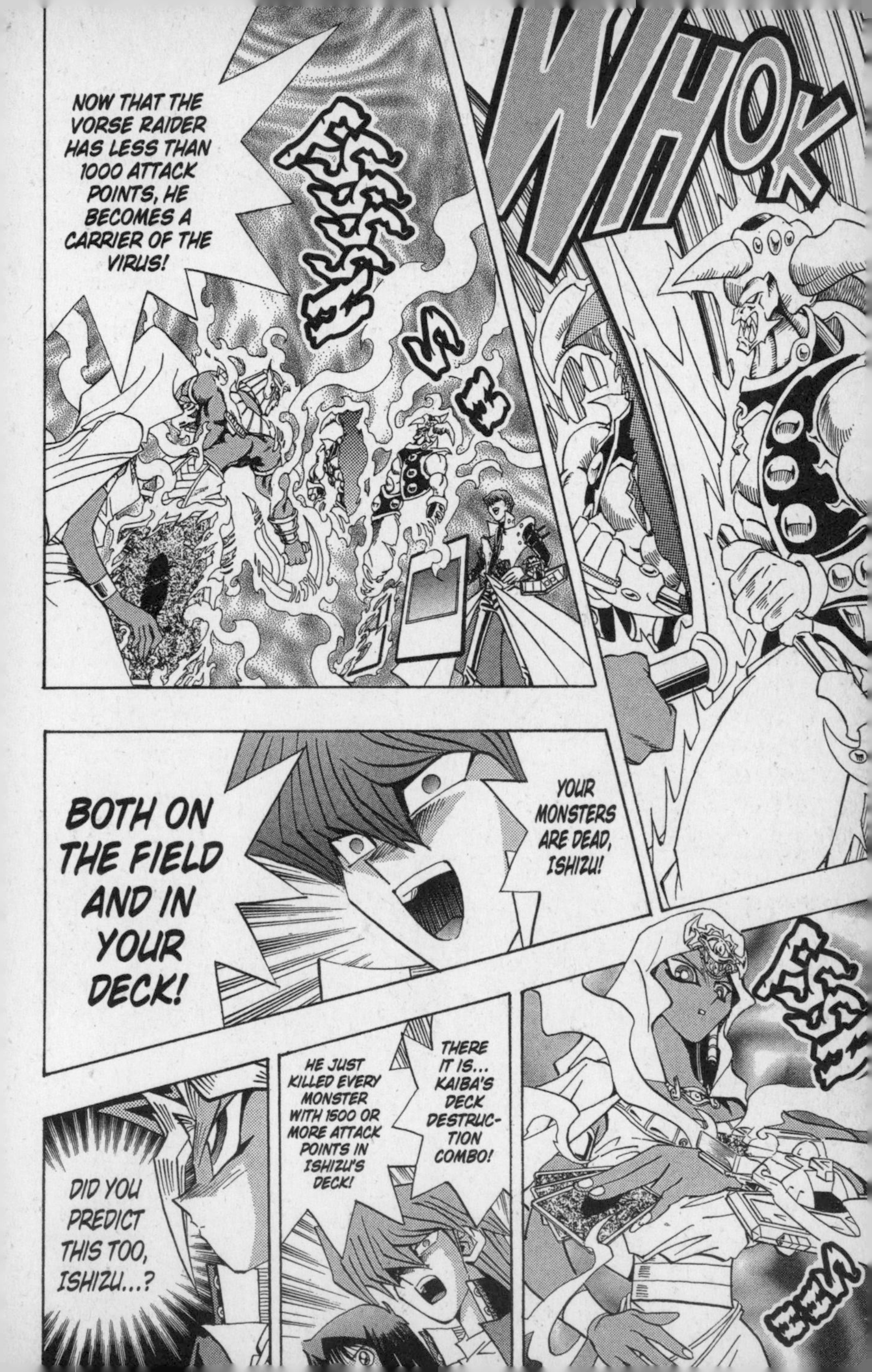
WHOK
NOW THAT THE VORSE RAIDER HAS LESS THAN 1000 ATTACK POINTS, HE BECOMES A CARRIER OF THE VIRUS!
YOUR MONSTERS ARE DEAD, ISHIZU!
BOTH ON THE FIELD AND IN YOUR DECK!
THERE IT IS... KAIBA'S DECK DESTRUCTION COMBO!
HE JUST KILLED EVERY MONSTER WITH 1500 OR MORE ATTACK POINTS IN ISHIZU'S DECK!
DID YOU PREDICT THIS TOO, ISHIZU...?

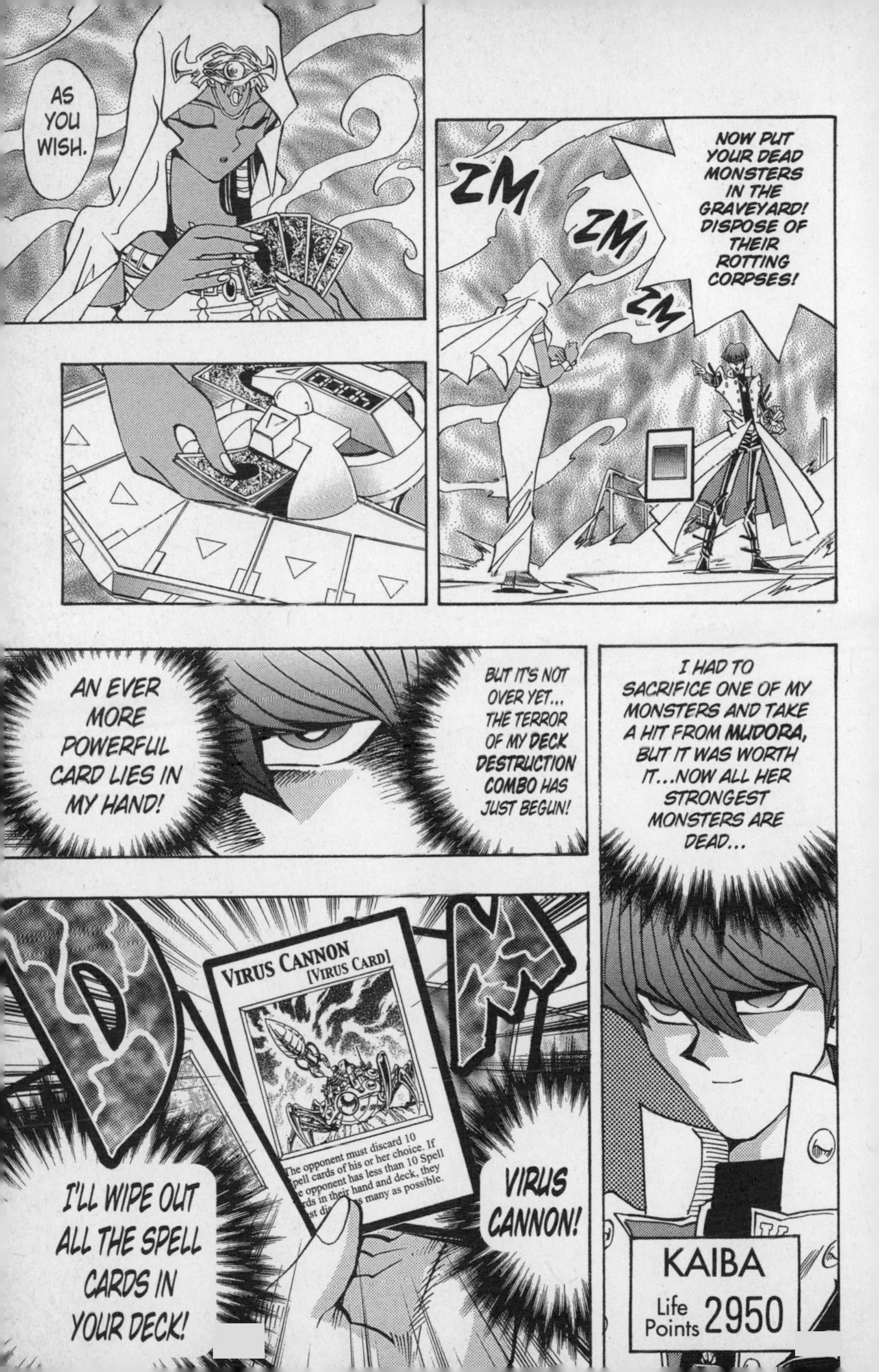
NOW PUT YOUR DEAD MONSTERS IN THE GRAVEYARD! DISPOSE OF THEIR ROTTING CORPSES!
ZM
ZM
ZM
AS YOU WISH.
I HAD TO SACRIFICE ONE OF MY MONSTERS AND TAKE A HIT FROM MUDORA, BUT IT WAS WORTH IT...NOW ALL HER STRONGEST MONSTERS ARE DEAD...
KAIBA
Life Points 2950
BUT IT'S NOT OVER YET... THE TERROR OF MY DECK DESTRUCTION COMBO HAS JUST BEGUN!
AN EVER MORE POWERFUL CARD LIES IN MY HAND!
VIRUS CANNON!
VIRUS CANNON
[VIRUS CARD]
The opponent must discard 10
I'LL WIPE OUT ALL THE SPELL CARDS IN YOUR DECK!

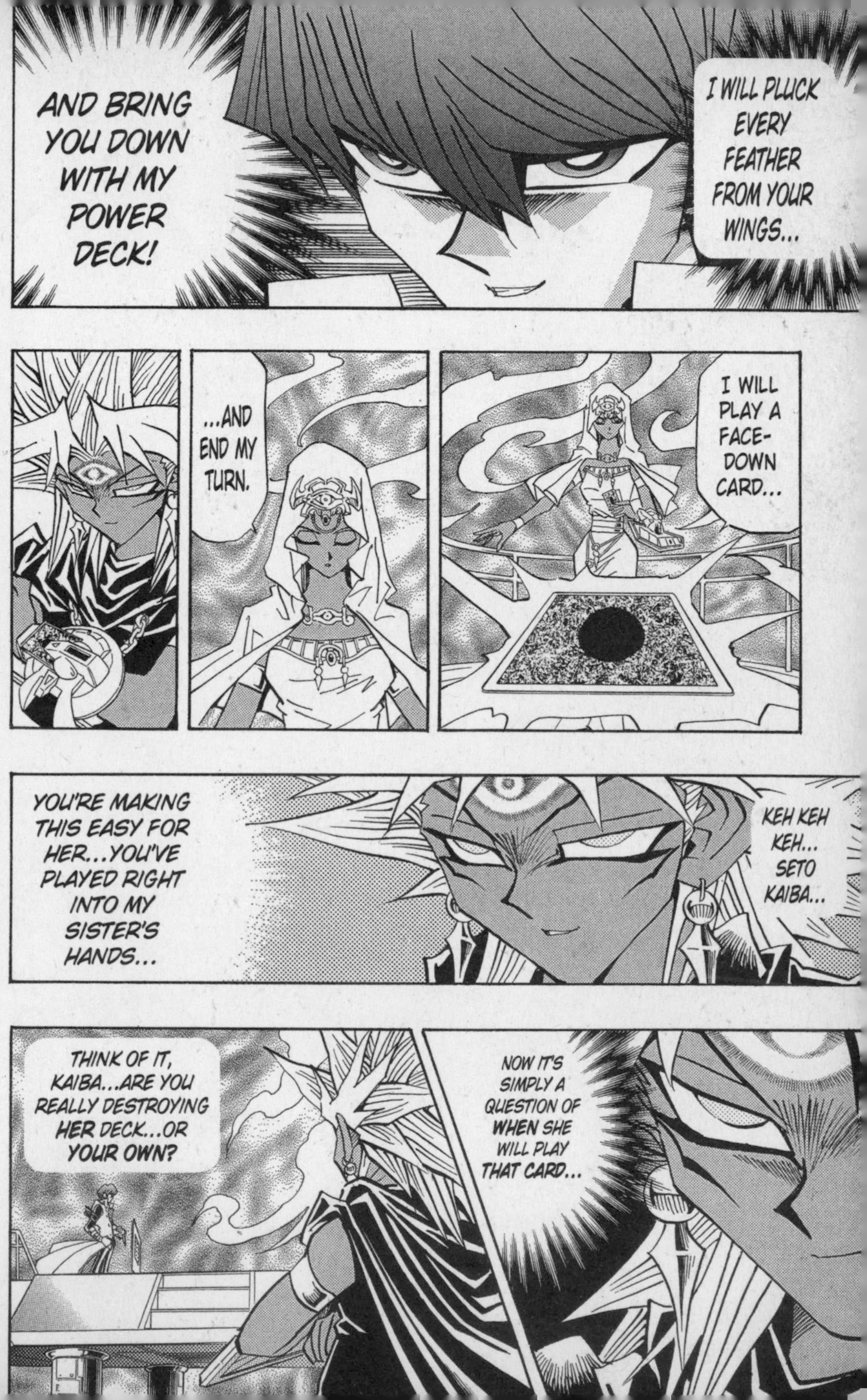
I WILL PLUCK EVERY FEATHER FROM YOUR WINGS...
AND BRING YOU DOWN WITH MY POWER DECK!
I WILL PLAY A FACE-DOWN CARD...
...AND END MY TURN.
KEH KEH KEH... SETO KAIBA...
YOU'RE MAKING THIS EASY FOR HER...YOU'VE PLAYED RIGHT INTO MY SISTER'S HANDS...
NOW IT'S SIMPLY A QUESTION OF WHEN SHE WILL PLAY THAT CARD...
THINK OF IT, KAIBA...ARE YOU REALLY DESTROYING HER DECK...OR YOUR OWN?

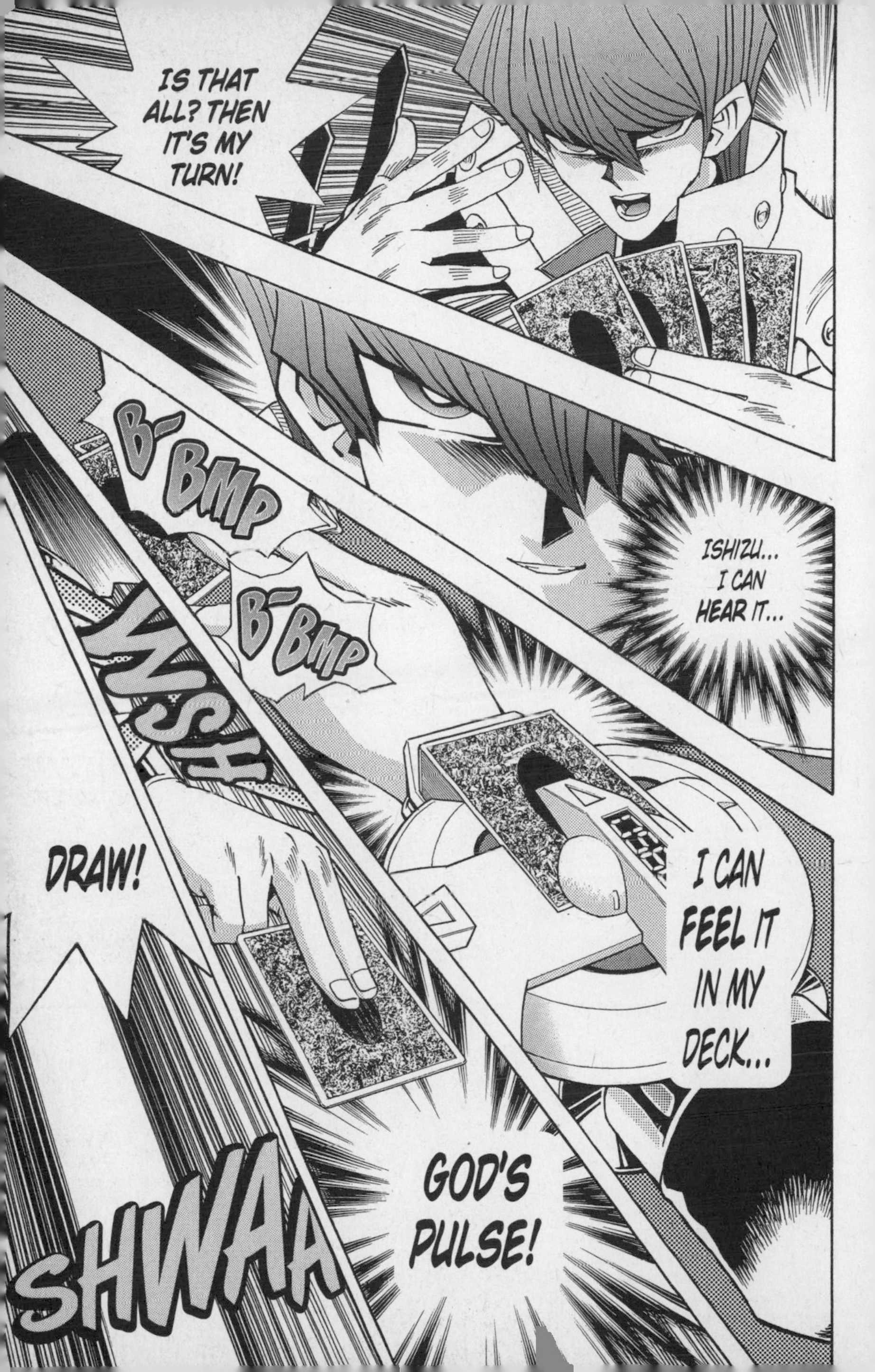
IS THAT ALL? THEN IT'S MY TURN!
ISHIZU... I CAN HEAR IT...
B-BMP
B-BMP
WSH
I CAN FEEL IT IN MY DECK...
DRAW!
GOD'S PULSE!
SHWAA

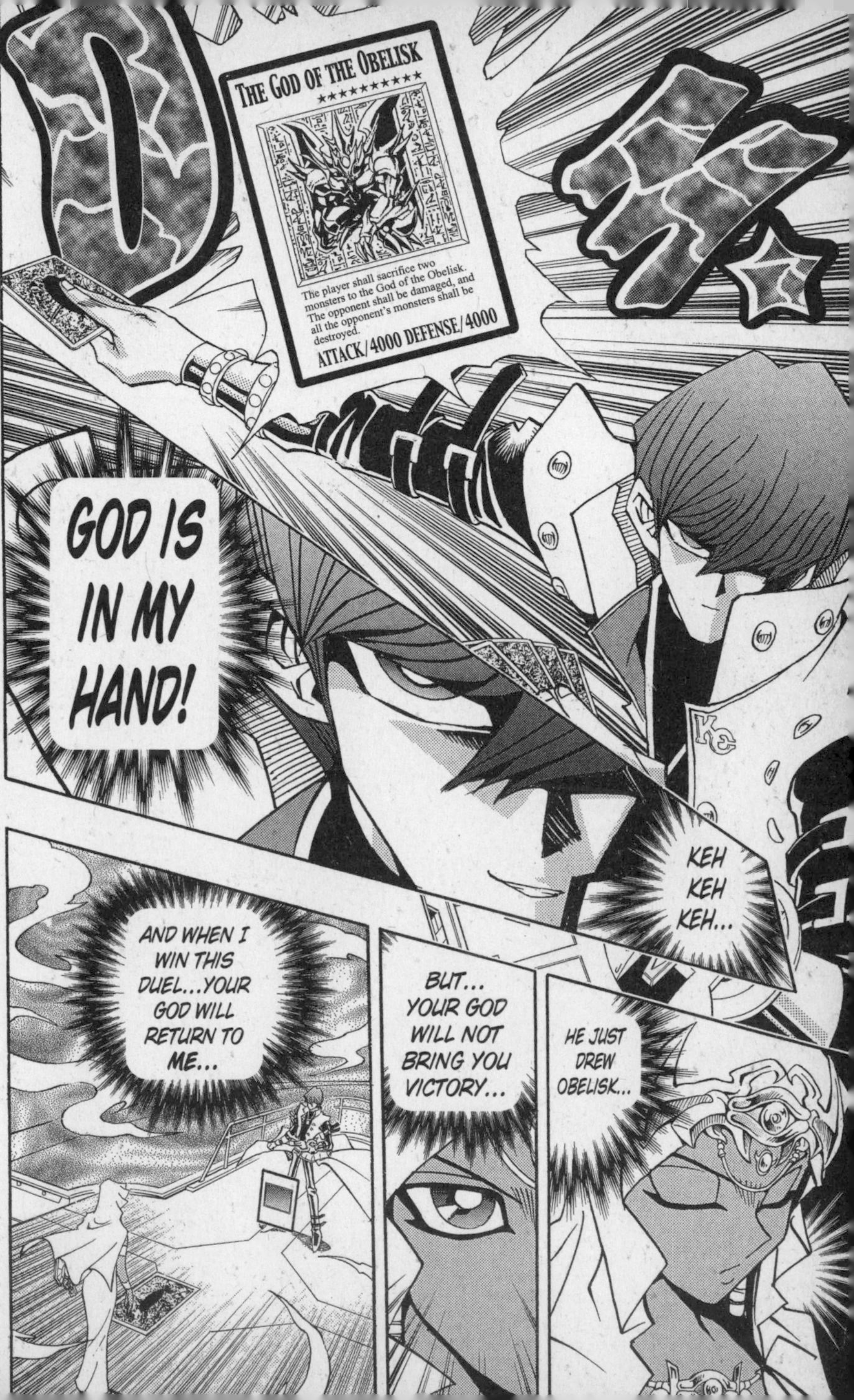
THE GOD OF THE OBELISK
★★★★★★★★★★
The player shall sacrifice two monsters to the God of the Obelisk. The opponent shall be damaged, and all the opponent's monsters shall be destroyed.
ATTACK/4000 DEFENSE/4000
GOD IS IN MY HAND!
KEH KEH KEH...
HE JUST DREW OBELISK...
BUT... YOUR GOD WILL NOT BRING YOU VICTORY...
AND WHEN I WIN THIS DUEL...YOUR GOD WILL RETURN TO ME...

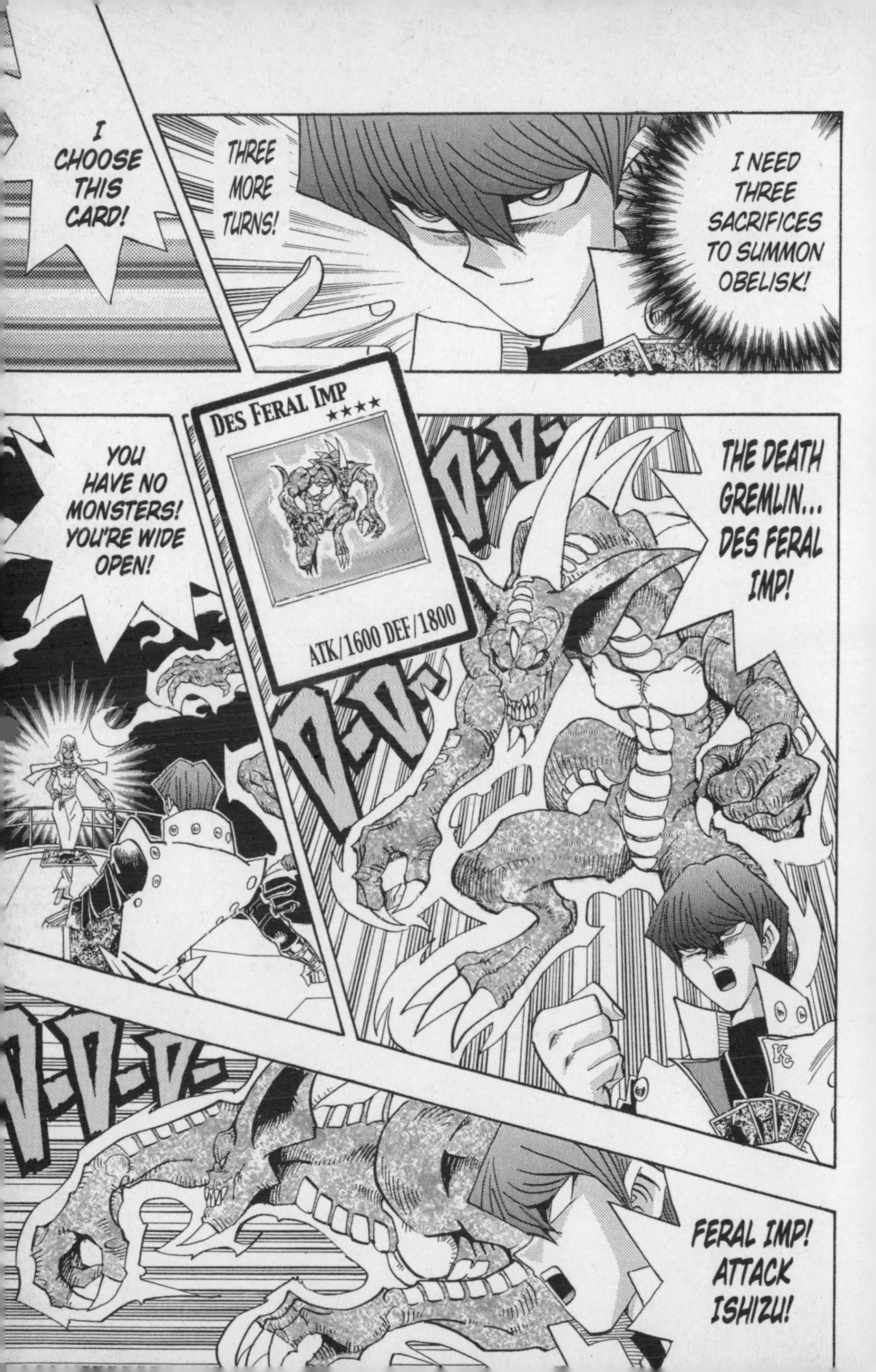
I NEED THREE SACRIFICES TO SUMMON OBELISK!
THREE MORE TURNS!
I CHOOSE THIS CARD!
THE DEATH GREMLIN... DES FERAL IMP!
DES FERAL IMP
ATK/1600 DEF/1800
YOU HAVE NO MONSTERS! YOU'RE WIDE OPEN!
FERAL IMP! ATTACK ISHIZU!

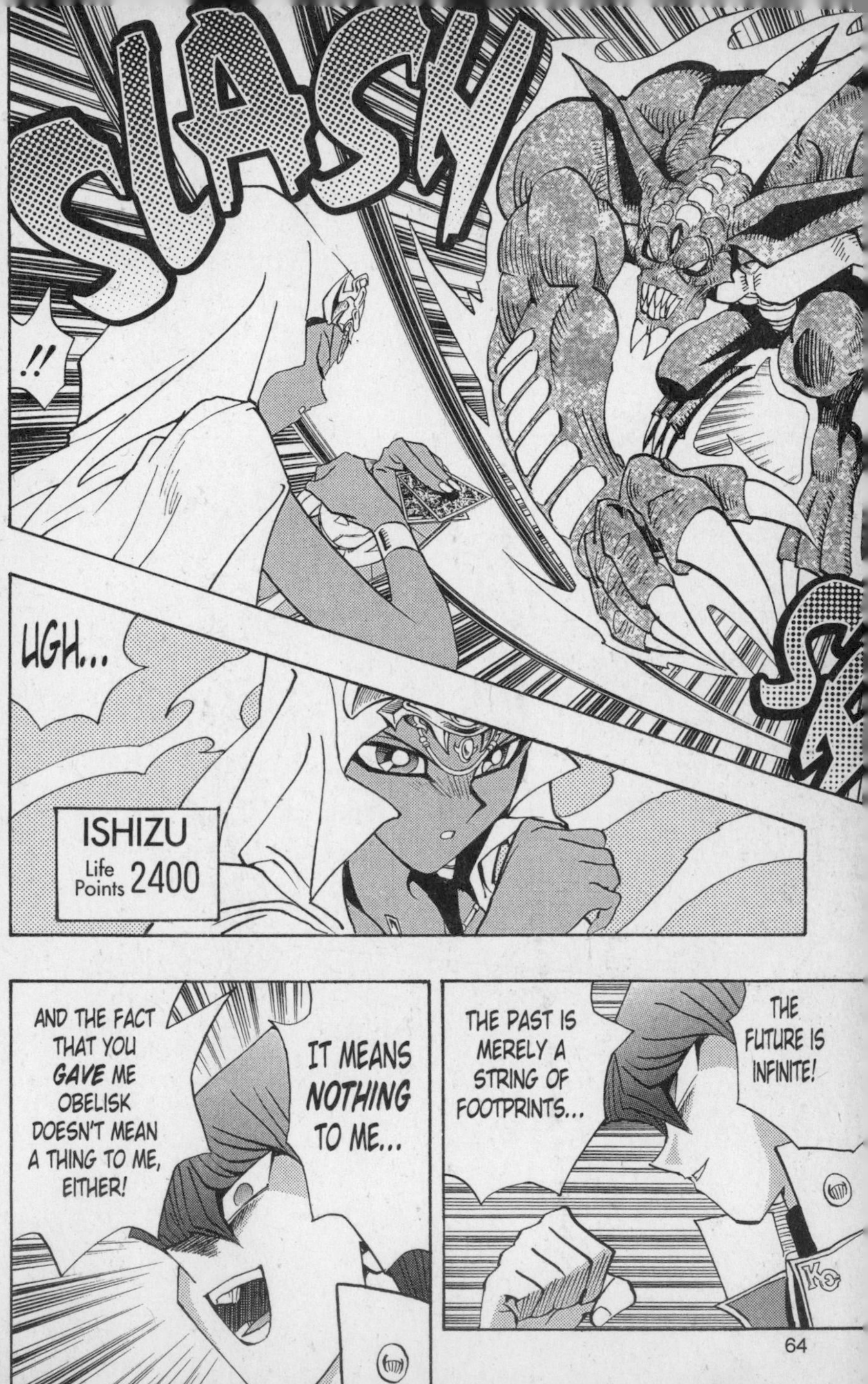
SLASH
!!
UGH...
ISHIZU
Life Points 2400
THE PAST IS MERELY A STRING OF FOOTPRINTS...
THE FUTURE IS INFINITE!
IT MEANS NOTHING TO ME...
AND THE FACT THAT YOU GAVE ME OBELISK DOESN'T MEAN A THING TO ME, EITHER!

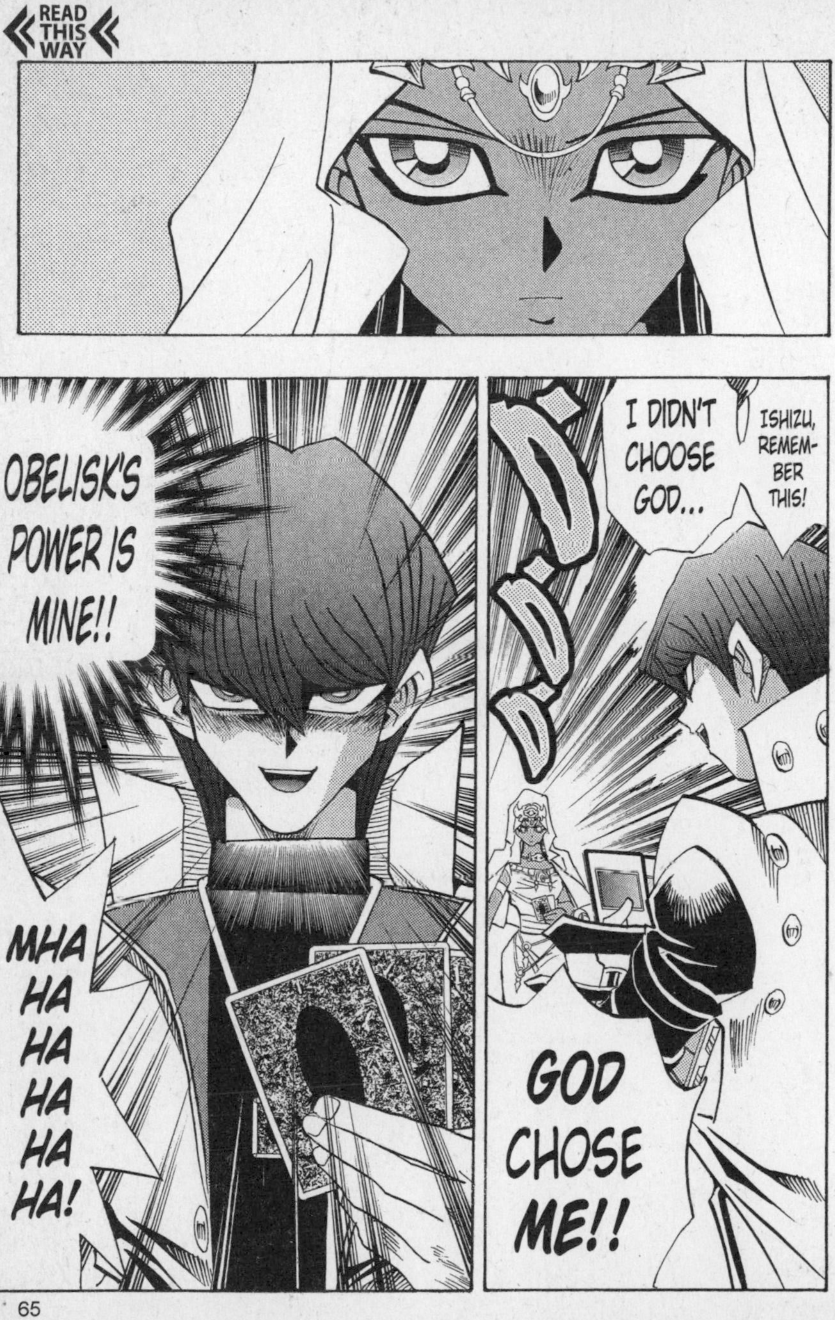
READ THIS WAY
I DIDN'T CHOOSE GOD...
ISHIZU, REMEM-BER THIS!
GOD CHOSE ME!!
OBELISK'S POWER IS MINE!!
MHA HA HA HA HA HA!

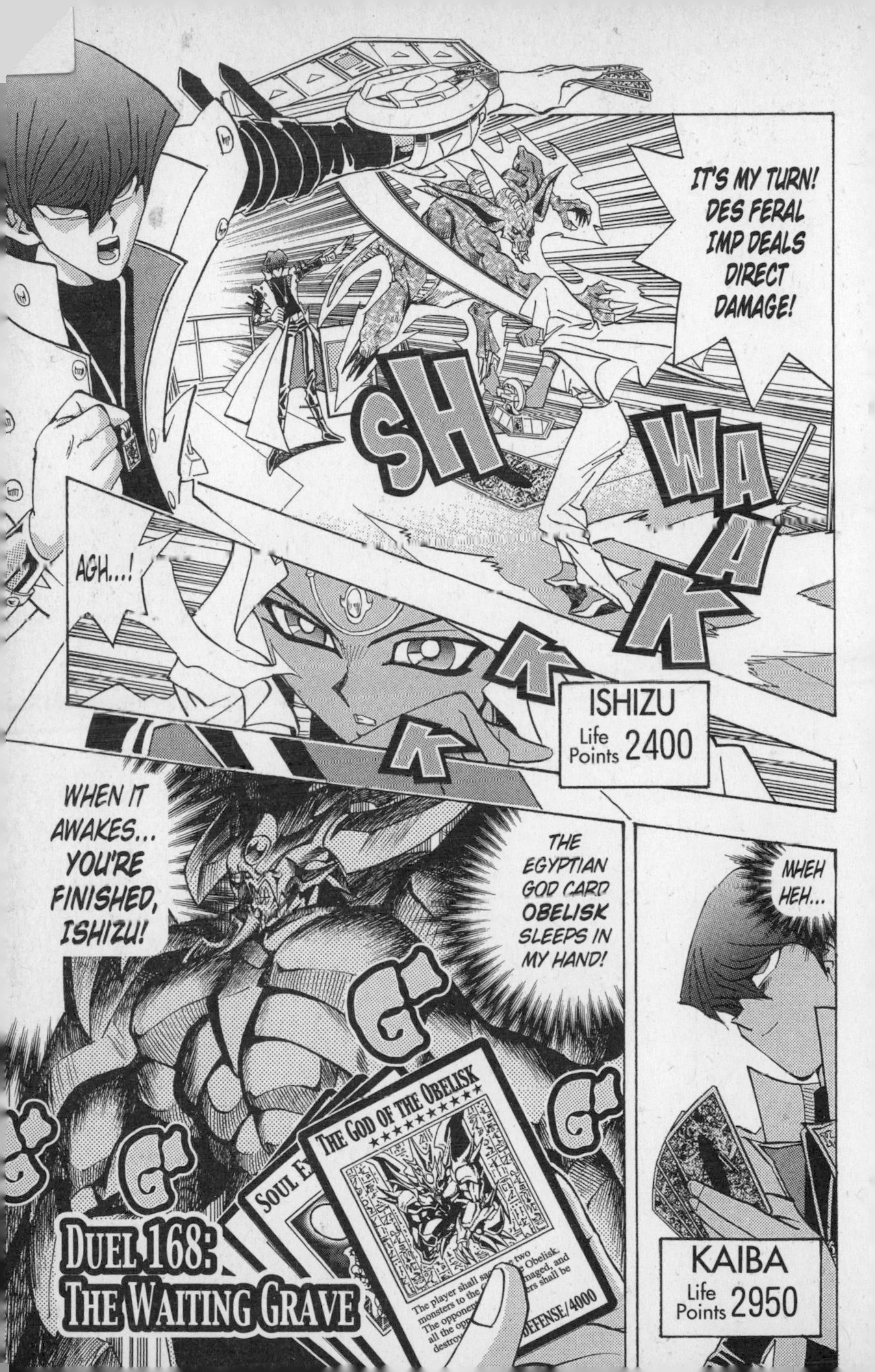
IT'S MY TURN! DES FERAL IMP DEALS DIRECT DAMAGE!
SH
WA
AK
AGH...!
K
K
ISHIZU
Life Points 2400
MHEH HEH...
KAIBA
Life Points 2950
THE EGYPTIAN GOD CARD OBELISK SLEEPS IN MY HAND!
WHEN IT AWAKES... YOU'RE FINISHED, ISHIZU!
G
G
G
G
THE GOD OF THE OBELISK
DEFENSE/4000
Duel 168:
The Waiting Grave

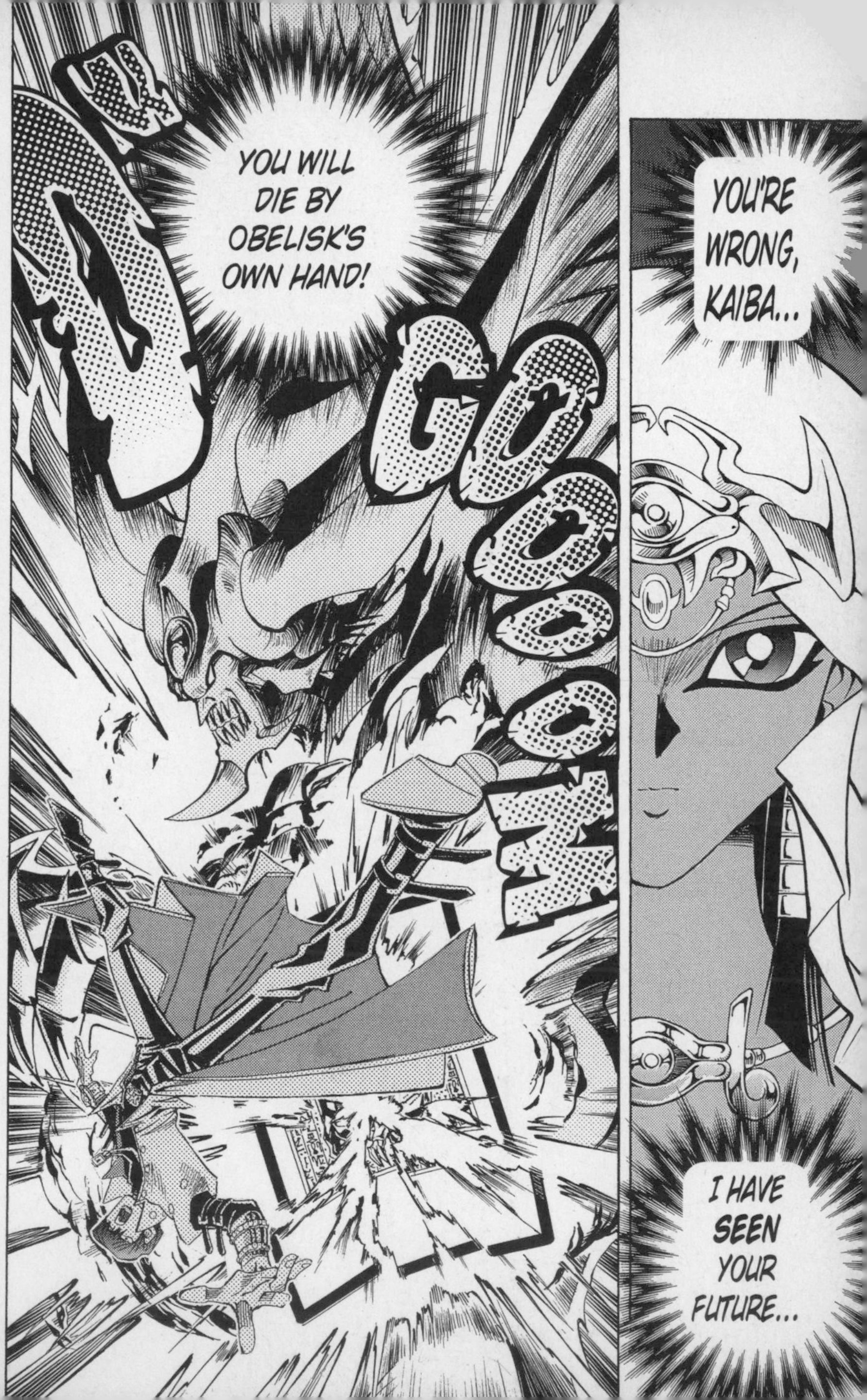
YOU'RE WRONG, KAIBA...
I HAVE SEEN YOUR FUTURE...
YOU WILL DIE BY OBELISK'S OWN HAND!
GOOOOM

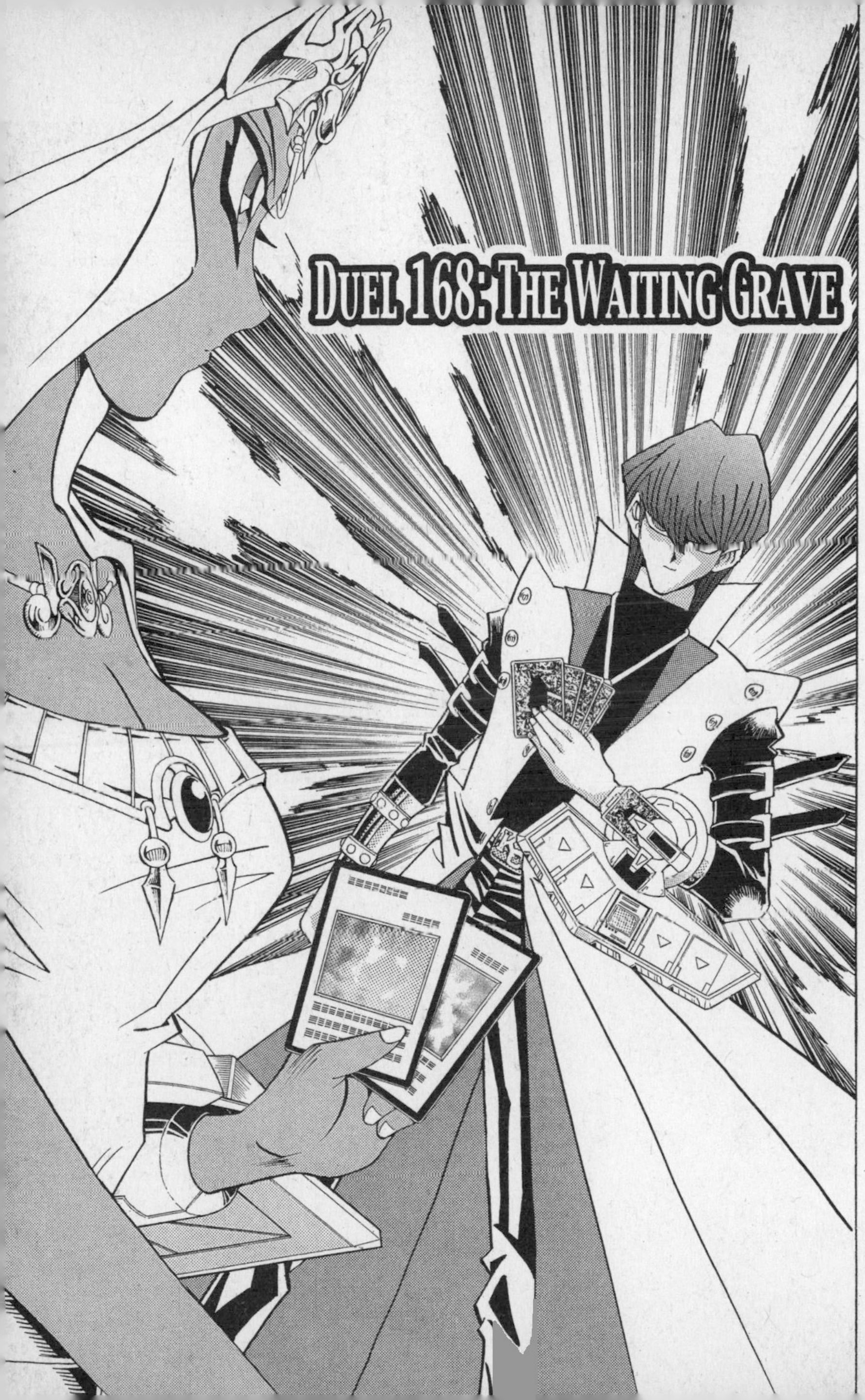
DUEL 168: THE WAITING GRAVE

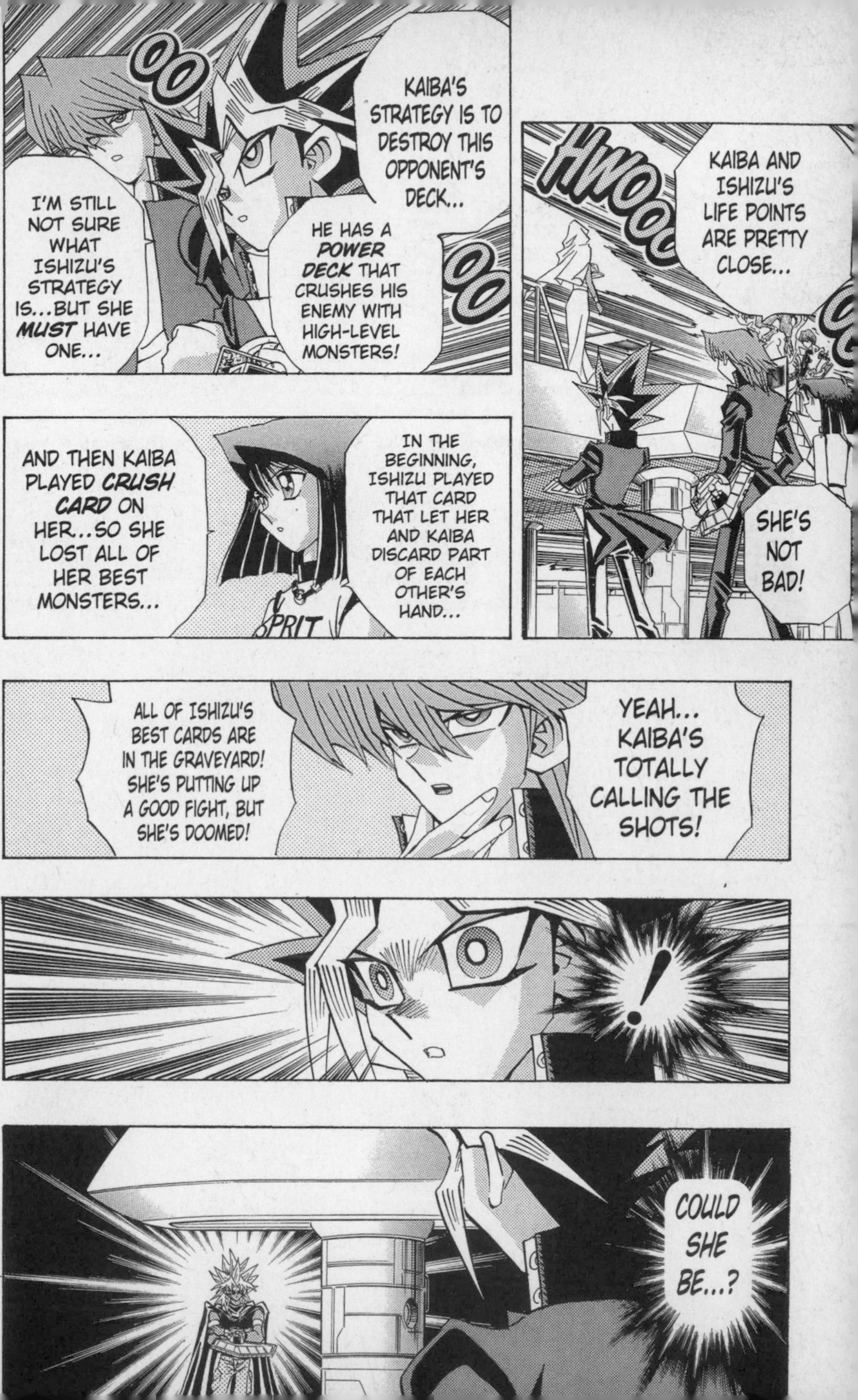
KAIBA AND ISHIZU'S LIFE POINTS ARE PRETTY CLOSE...
HWOOOOOOO
SHE'S NOT BAD!
KAIBA'S STRATEGY IS TO DESTROY THIS OPPONENT'S DECK...
HE HAS A **POWER DECK** THAT CRUSHES HIS ENEMY WITH HIGH-LEVEL MONSTERS!
I'M STILL NOT SURE WHAT ISHIZU'S STRATEGY IS...BUT SHE **MUST** HAVE ONE...
IN THE BEGINNING, ISHIZU PLAYED THAT CARD THAT LET HER AND KAIBA DISCARD PART OF EACH OTHER'S HAND...
AND THEN KAIBA PLAYED **CRUSH CARD** ON HER...SO SHE LOST ALL OF HER BEST MONSTERS...
YEAH... KAIBA'S TOTALLY CALLING THE SHOTS!
ALL OF ISHIZU'S BEST CARDS ARE IN THE GRAVEYARD! SHE'S PUTTING UP A GOOD FIGHT, BUT SHE'S DOOMED!
!
COULD SHE BE...?

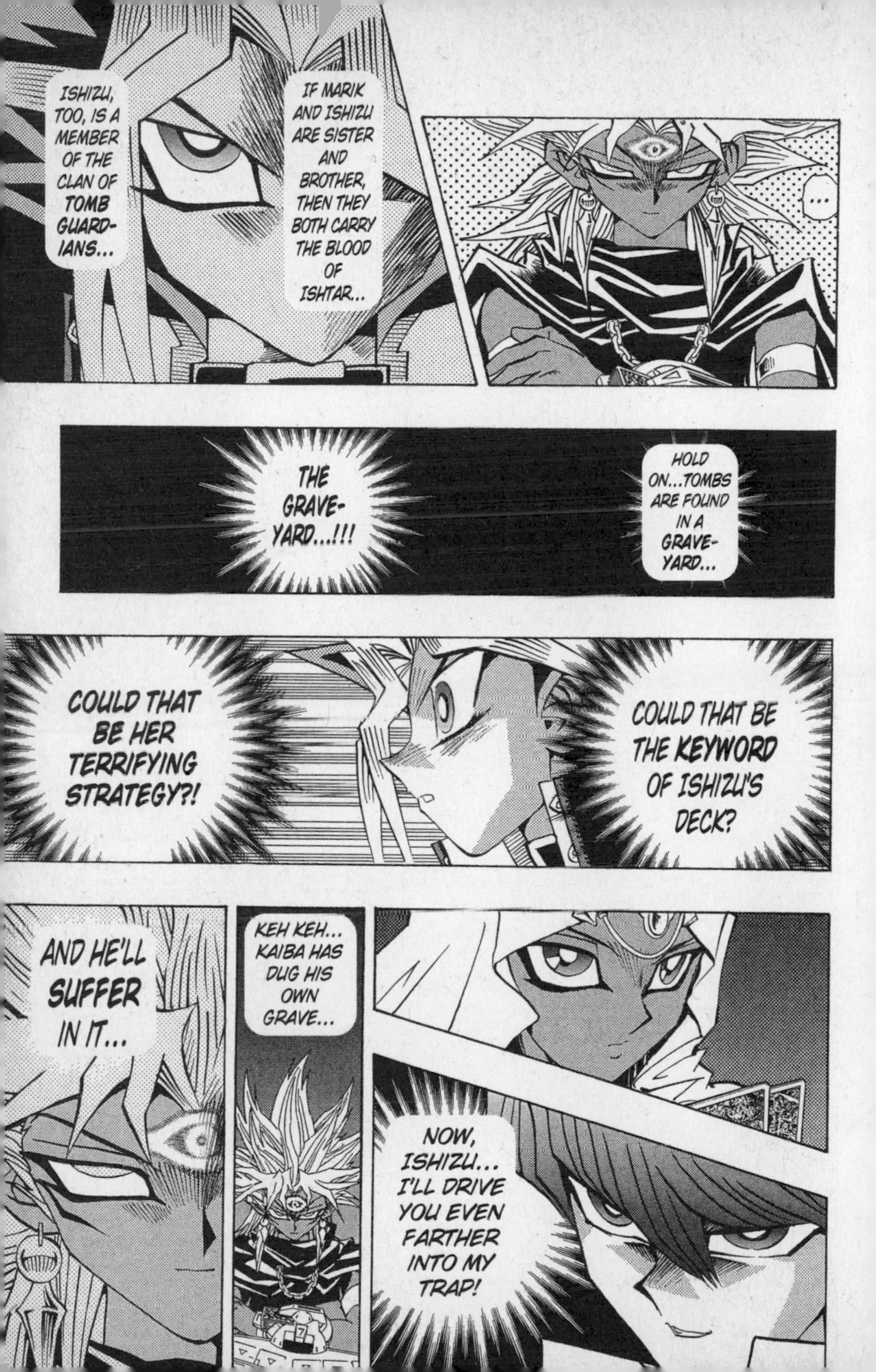
...
IF MARIK AND ISHIZU ARE SISTER AND BROTHER, THEN THEY BOTH CARRY THE BLOOD OF ISHTAR...
ISHIZU, TOO, IS A MEMBER OF THE CLAN OF TOMB GUARDIANS...
HOLD ON...TOMBS ARE FOUND IN A GRAVEYARD...
THE GRAVEYARD...!!!
COULD THAT BE THE KEYWORD OF ISHIZU'S DECK?
COULD THAT BE HER TERRIFYING STRATEGY?!
NOW, ISHIZU... I'LL DRIVE YOU EVEN FARTHER INTO MY TRAP!
KEH KEH... KAIBA HAS DUG HIS OWN GRAVE...
AND HE'LL SUFFER IN IT...

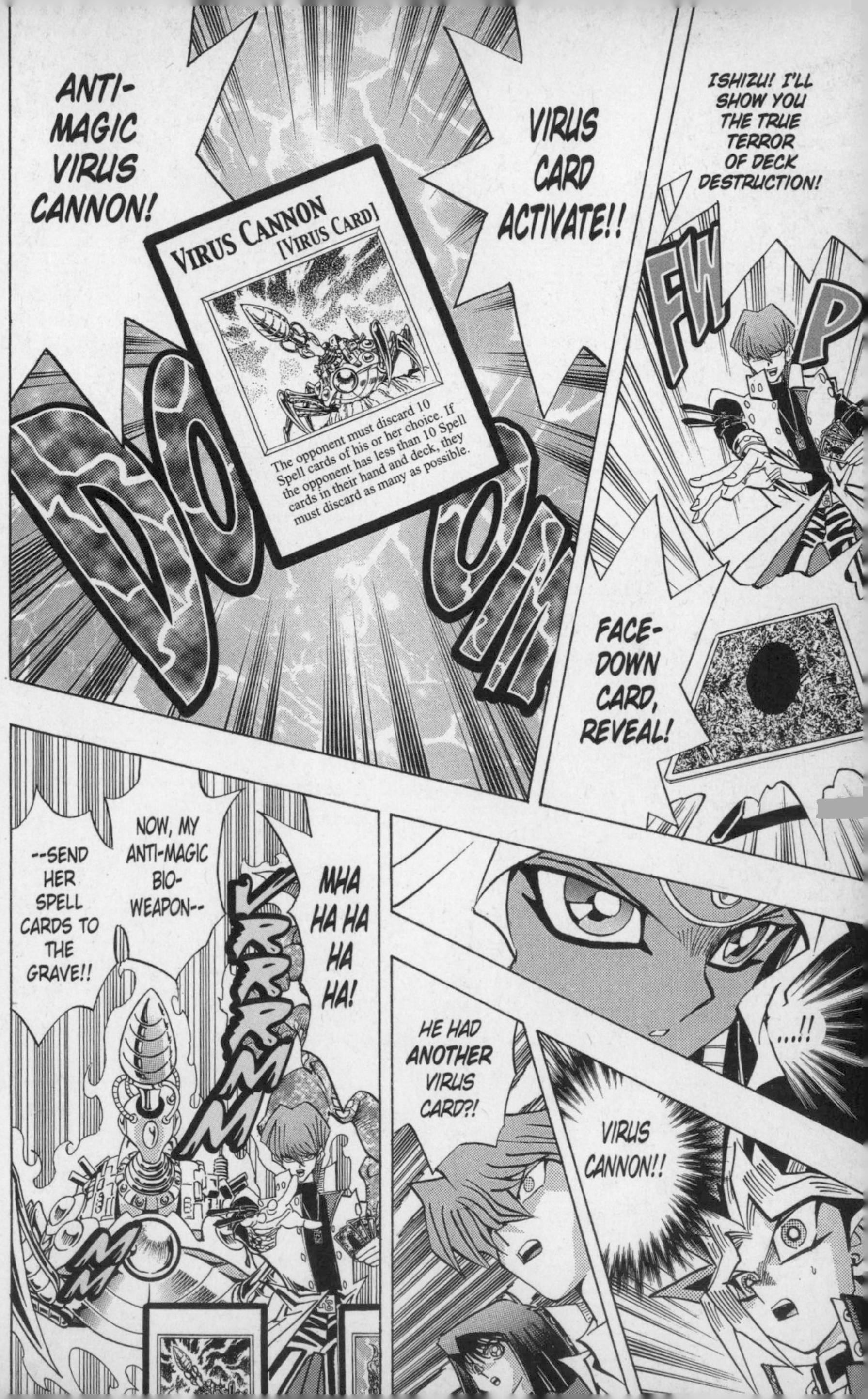
ISHIZU! I'LL SHOW YOU THE TRUE TERROR OF DECK DESTRUCTION!
FWP
FACE-DOWN CARD, REVEAL!
VIRUS CARD ACTIVATE!!
ANTI-MAGIC VIRUS CANNON!
VIRUS CANNON
[VIRUS CARD]
The opponent must discard 10 Spell cards of his or her choice. If the opponent has less than 10 Spell cards in their hand and deck, they must discard as many as possible.
DOOM
...!!
HE HAD ANOTHER VIRUS CARD?!
VIRUS CANNON!!
MHA HA HA HA HA!
NOW, MY ANTI-MAGIC BIO-WEAPON--
--SEND HER SPELL CARDS TO THE GRAVE!!

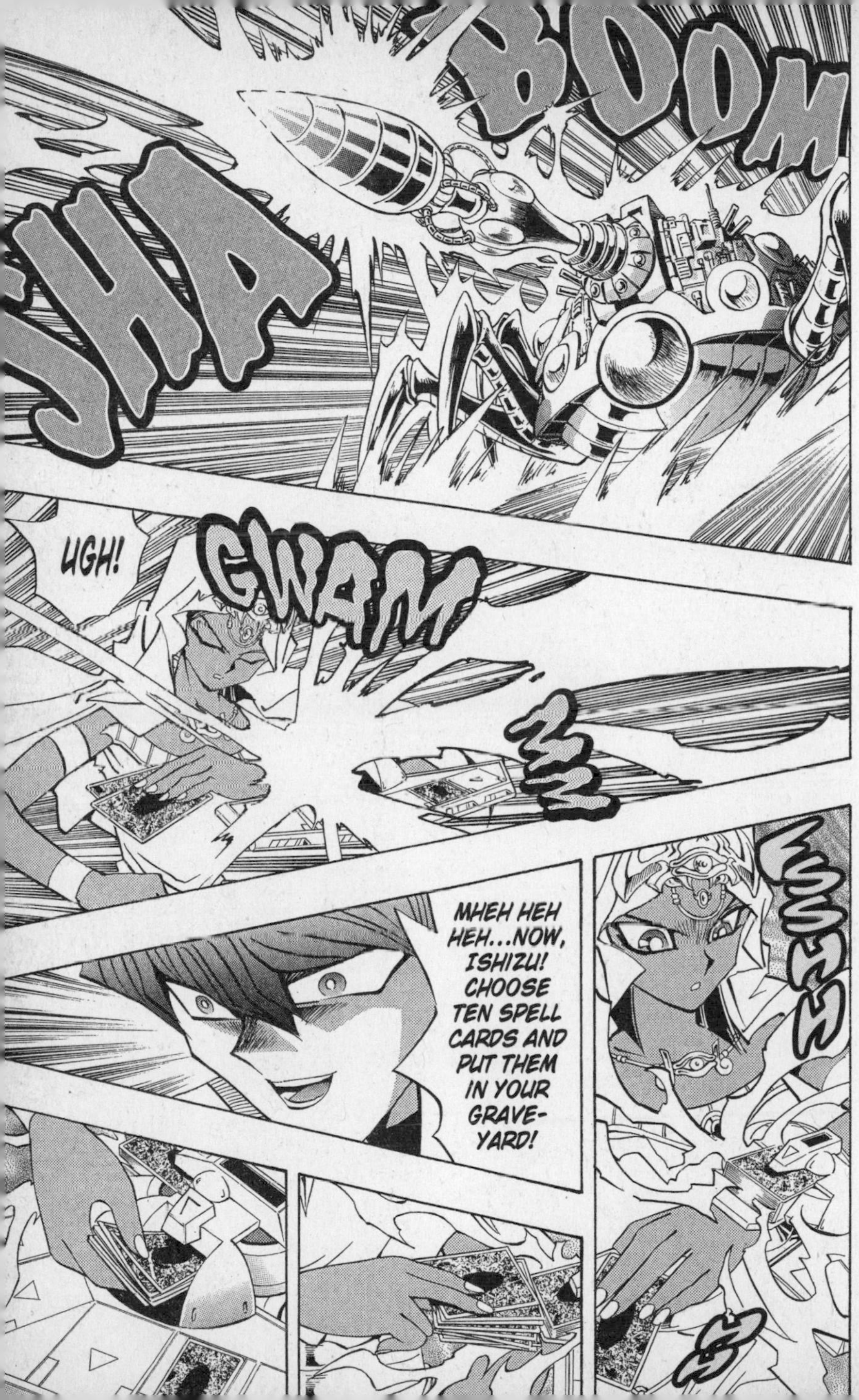
BOOM
JHA
GWAM
UGH!
MN
WUSHH
MHEH HEH HEH...NOW, ISHIZU! CHOOSE TEN SPELL CARDS AND PUT THEM IN YOUR GRAVE-YARD!

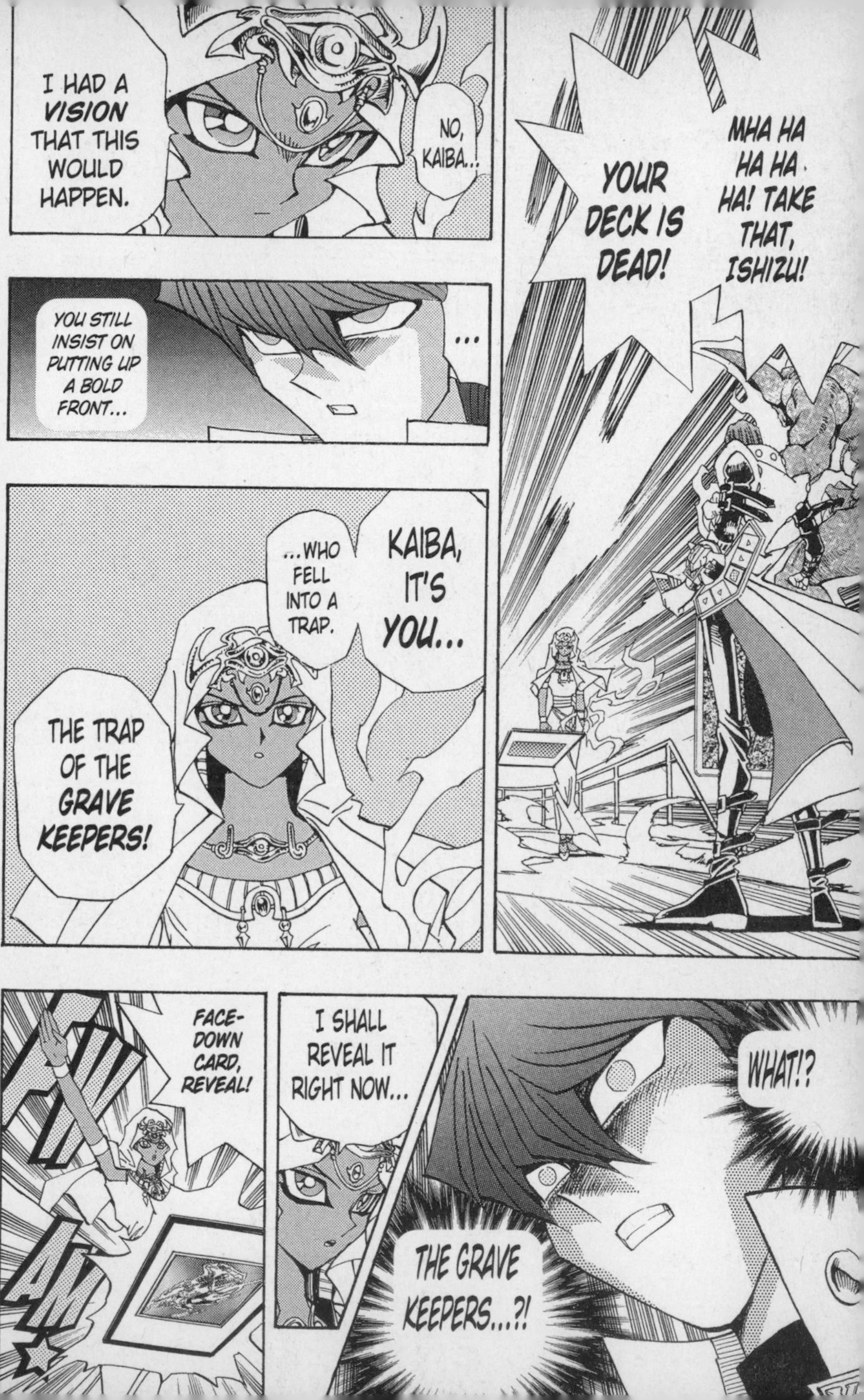
MHA HA HA HA. HA! TAKE THAT, ISHIZU!
YOUR DECK IS DEAD!
I HAD A VISION THAT THIS WOULD HAPPEN.
NO, KAIBA...
...
YOU STILL INSIST ON PUTTING UP A BOLD FRONT...
KAIBA, IT'S YOU...
...WHO FELL INTO A TRAP.
THE TRAP OF THE GRAVE KEEPERS!
WHAT!?
THE GRAVE KEEPERS...?!
I SHALL REVEAL IT RIGHT NOW...
FACE-DOWN CARD, REVEAL!

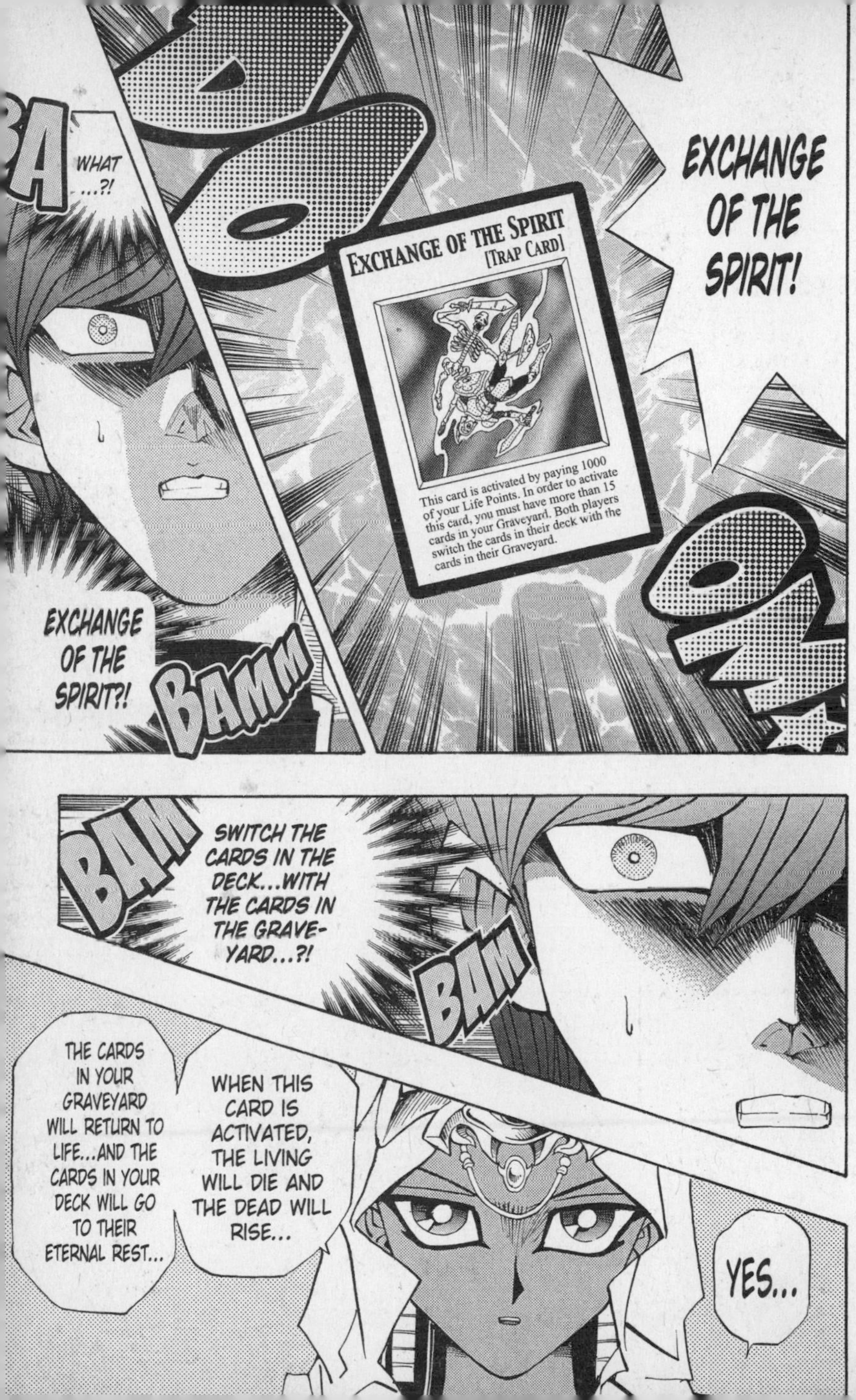
EXCHANGE OF THE SPIRIT!
EXCHANGE OF THE SPIRIT
[TRAP CARD]
This card is activated by paying 1000 of your Life Points. In order to activate this card, you must have more than 15 cards in your Graveyard. Both players switch the cards in their deck with the cards in their Graveyard.
WHAT ...?!
EXCHANGE OF THE SPIRIT?!
BAMM
SWITCH THE CARDS IN THE DECK...WITH THE CARDS IN THE GRAVE-YARD...?!
BAM
BAM
YES...
WHEN THIS CARD IS ACTIVATED, THE LIVING WILL DIE AND THE DEAD WILL RISE...
THE CARDS IN YOUR GRAVEYARD WILL RETURN TO LIFE...AND THE CARDS IN YOUR DECK WILL GO TO THEIR ETERNAL REST...

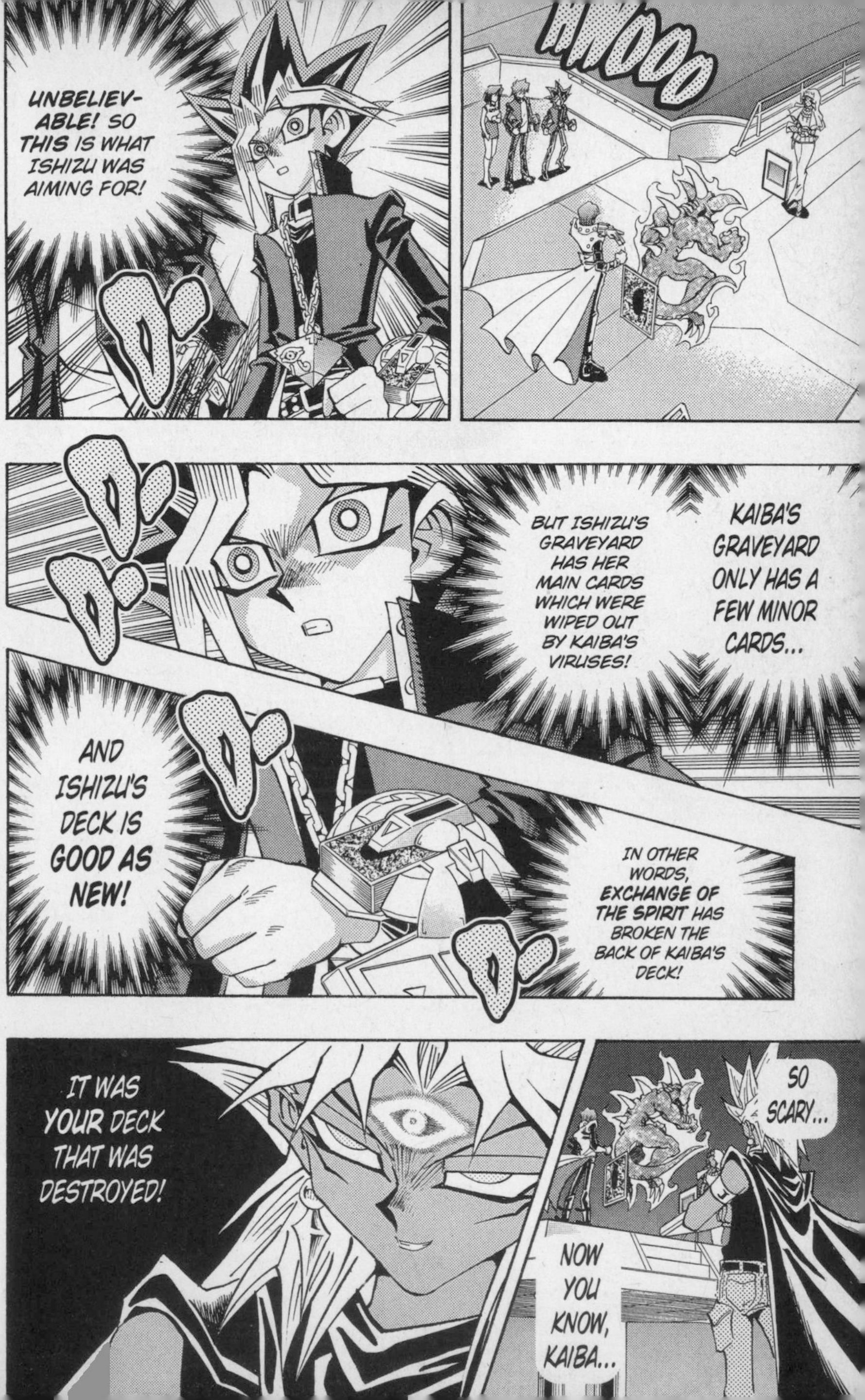
WHOOO
UNBELIEVABLE! SO THIS IS WHAT ISHIZU WAS AIMING FOR!
KAIBA'S GRAVEYARD ONLY HAS A FEW MINOR CARDS...
BUT ISHIZU'S GRAVEYARD HAS HER MAIN CARDS WHICH WERE WIPED OUT BY KAIBA'S VIRUSES!
AND ISHIZU'S DECK IS GOOD AS NEW!
IN OTHER WORDS, EXCHANGE OF THE SPIRIT HAS BROKEN THE BACK OF KAIBA'S DECK!
SO SCARY...
NOW YOU KNOW, KAIBA...
IT WAS YOUR DECK THAT WAS DESTROYED!

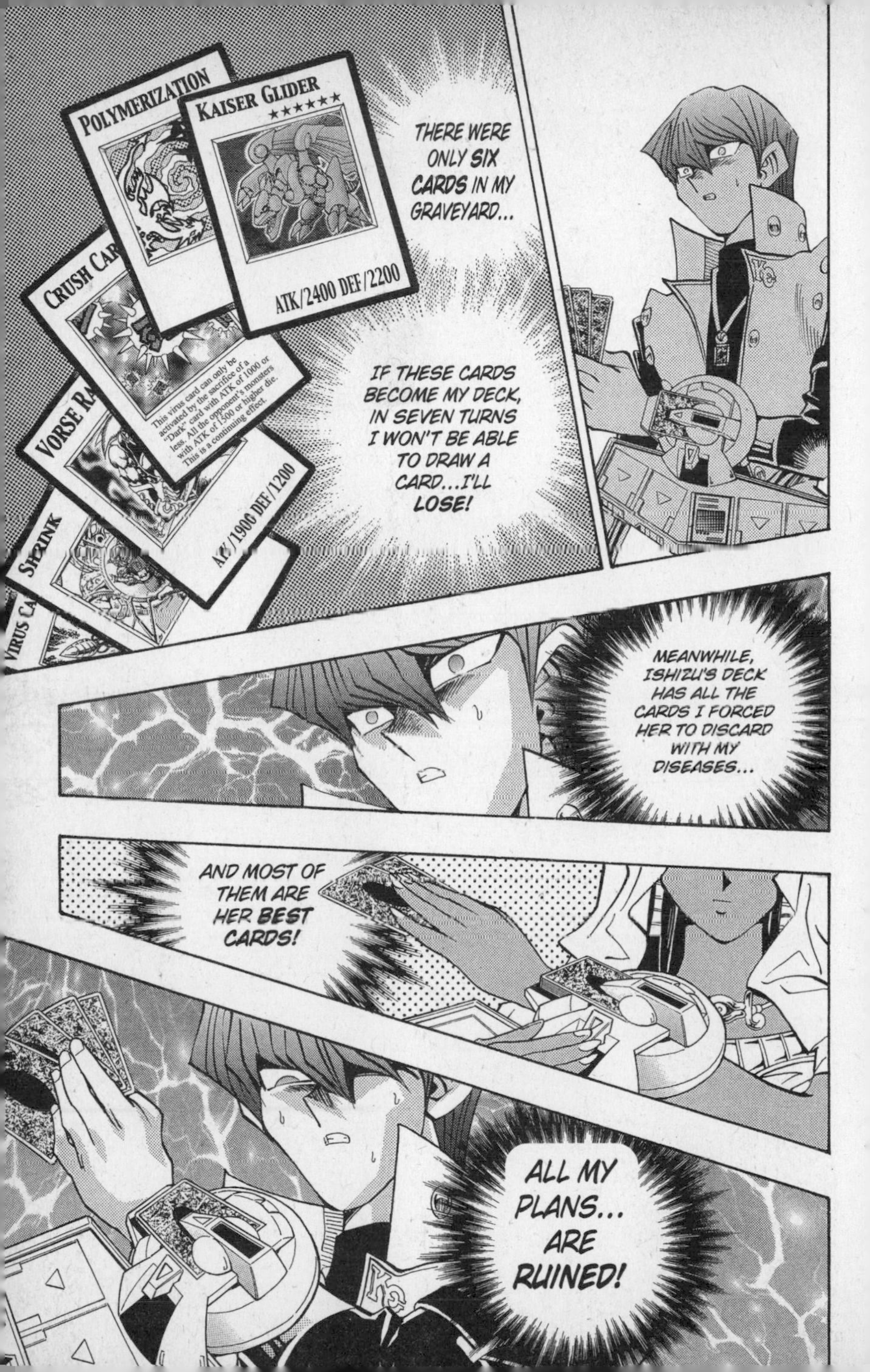
THERE WERE ONLY SIX CARDS IN MY GRAVEYARD...
IF THESE CARDS BECOME MY DECK, IN SEVEN TURNS I WON'T BE ABLE TO DRAW A CARD...I'LL LOSE!
POLYMERIZATION
KAISER GLIDER
ATK/2400 DEF/2200
This virus card can only be activated by the sacrifice of a "Dark" card with ATK of 1000 or less. All the opponent's monsters with ATK of 1500 or higher die. This is a continuing effect.
SHRINK
MEANWHILE, ISHIZU'S DECK HAS ALL THE CARDS I FORCED HER TO DISCARD WITH MY DISEASES...
AND MOST OF THEM ARE HER BEST CARDS!
ALL MY PLANS... ARE RUINED!

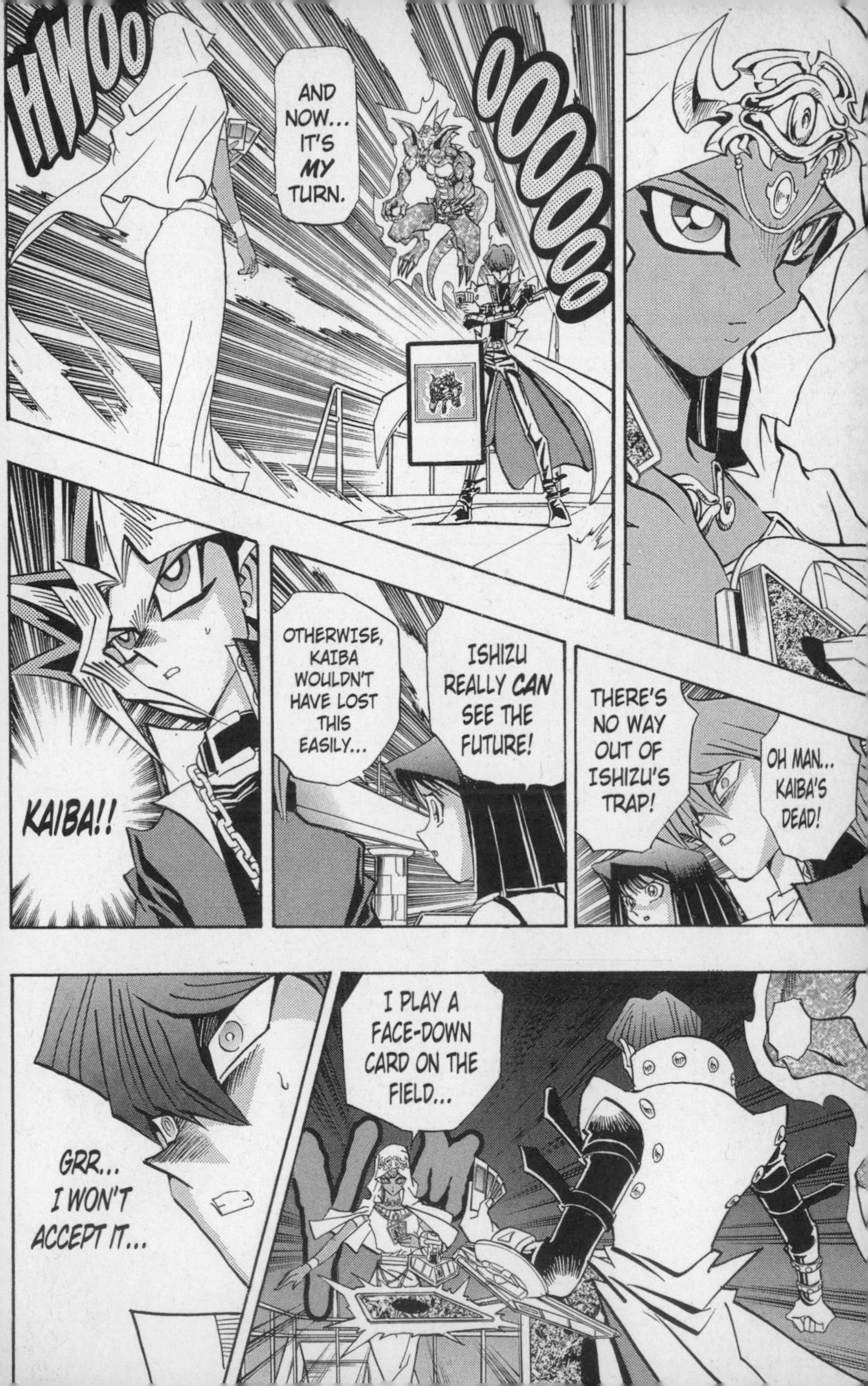
HWOOOOOOOO
AND NOW... IT'S *MY* TURN.
OH MAN... KAIBA'S DEAD!
THERE'S NO WAY OUT OF ISHIZU'S TRAP!
ISHIZU REALLY *CAN* SEE THE FUTURE!
OTHERWISE, KAIBA WOULDN'T HAVE LOST THIS EASILY...
KAIBA!!
I PLAY A FACE-DOWN CARD ON THE FIELD...
GRR... I WON'T ACCEPT IT...

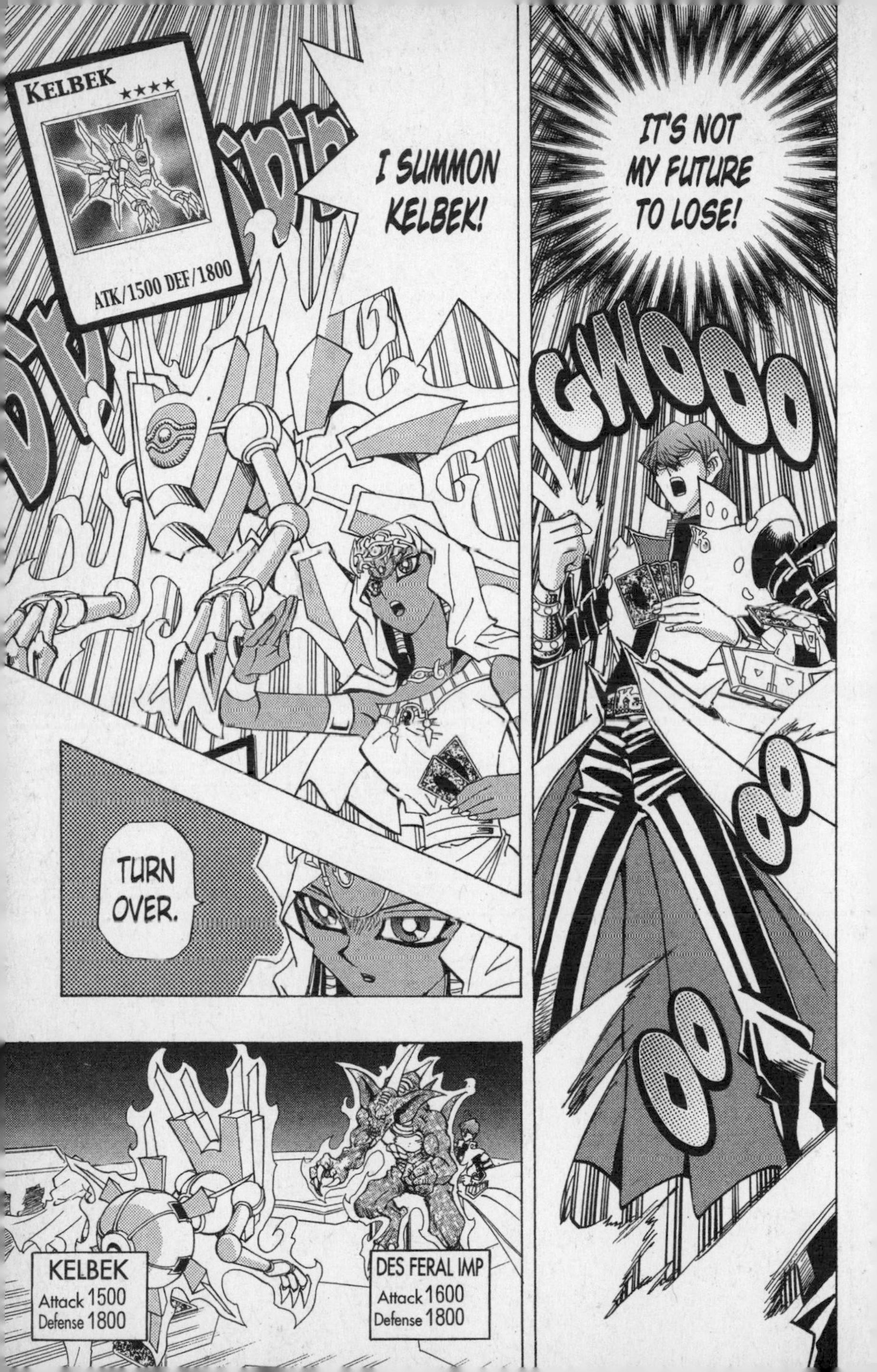
IT'S NOT MY FUTURE TO LOSE!
GWOOOOOOOOO
KELBEK ★★★★
ATK/1500 DEF/1800
I SUMMON KELBEK!
TURN OVER.
KELBEK
Attack 1500
Defense 1800
DES FERAL IMP
Attack 1600
Defense 1800

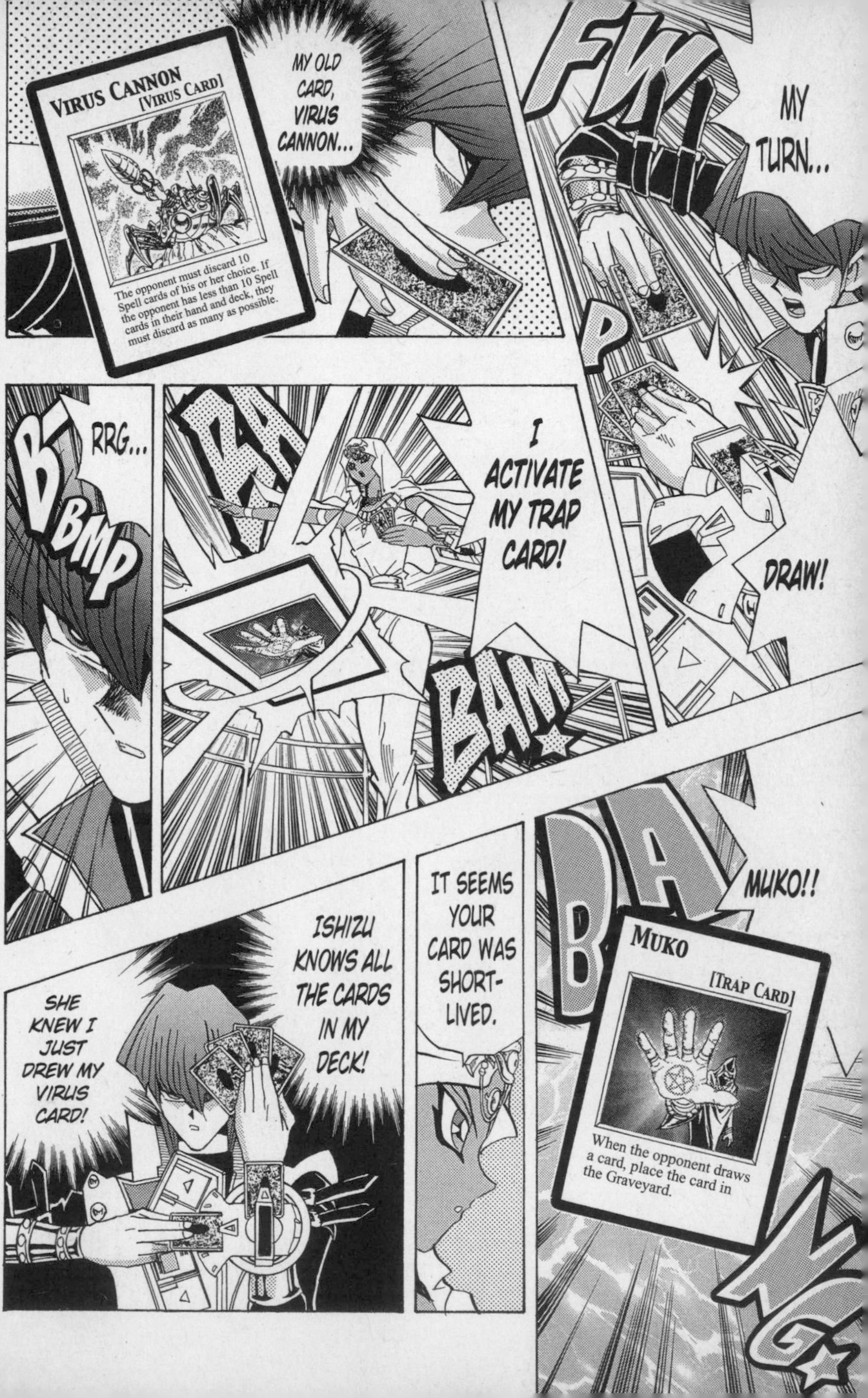
FW
MY TURN...
P
DRAW!
MY OLD CARD, VIRUS CANNON...
VIRUS CANNON
[VIRUS CARD]
The opponent must discard 10 Spell cards of his or her choice. If the opponent has less than 10 Spell cards in their hand and deck, they must discard as many as possible.
I ACTIVATE MY TRAP CARD!
BAM
RRG...
BBMP
MUKO!!
BA
MUKO
[TRAP CARD]
When the opponent draws a card, place the card in the Graveyard.
IT SEEMS YOUR CARD WAS SHORT-LIVED.
ISHIZU KNOWS ALL THE CARDS IN MY DECK!
SHE KNEW I JUST DREW MY VIRUS CARD!

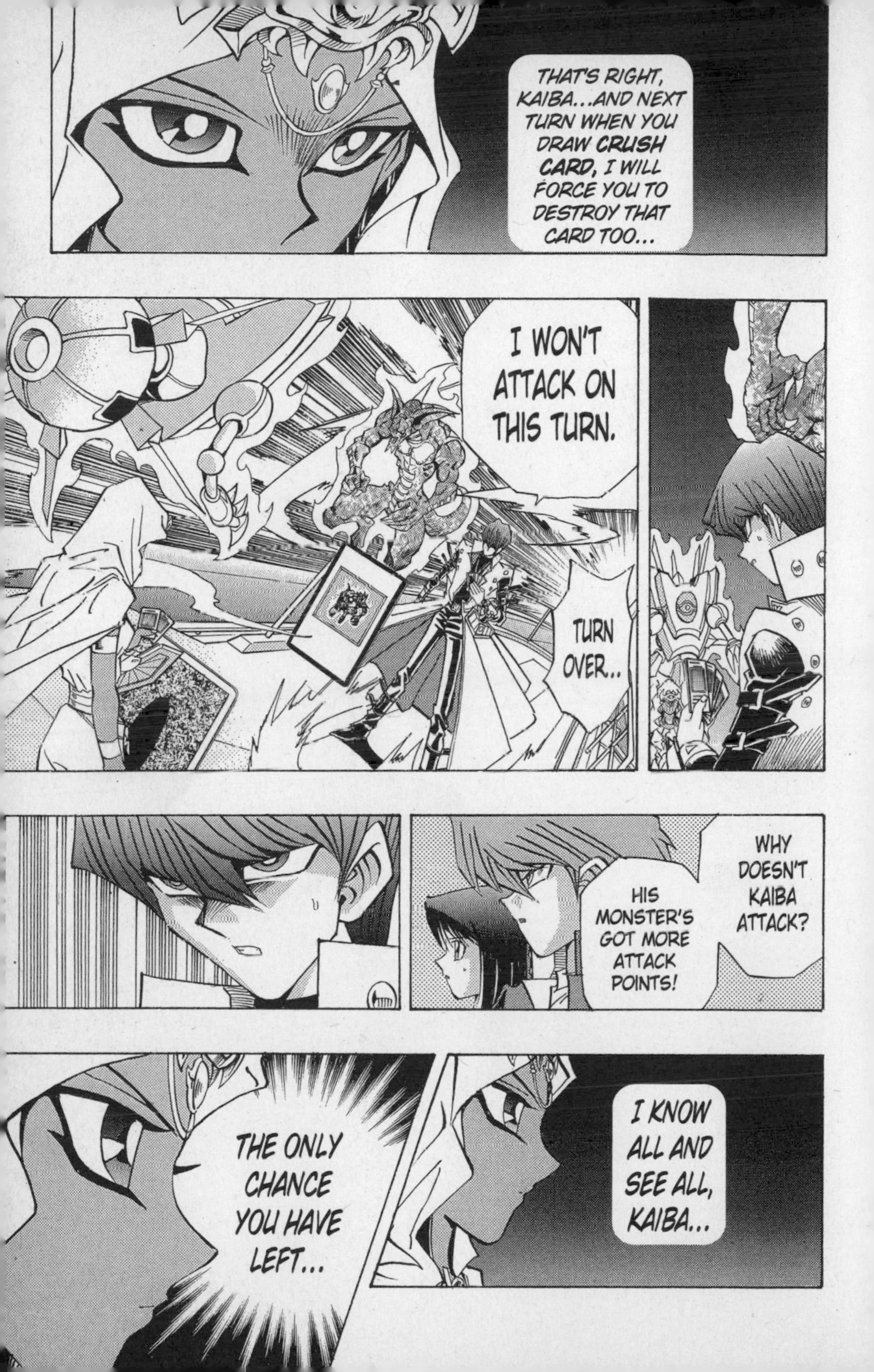
THAT'S RIGHT, KAIBA...AND NEXT TURN WHEN YOU DRAW CRUSH CARD, I WILL FORCE YOU TO DESTROY THAT CARD TOO...
I WON'T ATTACK ON THIS TURN.
TURN OVER...
WHY DOESN'T KAIBA ATTACK?
HIS MONSTER'S GOT MORE ATTACK POINTS!
I KNOW ALL AND SEE ALL, KAIBA...
THE ONLY CHANCE YOU HAVE LEFT...

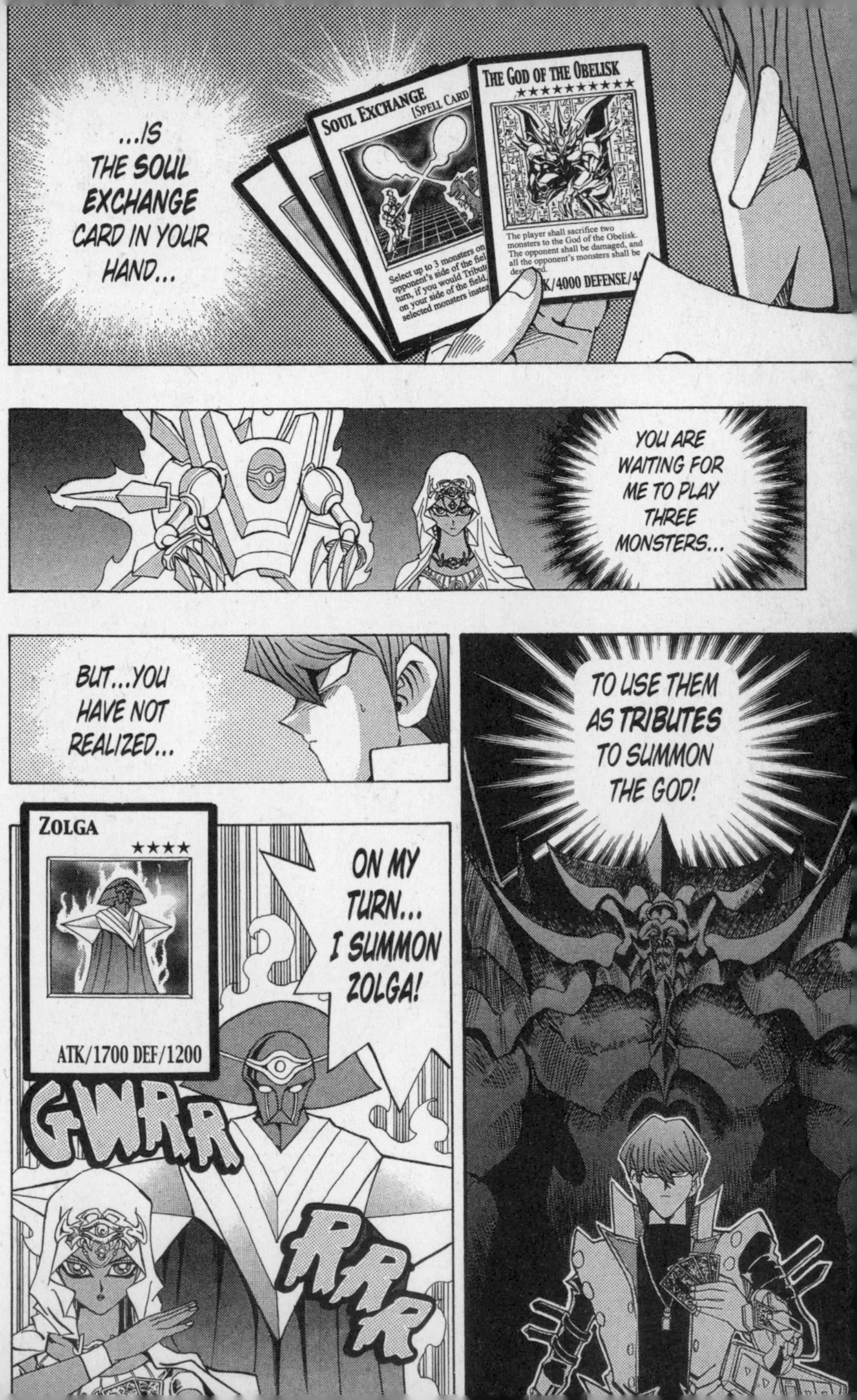
...IS THE SOUL EXCHANGE CARD IN YOUR HAND...
SOUL EXCHANGE
[SPELL CARD]
Select up to 3 monsters on opponent's side of the field turn, if you would Tribute on your side of the field, selected monsters instead
THE GOD OF THE OBELISK
The player shall sacrifice two monsters to the God of the Obelisk. The opponent shall be damaged, and all the opponent's monsters shall be destroyed.
K/4000 DEFENSE/4
YOU ARE WAITING FOR ME TO PLAY THREE MONSTERS...
TO USE THEM AS TRIBUTES TO SUMMON THE GOD!
BUT...YOU HAVE NOT REALIZED...
ZOLGA
ATK/1700 DEF/1200
ON MY TURN... I SUMMON ZOLGA!
GWRR
RRR

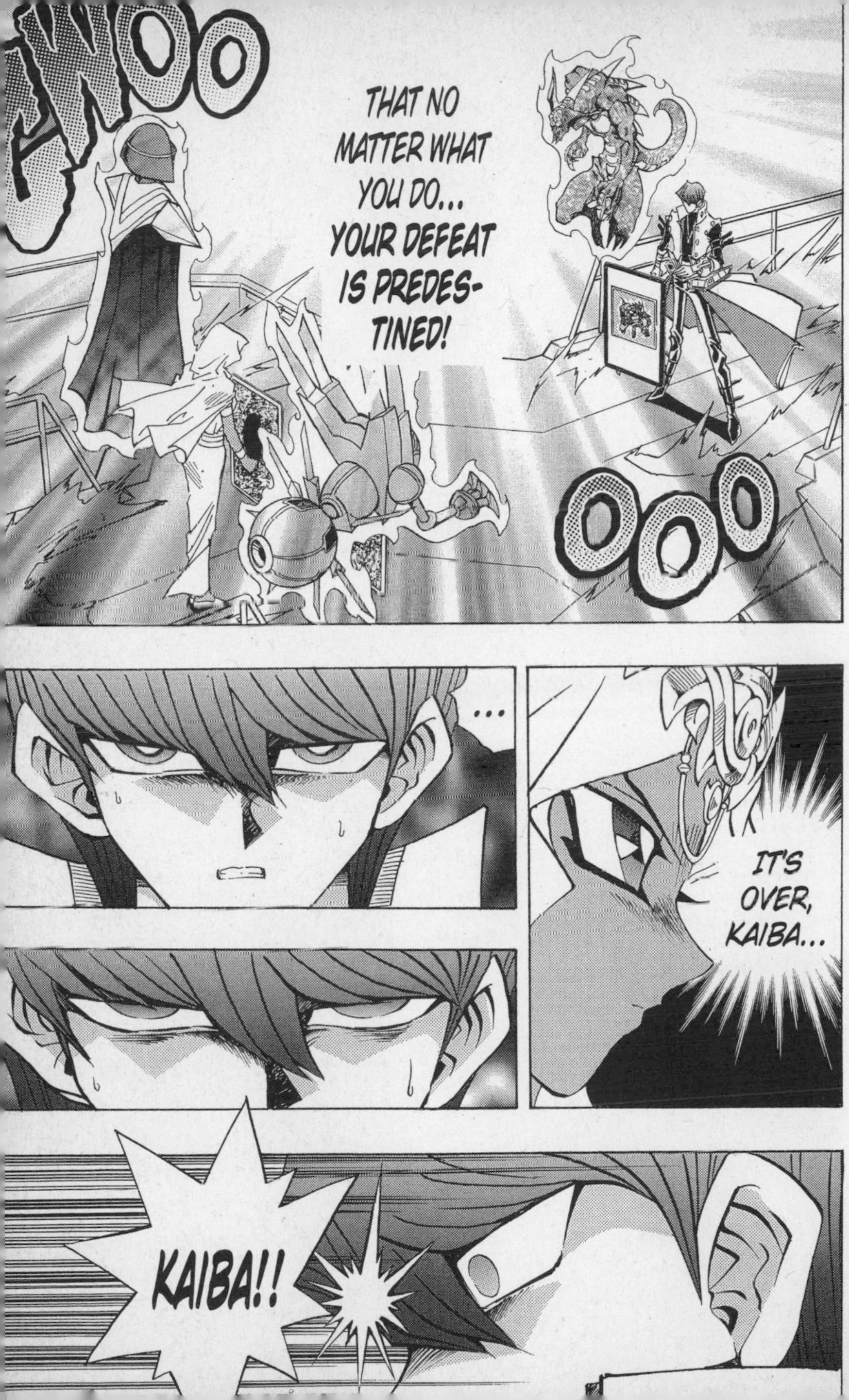
OOOO
THAT NO MATTER WHAT YOU DO... YOUR DEFEAT IS PREDES-TINED!
WOO
IT'S OVER, KAIBA...
...
KAIBA!!

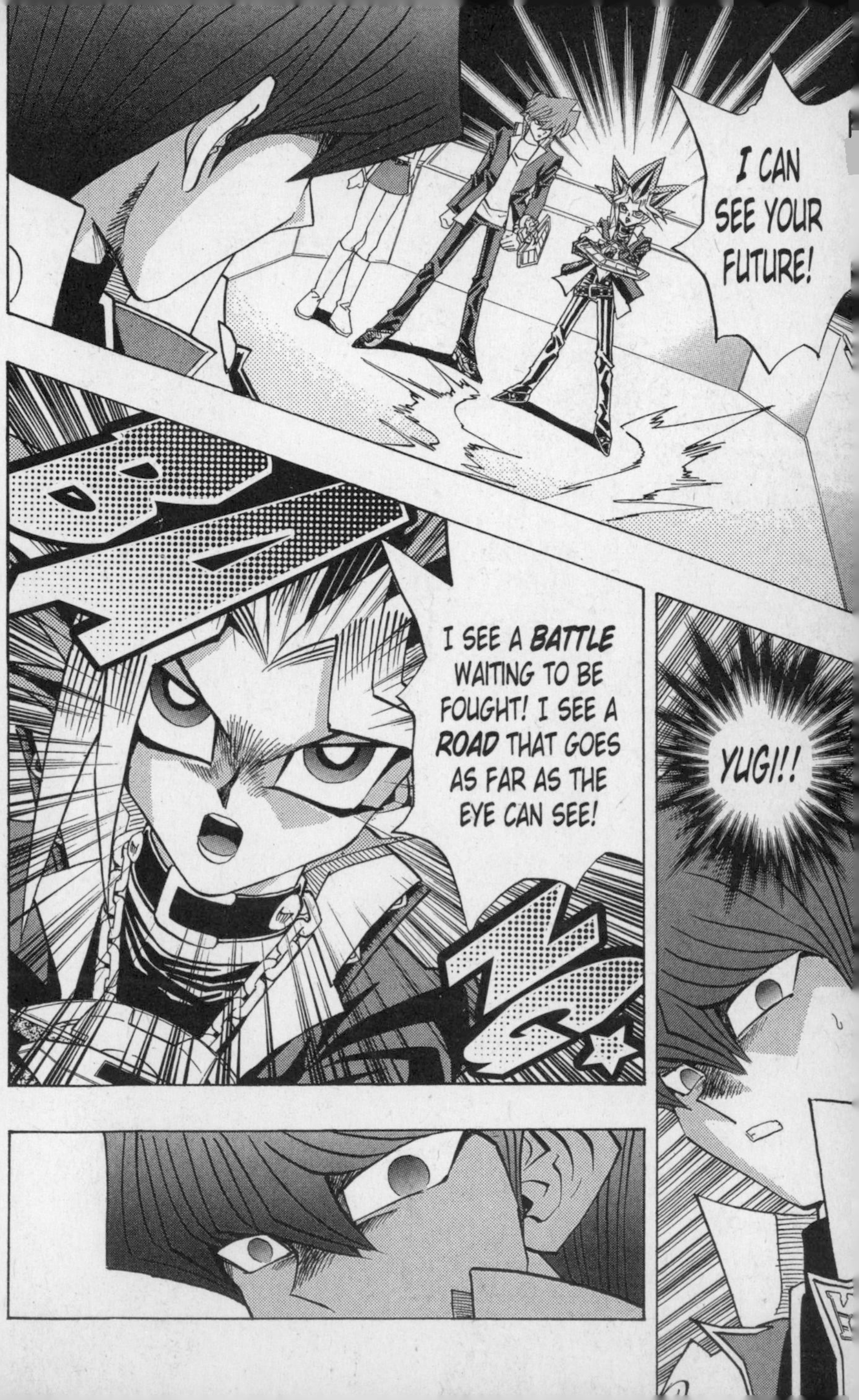
I CAN SEE YOUR FUTURE!
YUGI!!
I SEE A ***BATTLE*** WAITING TO BE FOUGHT! I SEE A ***ROAD*** THAT GOES AS FAR AS THE EYE CAN SEE!

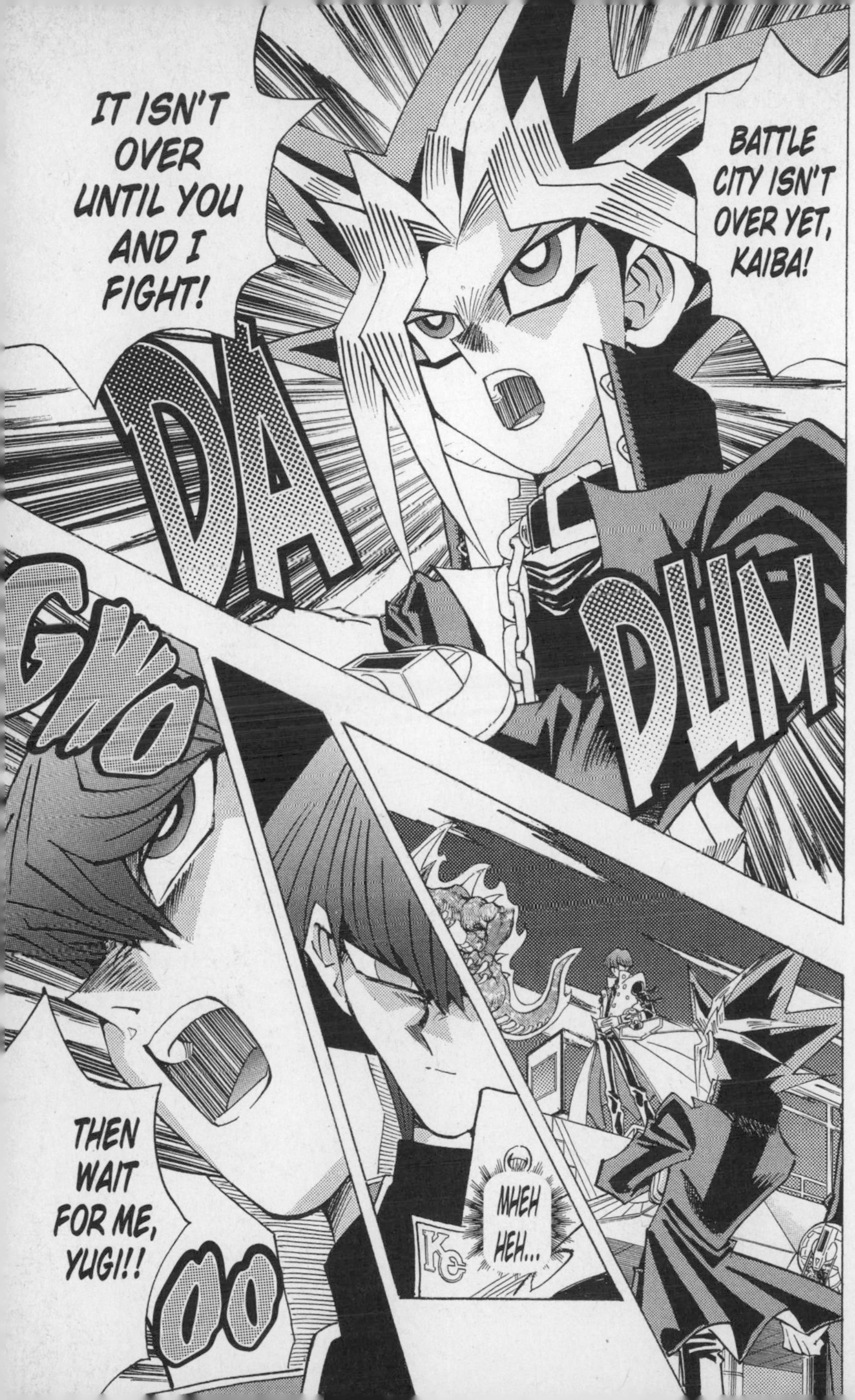
BATTLE CITY ISN'T OVER YET, KAIBA!
IT ISN'T OVER UNTIL YOU AND I FIGHT!
DA
DUM
MHEH HEH...
GWO
OO
THEN WAIT FOR ME, YUGI!!

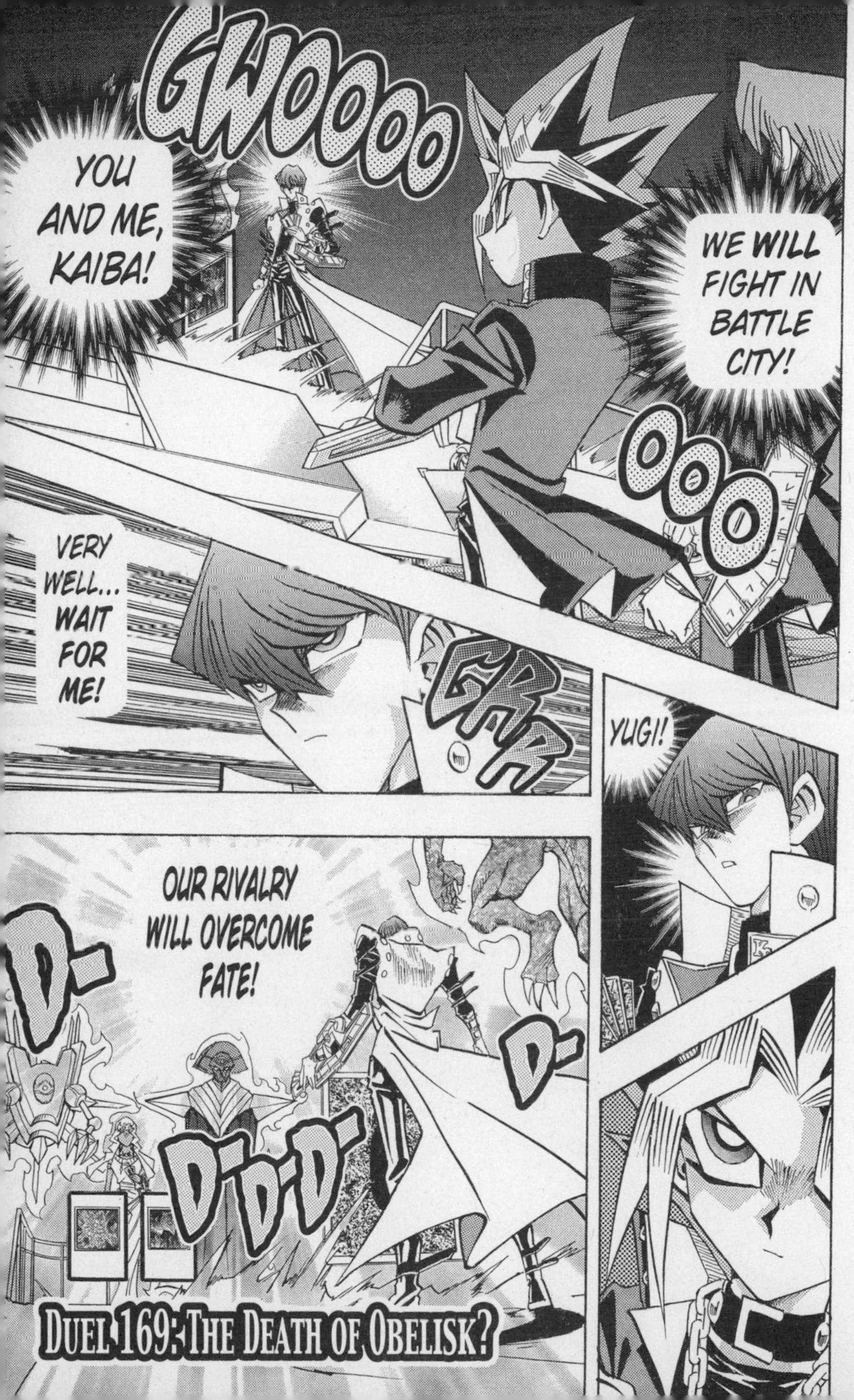
GWOOOO
WE WILL FIGHT IN BATTLE CITY!
YOU AND ME, KAIBA!
OOO
YUGI!
GRR
VERY WELL... WAIT FOR ME!
OUR RIVALRY WILL OVERCOME FATE!
D-
D-
D-D-D-
DUEL 169: THE DEATH OF OBELISK?

DUEL 169: THE DEATH OF OBELISK?

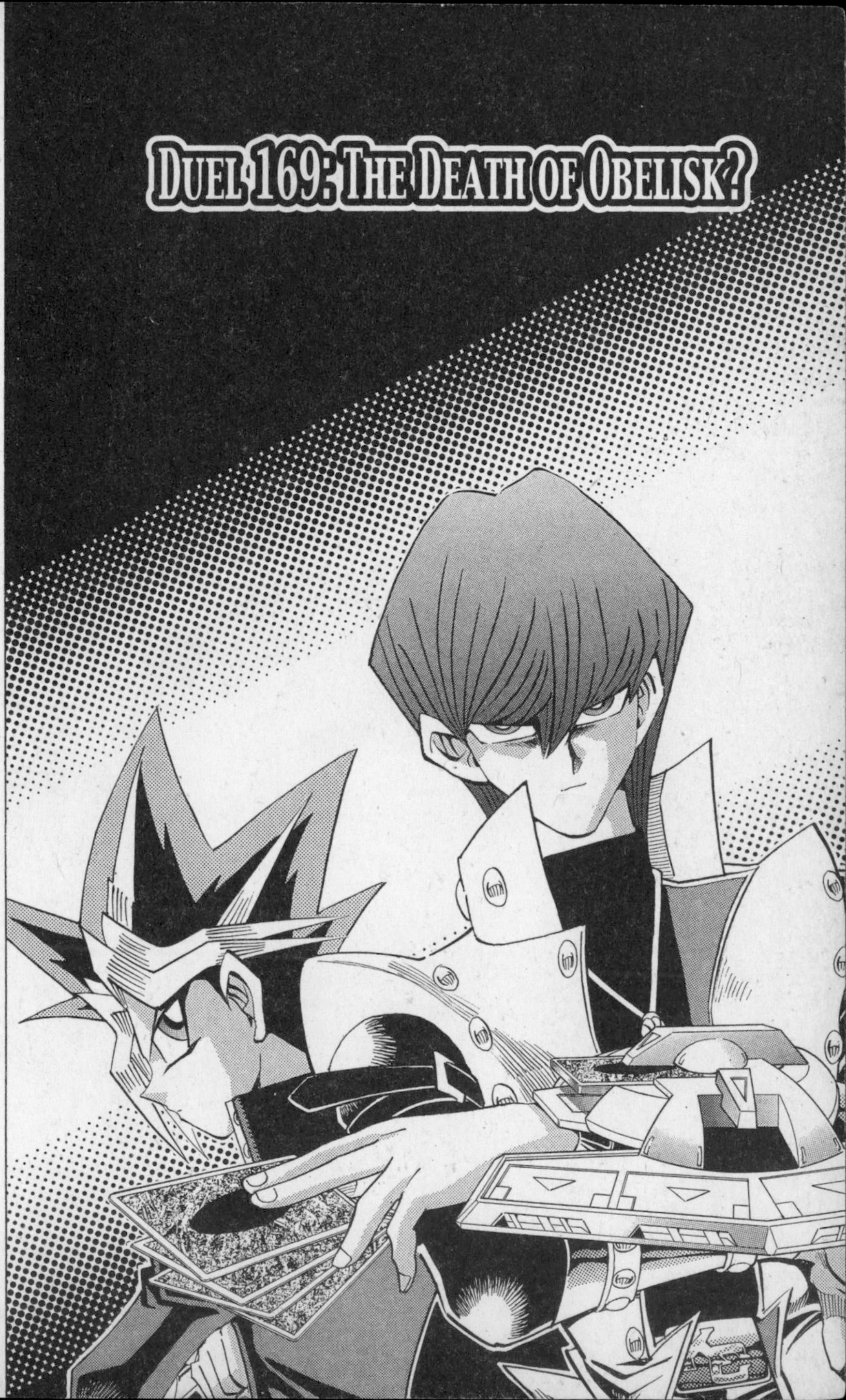

READ THIS WAY

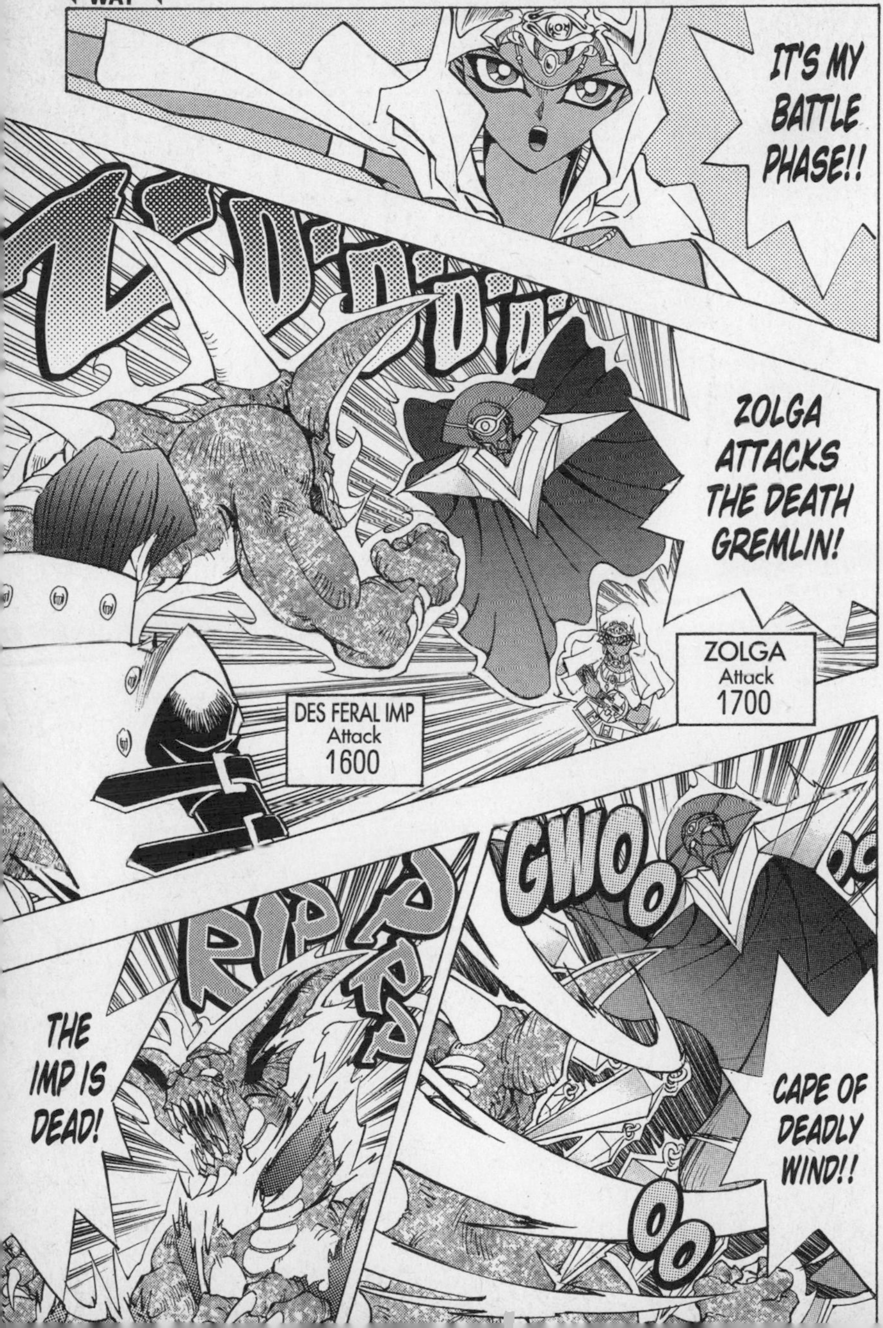
IT'S MY BATTLE PHASE!!
ZOLGA ATTACKS THE DEATH GREMLIN!
ZOLGA
Attack
1700
DES FERAL IMP
Attack
1600
GWOOOO
CAPE OF DEADLY WIND!!
RIP
THE IMP IS DEAD!

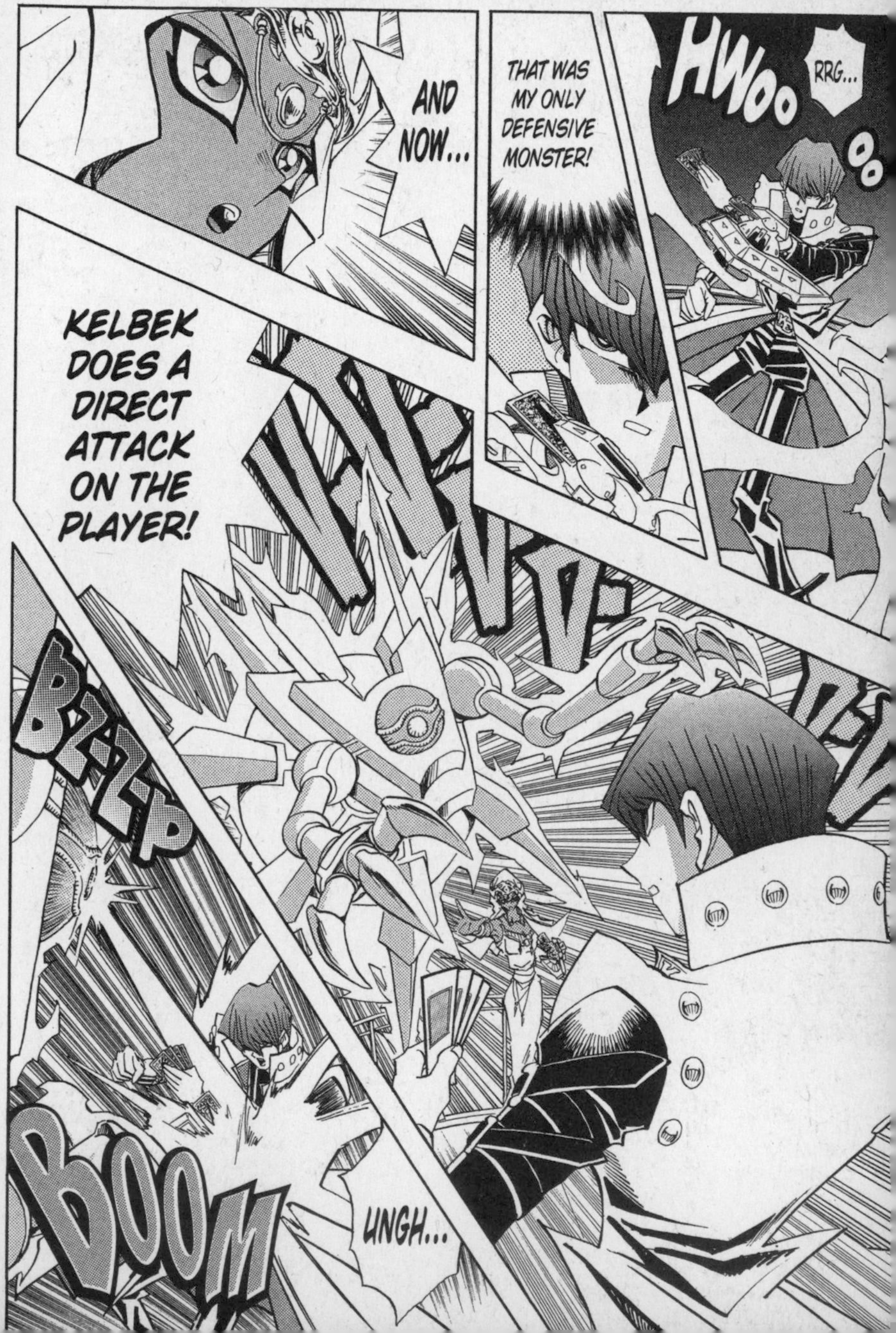
HWOOOO
RRG...
THAT WAS MY ONLY DEFENSIVE MONSTER!
AND NOW...
KELBEK DOES A DIRECT ATTACK ON THE PLAYER!
BZZZP
UNGH...
BOOM

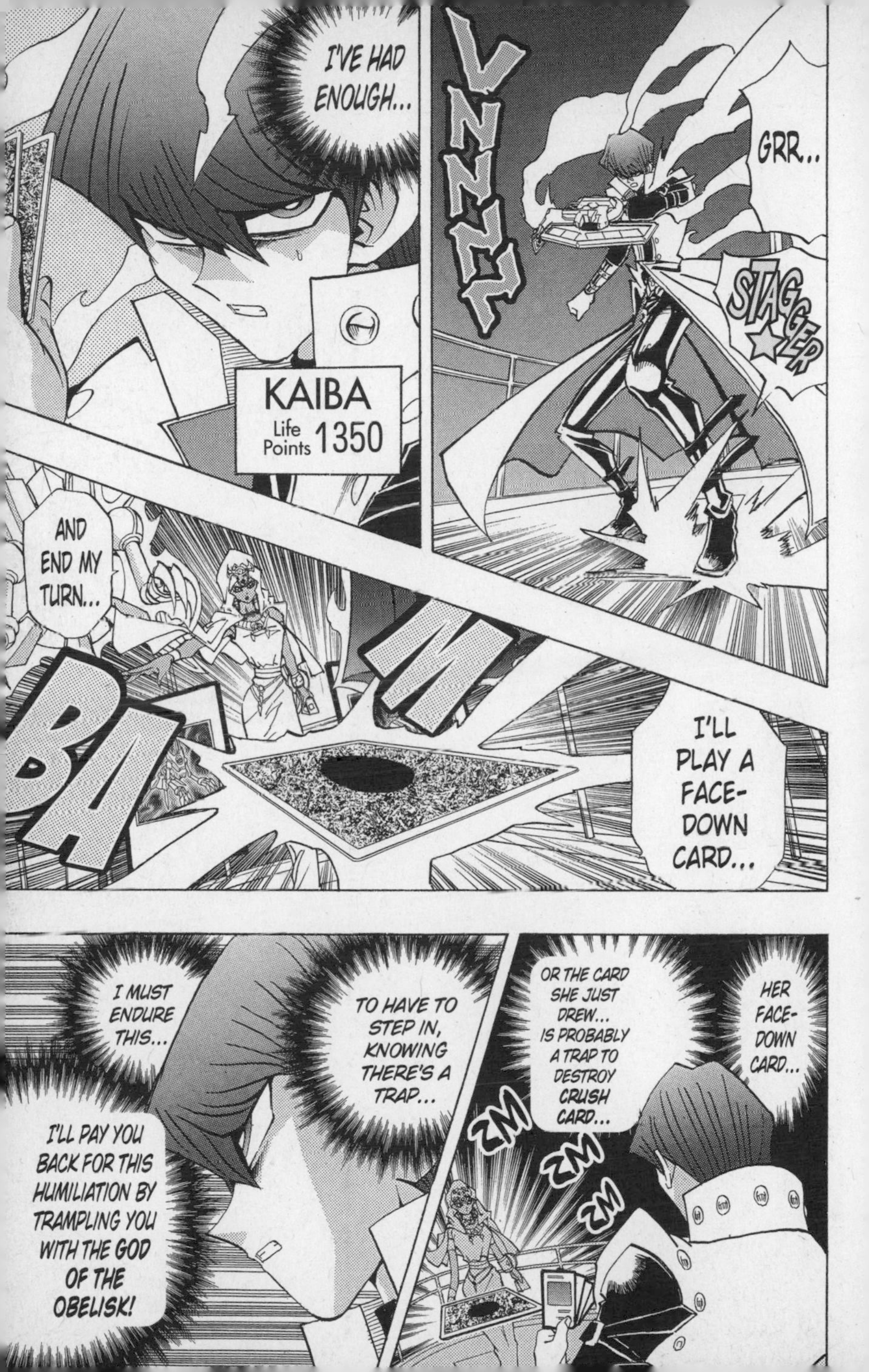
GRR...
STAGGER
VNNZZT
I'VE HAD ENOUGH...
KAIBA
Life Points 1350
I'LL PLAY A FACE-DOWN CARD...
AND END MY TURN...
HER FACE-DOWN CARD...
OR THE CARD SHE JUST DREW... IS PROBABLY A TRAP TO DESTROY CRUSH CARD...
ZM
ZM
ZM
TO HAVE TO STEP IN, KNOWING THERE'S A TRAP...
I MUST ENDURE THIS...
I'LL PAY YOU BACK FOR THIS HUMILIATION BY TRAMPLING YOU WITH THE GOD OF THE OBELISK!

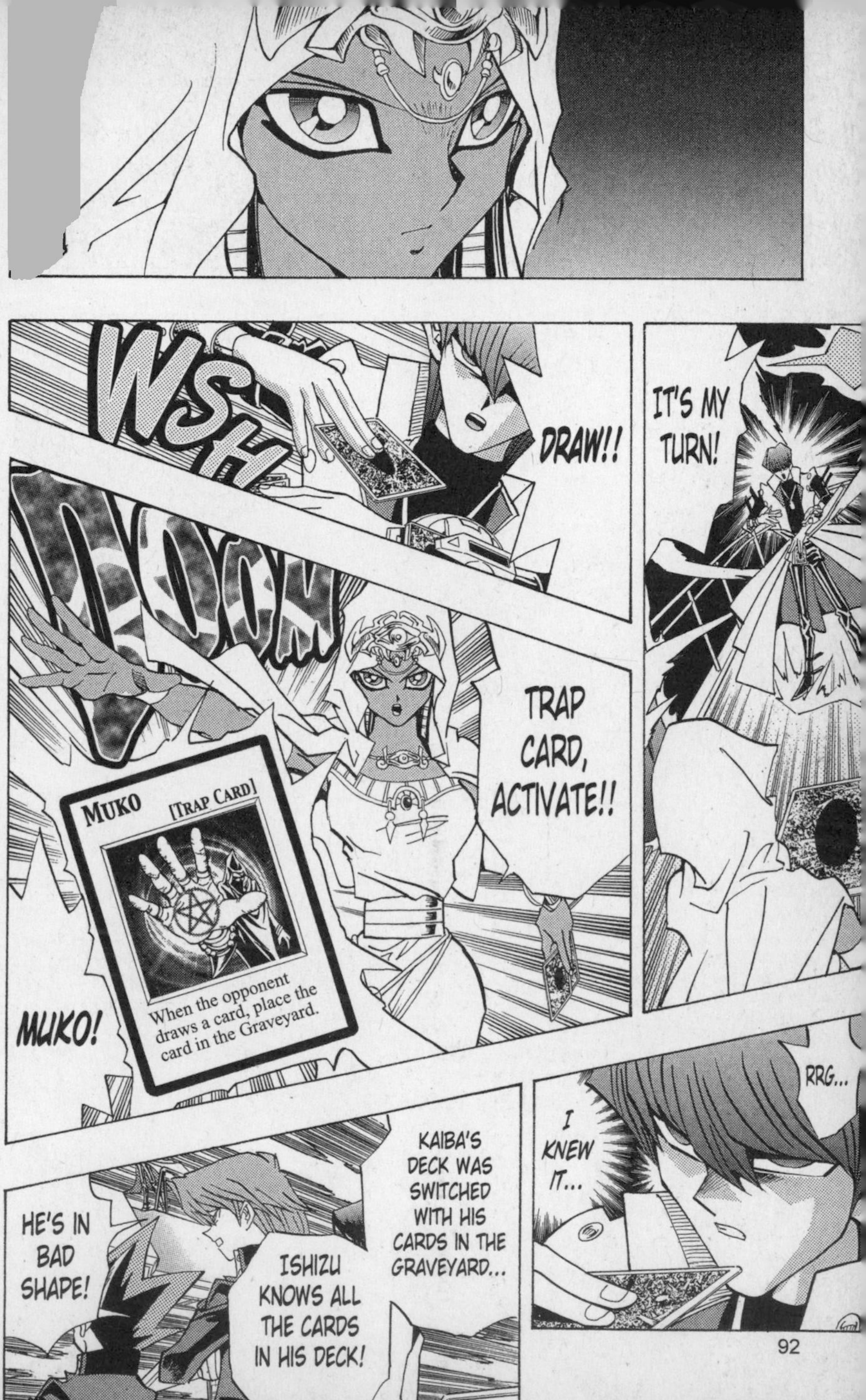
IT'S MY TURN!
DRAW!!
WSH
DOOM
TRAP CARD, ACTIVATE!!
MUKO [TRAP CARD]
When the opponent draws a card, place the card in the Graveyard.
MUKO!
RRG...
I KNEW IT...
KAIBA'S DECK WAS SWITCHED WITH HIS CARDS IN THE GRAVEYARD...
ISHIZU KNOWS ALL THE CARDS IN HIS DECK!
HE'S IN BAD SHAPE!

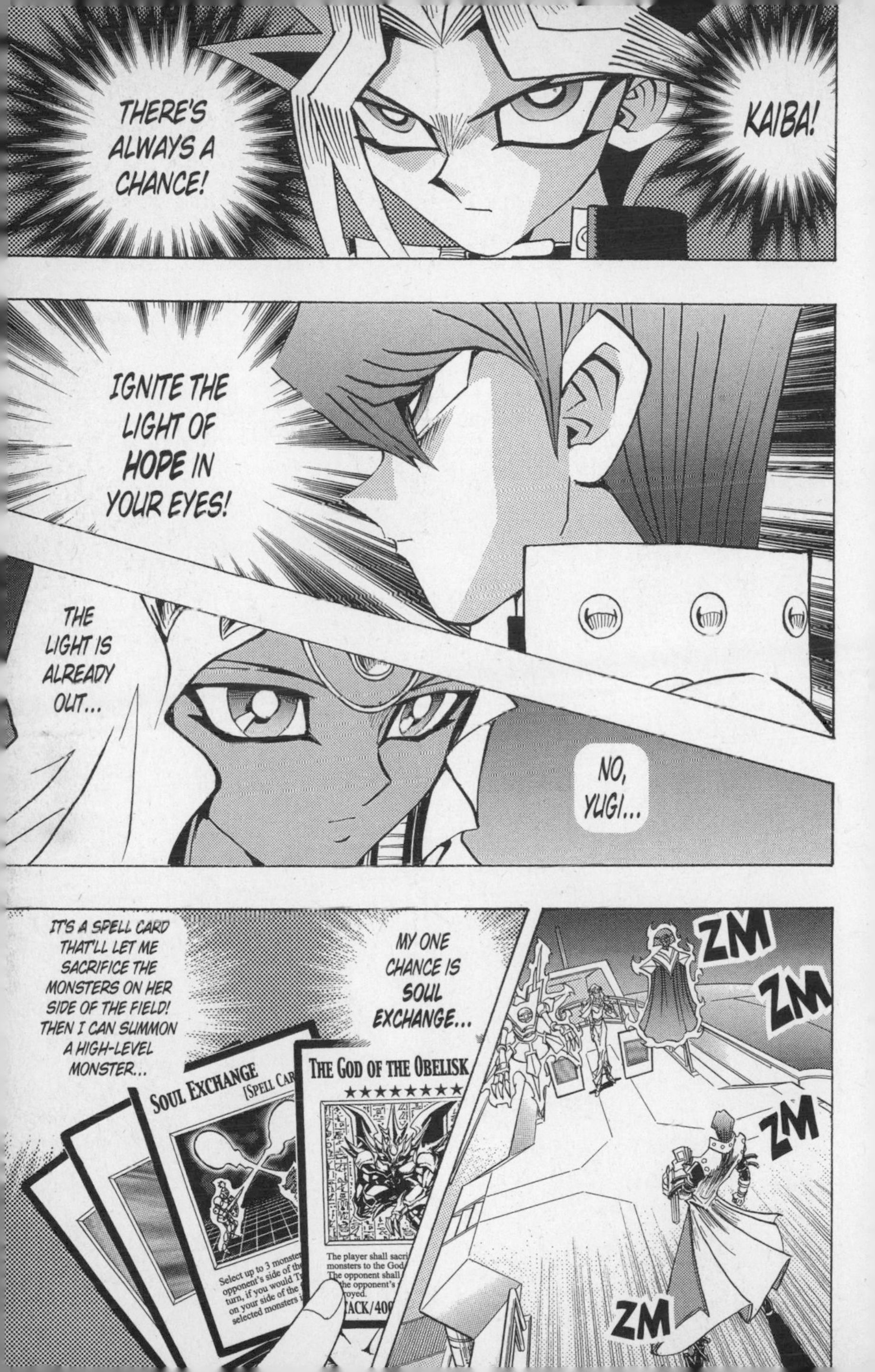
KAIBA!
THERE'S ALWAYS A CHANCE!
IGNITE THE LIGHT OF HOPE IN YOUR EYES!
NO, YUGI...
THE LIGHT IS ALREADY OUT...
ZM
ZM
ZM
ZM
MY ONE CHANCE IS SOUL EXCHANGE...
IT'S A SPELL CARD THAT'LL LET ME SACRIFICE THE MONSTERS ON HER SIDE OF THE FIELD! THEN I CAN SUMMON A HIGH-LEVEL MONSTER...
THE GOD OF THE OBELISK
SOUL EXCHANGE

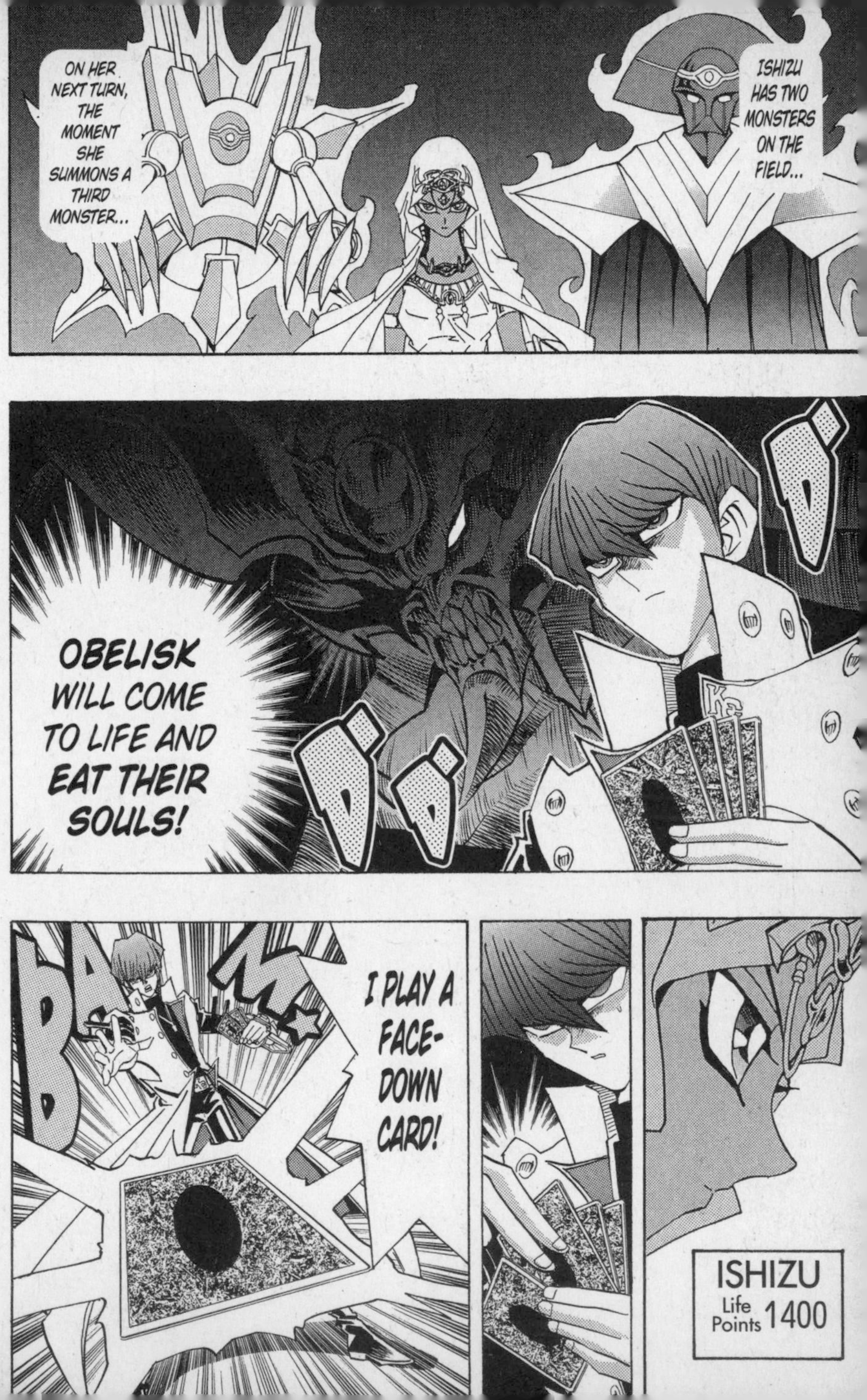
ISHIZU HAS TWO MONSTERS ON THE FIELD...
ON HER NEXT TURN, THE MOMENT SHE SUMMONS A THIRD MONSTER...
OBELISK WILL COME TO LIFE AND EAT THEIR SOULS!
ISHIZU Life Points 1400
I PLAY A FACE-DOWN CARD!
BAM

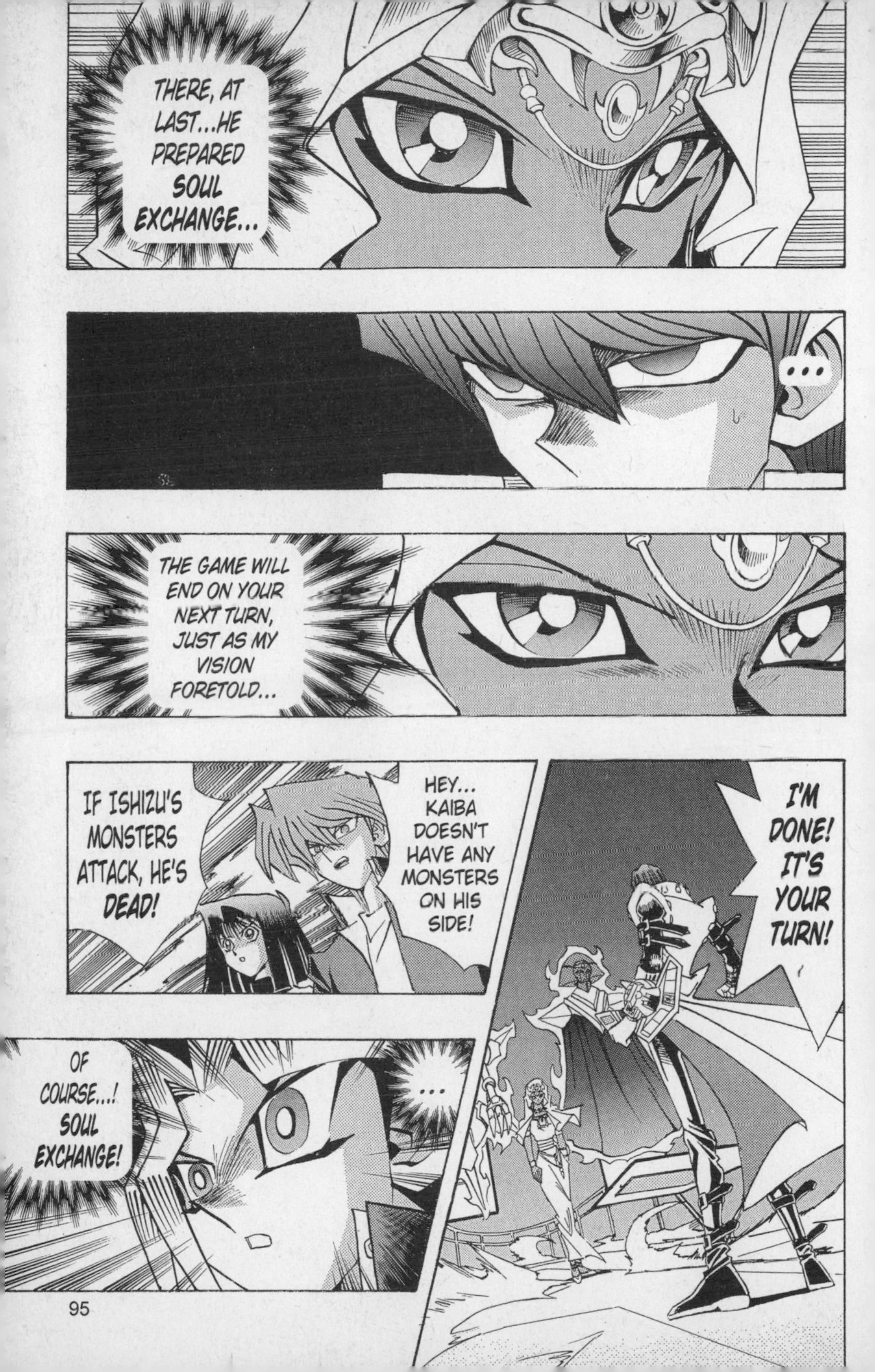
THERE, AT LAST...HE PREPARED SOUL EXCHANGE...
...
THE GAME WILL END ON YOUR NEXT TURN, JUST AS MY VISION FORETOLD...
I'M DONE! IT'S YOUR TURN!
HEY... KAIBA DOESN'T HAVE ANY MONSTERS ON HIS SIDE!
IF ISHIZU'S MONSTERS ATTACK, HE'S DEAD!
...
OF COURSE...! SOUL EXCHANGE!

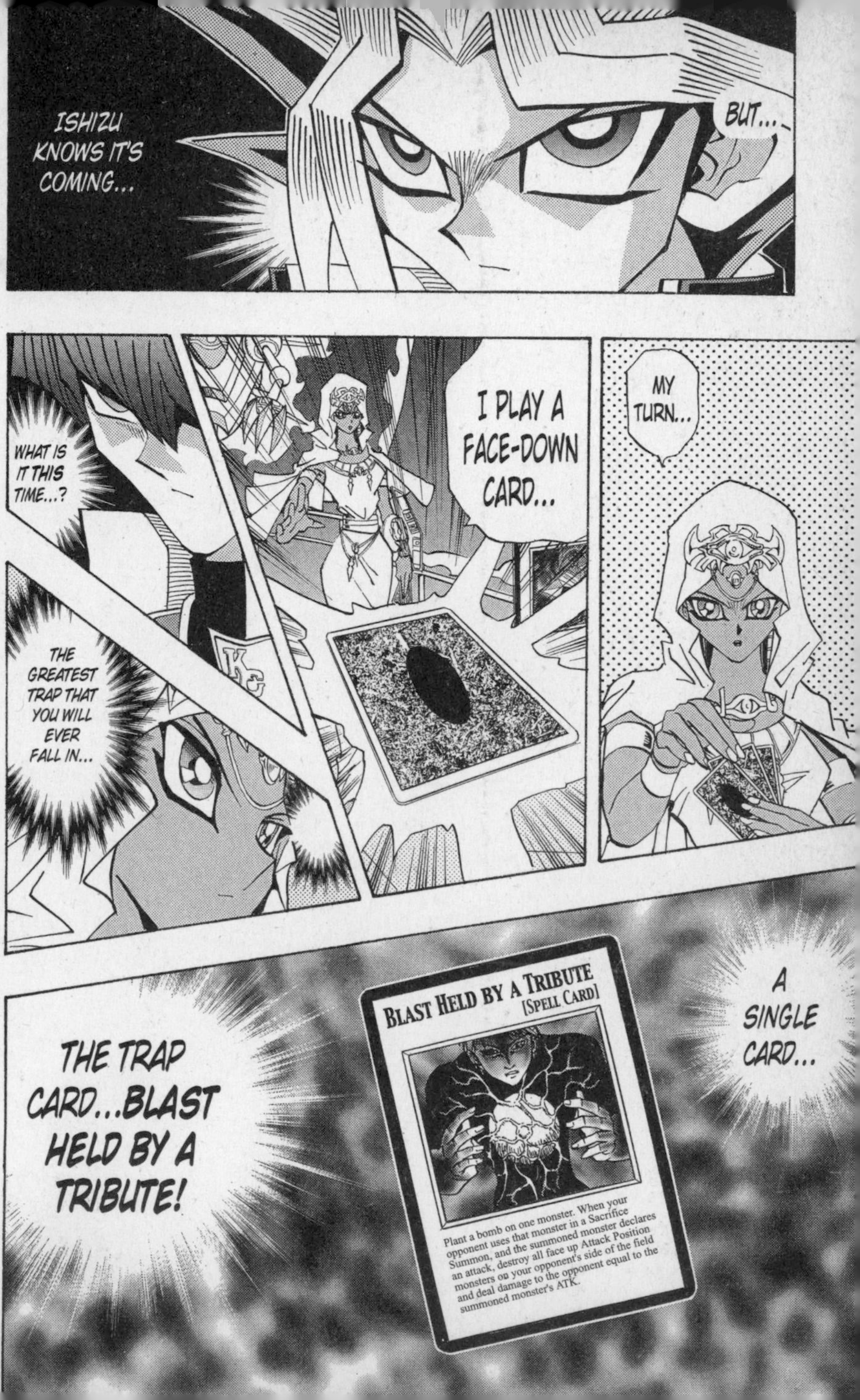
BUT...
ISHIZU KNOWS IT'S COMING...
MY TURN...
I PLAY A FACE-DOWN CARD...
WHAT IS IT THIS TIME...?
THE GREATEST TRAP THAT YOU WILL EVER FALL IN...
A SINGLE CARD...
BLAST HELD BY A TRIBUTE
[SPELL CARD]
Plant a bomb on one monster. When your opponent uses that monster in a Sacrifice Summon, and the summoned monster declares an attack, destroy all face up Attack Position monsters on your opponent's side of the field and deal damage to the opponent equal to the summoned monster's ATK.
THE TRAP CARD...BLAST HELD BY A TRIBUTE!

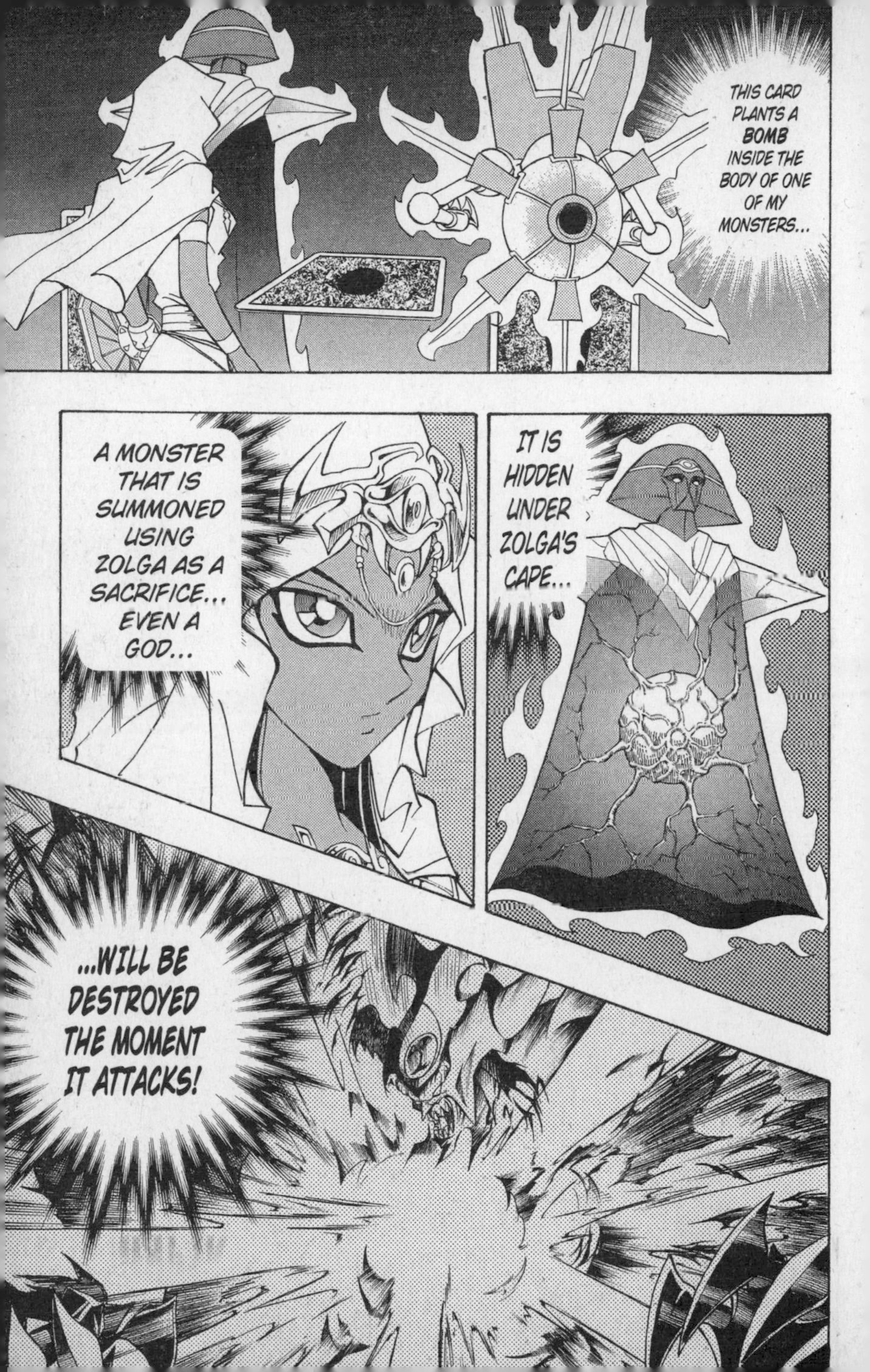
THIS CARD PLANTS A BOMB INSIDE THE BODY OF ONE OF MY MONSTERS...
IT IS HIDDEN UNDER ZOLGA'S CAPE...
A MONSTER THAT IS SUMMONED USING ZOLGA AS A SACRIFICE... EVEN A GOD...
...WILL BE DESTROYED THE MOMENT IT ATTACKS!

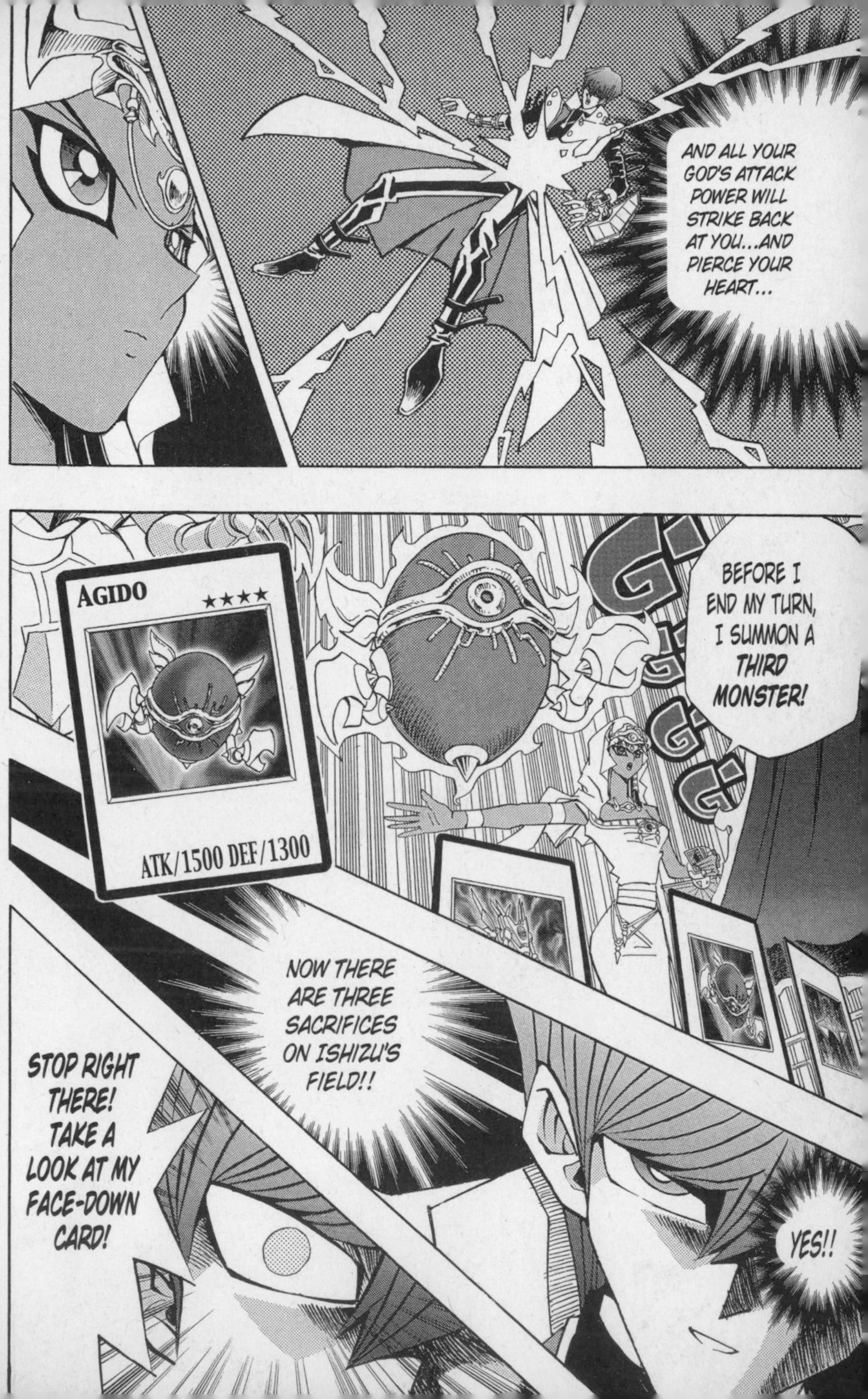
AND ALL YOUR GOD'S ATTACK POWER WILL STRIKE BACK AT YOU...AND PIERCE YOUR HEART...
BEFORE I END MY TURN, I SUMMON A THIRD MONSTER!
AGIDO
★★★★
ATK/1500 DEF/1300
NOW THERE ARE THREE SACRIFICES ON ISHIZU'S FIELD!!
YES!!
STOP RIGHT THERE! TAKE A LOOK AT MY FACE-DOWN CARD!

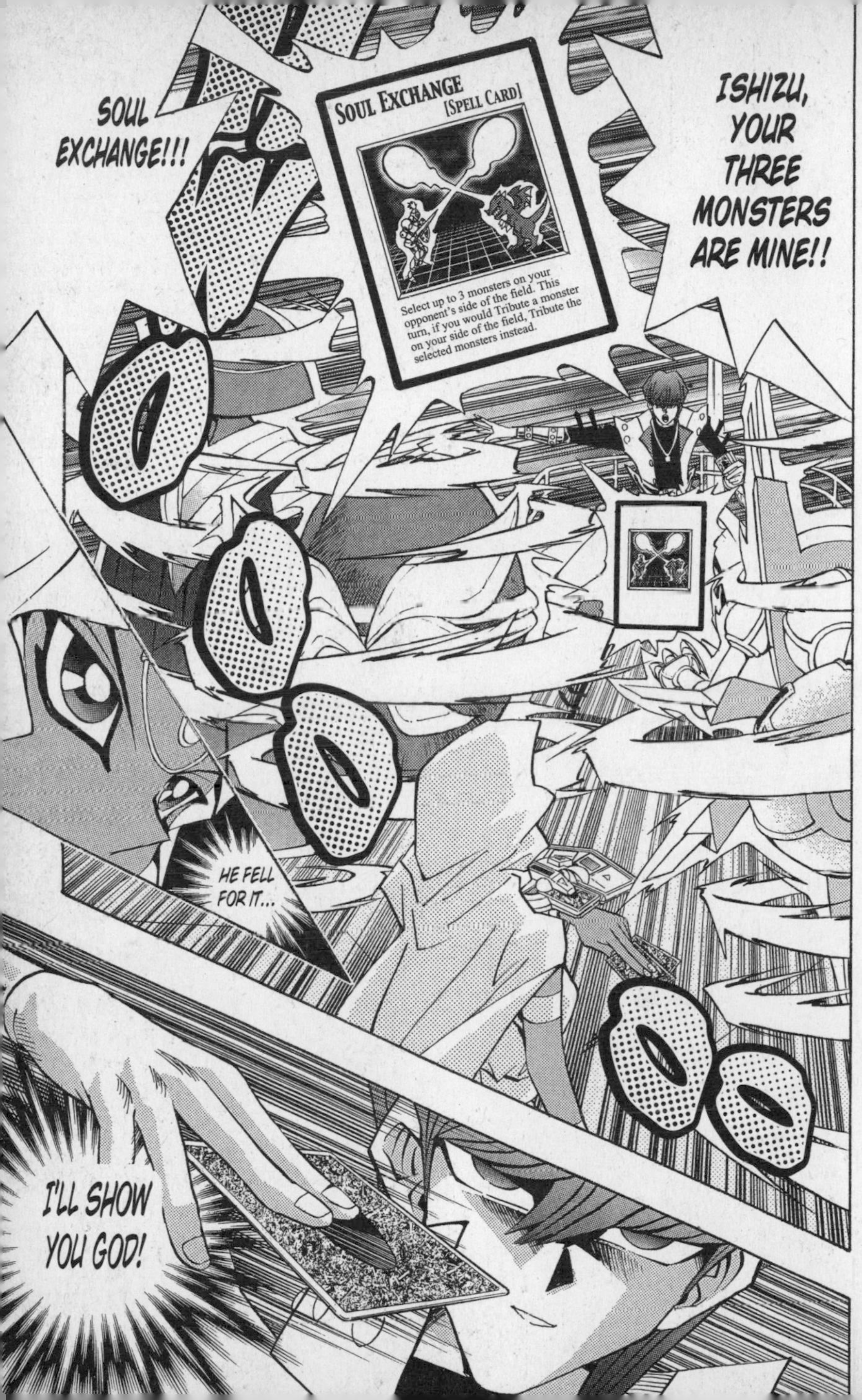
ISHIZU, YOUR THREE MONSTERS ARE MINE!!
SOUL EXCHANGE!!!
SOUL EXCHANGE
[SPELL CARD]
Select up to 3 monsters on your opponent's side of the field. This turn, if you would Tribute a monster on your side of the field, Tribute the selected monsters instead.
HE FELL FOR IT...
I'LL SHOW YOU GOD!

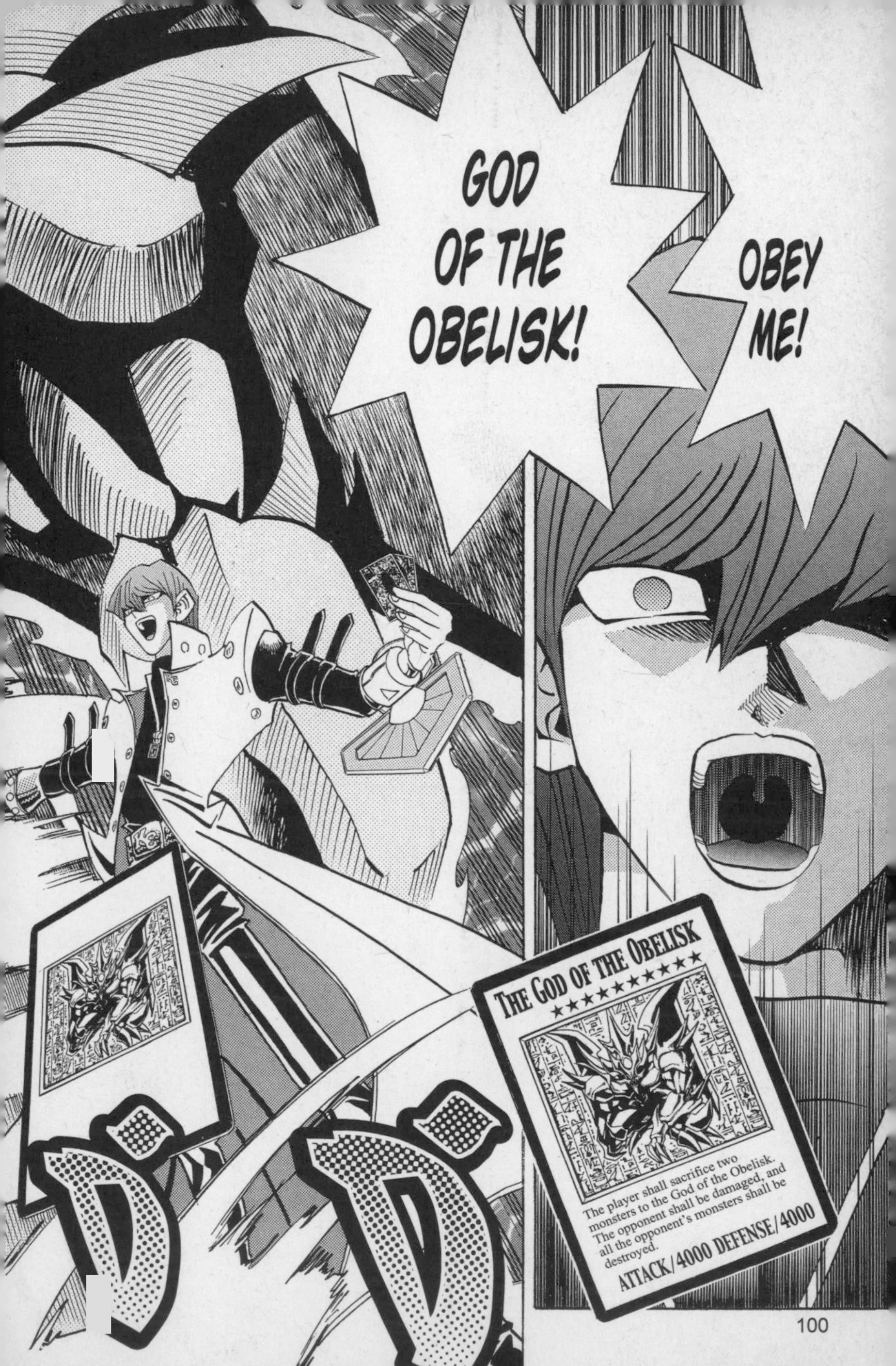
OBEY ME!
THE GOD OF THE OBELISK
The player shall sacrifice two monsters to the God of the Obelisk. The opponent shall be damaged, and all the opponent's monsters shall be destroyed.
ATTACK/4000 DEFENSE/4000
GOD OF THE OBELISK!
D D

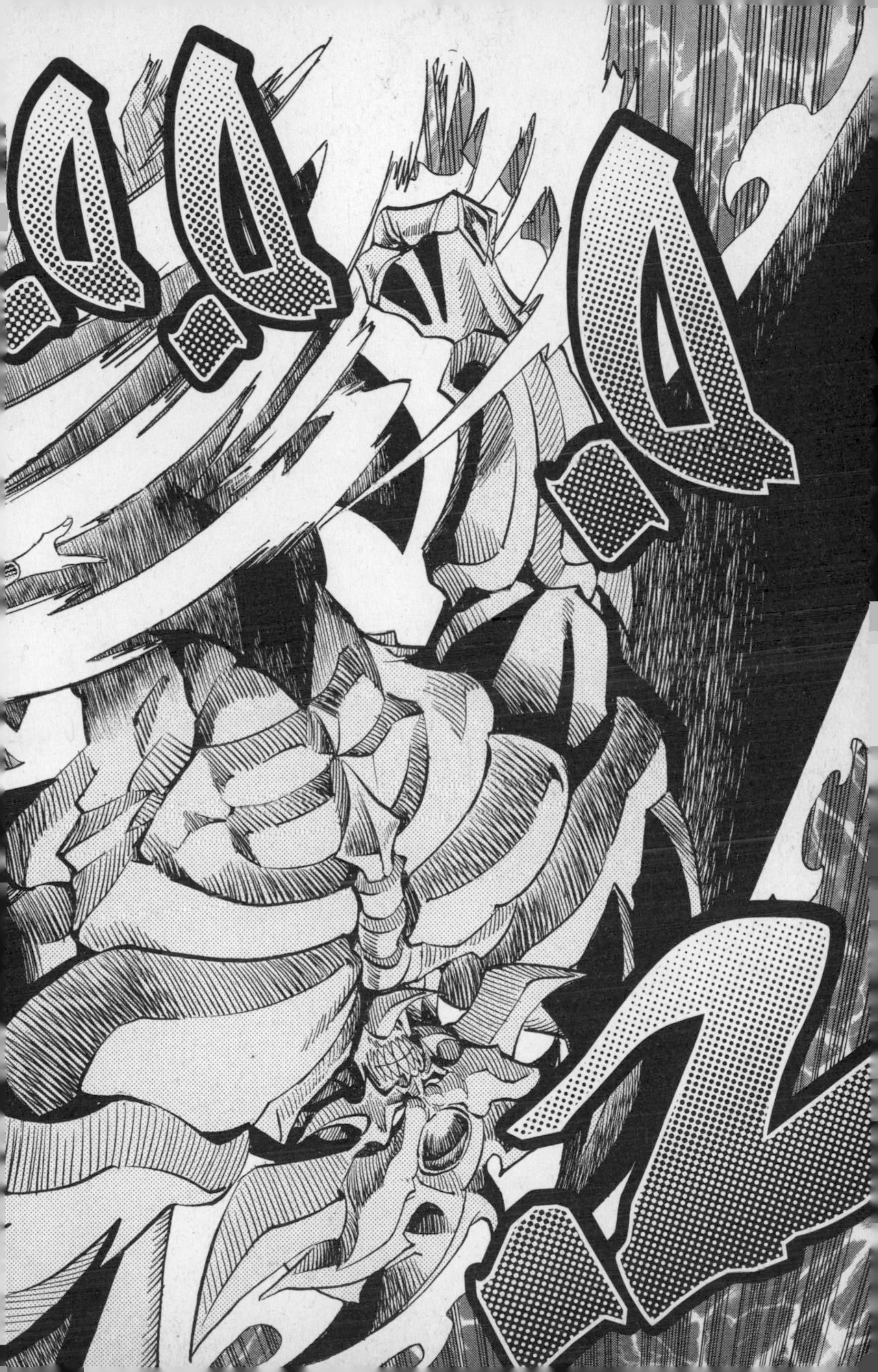

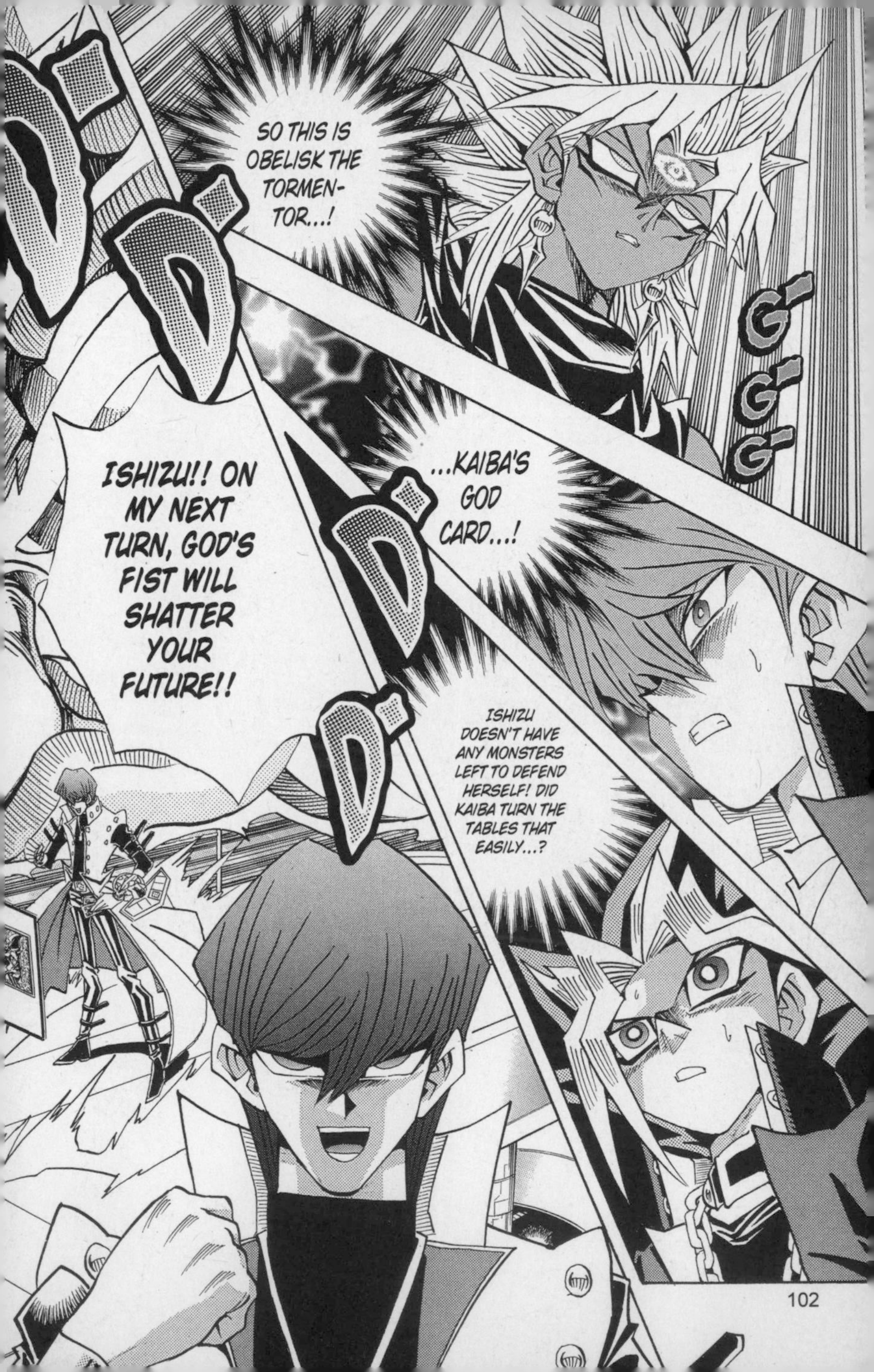
SO THIS IS OBELISK THE TORMENTOR...!
G-G-G-
...KAIBA'S GOD CARD...!
ISHIZU DOESN'T HAVE ANY MONSTERS LEFT TO DEFEND HERSELF! DID KAIBA TURN THE TABLES THAT EASILY...?
D-D-D-D
ISHIZU!! ON MY NEXT TURN, GOD'S FIST WILL SHATTER YOUR FUTURE!!

READ THIS WAY

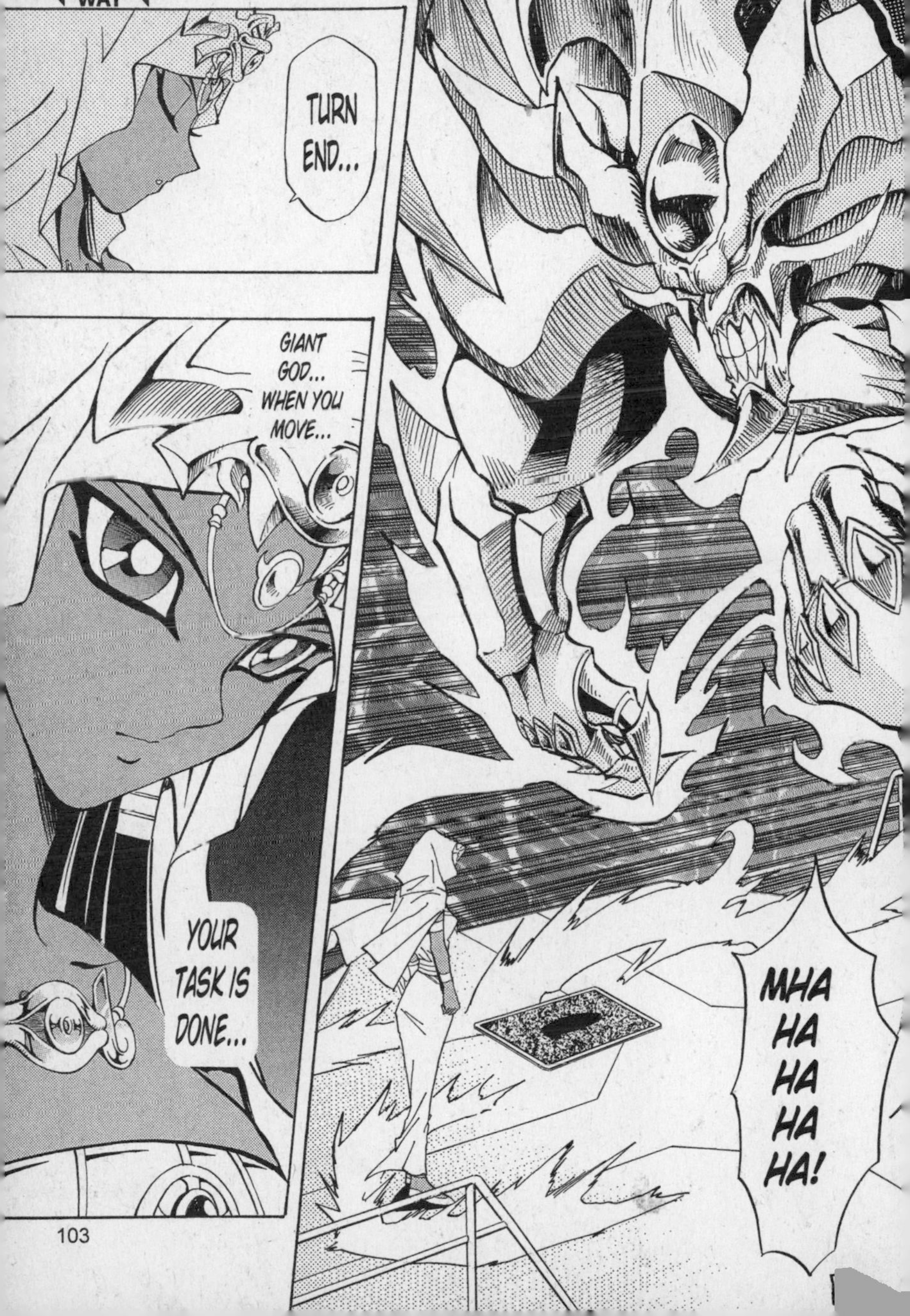
MHA HA HA HA HA HA!
TURN END...
GIANT GOD... WHEN YOU MOVE...
YOUR TASK IS DONE...

BLAST HELD BY A TRIBUTE

[SPELL CARD]

Plant a bomb on one monster. When your opponent uses that monster in a Sacrifice Summon, and the summoned monster declares an attack, destroy all face up Attack Position monsters on your opponent's side of the field and deal damage to the opponent equal to the summoned monster's ATK.

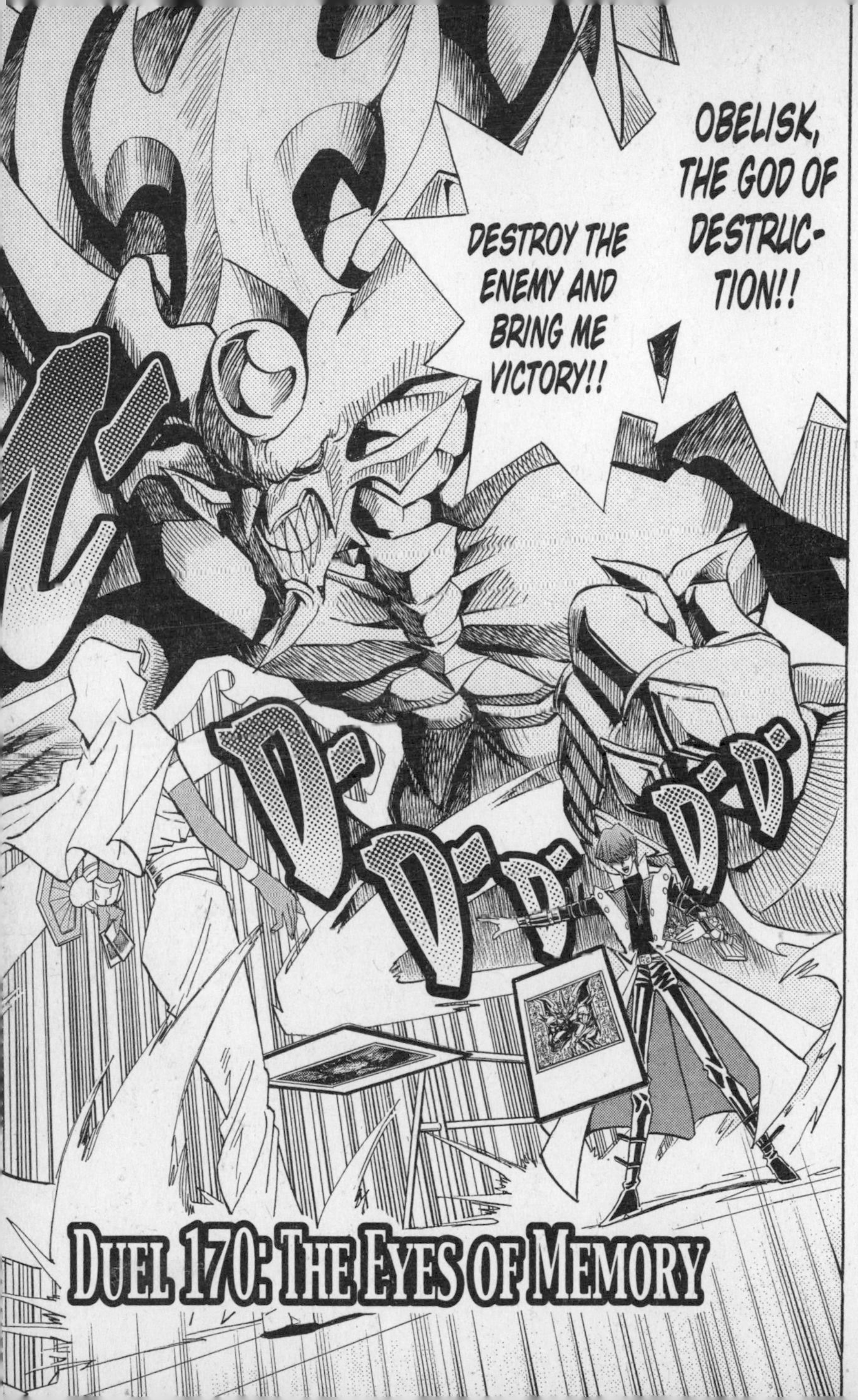
OBELISK, THE GOD OF DESTRUCTION!!
DESTROY THE ENEMY AND BRING ME VICTORY!!
DDDDD
DUEL 170: THE EYES OF MEMORY

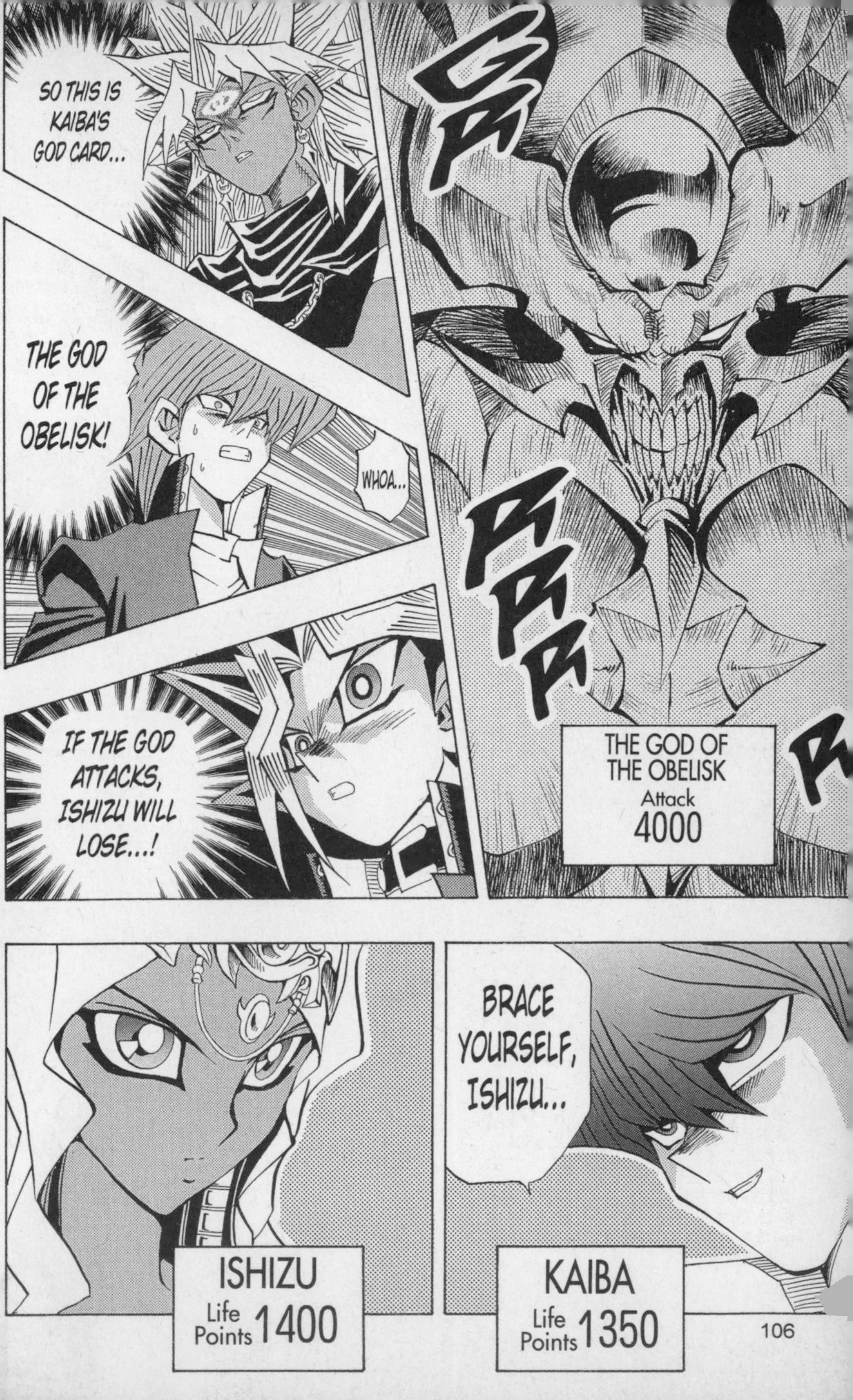
THE GOD OF THE OBELISK Attack 4000
SO THIS IS KAIBA'S GOD CARD...
THE GOD OF THE OBELISK!
WHOA...
IF THE GOD ATTACKS, ISHIZU WILL LOSE...!
BRACE YOURSELF, ISHIZU...
KAIBA Life Points 1350
ISHIZU Life Points 1400

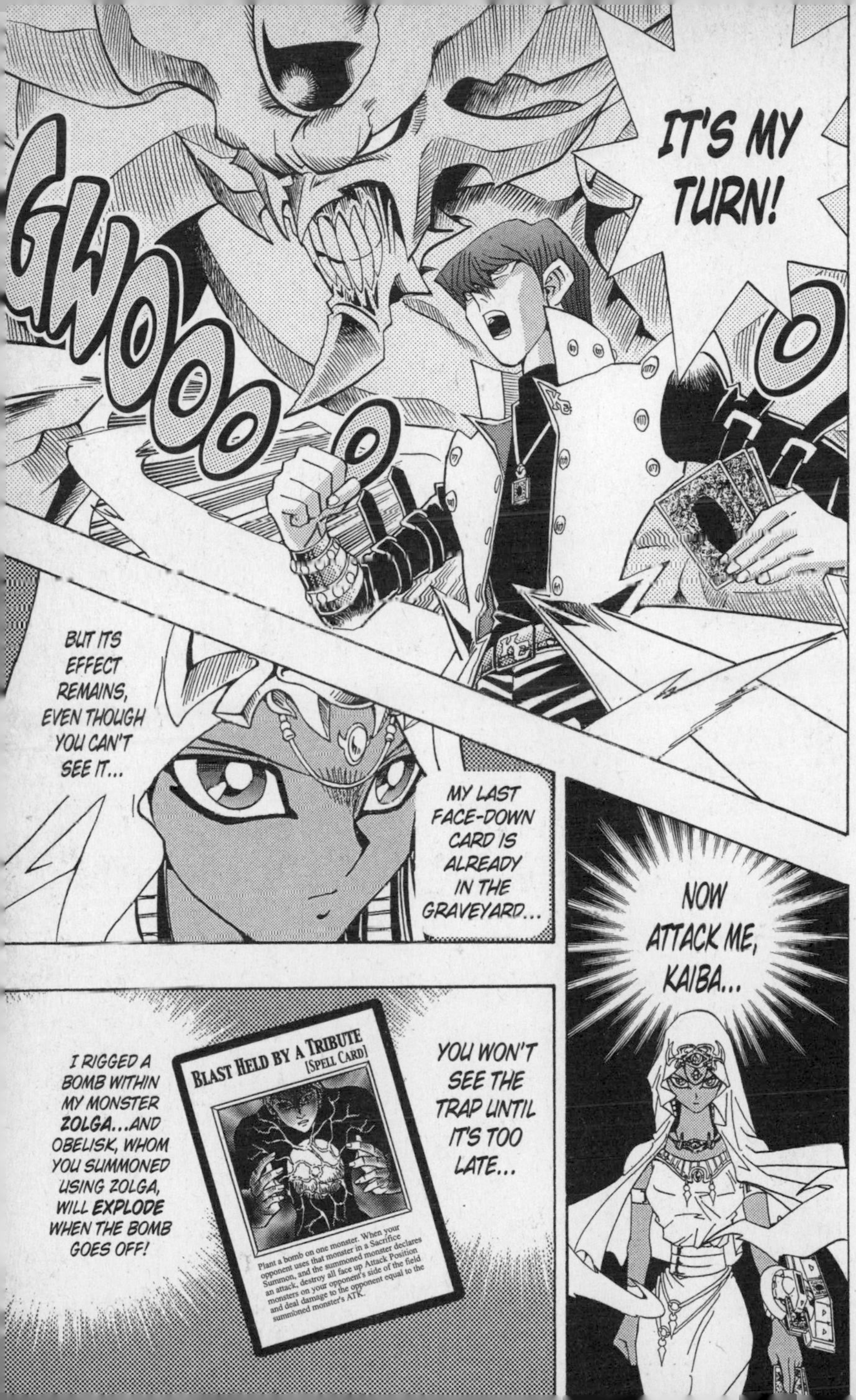
IT'S MY TURN!
GWOOOOOO
MY LAST FACE-DOWN CARD IS ALREADY IN THE GRAVEYARD...
BUT ITS EFFECT REMAINS, EVEN THOUGH YOU CAN'T SEE IT...
NOW ATTACK ME, KAIBA...
YOU WON'T SEE THE TRAP UNTIL IT'S TOO LATE...
I RIGGED A BOMB WITHIN MY MONSTER ZOLGA...AND OBELISK, WHOM YOU SUMMONED USING ZOLGA, WILL EXPLODE WHEN THE BOMB GOES OFF!
BLAST HELD BY A TRIBUTE
[SPELL CARD]
Plant a bomb on one monster. When your opponent uses that monster in a Sacrifice Summon, and the summoned monster declares an attack, destroy all face up Attack Position monsters on your opponent's side of the field and deal damage to the opponent equal to the summoned monster's ATK.

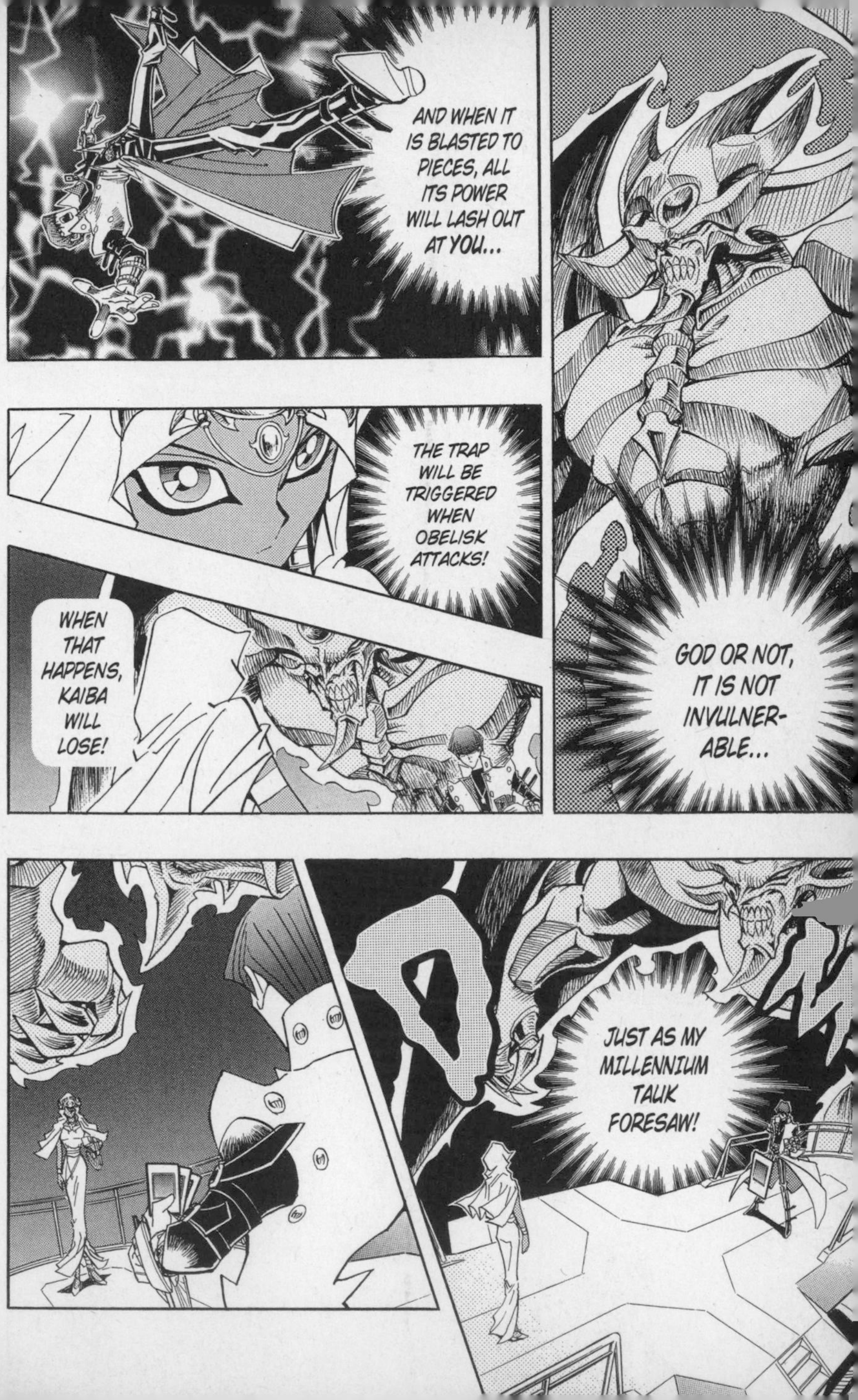
GOD OR NOT, IT IS NOT INVULNER-ABLE...
AND WHEN IT IS BLASTED TO PIECES, ALL ITS POWER WILL LASH OUT AT YOU...
THE TRAP WILL BE TRIGGERED WHEN OBELISK ATTACKS!
WHEN THAT HAPPENS, KAIBA WILL LOSE!
JUST AS MY MILLENNIUM TAUK FORESAW!

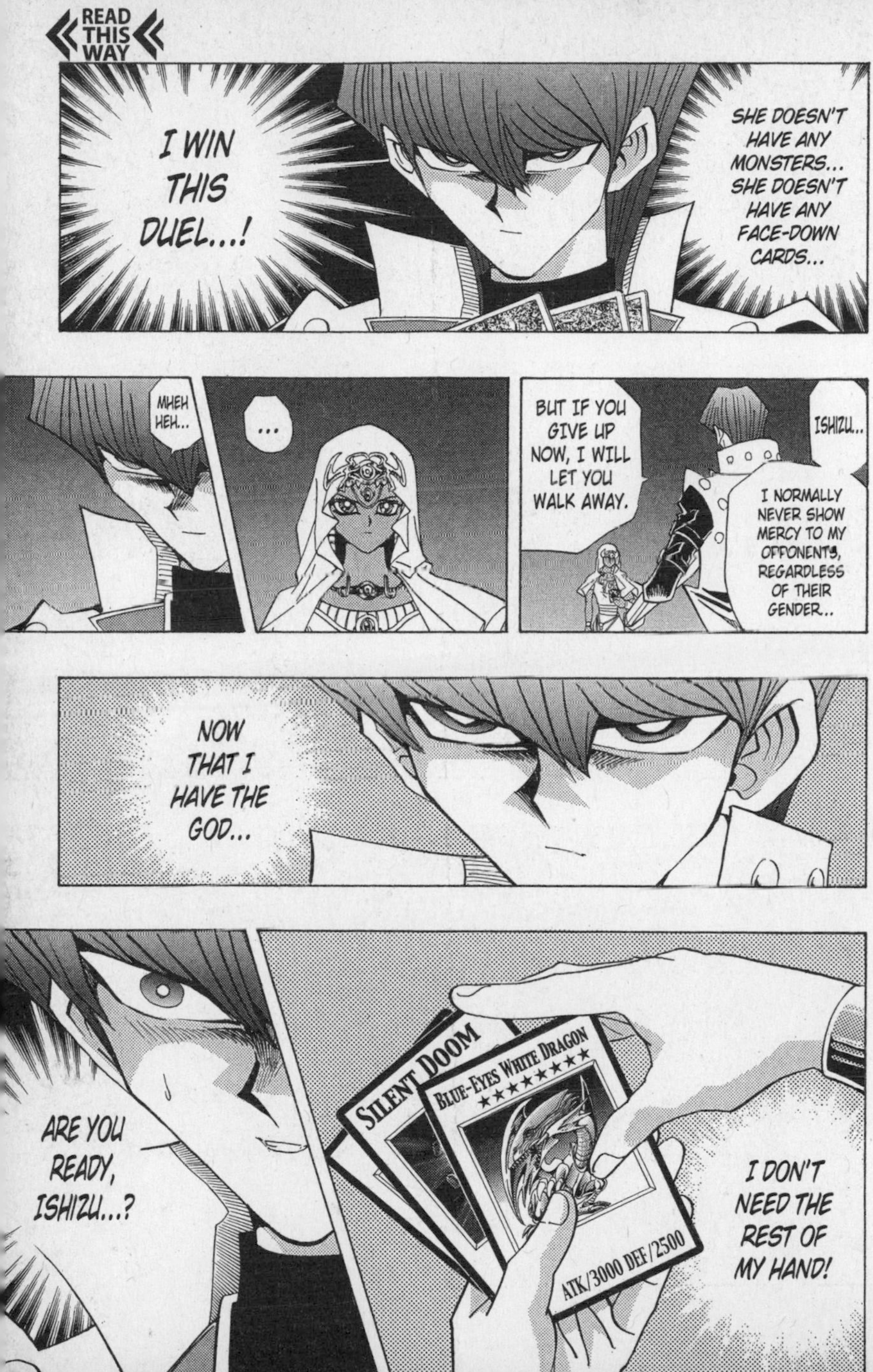
READ THIS WAY
SHE DOESN'T HAVE ANY MONSTERS... SHE DOESN'T HAVE ANY FACE-DOWN CARDS...
I WIN THIS DUEL...!
ISHIZU...
I NORMALLY NEVER SHOW MERCY TO MY OPPONENTS, REGARDLESS OF THEIR GENDER...
BUT IF YOU GIVE UP NOW, I WILL LET YOU WALK AWAY.
...
MHEH HEH...
NOW THAT I HAVE THE GOD...
I DON'T NEED THE REST OF MY HAND!
SILENT DOOM
BLUE-EYES WHITE DRAGON
ATK/3000 DEF/2500
ARE YOU READY, ISHIZU...?

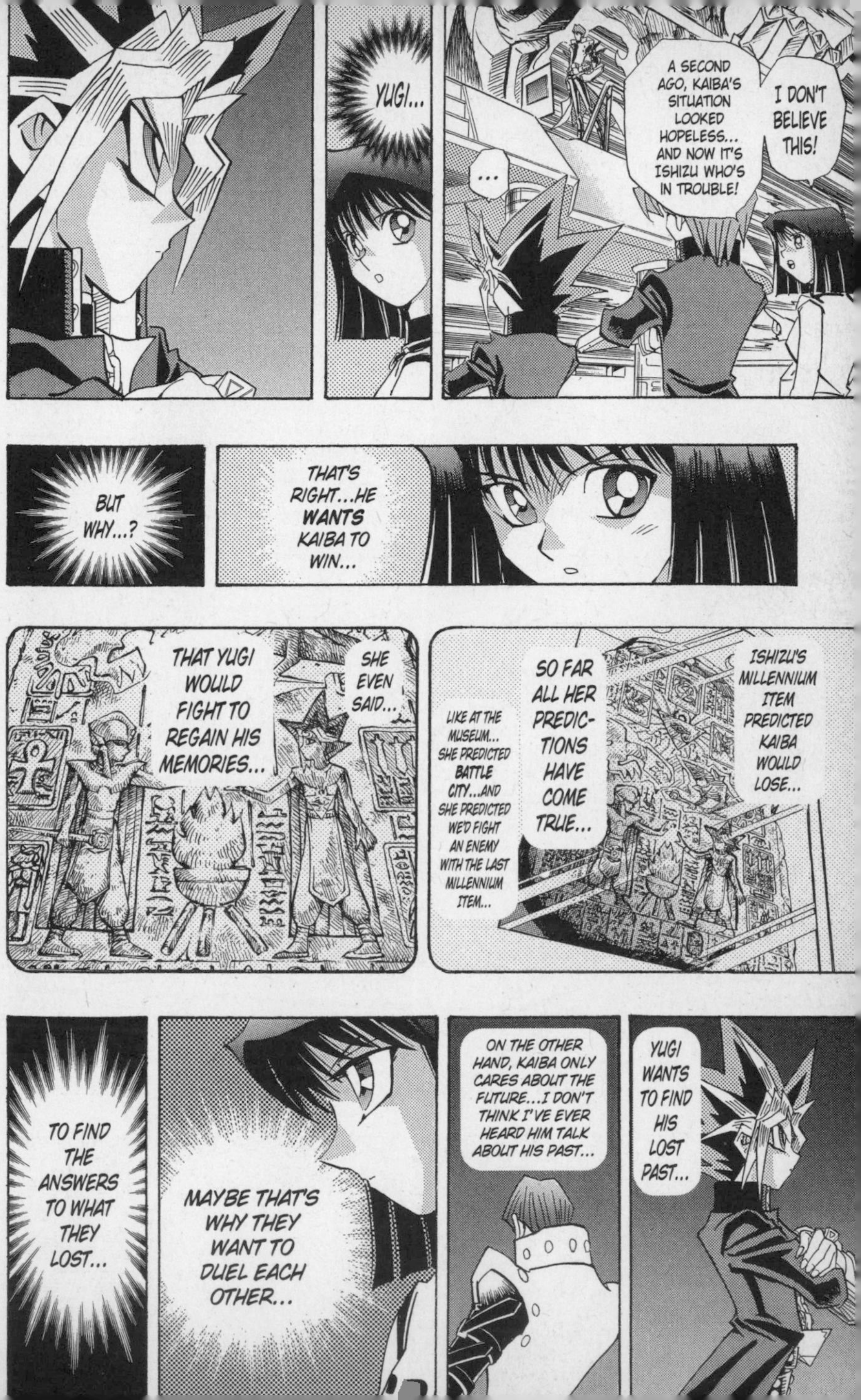
I DON'T BELIEVE THIS!
A SECOND AGO, KAIBA'S SITUATION LOOKED HOPELESS... AND NOW IT'S ISHIZU WHO'S IN TROUBLE!
...
YUGI...
THAT'S RIGHT...HE WANTS KAIBA TO WIN...
BUT WHY...?
ISHIZU'S MILLENNIUM ITEM PREDICTED KAIBA WOULD LOSE...
SO FAR ALL HER PREDIC-TIONS HAVE COME TRUE...
LIKE AT THE MUSEUM... SHE PREDICTED BATTLE CITY...AND SHE PREDICTED WE'D FIGHT AN ENEMY WITH THE LAST MILLENNIUM ITEM...
SHE EVEN SAID...
THAT YUGI WOULD FIGHT TO REGAIN HIS MEMORIES...
YUGI WANTS TO FIND HIS LOST PAST...
ON THE OTHER HAND, KAIBA ONLY CARES ABOUT THE FUTURE...I DON'T THINK I'VE EVER HEARD HIM TALK ABOUT HIS PAST...
MAYBE THAT'S WHY THEY WANT TO DUEL EACH OTHER...
TO FIND THE ANSWERS TO WHAT THEY LOST...

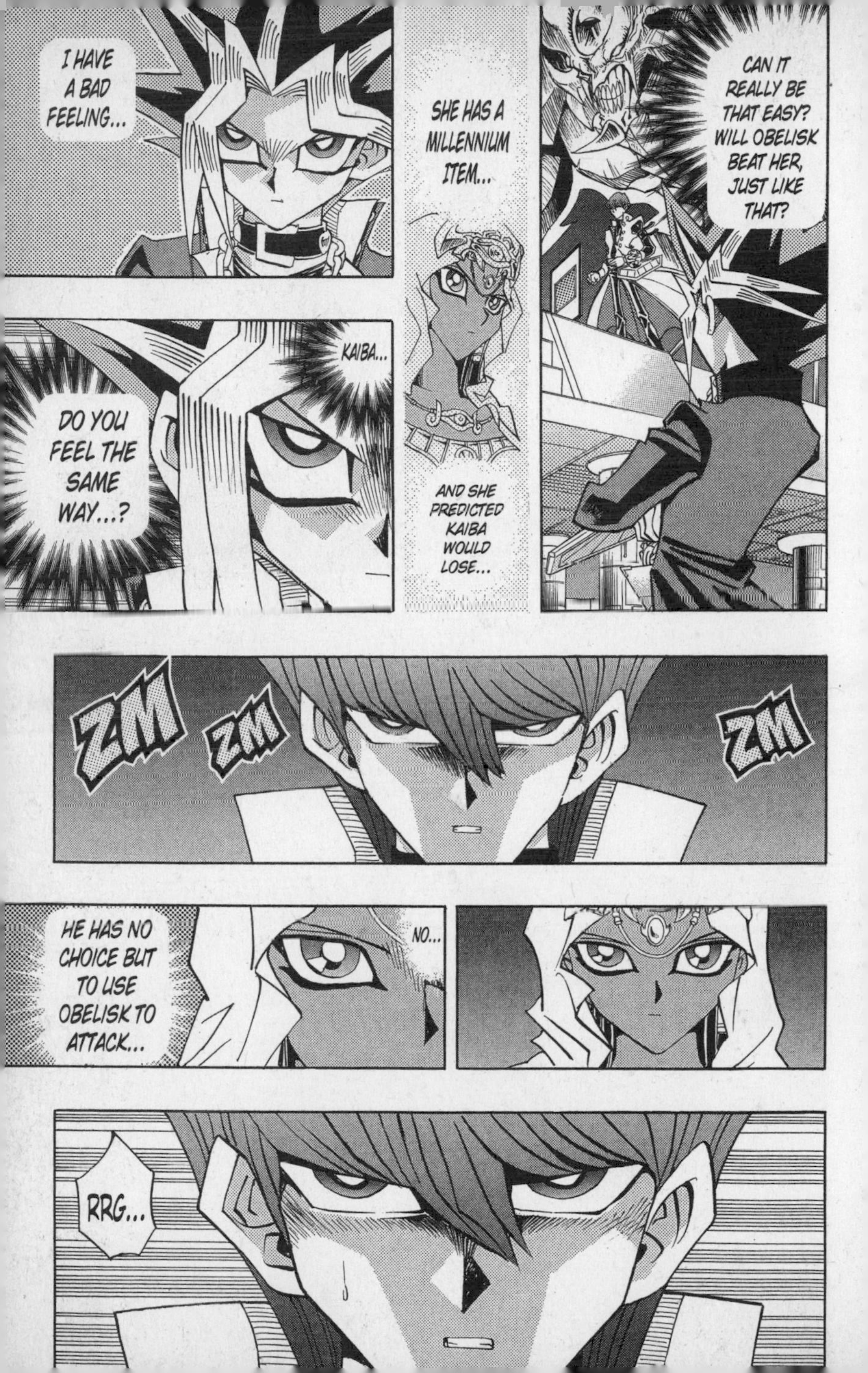
CAN IT REALLY BE THAT EASY? WILL OBELISK BEAT HER, JUST LIKE THAT?
SHE HAS A MILLENNIUM ITEM...
AND SHE PREDICTED KAIBA WOULD LOSE...
I HAVE A BAD FEELING...
KAIBA...
DO YOU FEEL THE SAME WAY...?
ZM
ZM
ZM
NO...
HE HAS NO CHOICE BUT TO USE OBELISK TO ATTACK...
RRG...

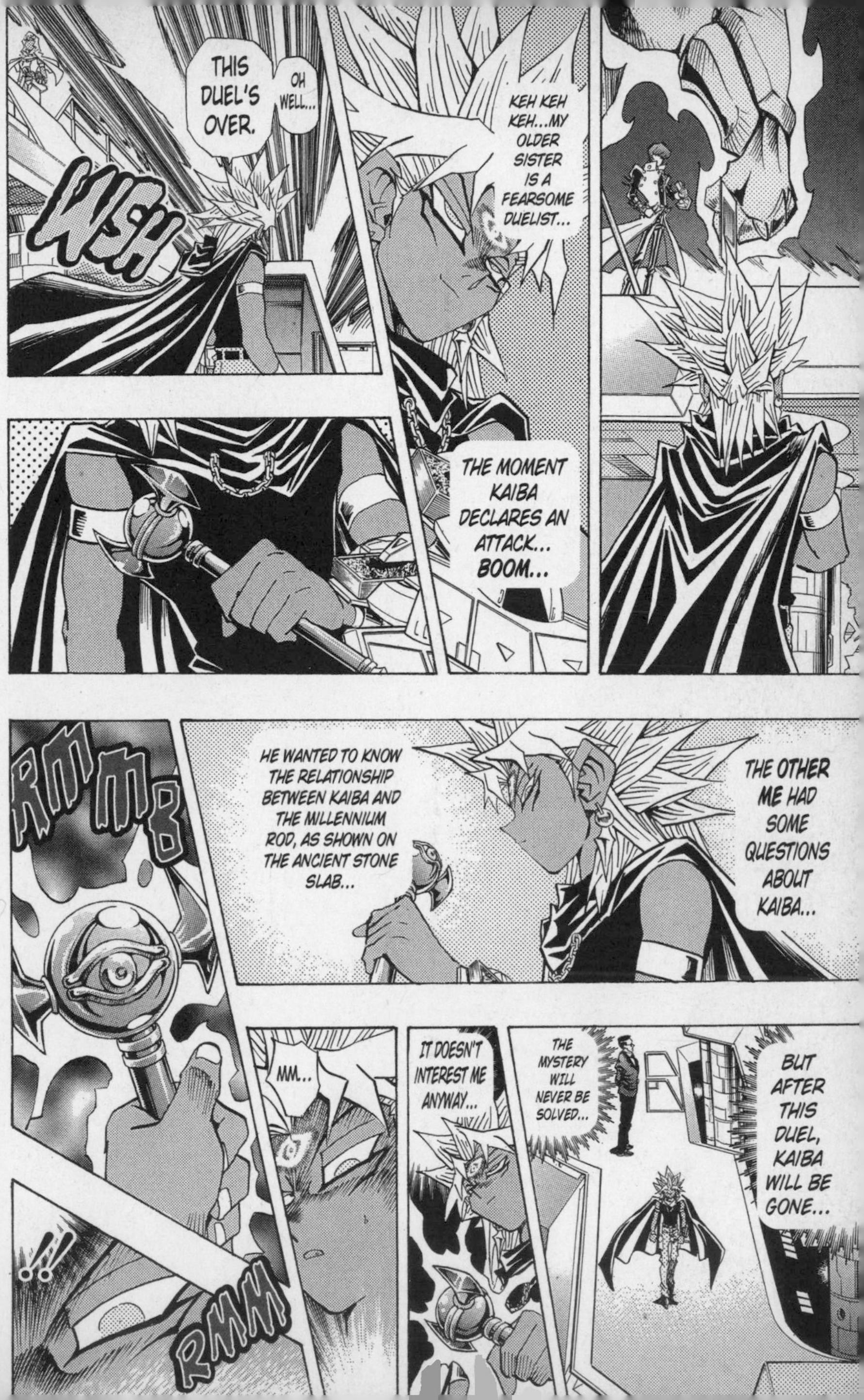
KEH KEH KEH...MY OLDER SISTER IS A FEARSOME DUELIST...
THE MOMENT KAIBA DECLARES AN ATTACK... BOOM...
THIS DUEL'S OVER.
OH WELL...
WSH
THE OTHER ME HAD SOME QUESTIONS ABOUT KAIBA...
HE WANTED TO KNOW THE RELATIONSHIP BETWEEN KAIBA AND THE MILLENNIUM ROD, AS SHOWN ON THE ANCIENT STONE SLAB...
BUT AFTER THIS DUEL, KAIBA WILL BE GONE...
THE MYSTERY WILL NEVER BE SOLVED...
IT DOESN'T INTEREST ME ANYWAY...
MM...
RMMB
!!
RMM

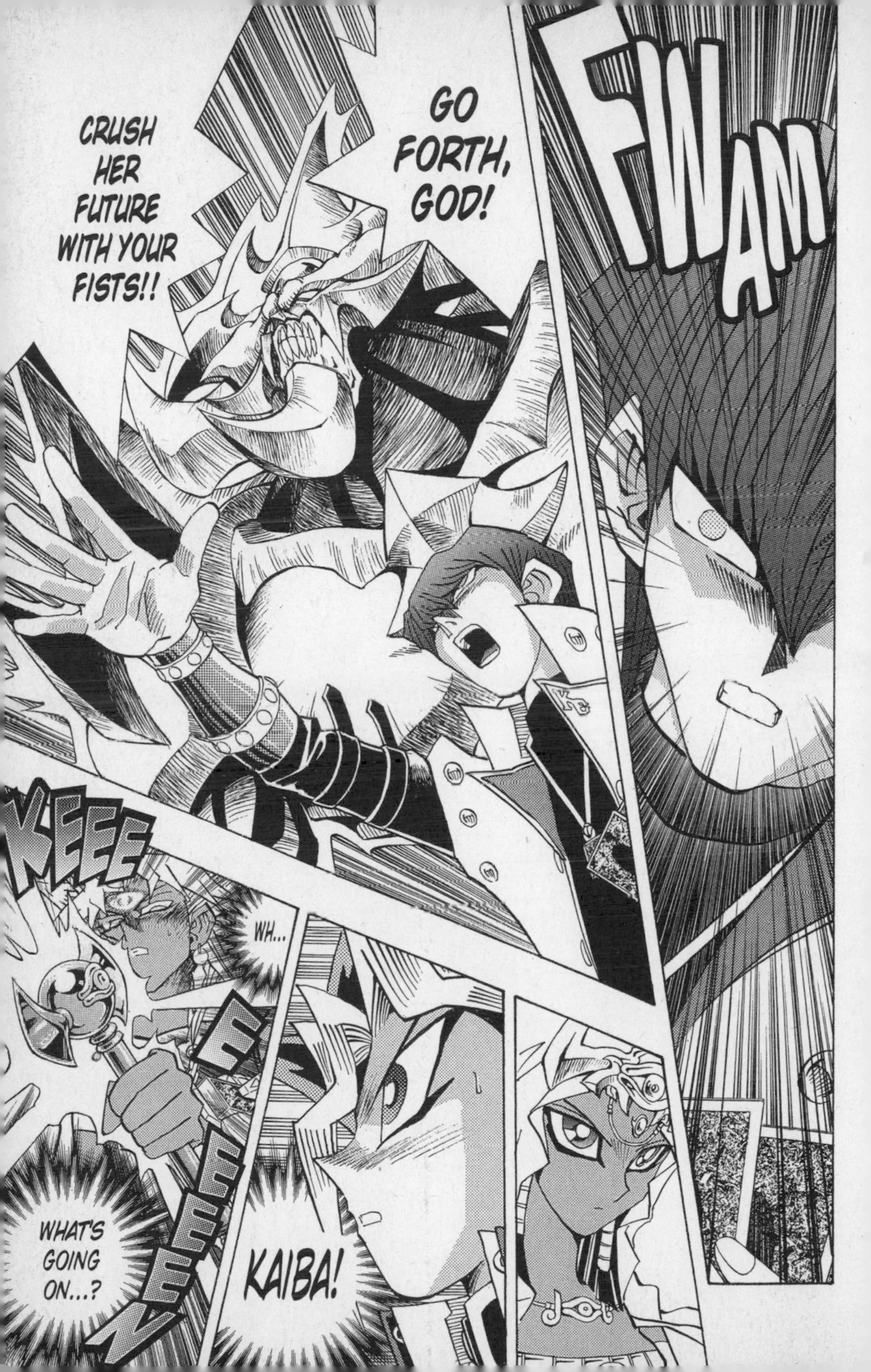
FWAM
GO FORTH, GOD!
CRUSH HER FUTURE WITH YOUR FISTS!!
KAIBA!
KEEE
WH...
E
EEEEN
WHAT'S GOING ON...?

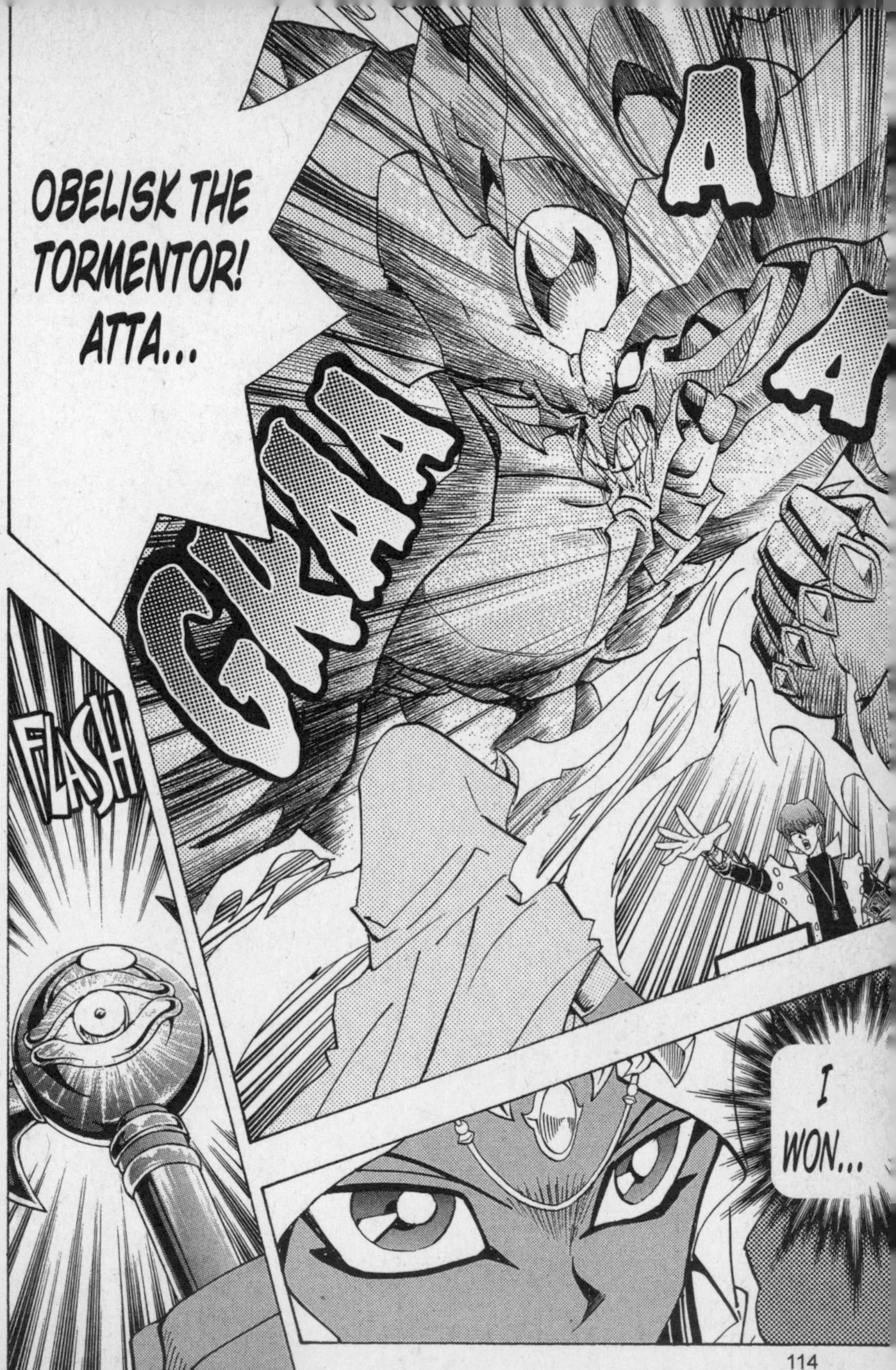
OBELISK THE TORMENTOR! ATTA...
CHAA
A
A
I WON...
FLASH

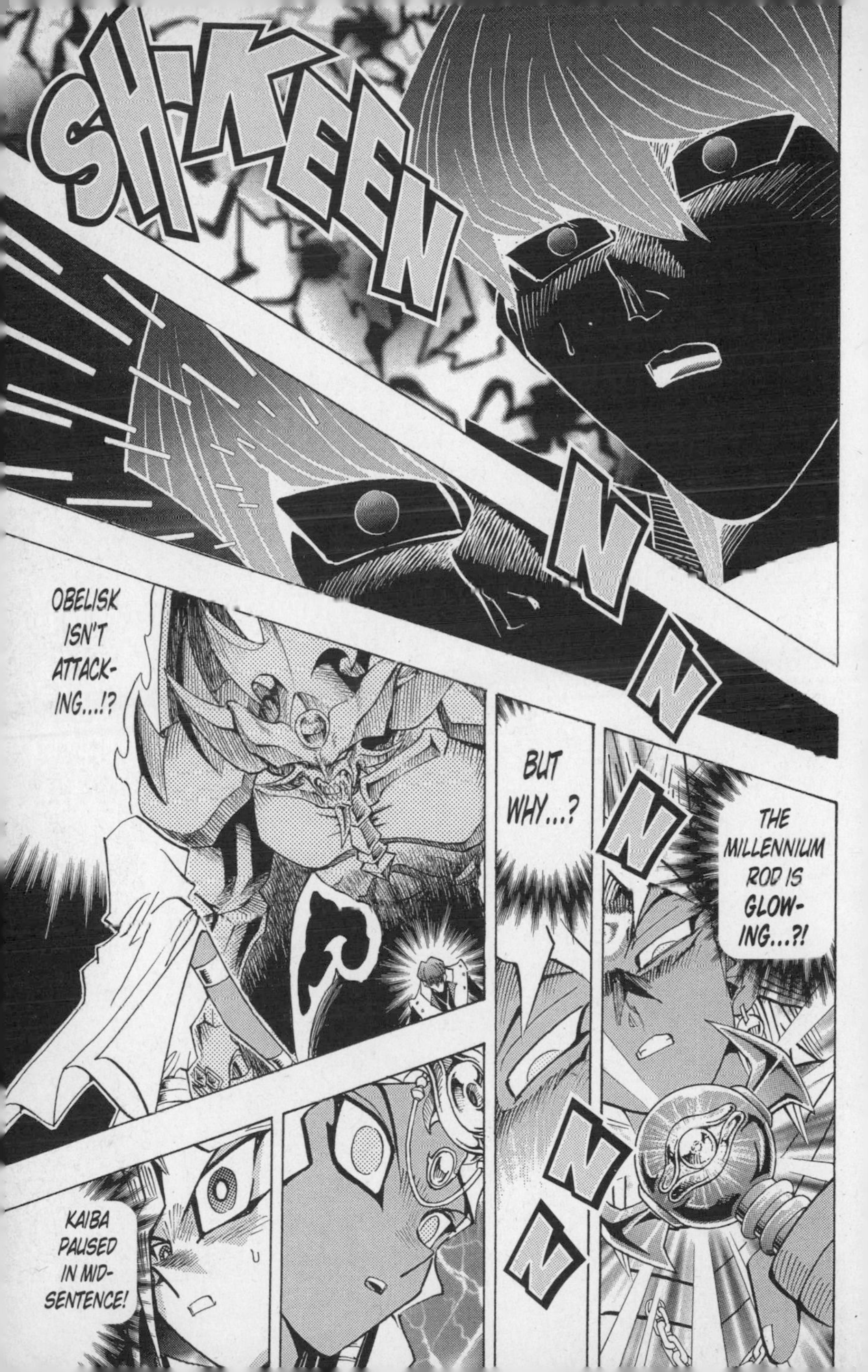
SHI-KEEN
NNNNN
OBELISK ISN'T ATTACKING...!?
THE MILLENNIUM ROD IS GLOWING...?!
BUT WHY...?
KAIBA PAUSED IN MID-SENTENCE!

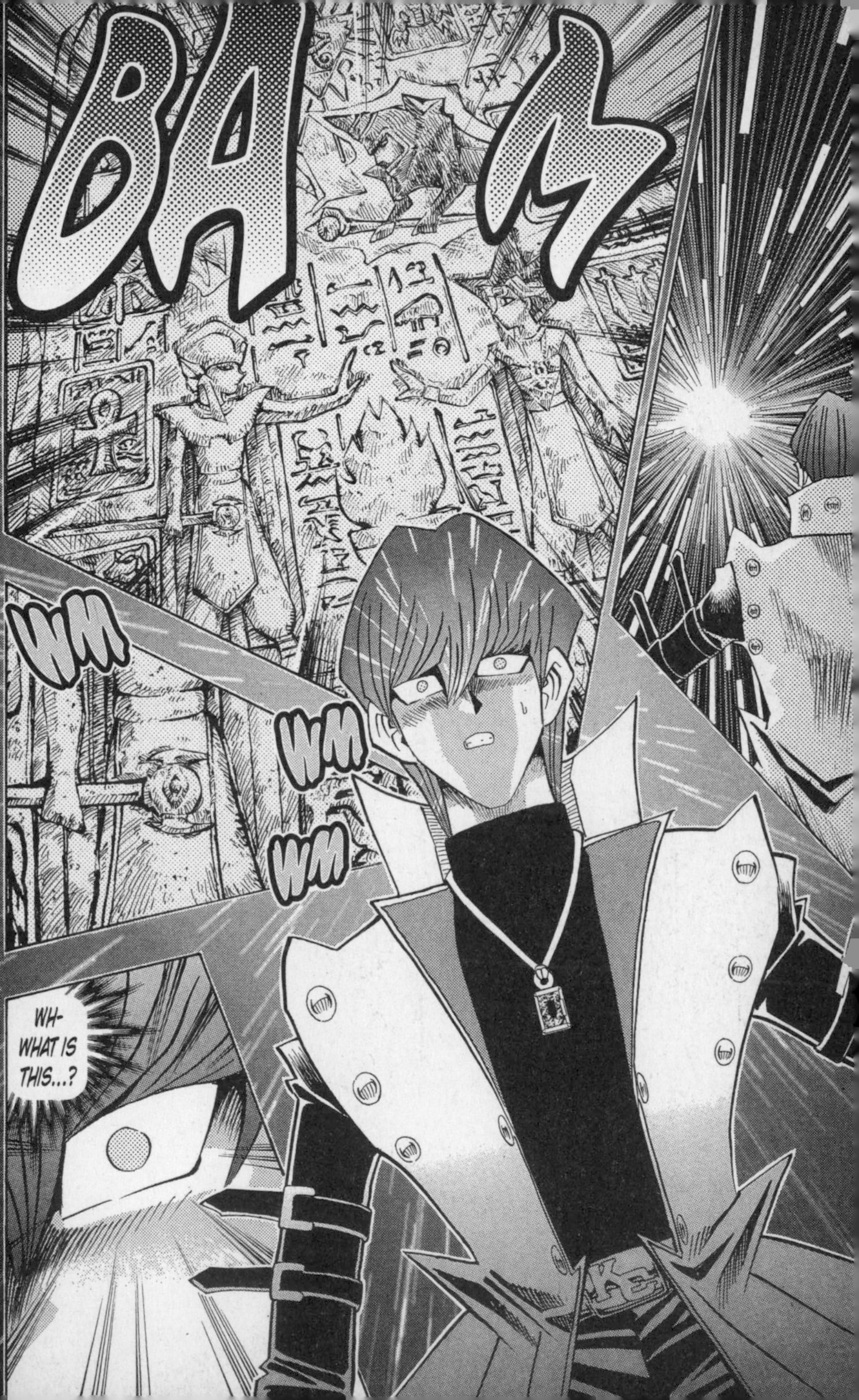
BAM
WM
WM
WM
WH-
WHAT IS
THIS...?

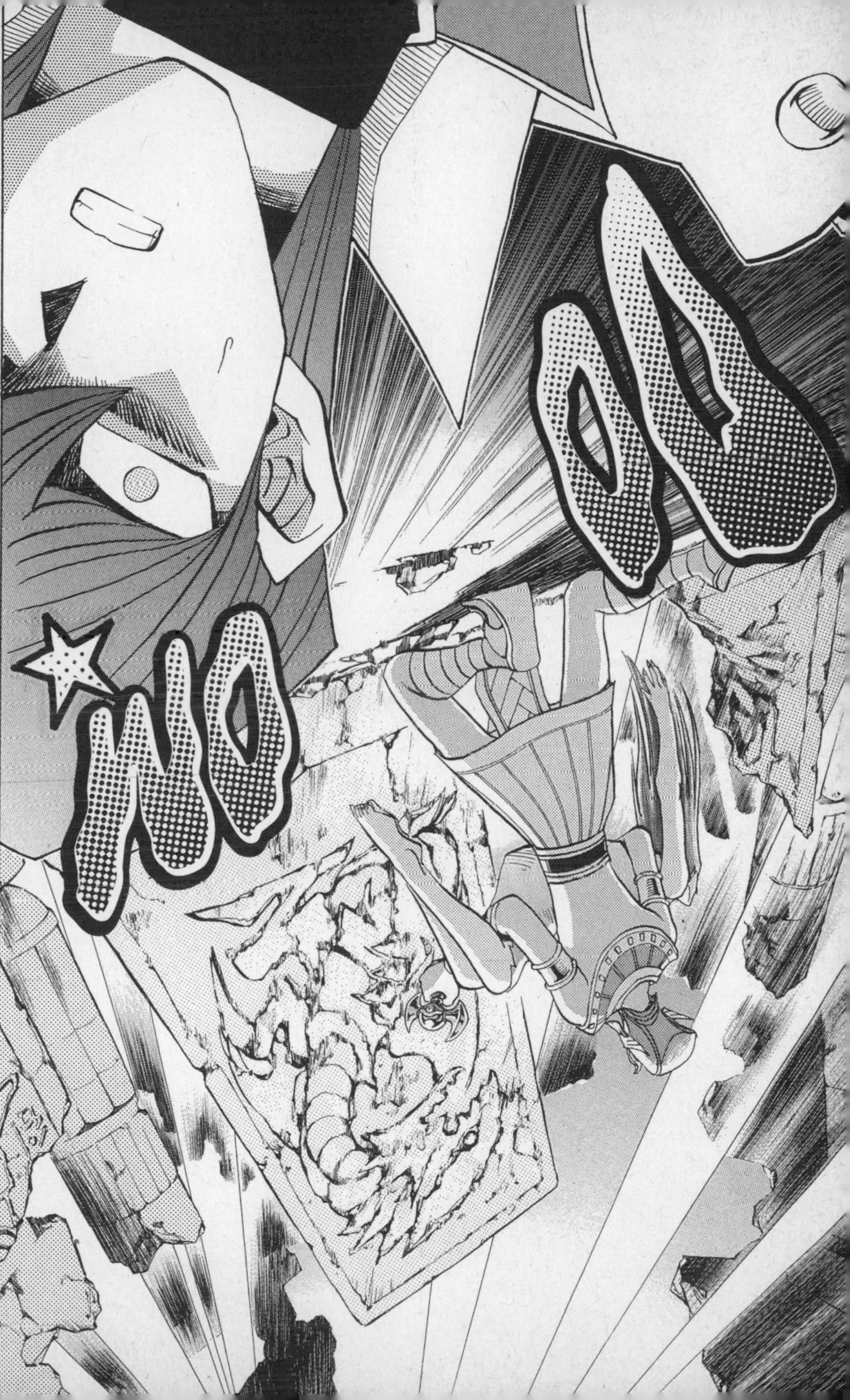
NO
OO

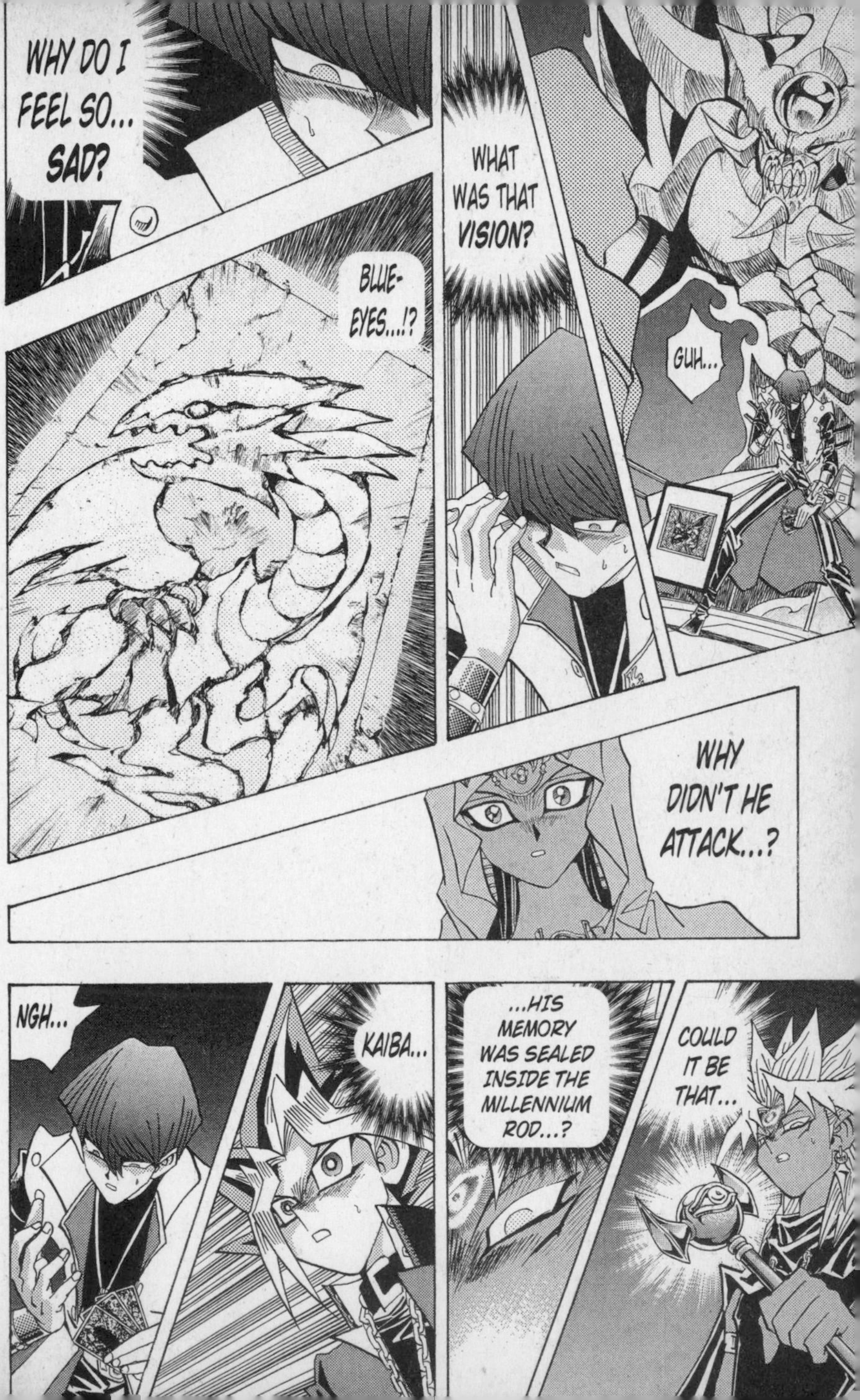
GUH...
WHAT WAS THAT VISION?
WHY DO I FEEL SO... SAD?
BLUE-EYES...!?
WHY DIDN'T HE ATTACK...?
COULD IT BE THAT...
...HIS MEMORY WAS SEALED INSIDE THE MILLENNIUM ROD...?
KAIBA...
NGH...

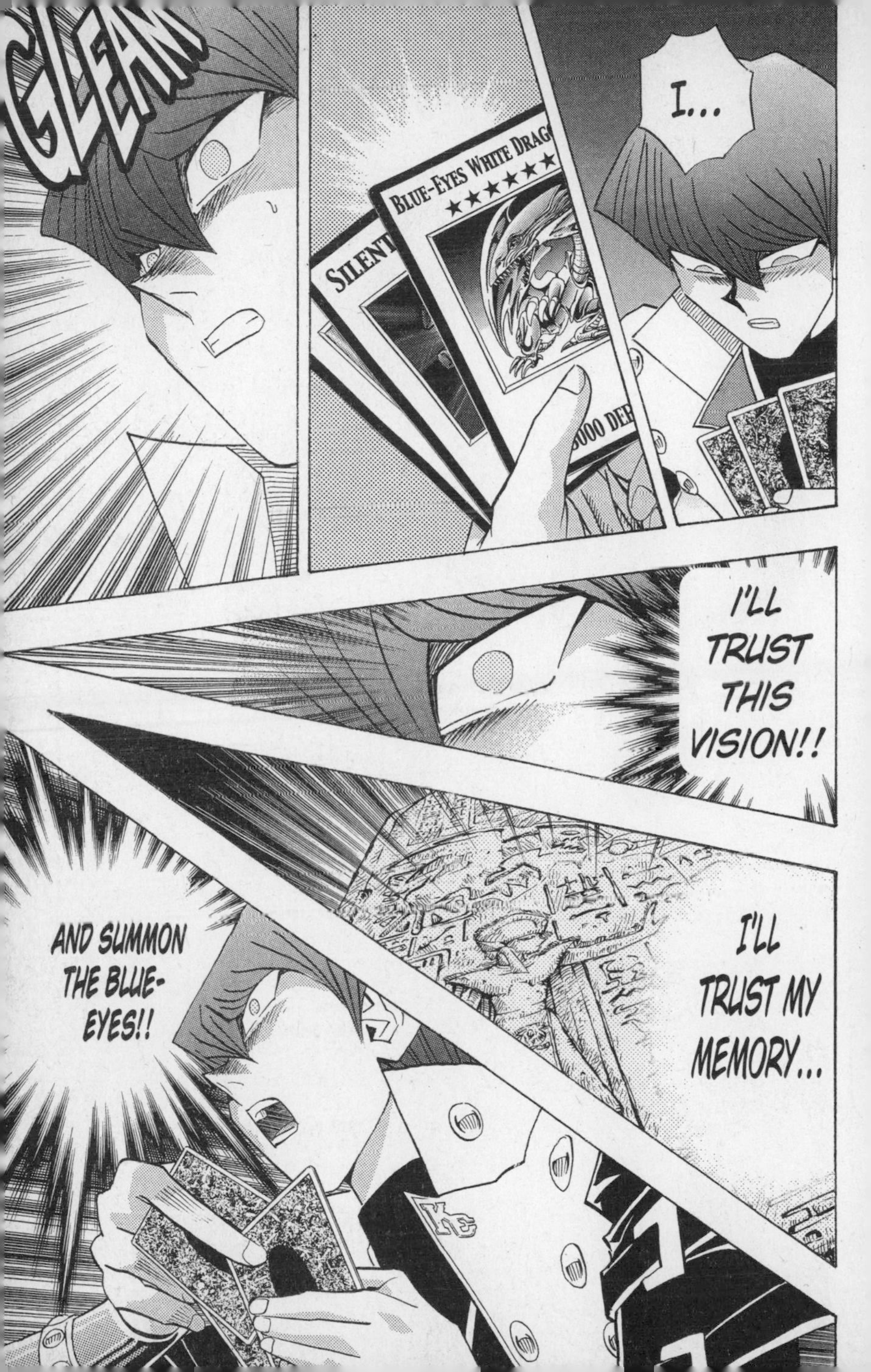
I...
BLUE-EYES WHITE DRAG
SILENT
3000 DEF
GLEAM
I'LL TRUST THIS VISION!!
I'LL TRUST MY MEMORY...
AND SUMMON THE BLUE-EYES!!

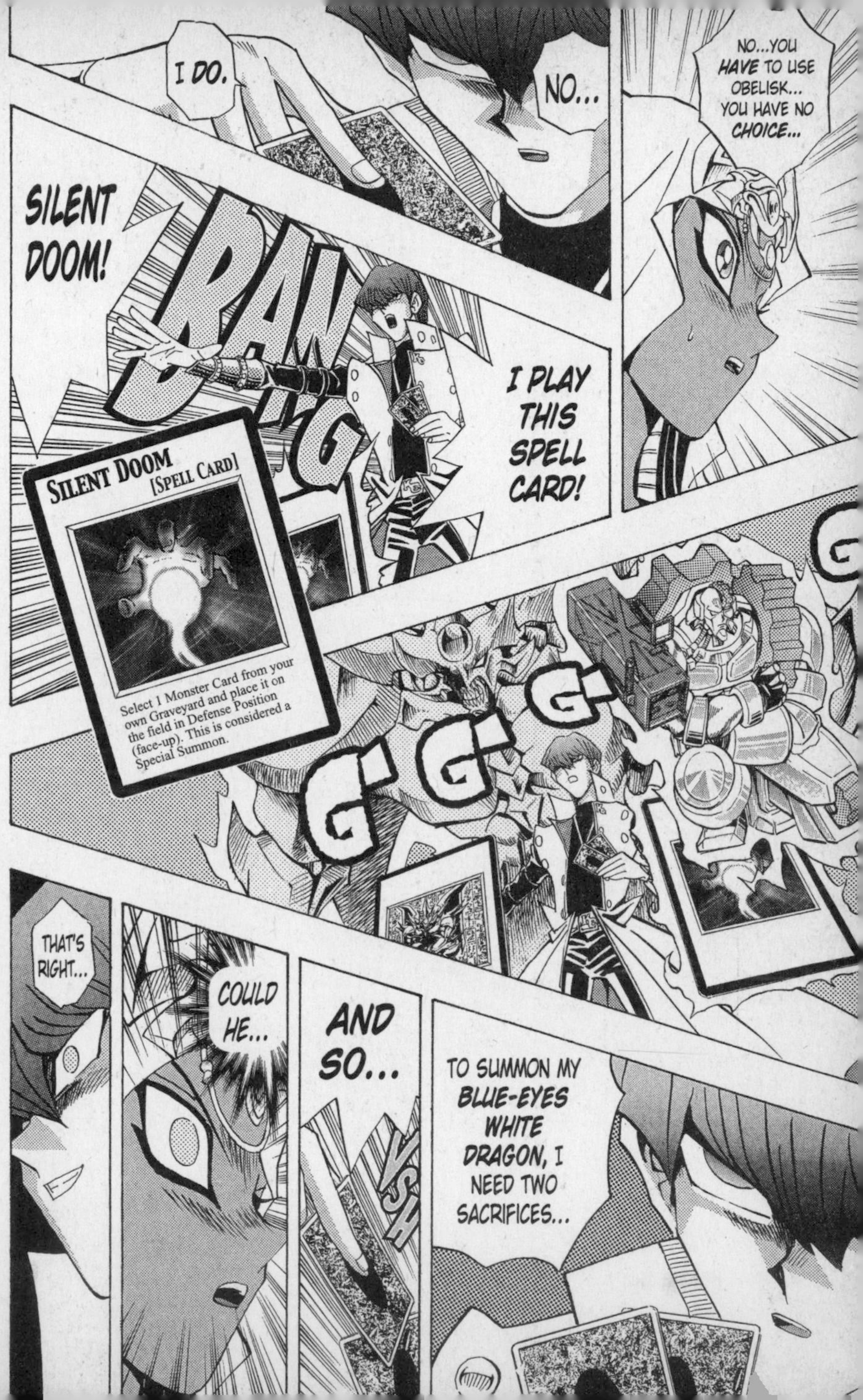
NO...YOU HAVE TO USE OBELISK... YOU HAVE NO CHOICE...
NO...
I DO.
I PLAY THIS SPELL CARD!
BANG
SILENT DOOM!
SILENT DOOM [SPELL CARD]
Select 1 Monster Card from your own Graveyard and place it on the field in Defense Position (face-up). This is considered a Special Summon.
G G G G
TO SUMMON MY BLUE-EYES WHITE DRAGON, I NEED TWO SACRIFICES...
VSH
AND SO...
COULD HE...
THAT'S RIGHT...

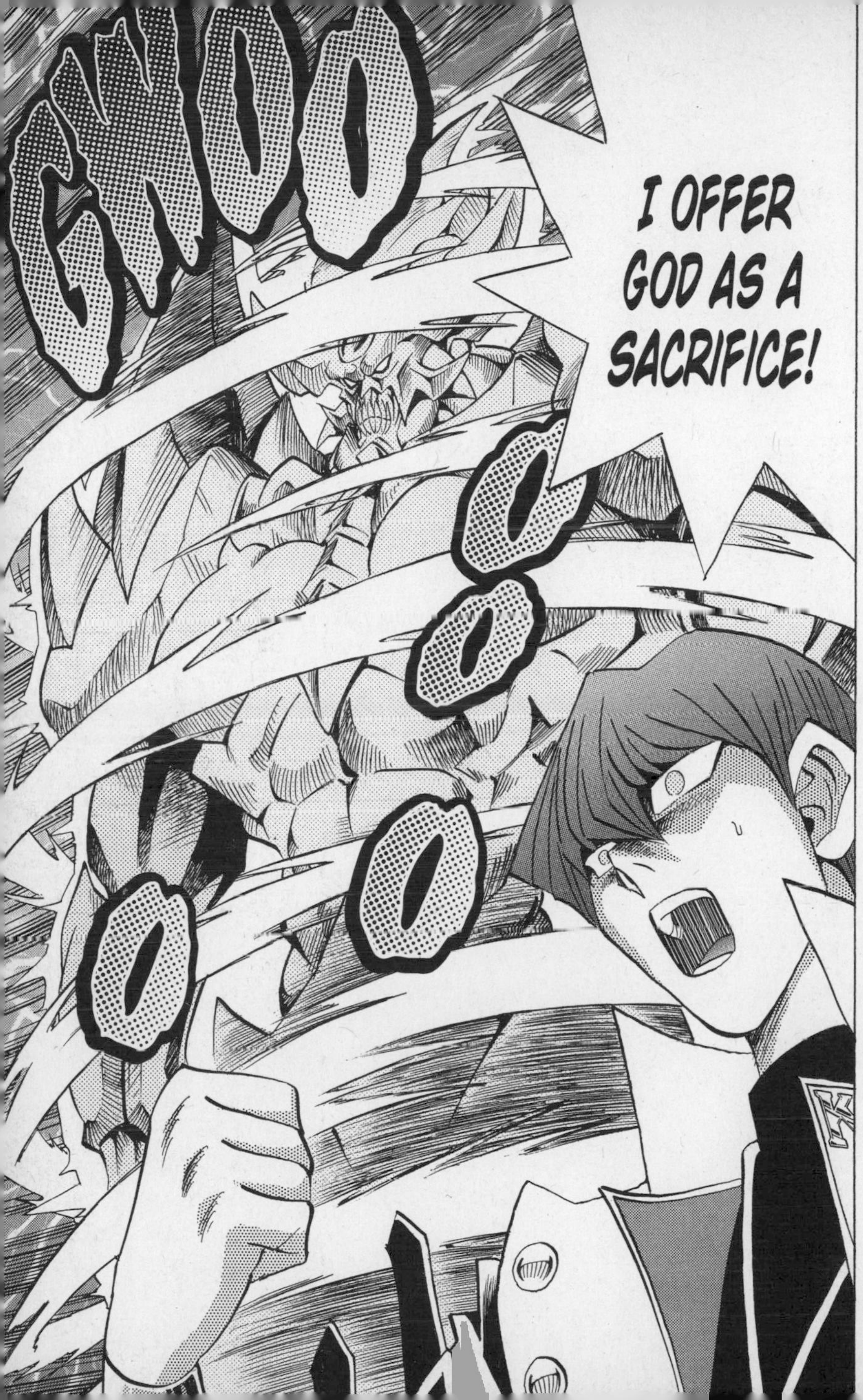
I OFFER GOD AS A SACRIFICE!
GWOOOOOO

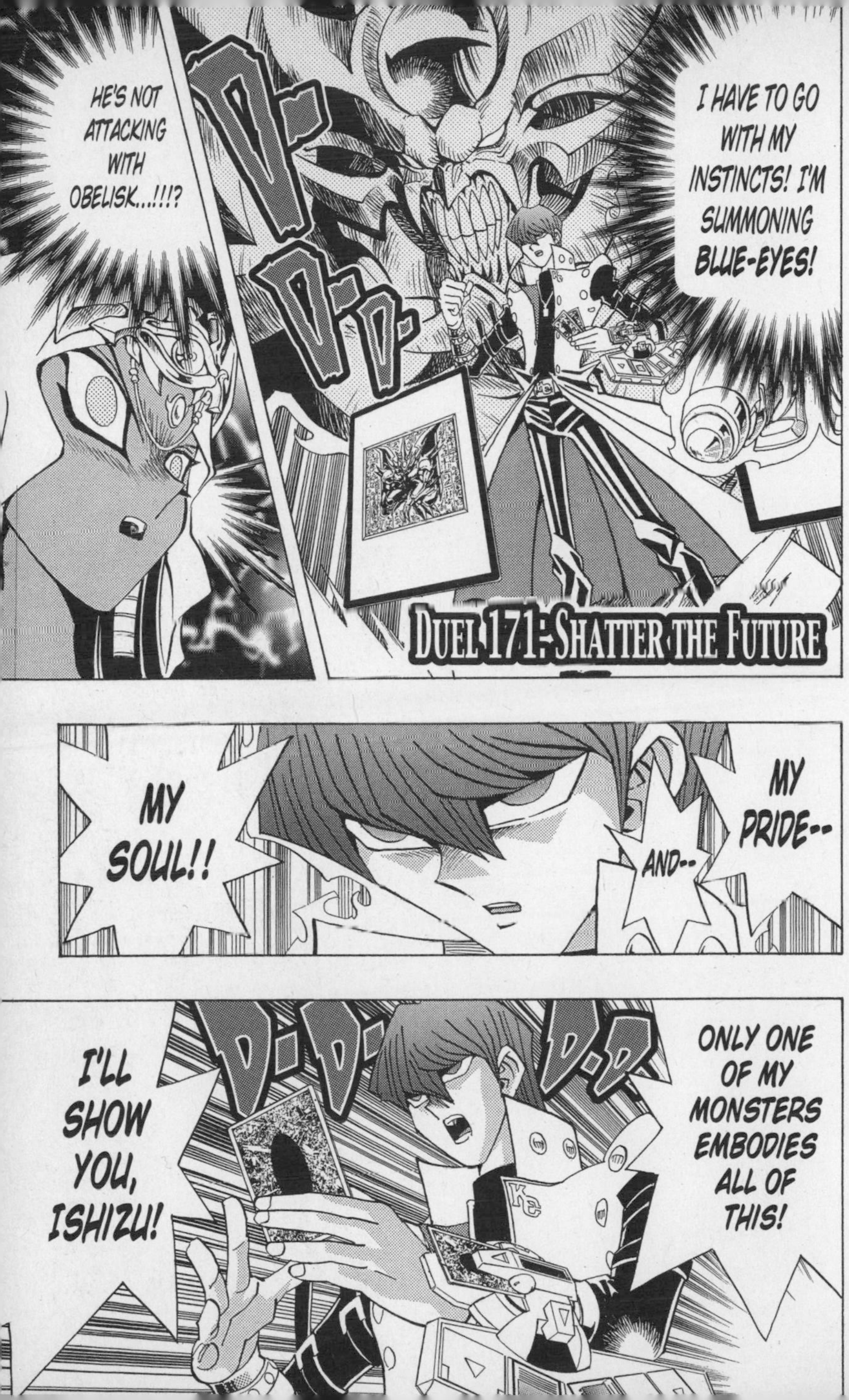
I HAVE TO GO WITH MY INSTINCTS! I'M SUMMONING BLUE-EYES!
HE'S NOT ATTACKING WITH OBELISK...!!!?
DUEL 171: SHATTER THE FUTURE
MY PRIDE--
AND--
MY SOUL!!
ONLY ONE OF MY MONSTERS EMBODIES ALL OF THIS!
I'LL SHOW YOU, ISHIZU!

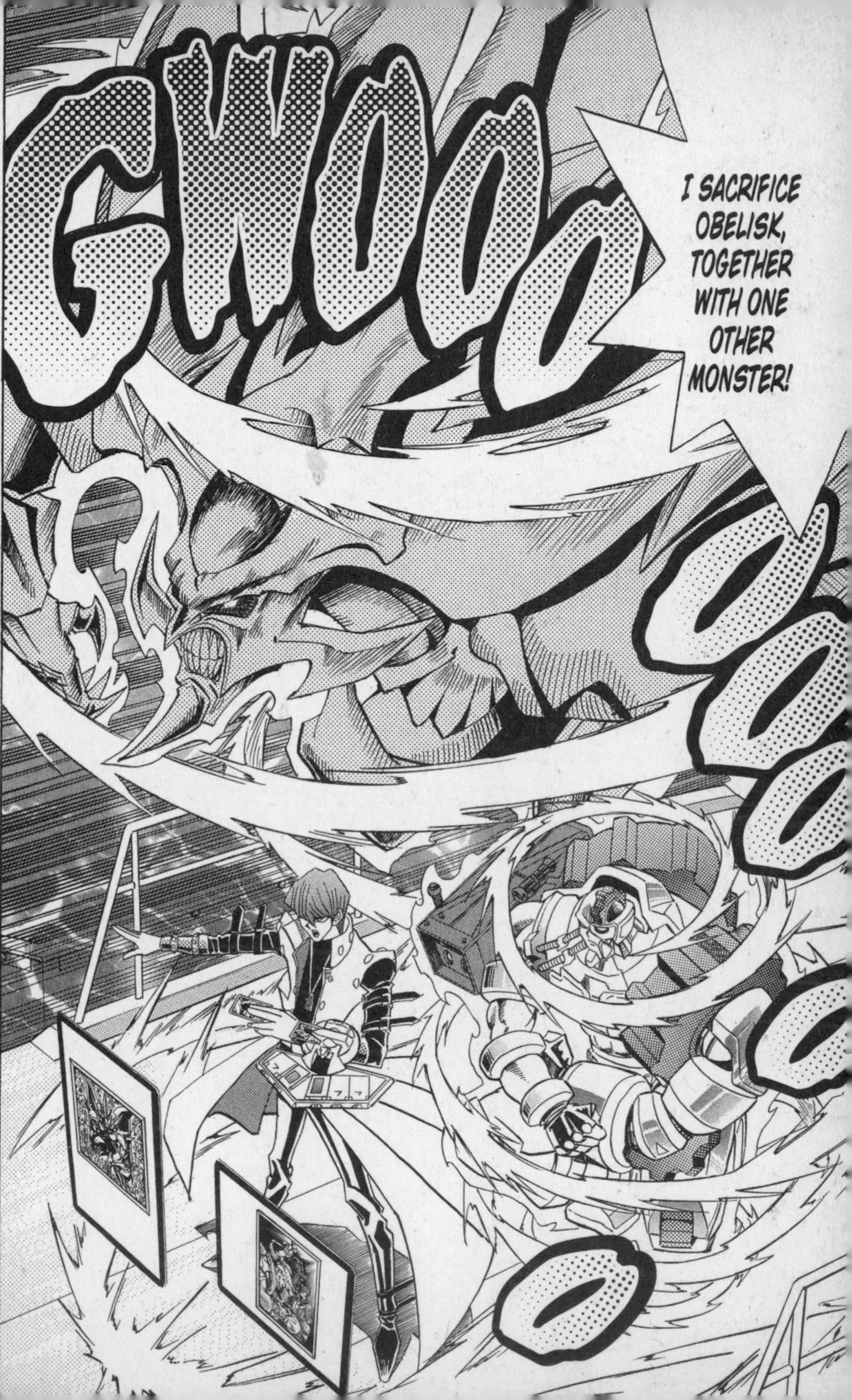
I SACRIFICE OBELISK, TOGETHER WITH ONE OTHER MONSTER!
GWOOOOOOOO

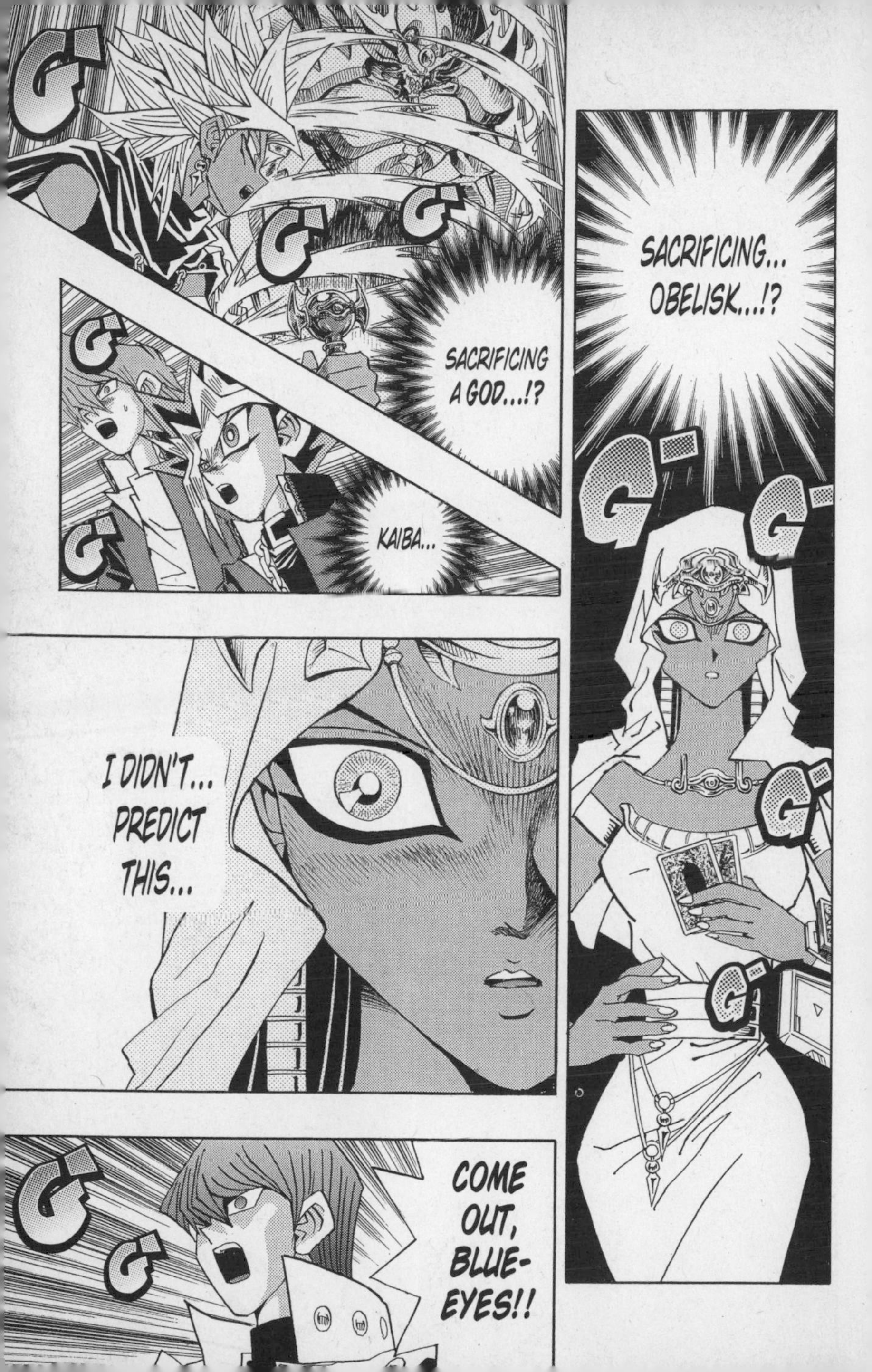
SACRIFICING... OBELISK...!?
G G
G
G
G
G G G
SACRIFICING A GOD...!?
G G
KAIBA...
I DIDN'T... PREDICT THIS...
G G
COME OUT, BLUE-EYES!!

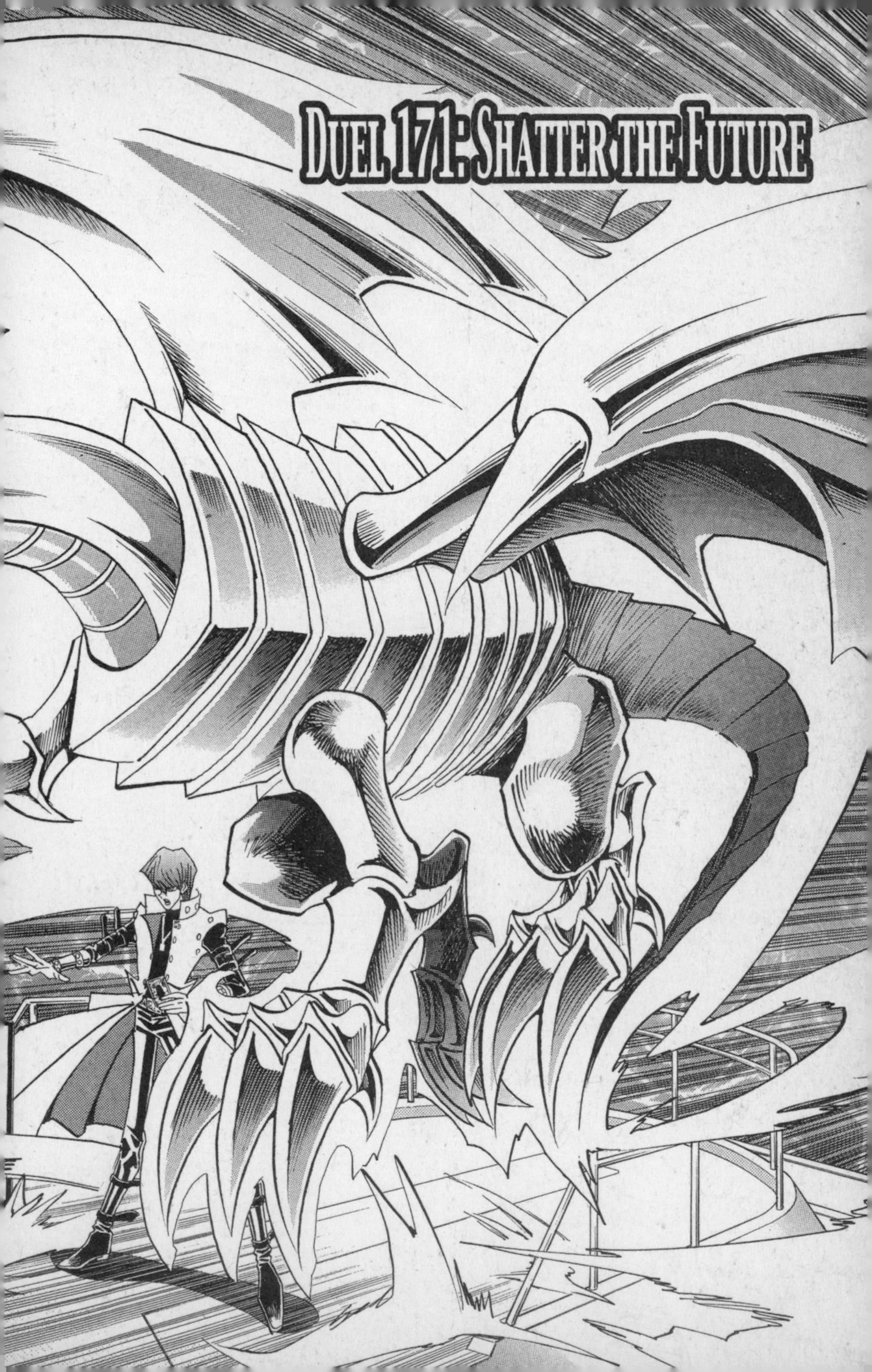
DUEL 171: SHATTER THE FUTURE

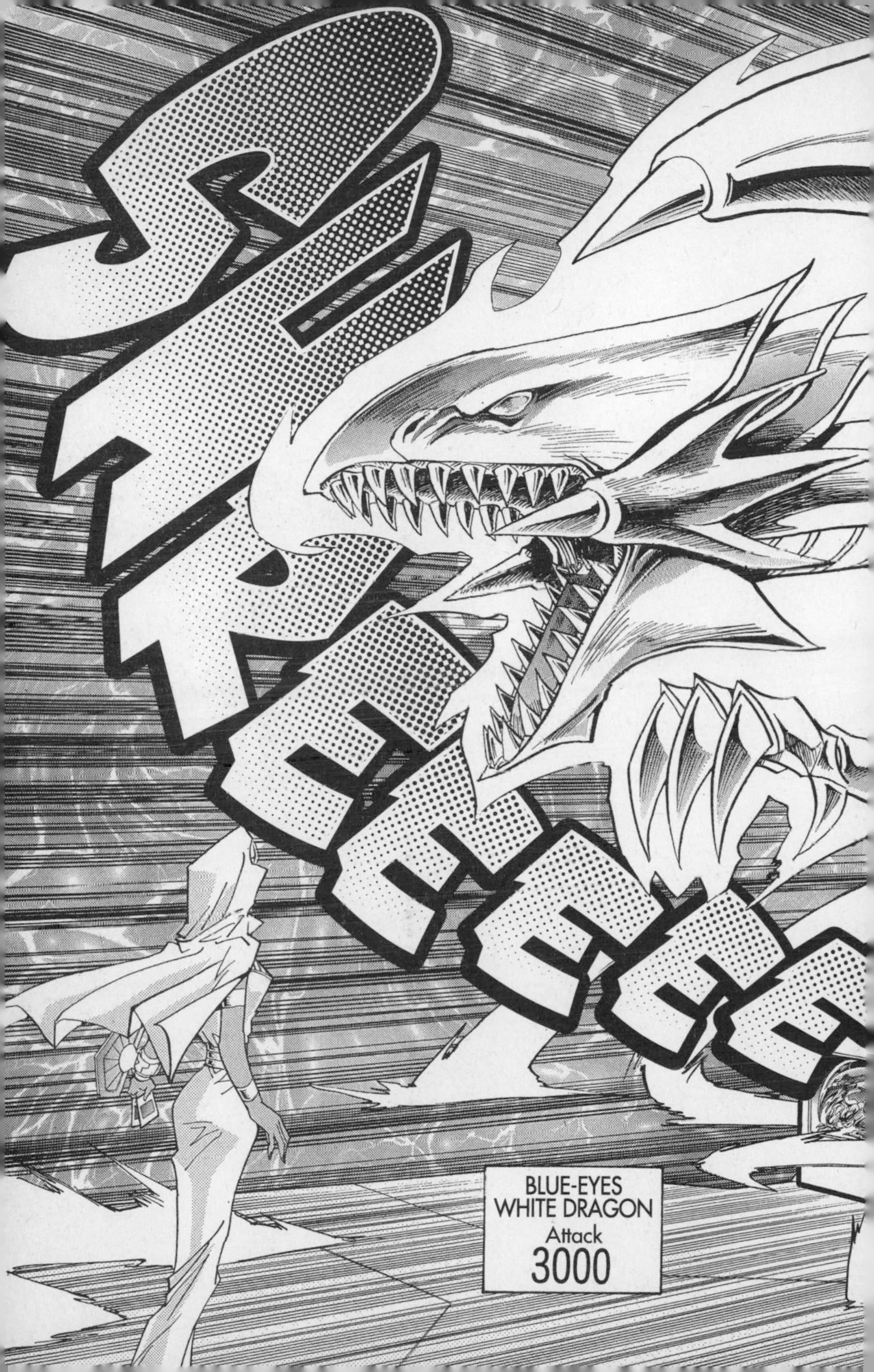
BLUE-EYES WHITE DRAGON Attack 3000

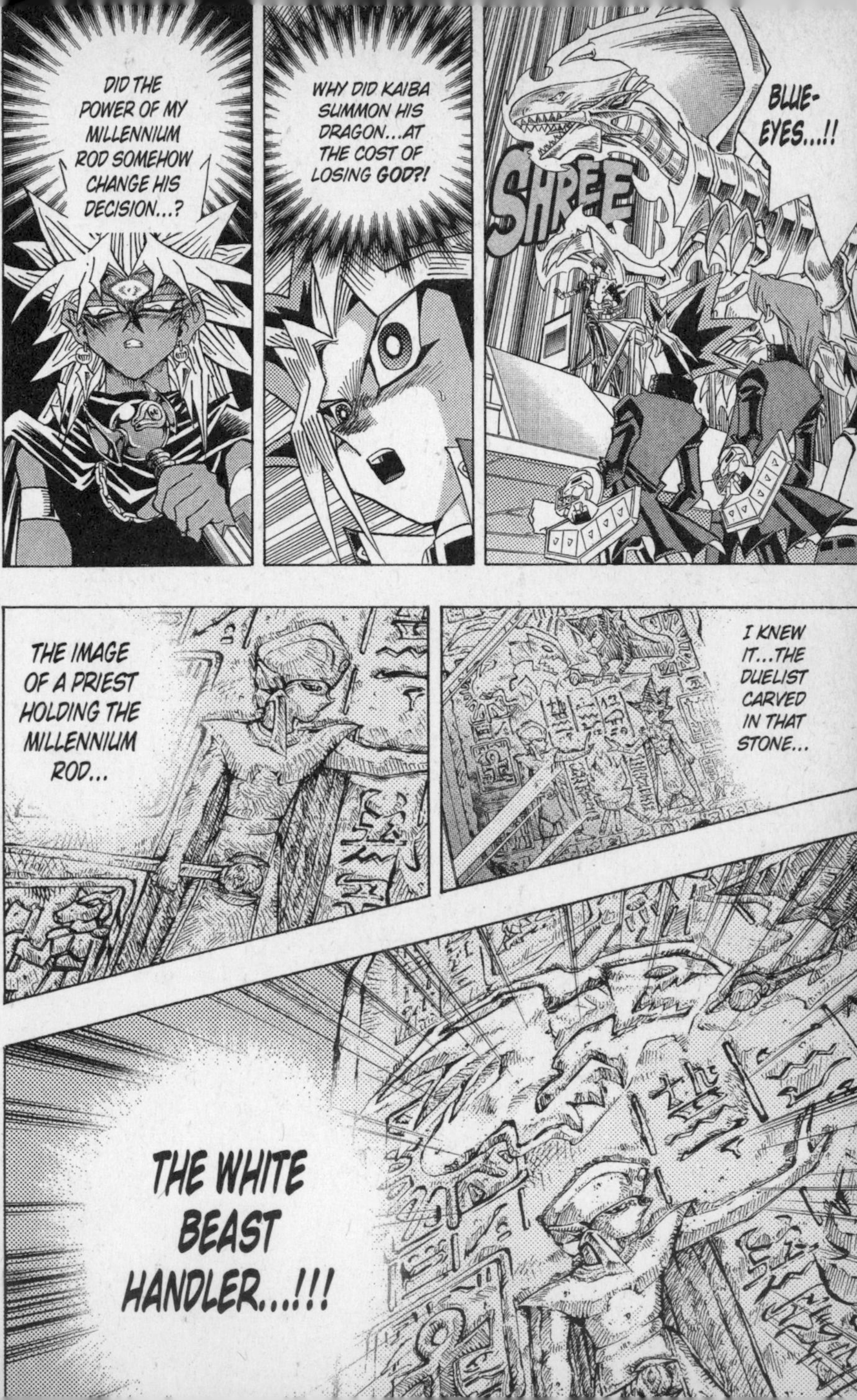
BLUE-EYES...!!
SHREE
WHY DID KAIBA SUMMON HIS DRAGON...AT THE COST OF LOSING GOD?!
DID THE POWER OF MY MILLENNIUM ROD SOMEHOW CHANGE HIS DECISION...?
I KNEW IT...THE DUELIST CARVED IN THAT STONE...
THE IMAGE OF A PRIEST HOLDING THE MILLENNIUM ROD...
THE WHITE BEAST HANDLER...!!!

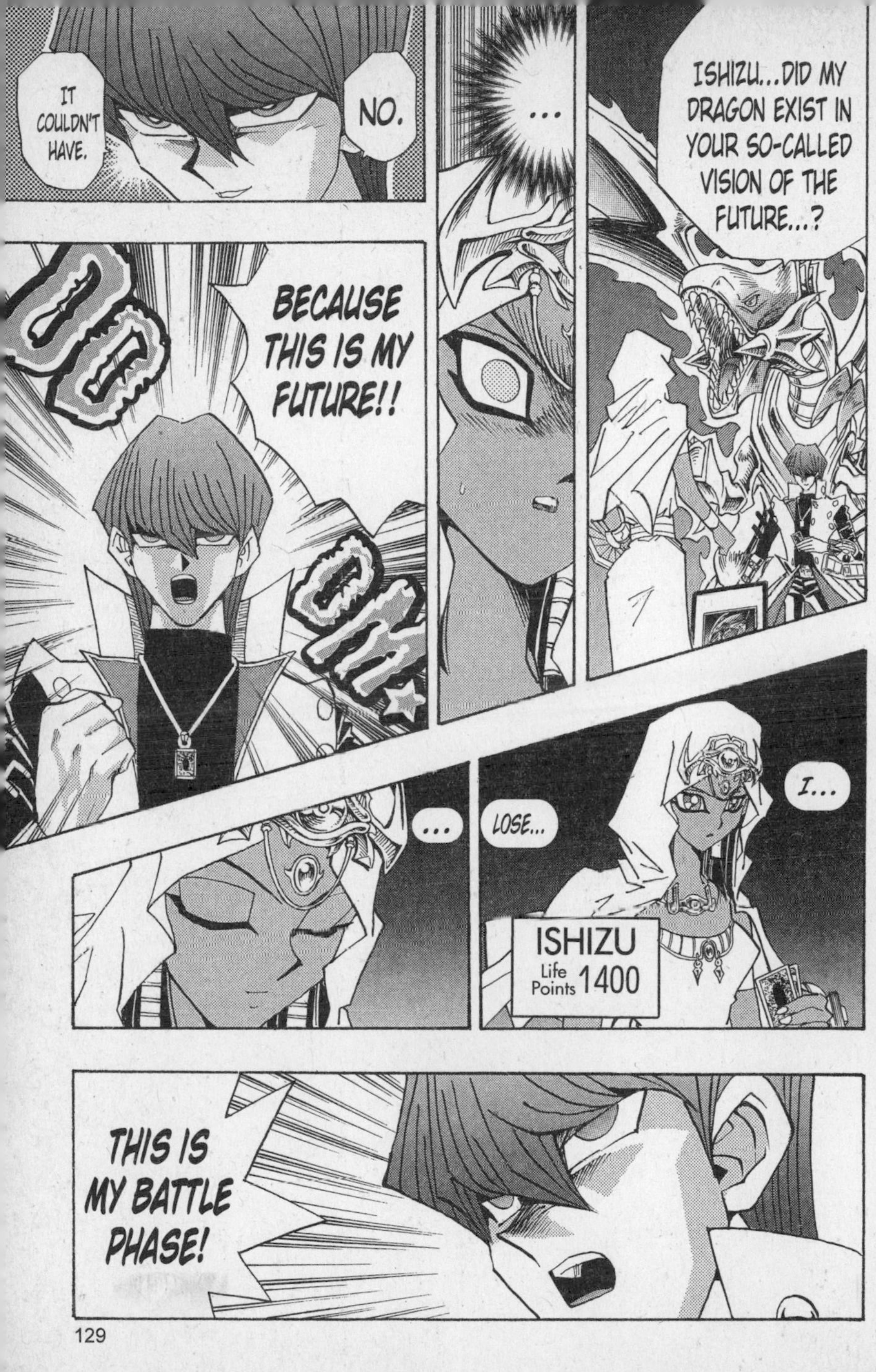
ISHIZU...DID MY DRAGON EXIST IN YOUR SO-CALLED VISION OF THE FUTURE...?
...
NO.
IT COULDN'T HAVE.
BECAUSE THIS IS MY FUTURE!!
I...
LOSE...
ISHIZU
Life Points 1400
...
THIS IS MY BATTLE PHASE!

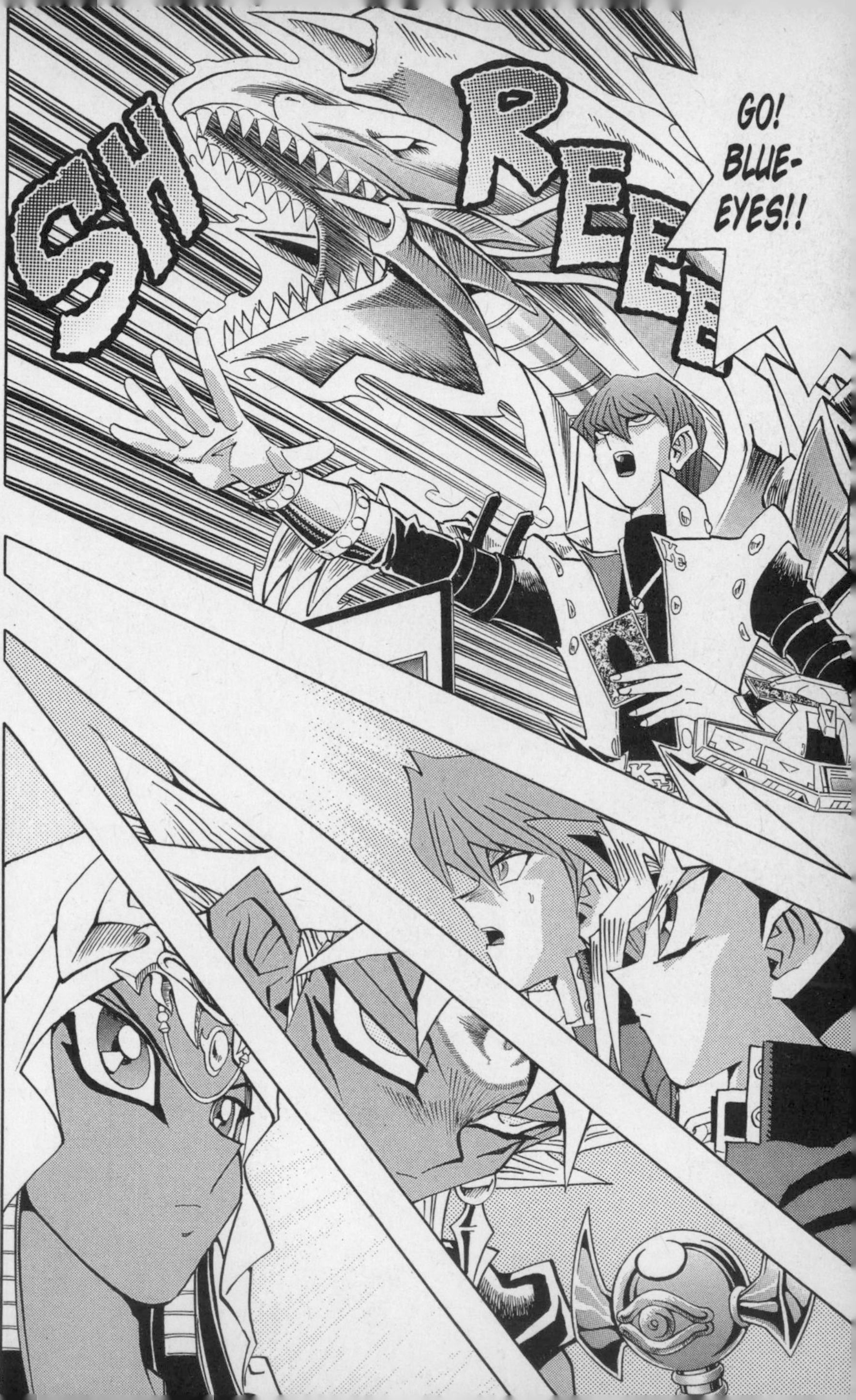
GO! BLUE-EYES!!
SHREEEE

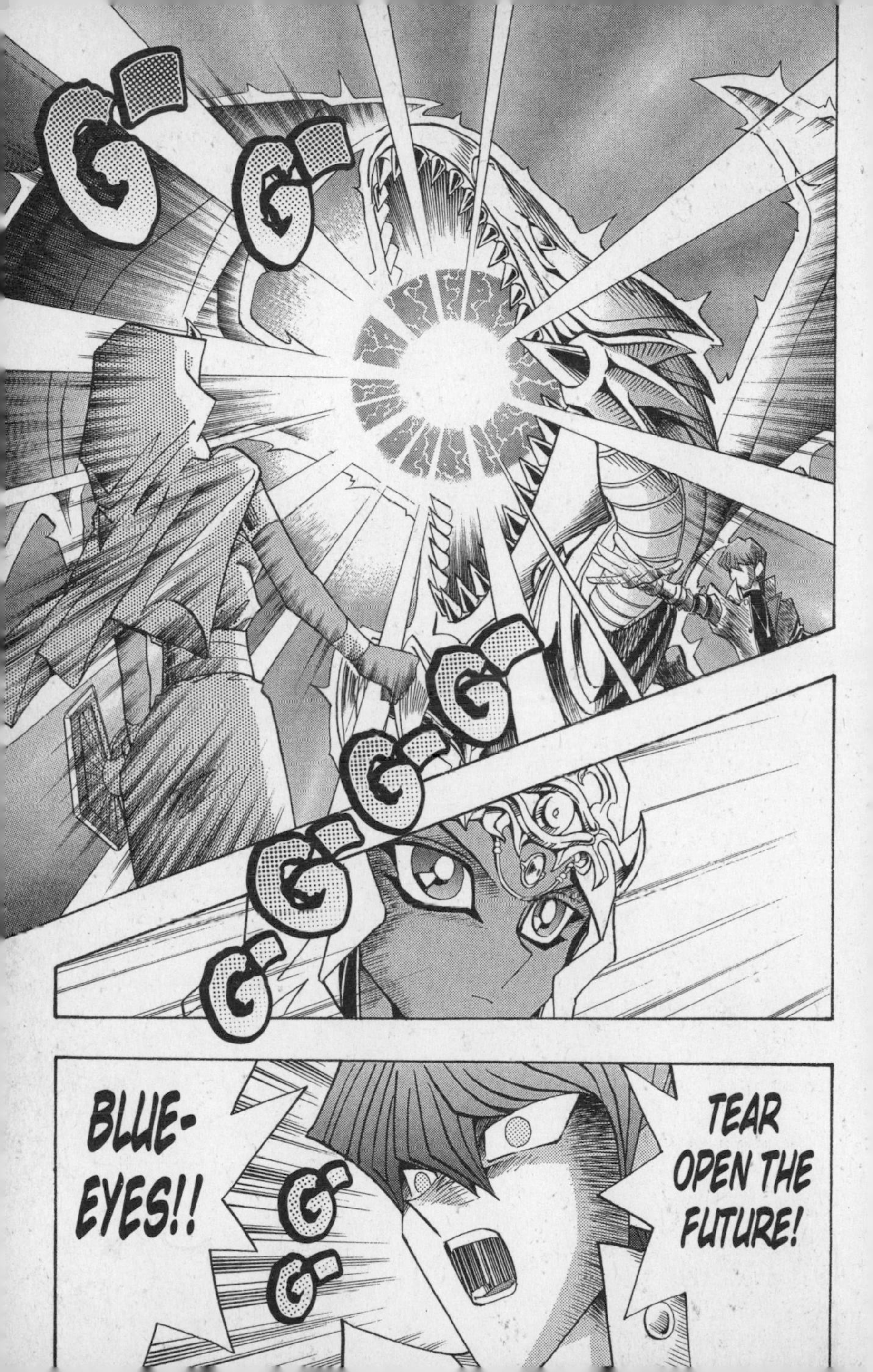
GG
GGGGGGG
TEAR OPEN THE FUTURE!
BLUE-EYES!!
GG

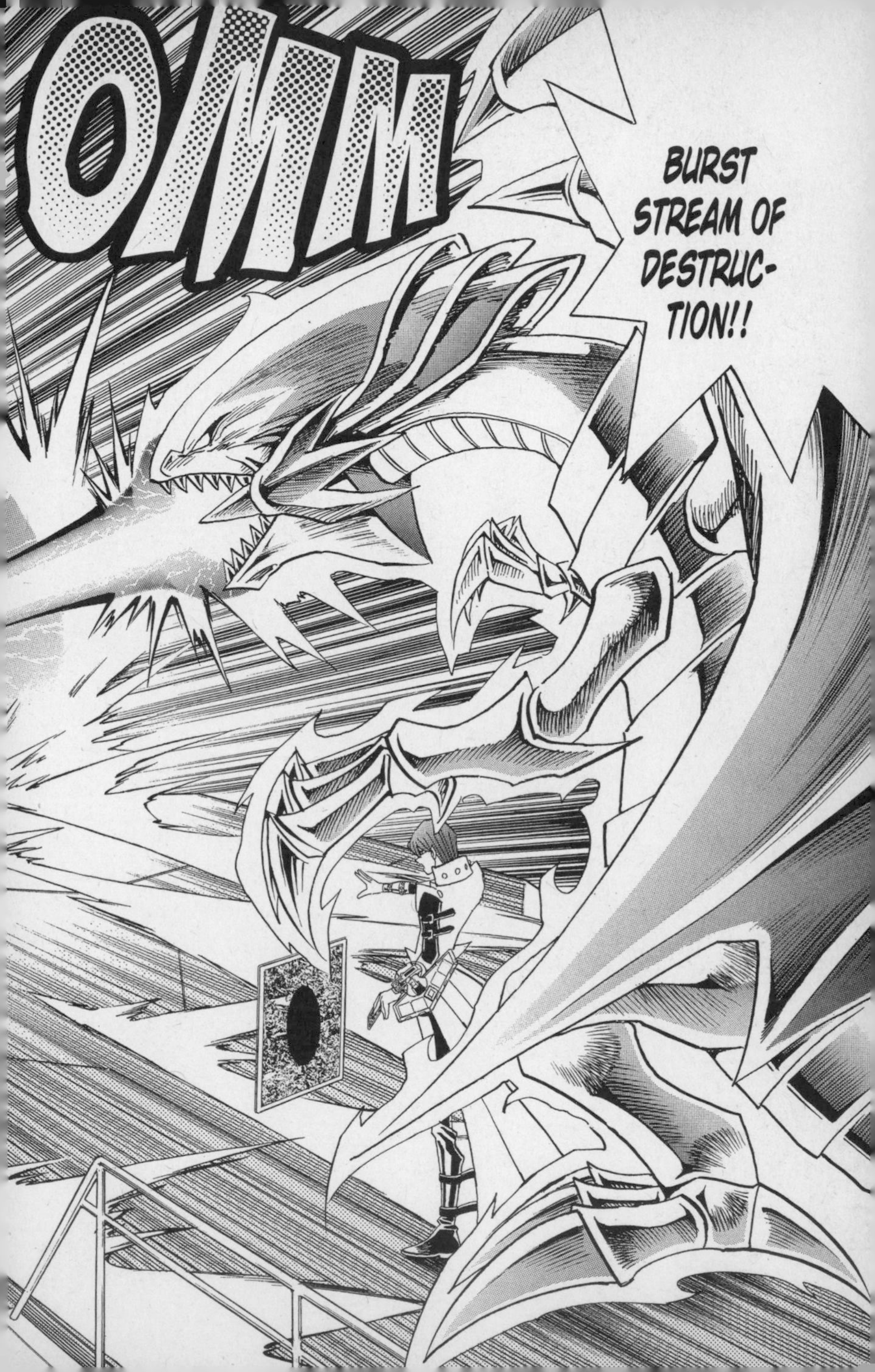
BURST STREAM OF DESTRUCTION!!
OMM

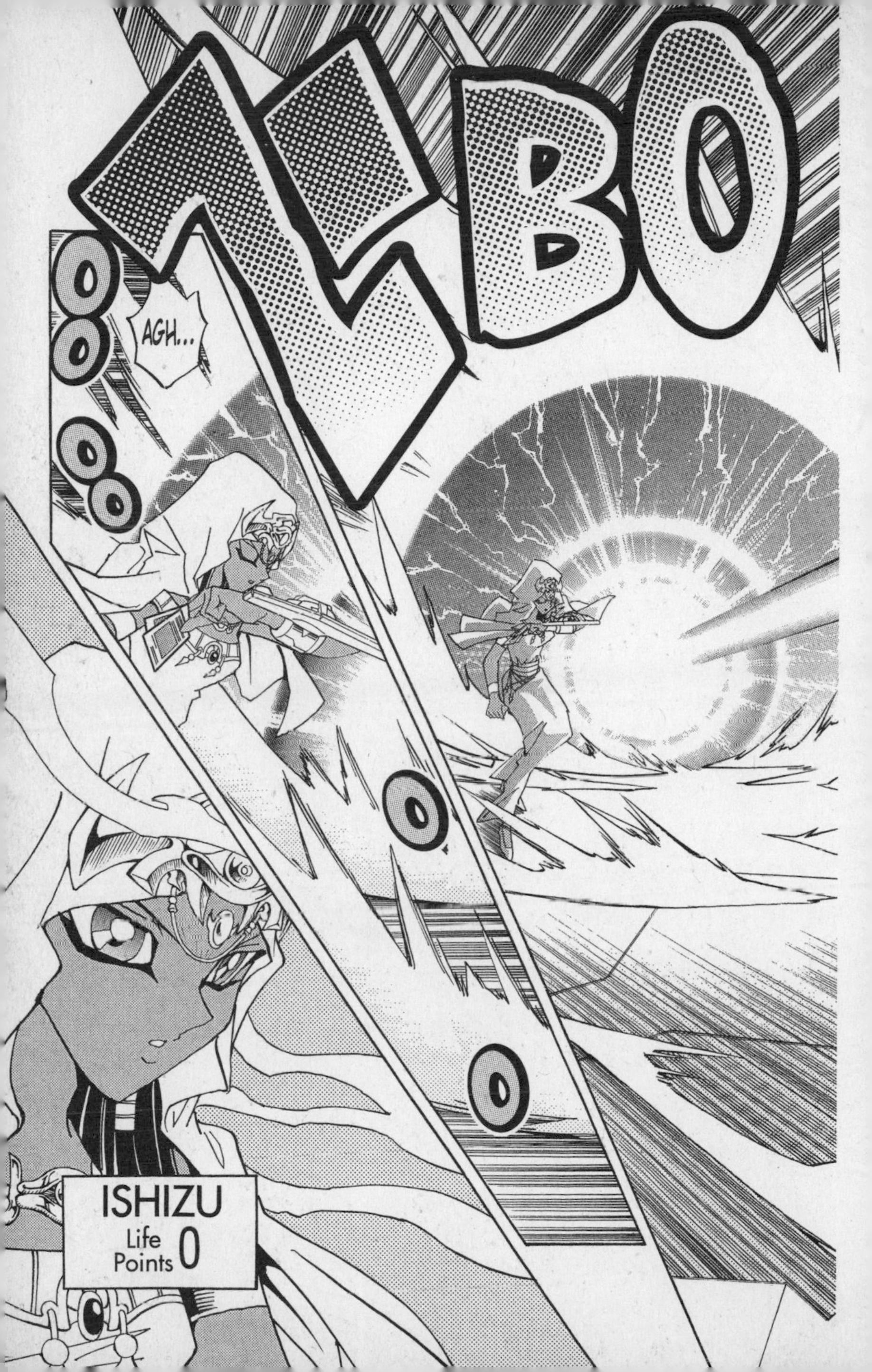
AGH...
ISHIZU
Life Points 0

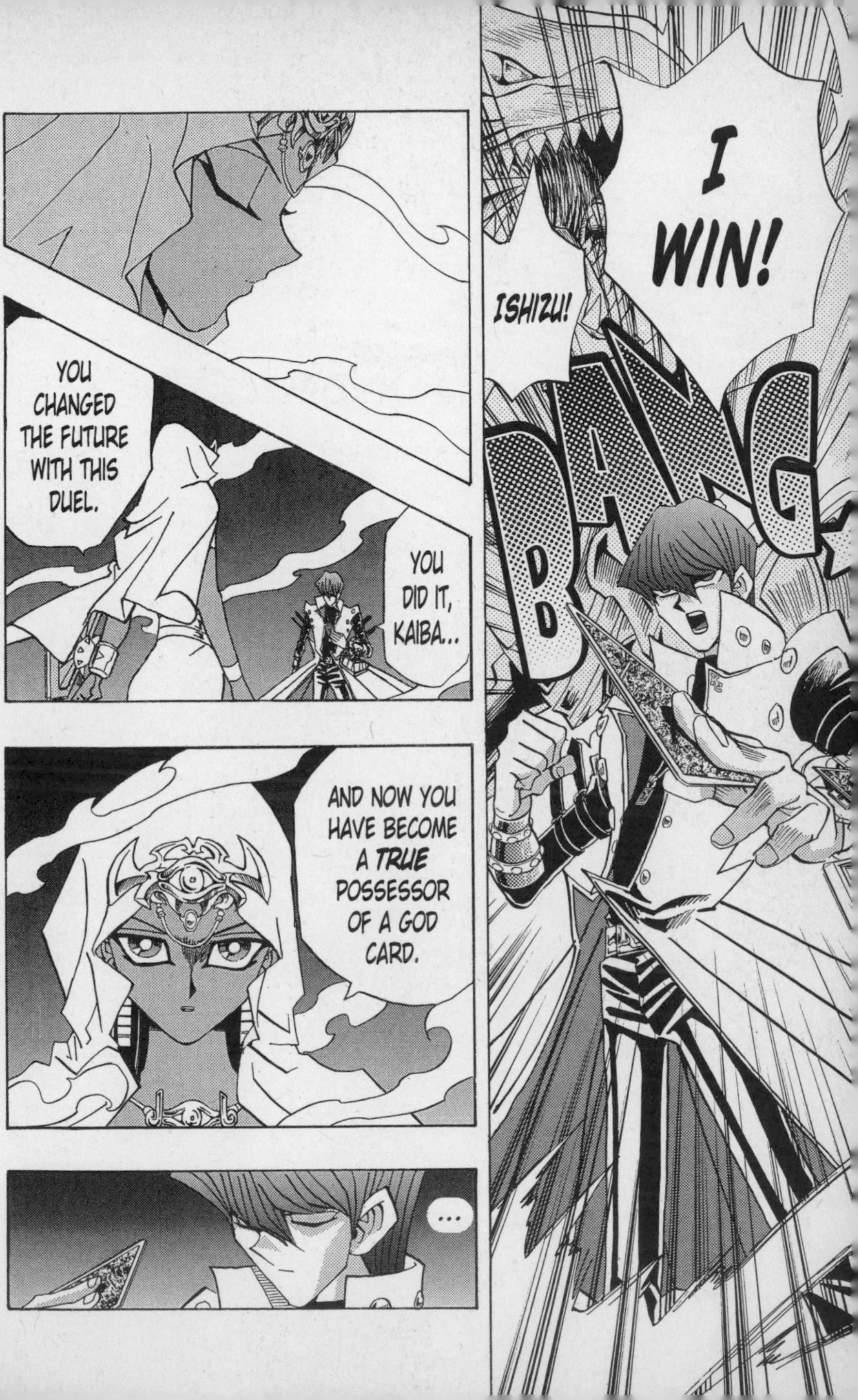
I WIN!
ISHIZU!
BANG
YOU CHANGED THE FUTURE WITH THIS DUEL.
YOU DID IT, KAIBA...
AND NOW YOU HAVE BECOME A *TRUE* POSSESSOR OF A GOD CARD.
...

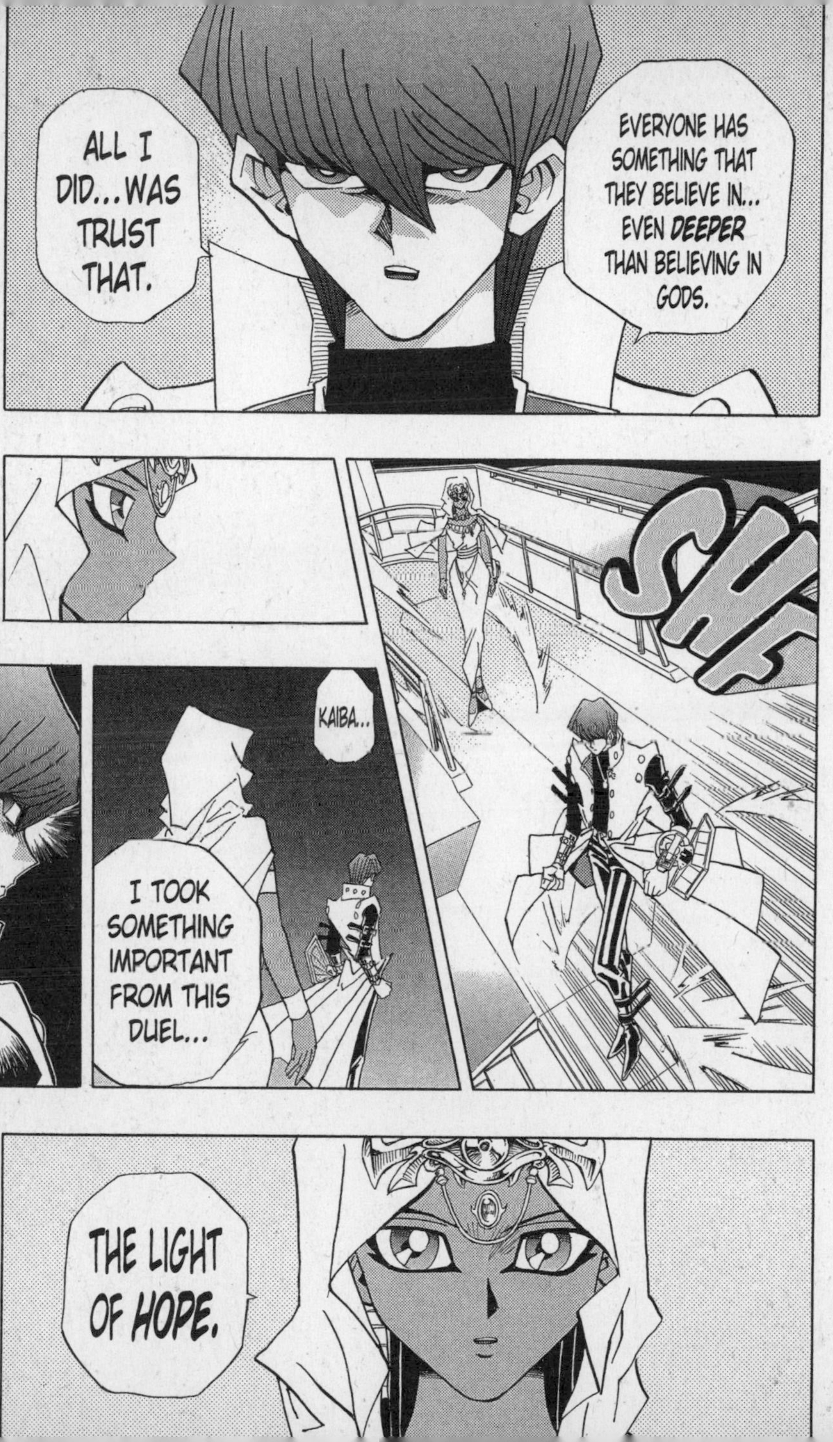
EVERYONE HAS SOMETHING THAT THEY BELIEVE IN... EVEN DEEPER THAN BELIEVING IN GODS.
ALL I DID...WAS TRUST THAT.
SHF
KAIBA...
I TOOK SOMETHING IMPORTANT FROM THIS DUEL...
THE LIGHT OF HOPE.

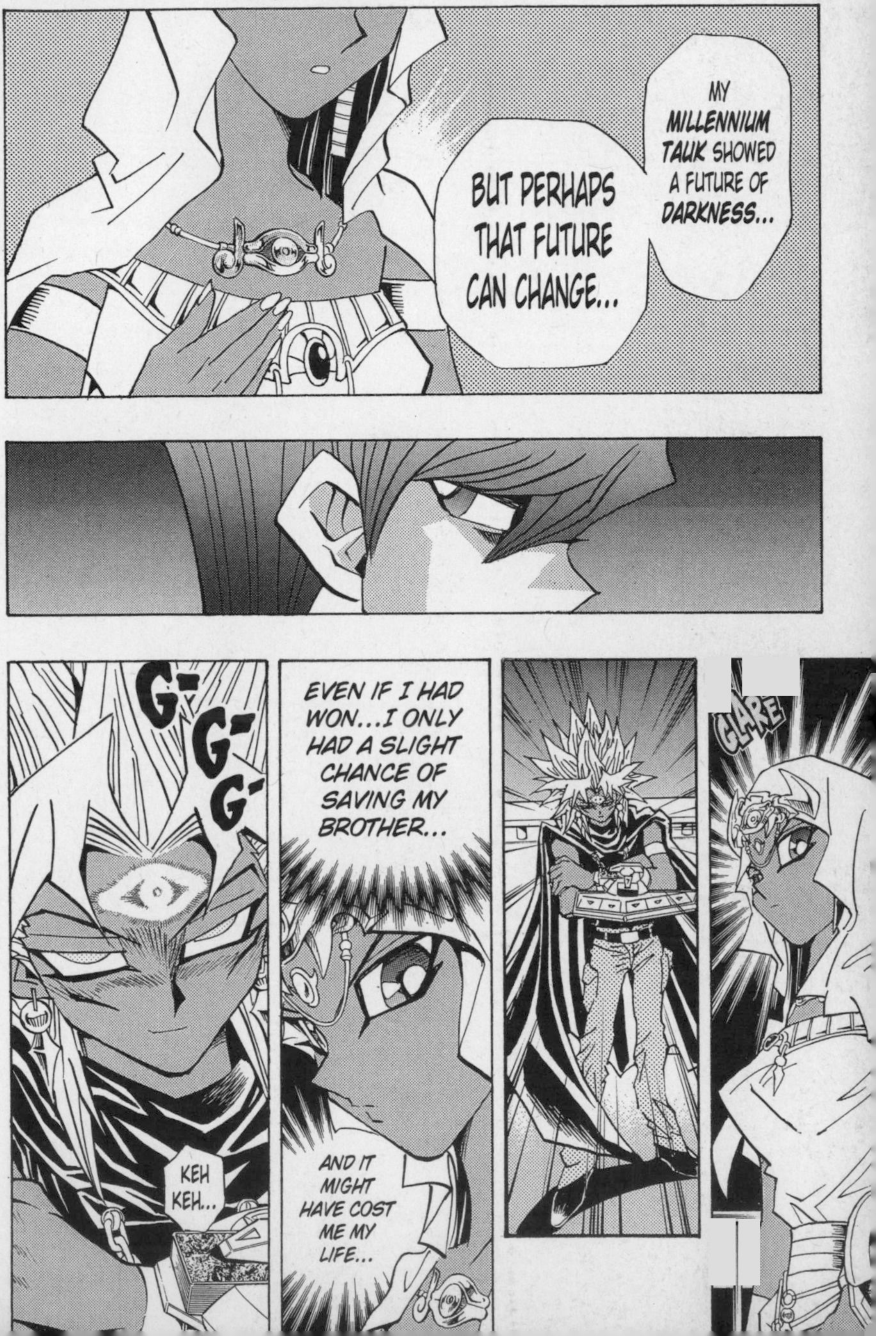
MY MILLENNIUM TAUK SHOWED A FUTURE OF DARKNESS...
BUT PERHAPS THAT FUTURE CAN CHANGE...
GLARE
EVEN IF I HAD WON...I ONLY HAD A SLIGHT CHANCE OF SAVING MY BROTHER...
AND IT MIGHT HAVE COST ME MY LIFE...
G- G- G-
KEH KEH...

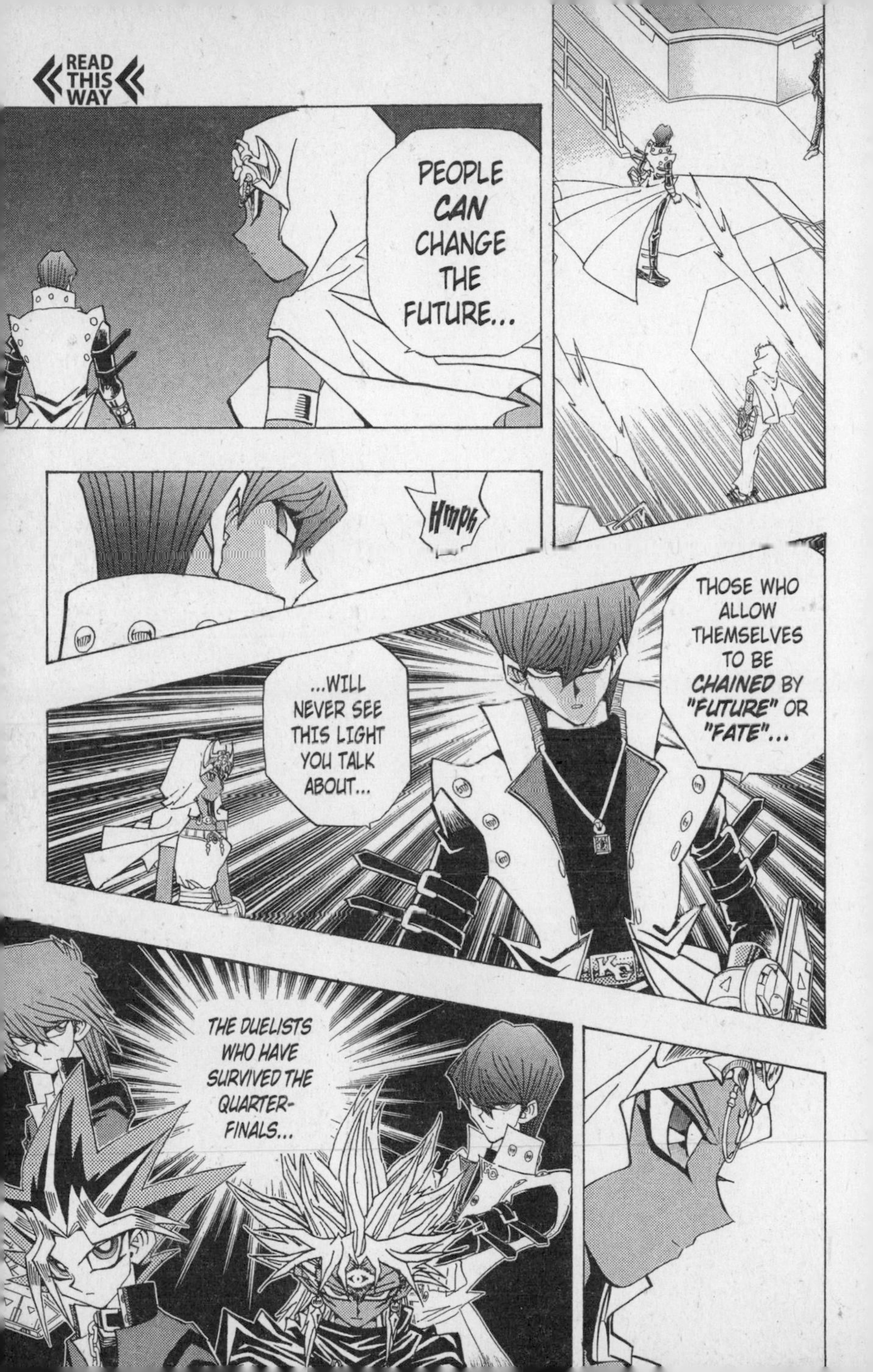
READ THIS WAY
PEOPLE CAN CHANGE THE FUTURE...
Hmph
THOSE WHO ALLOW THEMSELVES TO BE CHAINED BY "FUTURE" OR "FATE"...
...WILL NEVER SEE THIS LIGHT YOU TALK ABOUT...
THE DUELISTS WHO HAVE SURVIVED THE QUARTER-FINALS...

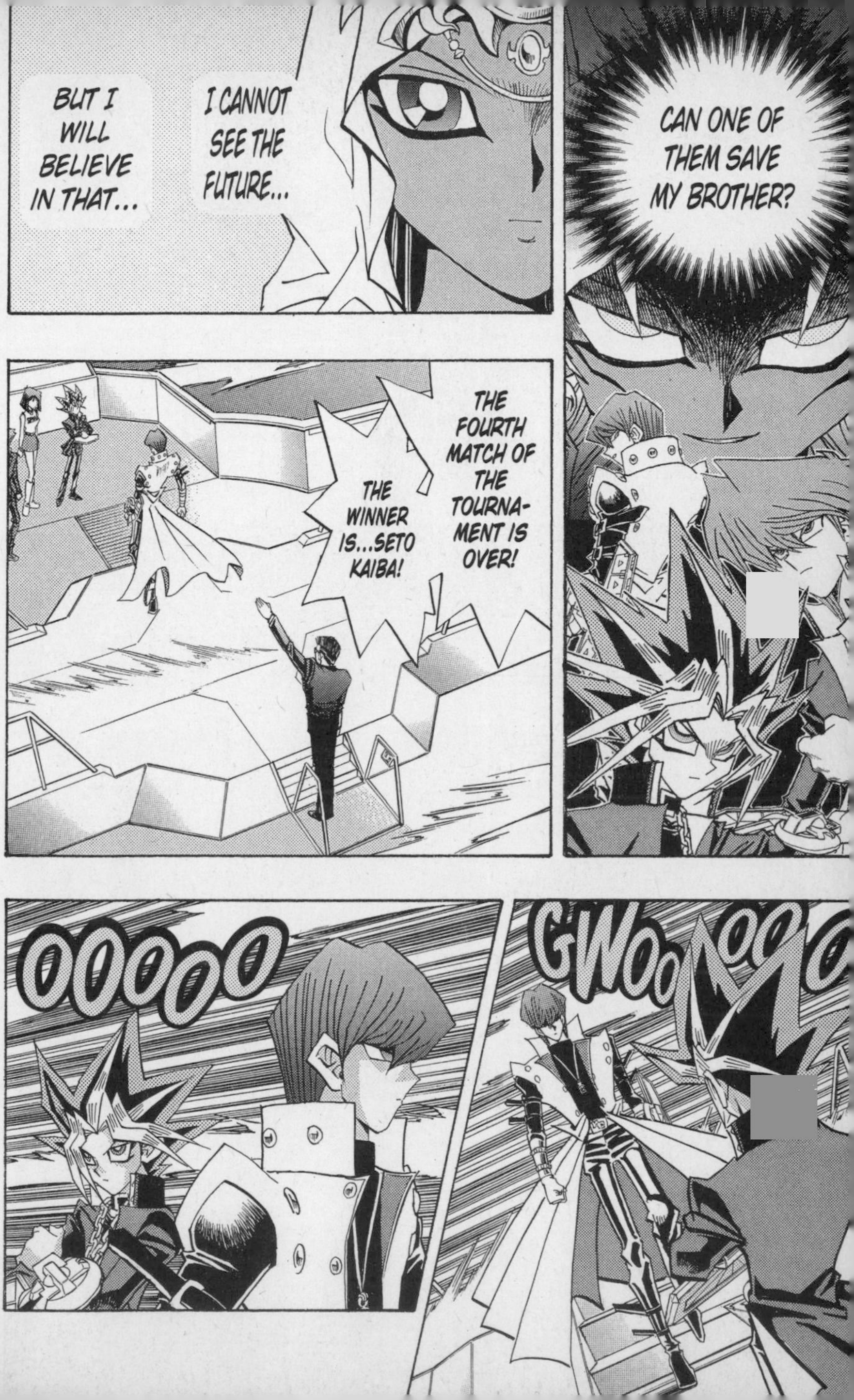
CAN ONE OF THEM SAVE MY BROTHER?
I CANNOT SEE THE FUTURE...
BUT I WILL BELIEVE IN THAT...
THE FOURTH MATCH OF THE TOURNAMENT IS OVER!
THE WINNER IS...SETO KAIBA!
GWOOOOO
OOOOO

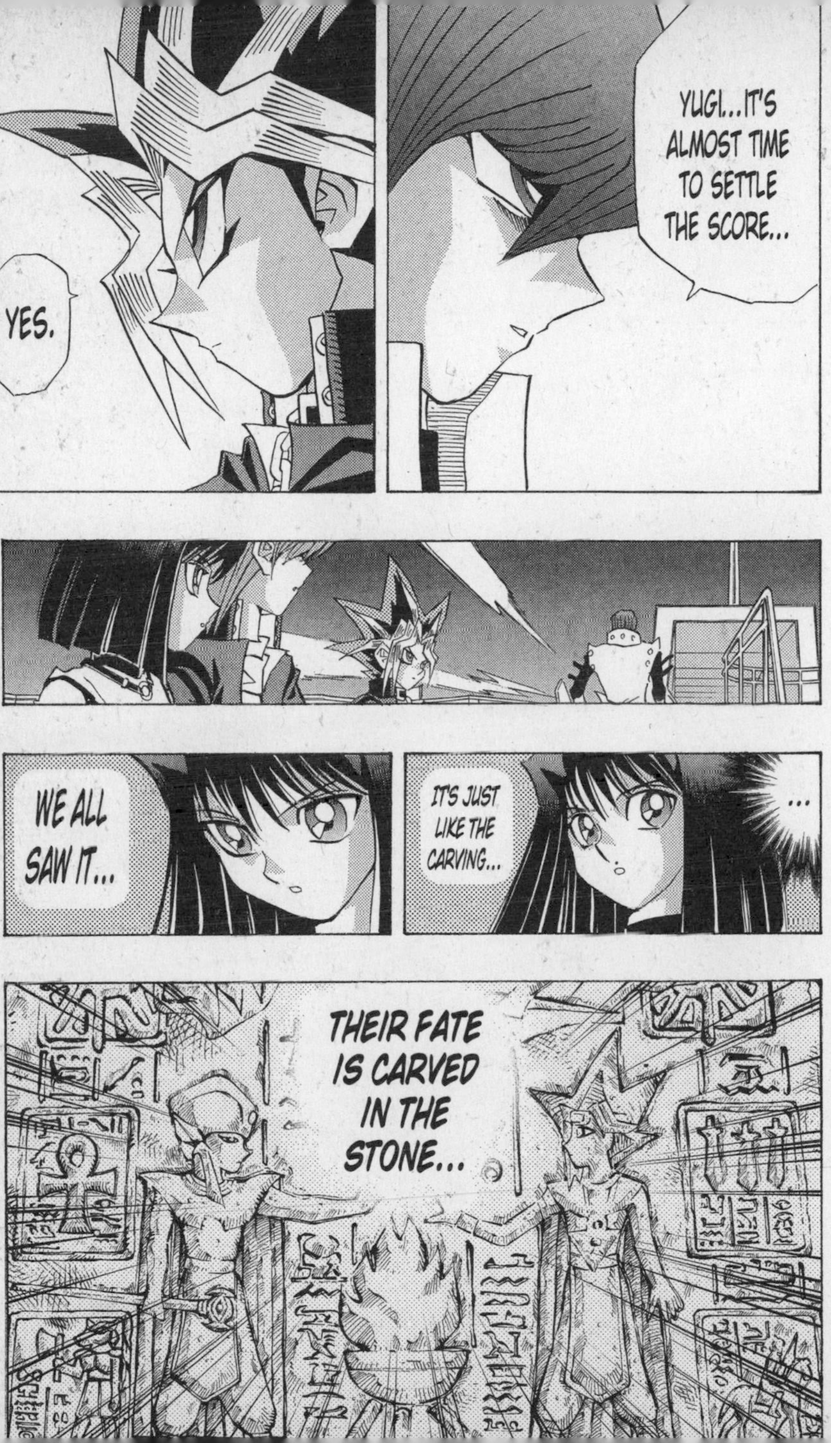
YUGI...IT'S ALMOST TIME TO SETTLE THE SCORE...
YES.
...
IT'S JUST LIKE THE CARVING...
WE ALL SAW IT...
THEIR FATE IS CARVED IN THE STONE...

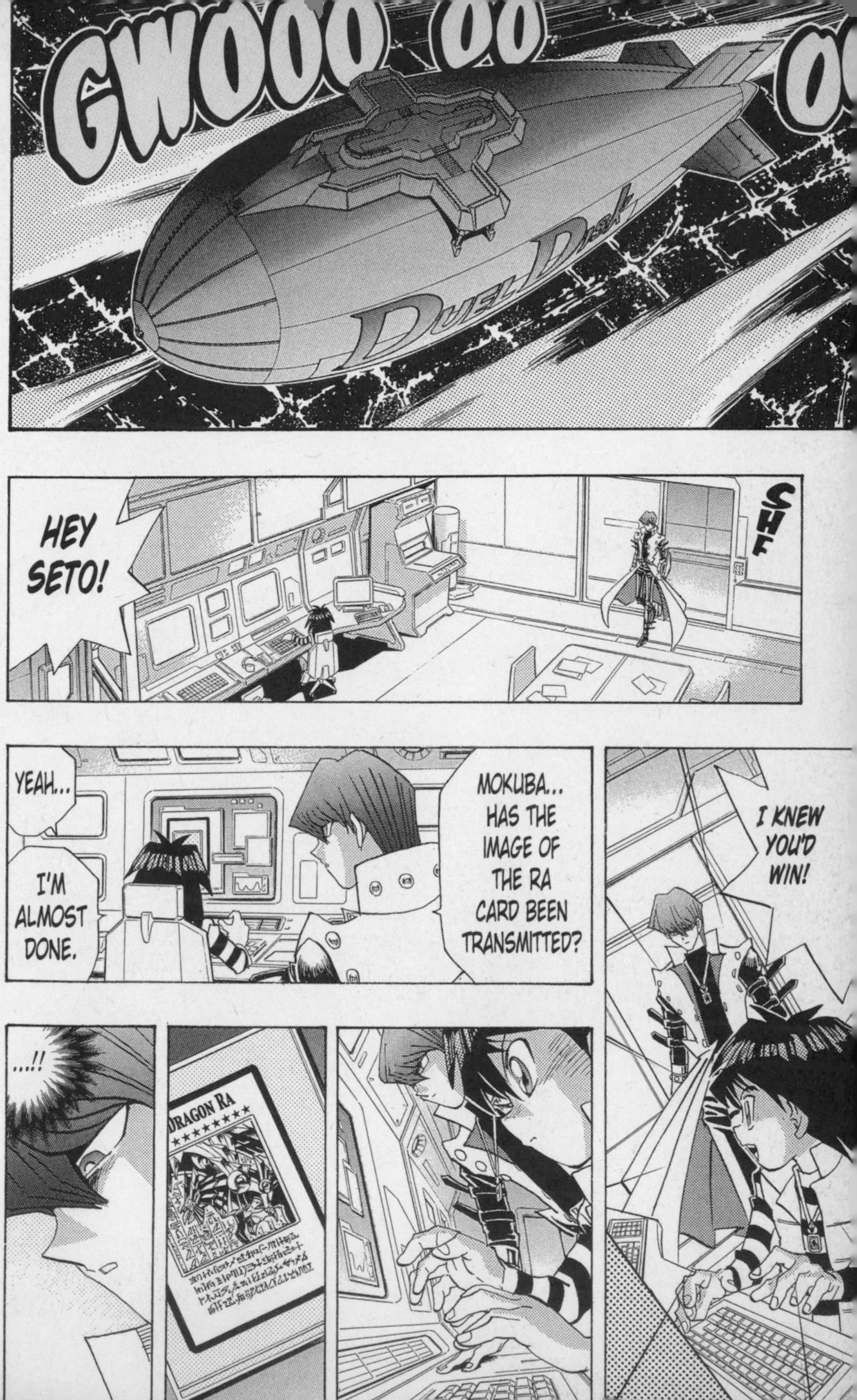
GWOOO OO OO
DUEL DISK
SHF
HEY SETO!
I KNEW YOU'D WIN!
MOKUBA... HAS THE IMAGE OF THE RA CARD BEEN TRANSMITTED?
YEAH...
I'M ALMOST DONE.
DRAGON RA
...!!

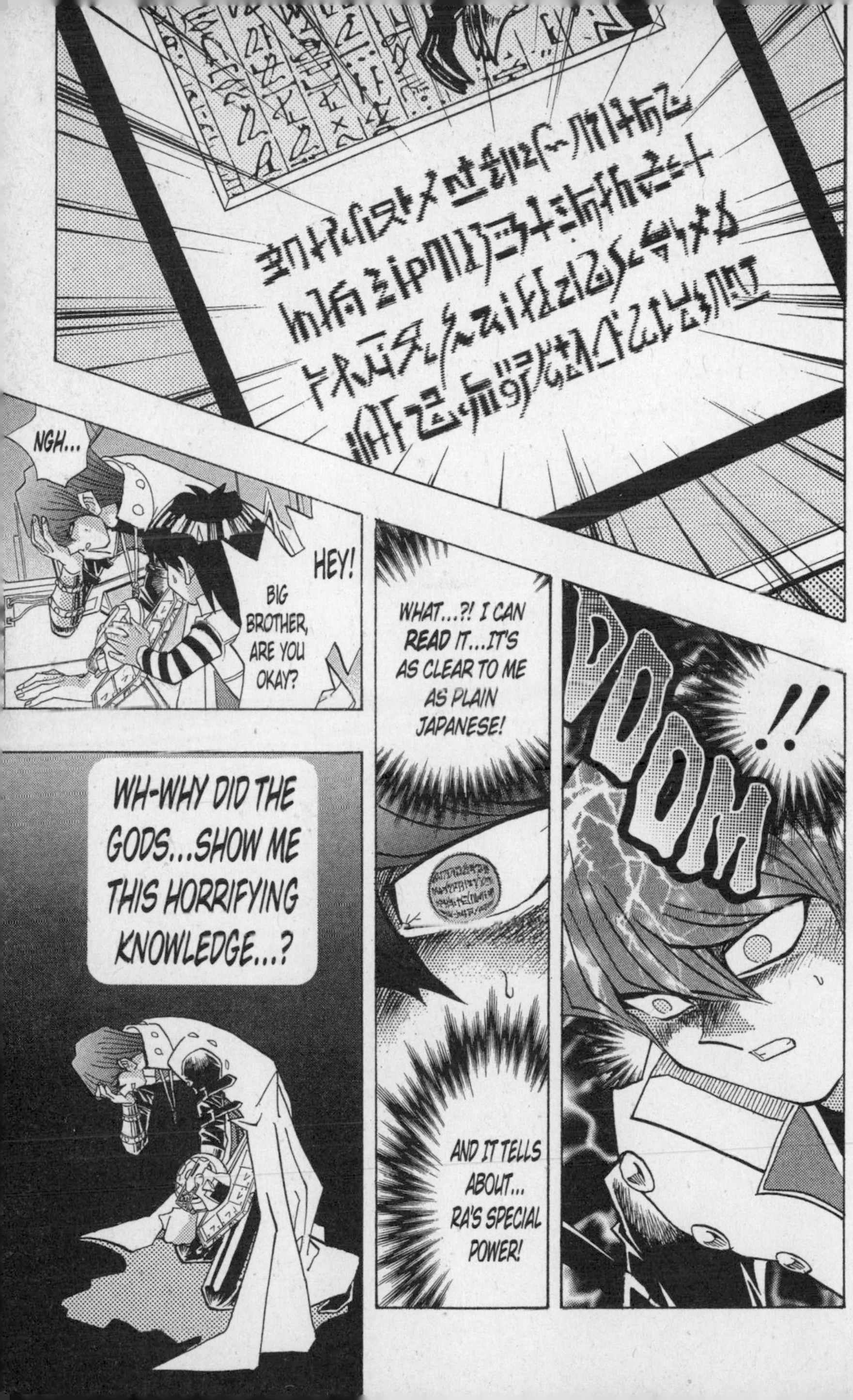
DOOM!!
WHAT...?! I CAN READ IT...IT'S AS CLEAR TO ME AS PLAIN JAPANESE!
AND IT TELLS ABOUT... RA'S SPECIAL POWER!
NGH...
HEY!
BIG BROTHER, ARE YOU OKAY?
WH-WHY DID THE GODS...SHOW ME THIS HORRIFYING KNOWLEDGE...?

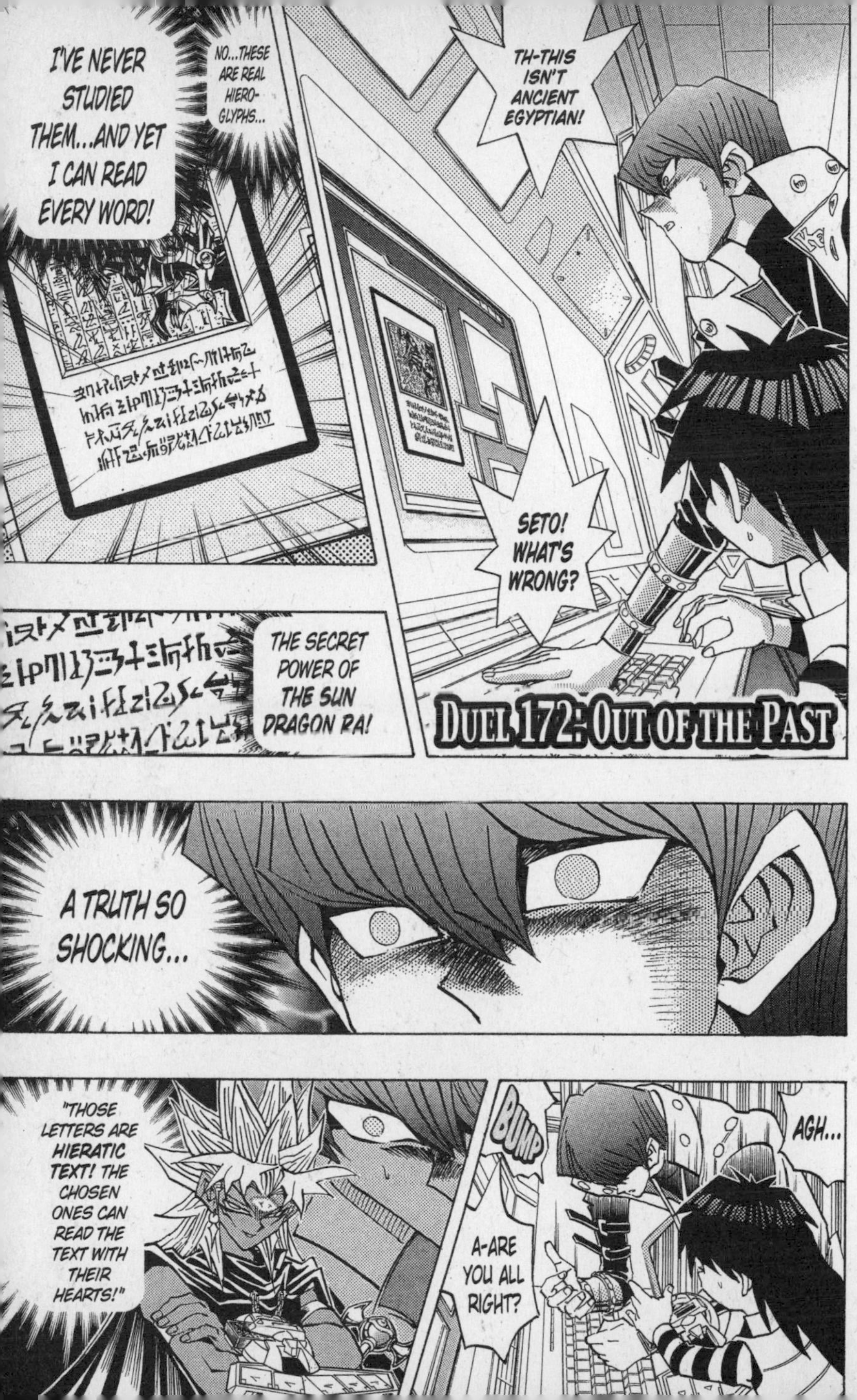
TH-THIS ISN'T ANCIENT EGYPTIAN!
SETO! WHAT'S WRONG?
DUEL 172: OUT OF THE PAST
I'VE NEVER STUDIED THEM...AND YET I CAN READ EVERY WORD!
NO...THESE ARE REAL HIERO-GLYPHS...
THE SECRET POWER OF THE SUN DRAGON RA!
A TRUTH SO SHOCKING...
AGH...
BUMP
A-ARE YOU ALL RIGHT?
"THOSE LETTERS ARE HIERATIC TEXT! THE CHOSEN ONES CAN READ THE TEXT WITH THEIR HEARTS!"

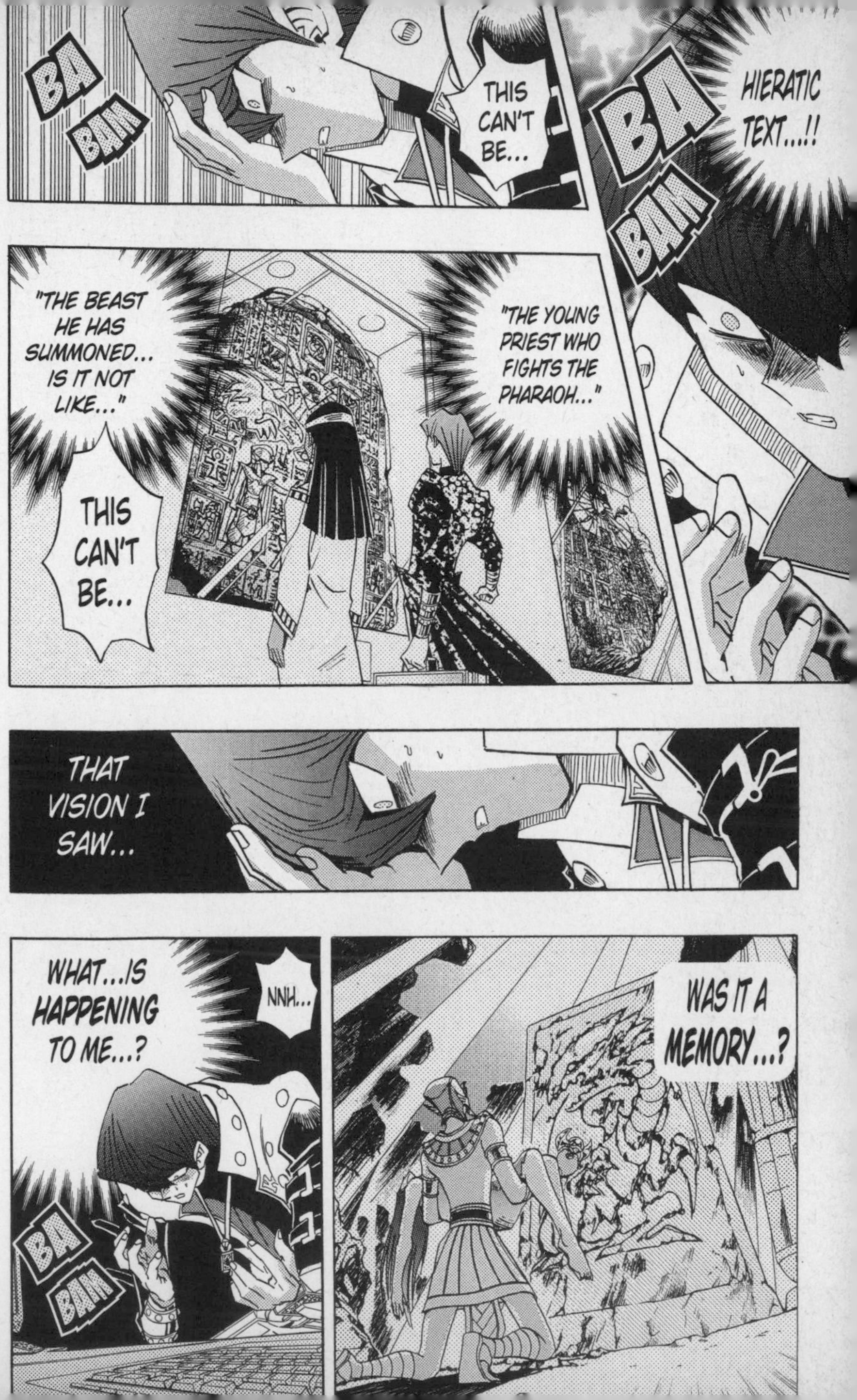
HIERATIC TEXT...!!
BA BAM
BA BAM
THIS CAN'T BE...
"THE YOUNG PRIEST WHO FIGHTS THE PHARAOH..."
"THE BEAST HE HAS SUMMONED... IS IT NOT LIKE..."
THIS CAN'T BE...
THAT VISION I SAW...
WAS IT A MEMORY...?
NNH...
WHAT...IS HAPPENING TO ME...?
BA BAM

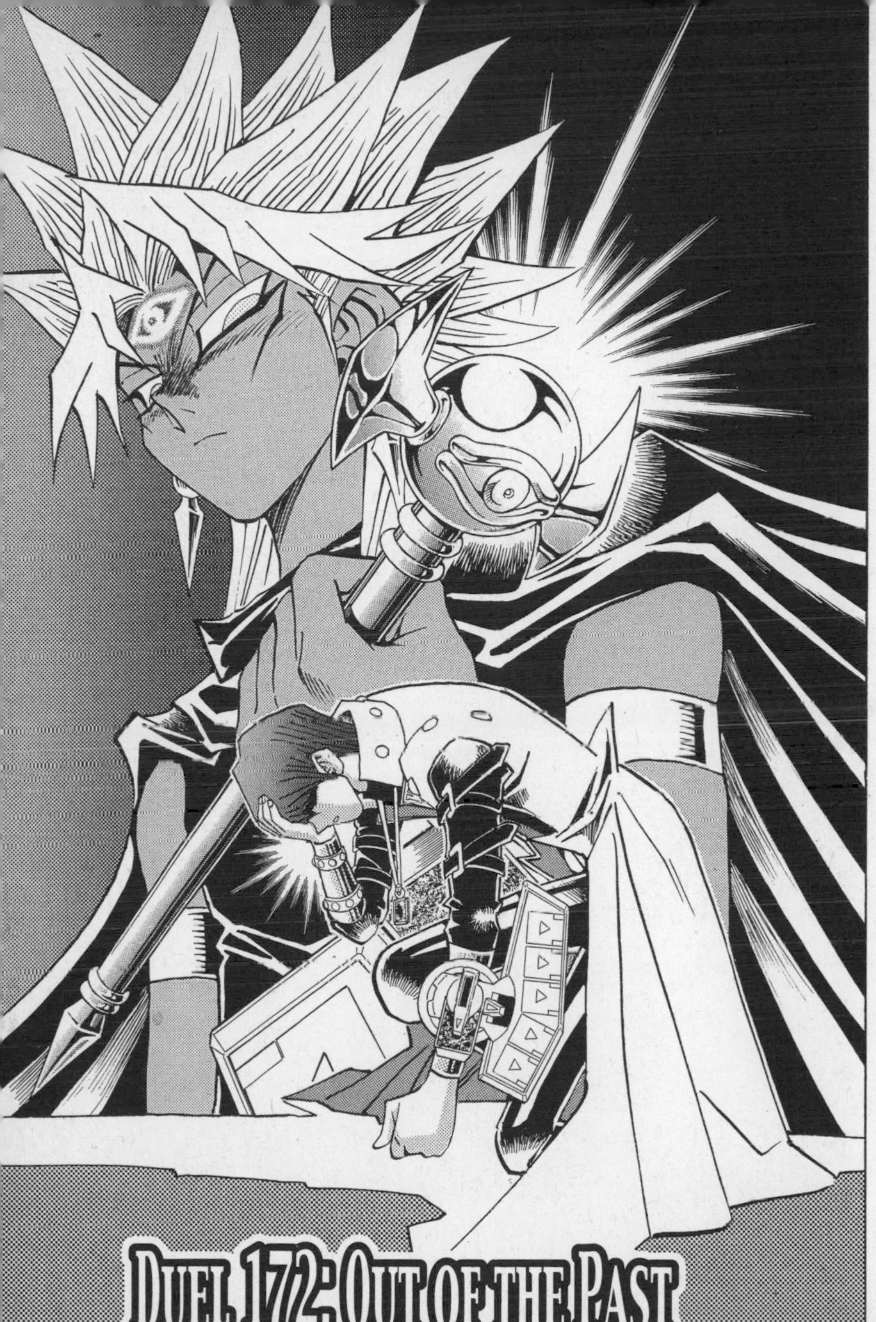

Duel 172: Out of the Past

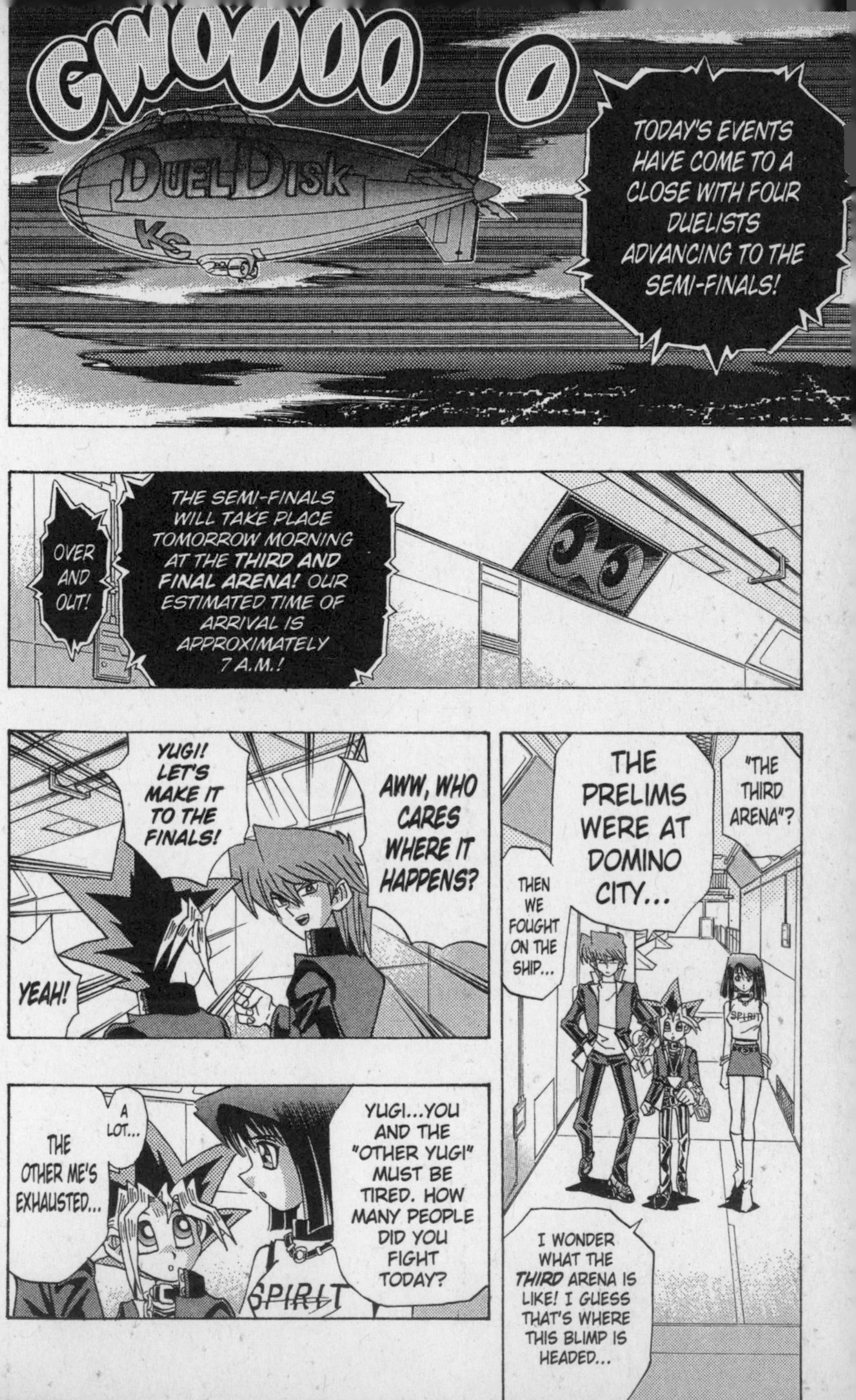
GWOOOO O
TODAY'S EVENTS HAVE COME TO A CLOSE WITH FOUR DUELISTS ADVANCING TO THE SEMI-FINALS!
THE SEMI-FINALS WILL TAKE PLACE TOMORROW MORNING AT THE THIRD AND FINAL ARENA! OUR ESTIMATED TIME OF ARRIVAL IS APPROXIMATELY 7 A.M.!
OVER AND OUT!
"THE THIRD ARENA"?
THE PRELIMS WERE AT DOMINO CITY...
THEN WE FOUGHT ON THE SHIP...
SPIRIT
I WONDER WHAT THE THIRD ARENA IS LIKE! I GUESS THAT'S WHERE THIS BLIMP IS HEADED...
AWW, WHO CARES WHERE IT HAPPENS?
YUGI! LET'S MAKE IT TO THE FINALS!
YEAH!
YUGI...YOU AND THE "OTHER YUGI" MUST BE TIRED. HOW MANY PEOPLE DID YOU FIGHT TODAY?
A LOT...
THE OTHER ME'S EXHAUSTED...
SPIRIT

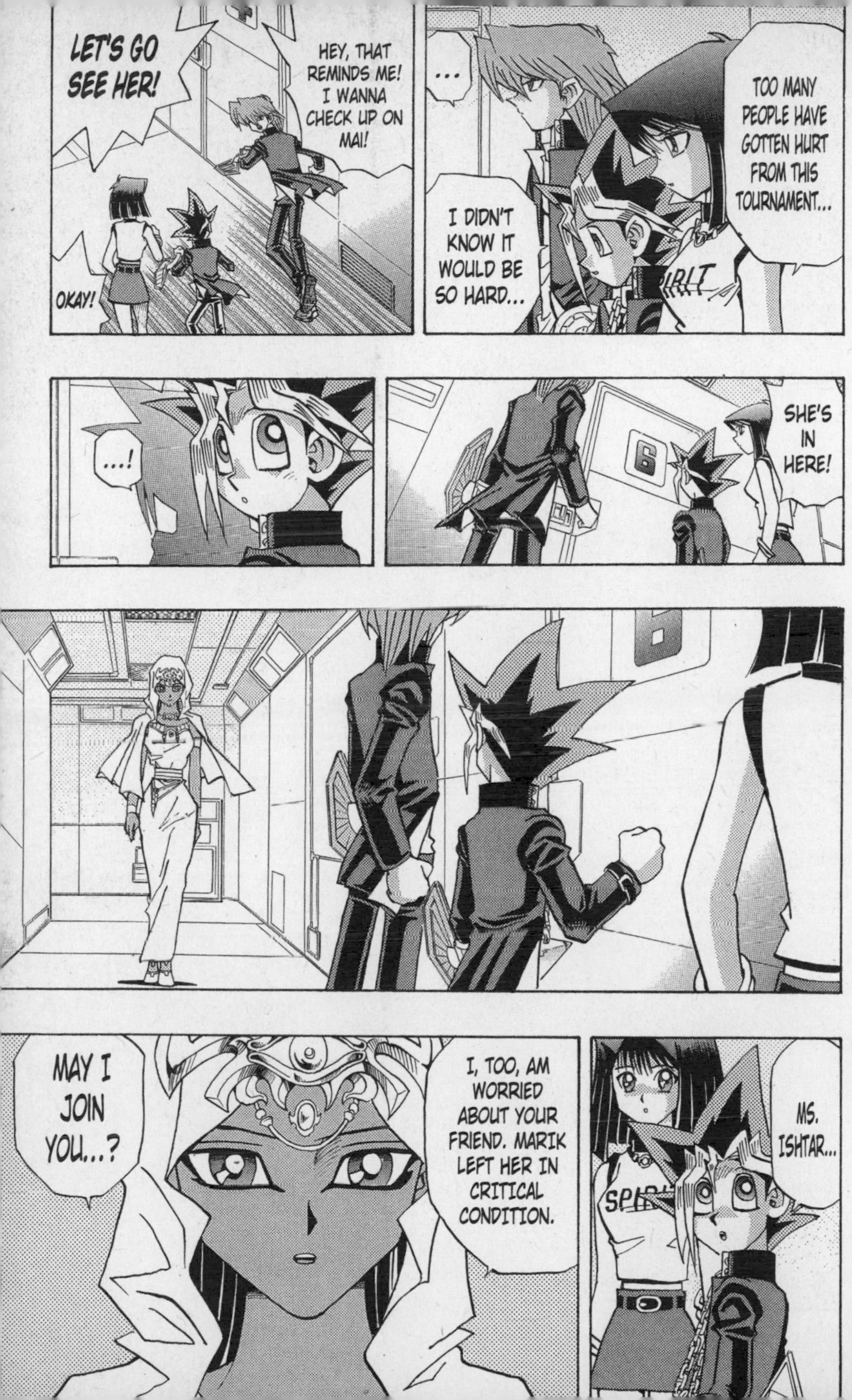
TOO MANY PEOPLE HAVE GOTTEN HURT FROM THIS TOURNAMENT...
I DIDN'T KNOW IT WOULD BE SO HARD...
...
HEY, THAT REMINDS ME! I WANNA CHECK UP ON MAI!
LET'S GO SEE HER!
OKAY!
SHE'S IN HERE!
...!
MS. ISHTAR...
I, TOO, AM WORRIED ABOUT YOUR FRIEND. MARIK LEFT HER IN CRITICAL CONDITION.
MAY I JOIN YOU...?

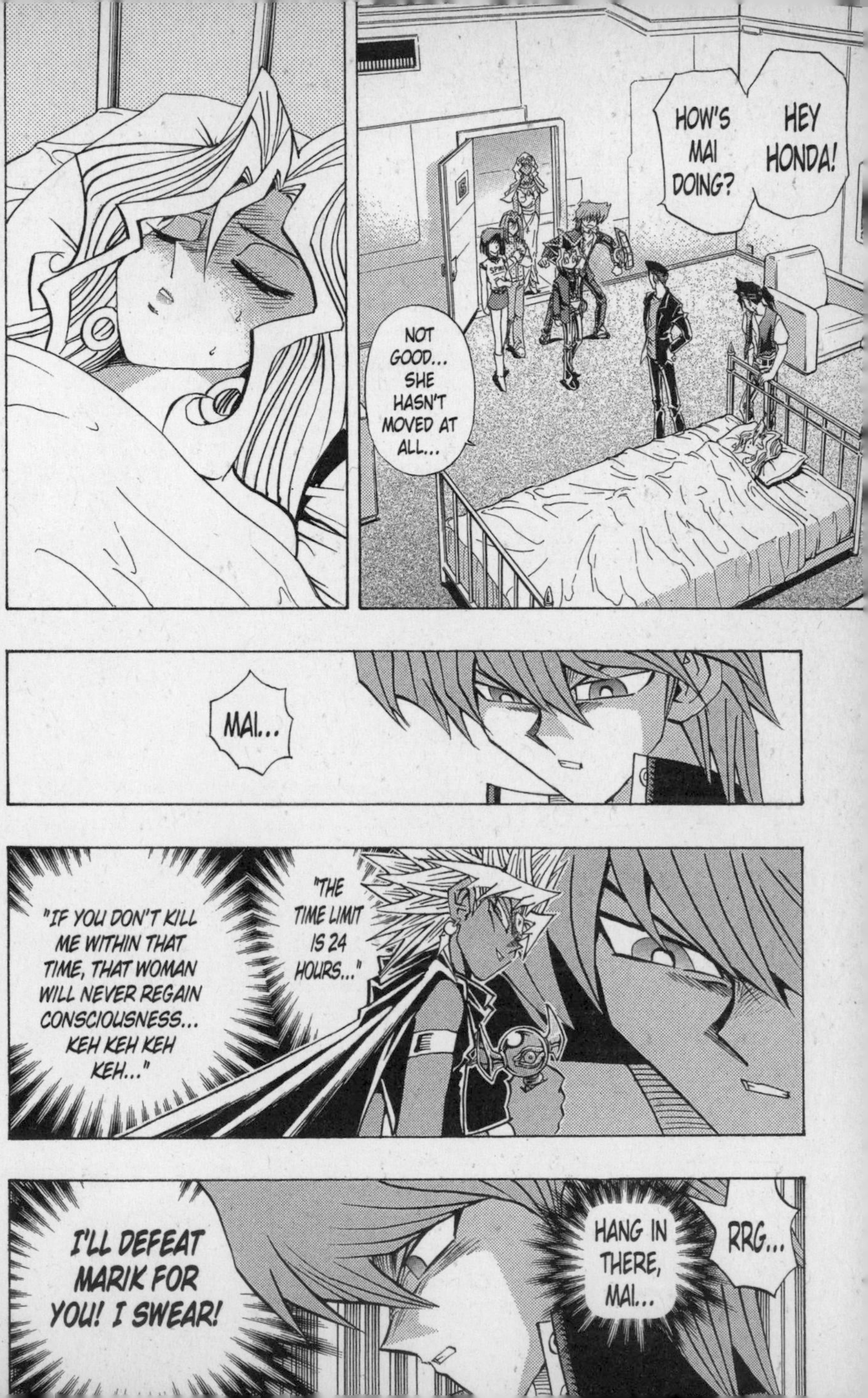
HEY HONDA!
HOW'S MAI DOING?
NOT GOOD... SHE HASN'T MOVED AT ALL...
MAI...
"THE TIME LIMIT IS 24 HOURS..."
"IF YOU DON'T KILL ME WITHIN THAT TIME, THAT WOMAN WILL NEVER REGAIN CONSCIOUSNESS... KEH KEH KEH KEH..."
RRG...
HANG IN THERE, MAI...
I'LL DEFEAT MARIK FOR YOU! I SWEAR!

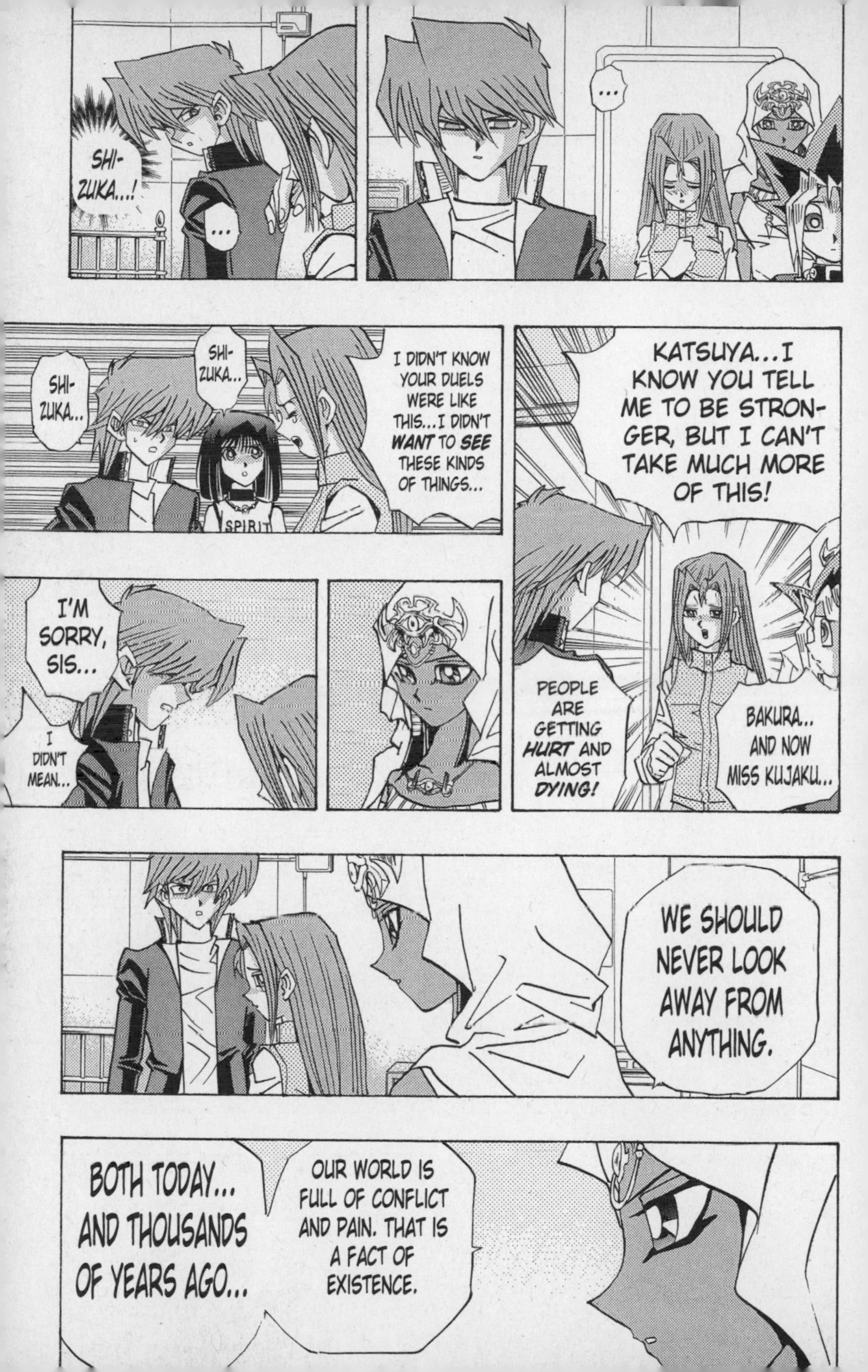
...
SHI-ZUKA...!
...
KATSUYA...I KNOW YOU TELL ME TO BE STRONGER, BUT I CAN'T TAKE MUCH MORE OF THIS!
BAKURA... AND NOW MISS KUJAKU...
PEOPLE ARE GETTING *HURT* AND ALMOST *DYING!*
I DIDN'T KNOW YOUR DUELS WERE LIKE THIS...I DIDN'T *WANT* TO *SEE* THESE KINDS OF THINGS...
SHI-ZUKA...
SHI-ZUKA...
I'M SORRY, SIS...
I DIDN'T MEAN...
WE SHOULD NEVER LOOK AWAY FROM ANYTHING.
OUR WORLD IS FULL OF CONFLICT AND PAIN. THAT IS A FACT OF EXISTENCE.
BOTH TODAY... AND THOUSANDS OF YEARS AGO...

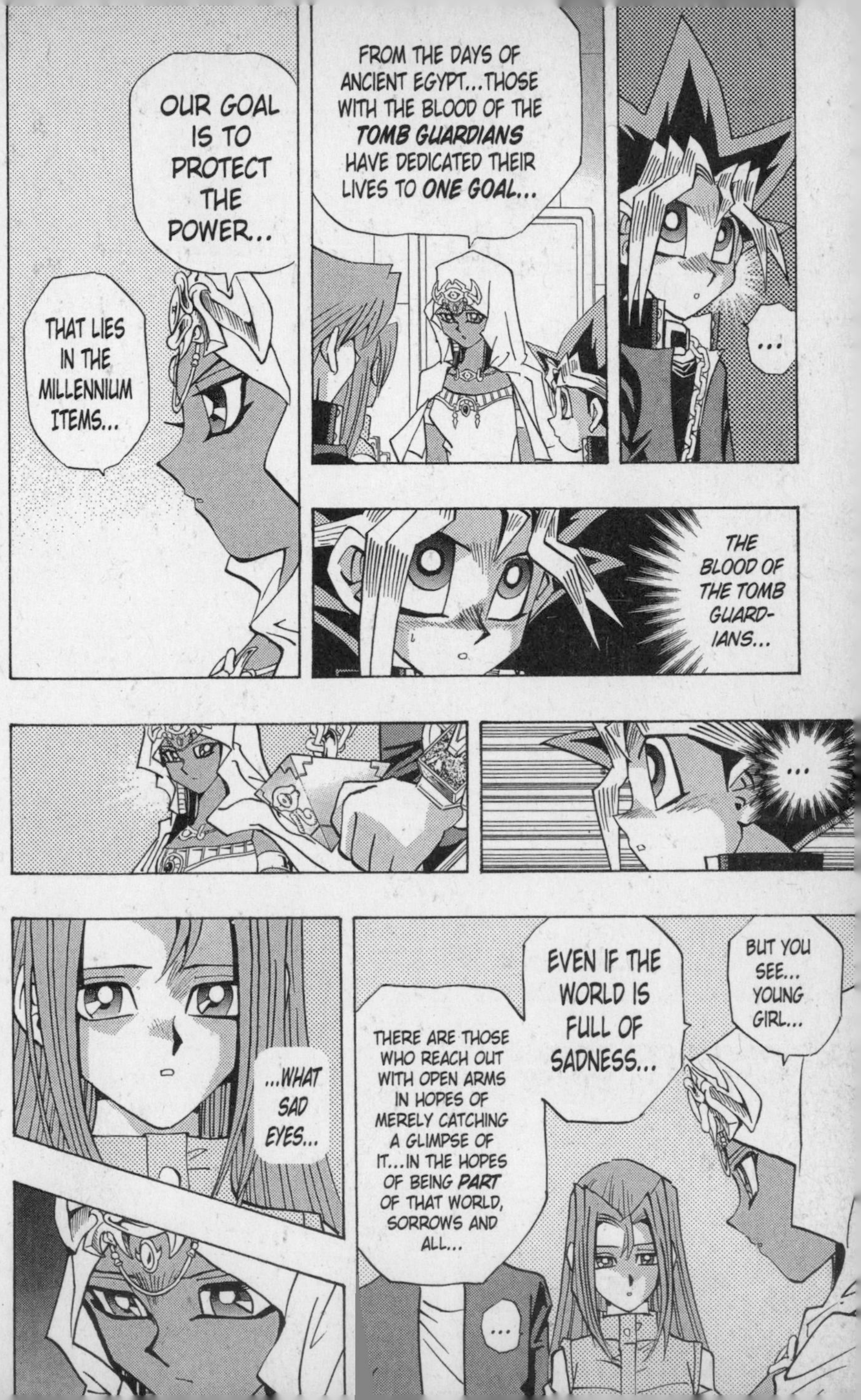
...
FROM THE DAYS OF ANCIENT EGYPT...THOSE WITH THE BLOOD OF THE **TOMB GUARDIANS** HAVE DEDICATED THEIR LIVES TO **ONE GOAL...**
THE BLOOD OF THE TOMB GUARD-IANS...
OUR GOAL IS TO PROTECT THE POWER...
THAT LIES IN THE MILLENNIUM ITEMS...
...
BUT YOU SEE... YOUNG GIRL...
EVEN IF THE WORLD IS FULL OF SADNESS...
THERE ARE THOSE WHO REACH OUT WITH OPEN ARMS IN HOPES OF MERELY CATCHING A GLIMPSE OF IT...IN THE HOPES OF BEING **PART** OF THAT WORLD, SORROWS AND ALL...
...
...WHAT SAD EYES...

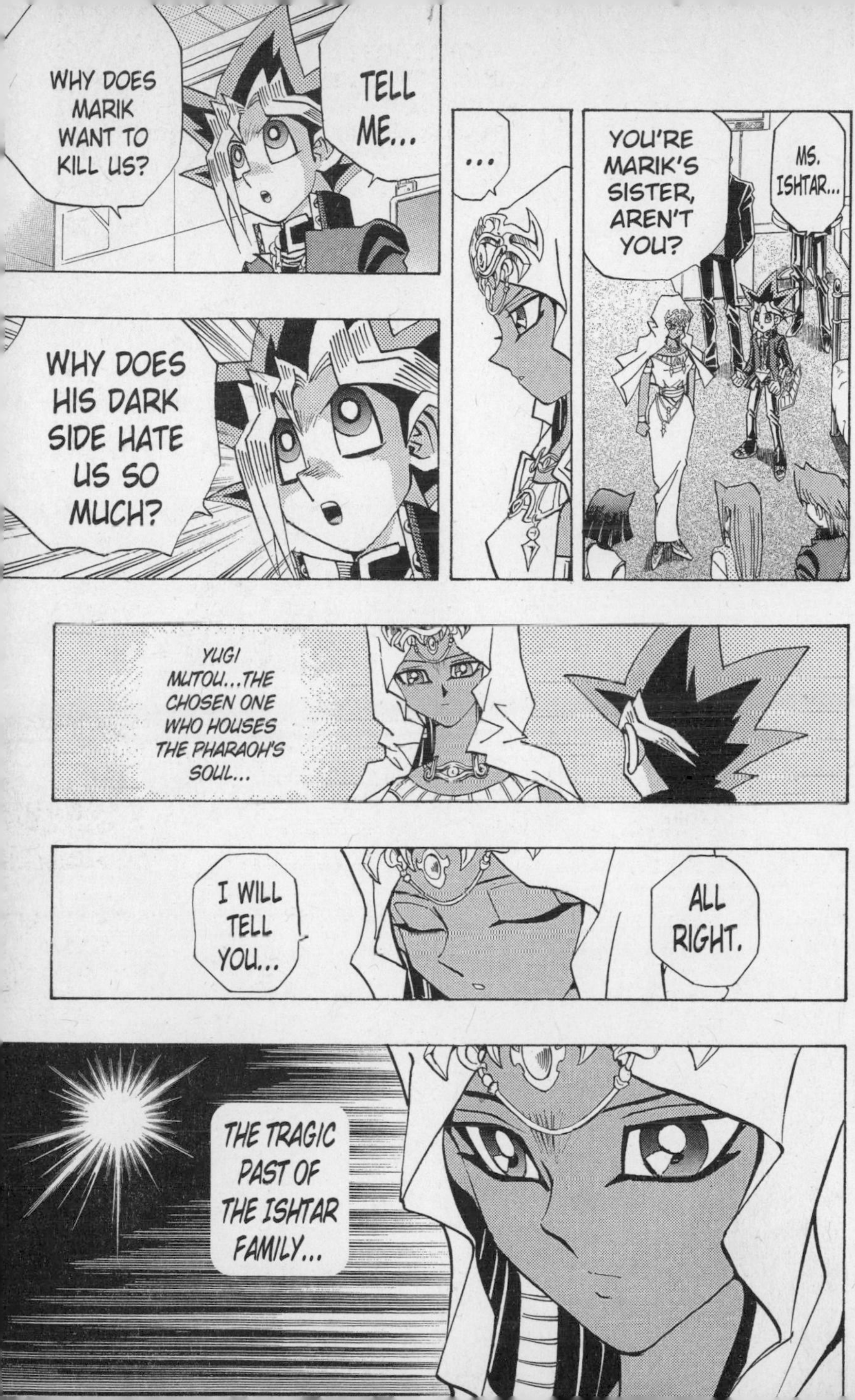
MS. ISHTAR...
YOU'RE MARIK'S SISTER, AREN'T YOU?
...
TELL ME...
WHY DOES MARIK WANT TO KILL US?
WHY DOES HIS DARK SIDE HATE US SO MUCH?
YUGI MUTOU...THE CHOSEN ONE WHO HOUSES THE PHARAOH'S SOUL...
ALL RIGHT.
I WILL TELL YOU...
THE TRAGIC PAST OF THE ISHTAR FAMILY...

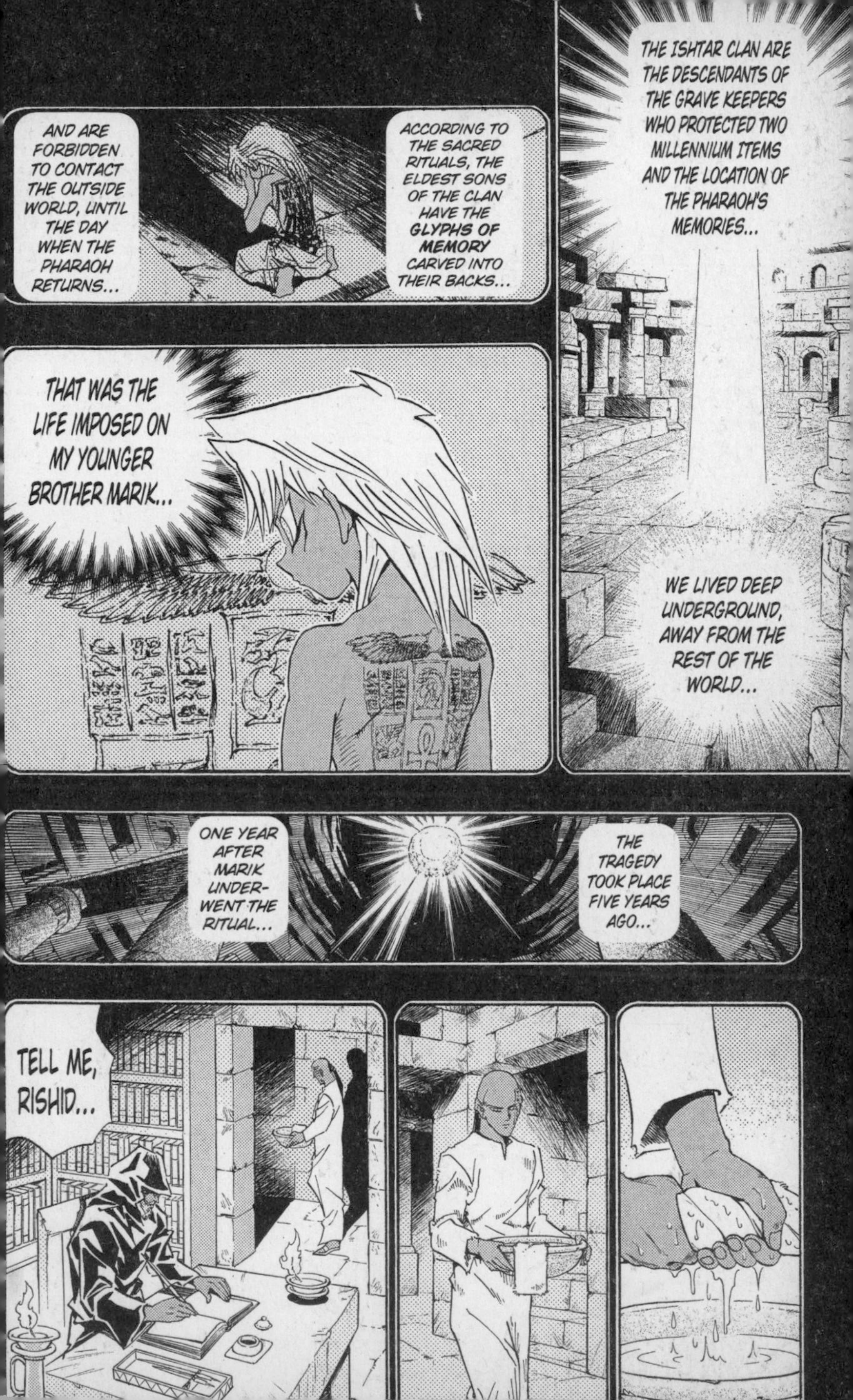
THE ISHTAR CLAN ARE THE DESCENDANTS OF THE GRAVE KEEPERS WHO PROTECTED TWO MILLENNIUM ITEMS AND THE LOCATION OF THE PHARAOH'S MEMORIES...
WE LIVED DEEP UNDERGROUND, AWAY FROM THE REST OF THE WORLD...
ACCORDING TO THE SACRED RITUALS, THE ELDEST SONS OF THE CLAN HAVE THE GLYPHS OF MEMORY CARVED INTO THEIR BACKS...
AND ARE FORBIDDEN TO CONTACT THE OUTSIDE WORLD, UNTIL THE DAY WHEN THE PHARAOH RETURNS...
THAT WAS THE LIFE IMPOSED ON MY YOUNGER BROTHER MARIK...
THE TRAGEDY TOOK PLACE FIVE YEARS AGO...
ONE YEAR AFTER MARIK UNDER-WENT THE RITUAL...
TELL ME, RISHID...

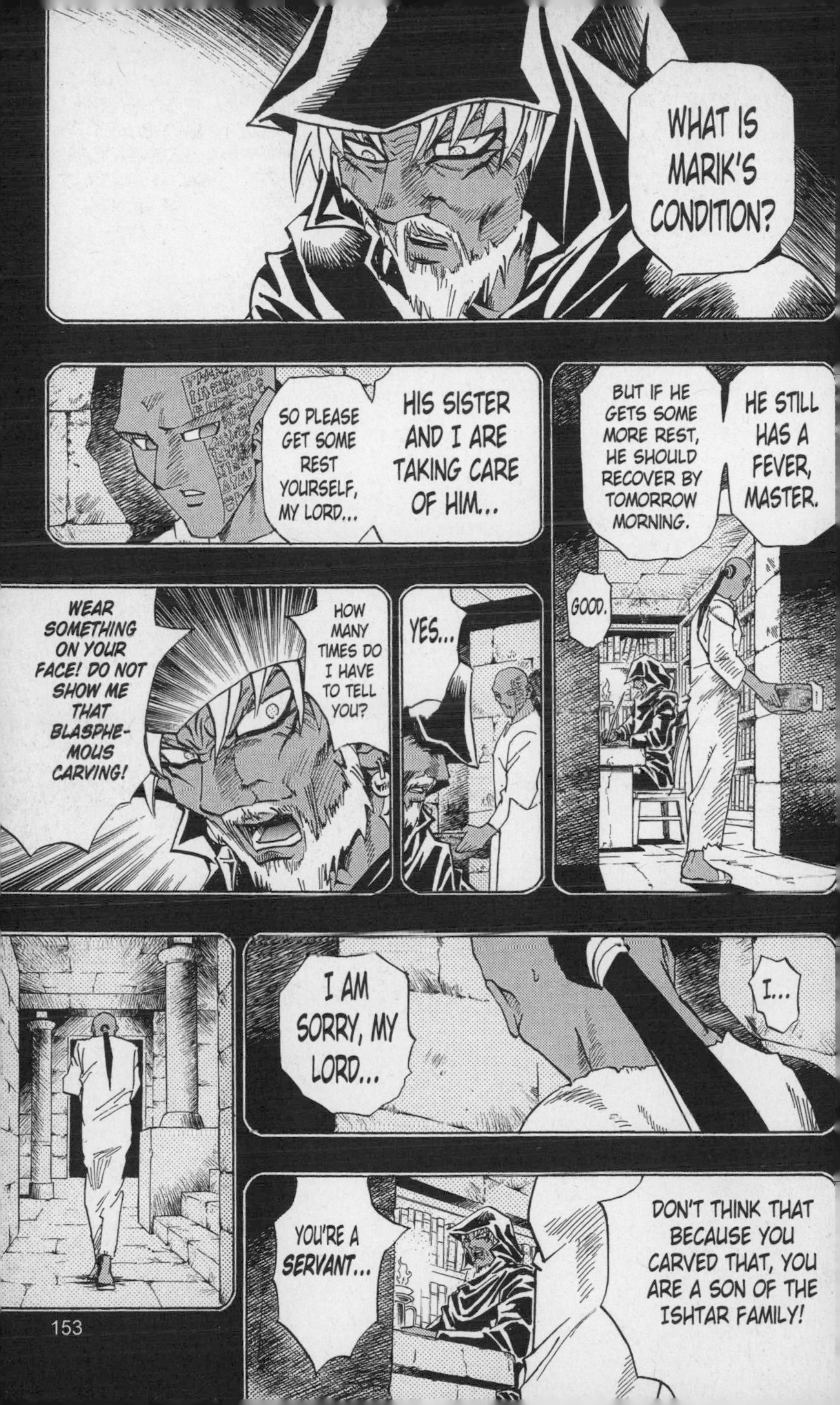
WHAT IS MARIK'S CONDITION?
HE STILL HAS A FEVER, MASTER.
BUT IF HE GETS SOME MORE REST, HE SHOULD RECOVER BY TOMORROW MORNING.
GOOD.
HIS SISTER AND I ARE TAKING CARE OF HIM...
SO PLEASE GET SOME REST YOURSELF, MY LORD...
YES...
HOW MANY TIMES DO I HAVE TO TELL YOU?
WEAR SOMETHING ON YOUR FACE! DO NOT SHOW ME THAT BLASPHE-MOUS CARVING!
I...
I AM SORRY, MY LORD...
DON'T THINK THAT BECAUSE YOU CARVED THAT, YOU ARE A SON OF THE ISHTAR FAMILY!
YOU'RE A SERVANT...

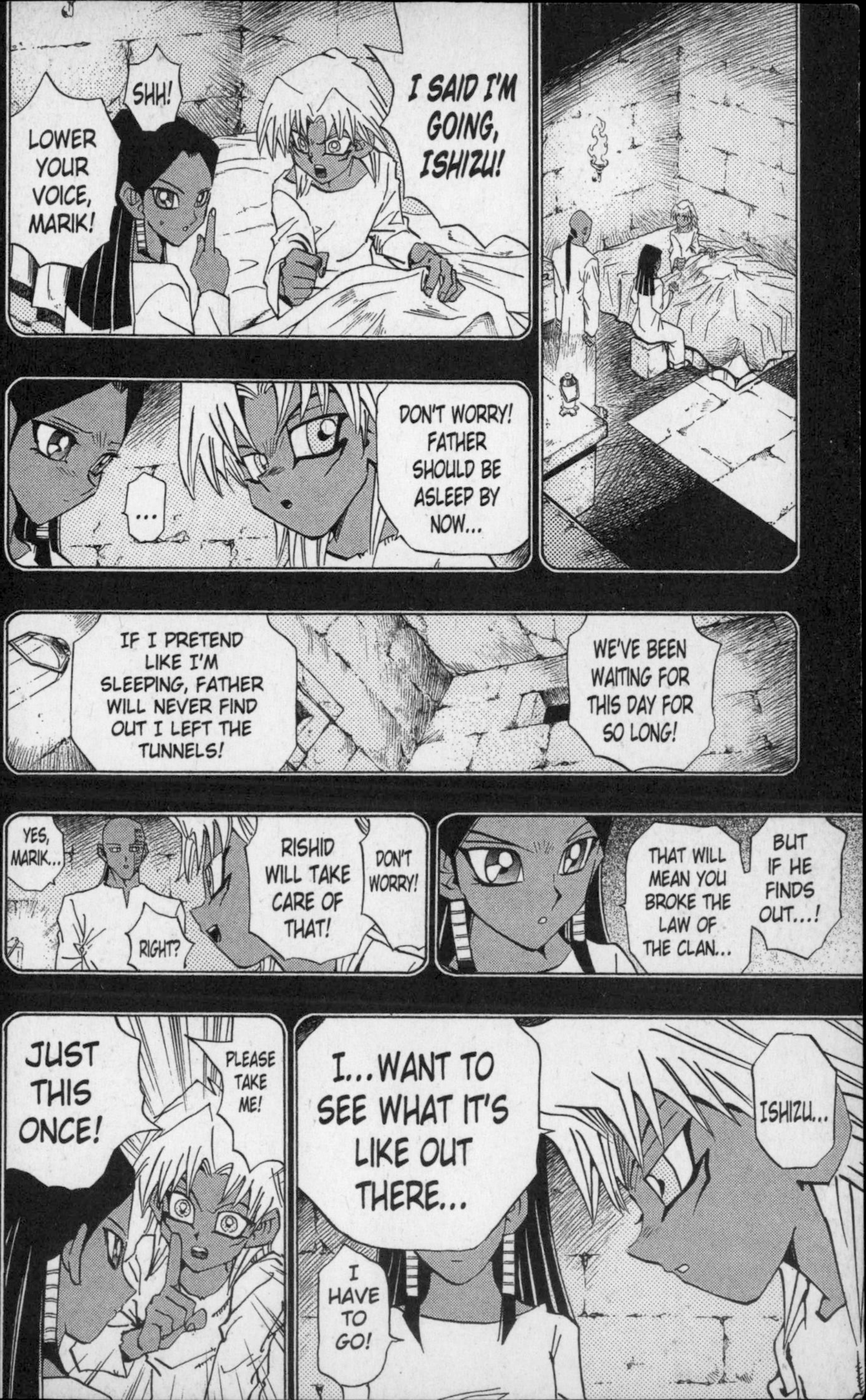
I SAID I'M GOING, ISHIZU!
SHH!
LOWER YOUR VOICE, MARIK!
DON'T WORRY! FATHER SHOULD BE ASLEEP BY NOW...
...
WE'VE BEEN WAITING FOR THIS DAY FOR SO LONG!
IF I PRETEND LIKE I'M SLEEPING, FATHER WILL NEVER FIND OUT I LEFT THE TUNNELS!
BUT IF HE FINDS OUT...!
THAT WILL MEAN YOU BROKE THE LAW OF THE CLAN...
DON'T WORRY!
RISHID WILL TAKE CARE OF THAT!
RIGHT?
YES, MARIK...
ISHIZU...
I...WANT TO SEE WHAT IT'S LIKE OUT THERE...
I HAVE TO GO!
PLEASE TAKE ME!
JUST THIS ONCE!

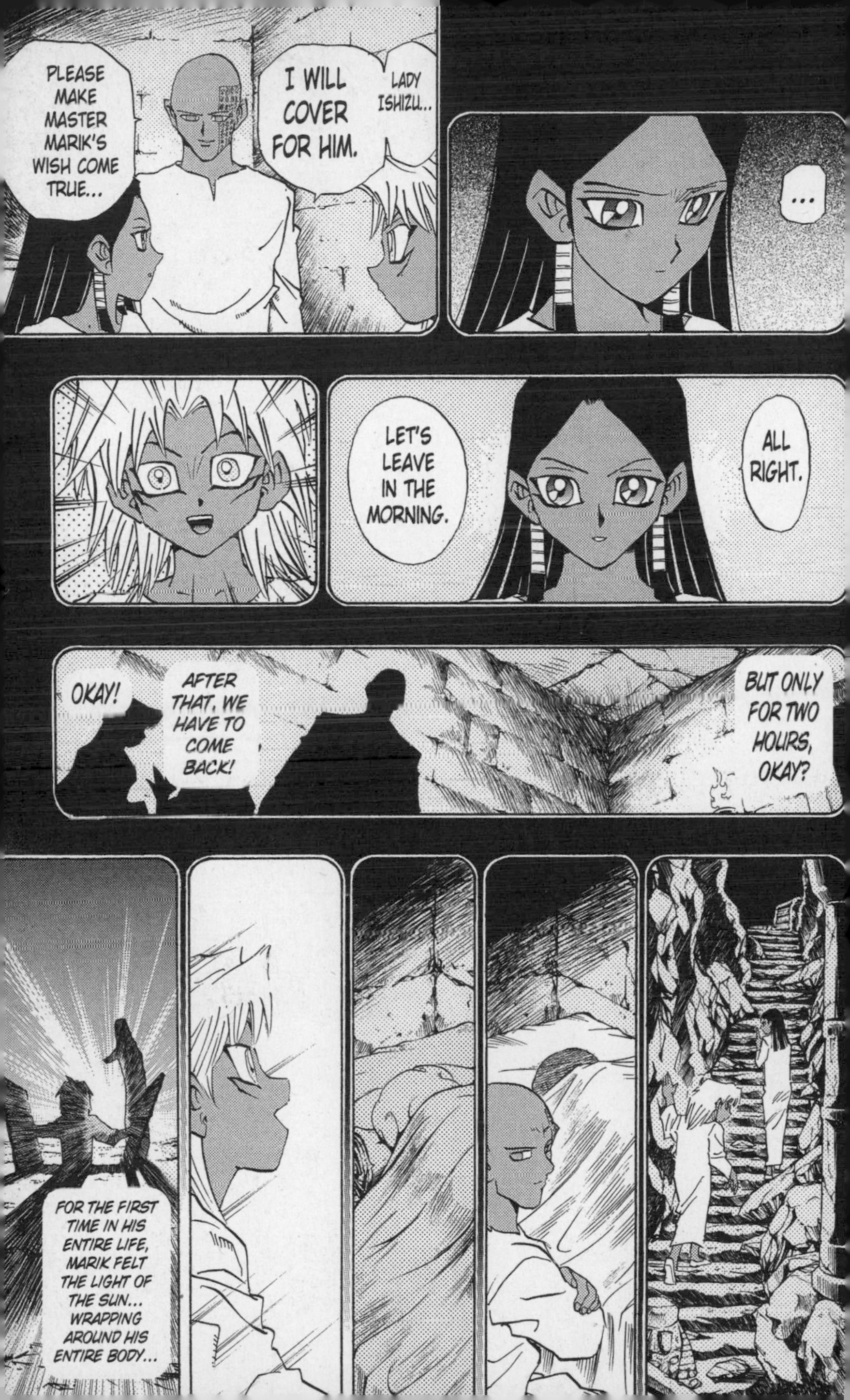
...
LADY ISHIZU...
I WILL COVER FOR HIM.
PLEASE MAKE MASTER MARIK'S WISH COME TRUE...
ALL RIGHT.
LET'S LEAVE IN THE MORNING.
BUT ONLY FOR TWO HOURS, OKAY?
AFTER THAT, WE HAVE TO COME BACK!
OKAY!
FOR THE FIRST TIME IN HIS ENTIRE LIFE, MARIK FELT THE LIGHT OF THE SUN... WRAPPING AROUND HIS ENTIRE BODY...

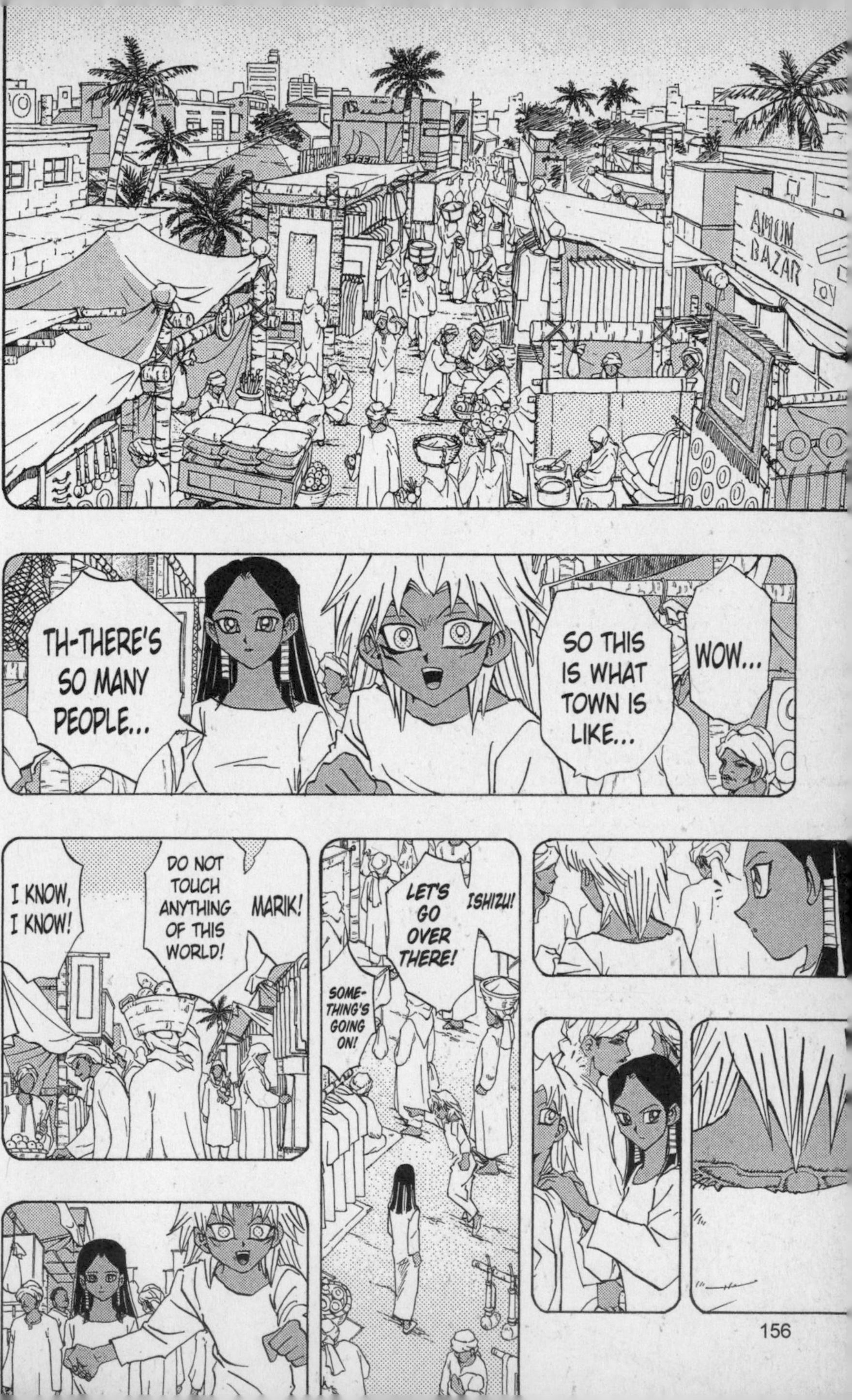
AMUN BAZAR
WOW...
SO THIS IS WHAT TOWN IS LIKE...
TH-THERE'S SO MANY PEOPLE...
ISHIZU!
LET'S GO OVER THERE!
SOME-THING'S GOING ON!
MARIK!
DO NOT TOUCH ANYTHING OF THIS WORLD!
I KNOW, I KNOW!

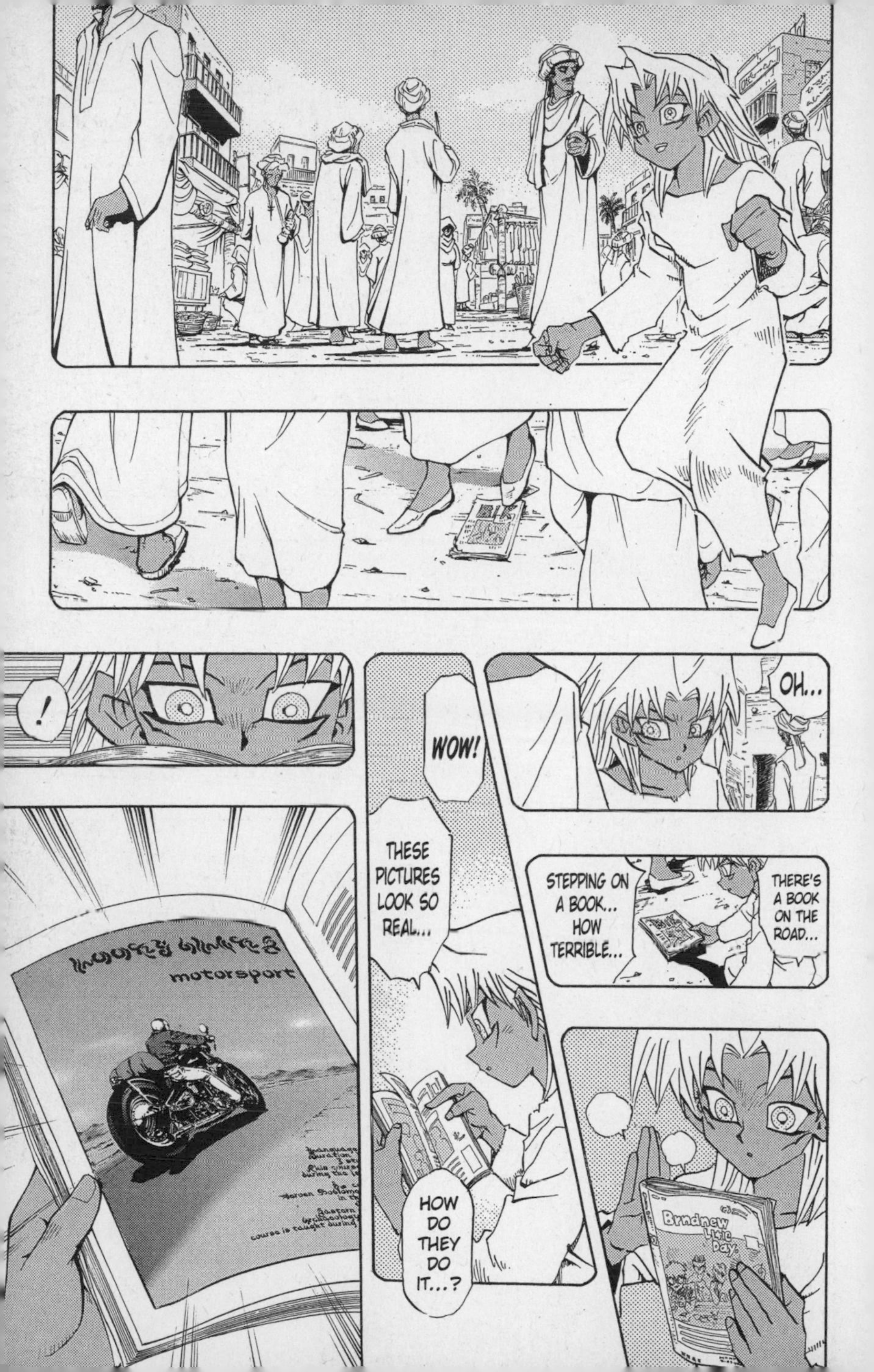
OH...
THERE'S A BOOK ON THE ROAD...
STEPPING ON A BOOK... HOW TERRIBLE...
WOW!
THESE PICTURES LOOK SO REAL...
HOW DO THEY DO IT...?
!
motorsport

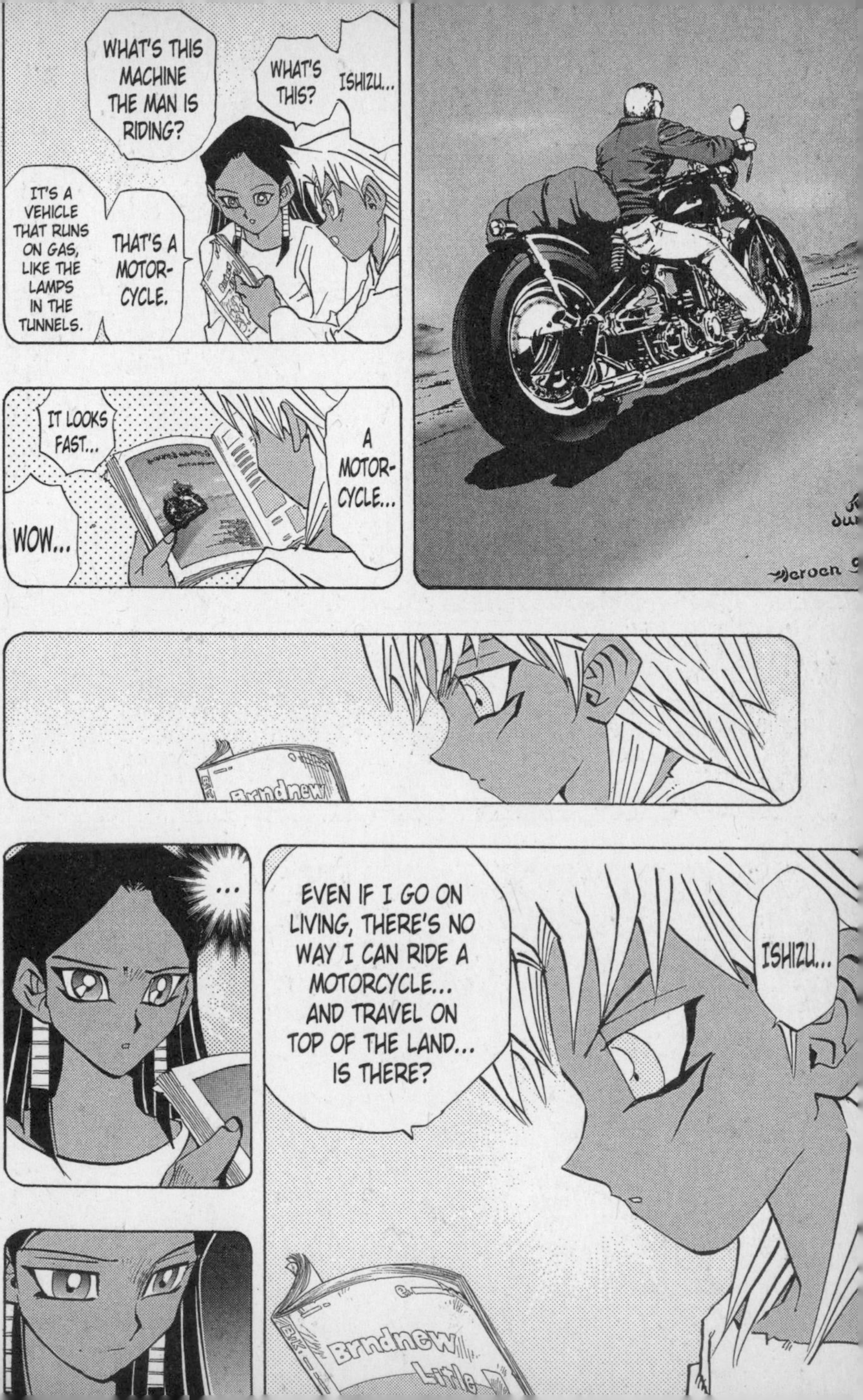
ISHIZU...
WHAT'S THIS?
WHAT'S THIS MACHINE THE MAN IS RIDING?
THAT'S A MOTORCYCLE.
IT'S A VEHICLE THAT RUNS ON GAS, LIKE THE LAMPS IN THE TUNNELS.
A MOTORCYCLE...
IT LOOKS FAST...
WOW...
Brndnew
ISHIZU...
EVEN IF I GO ON LIVING, THERE'S NO WAY I CAN RIDE A MOTORCYCLE... AND TRAVEL ON TOP OF THE LAND... IS THERE?
...
Brndnew
Litle

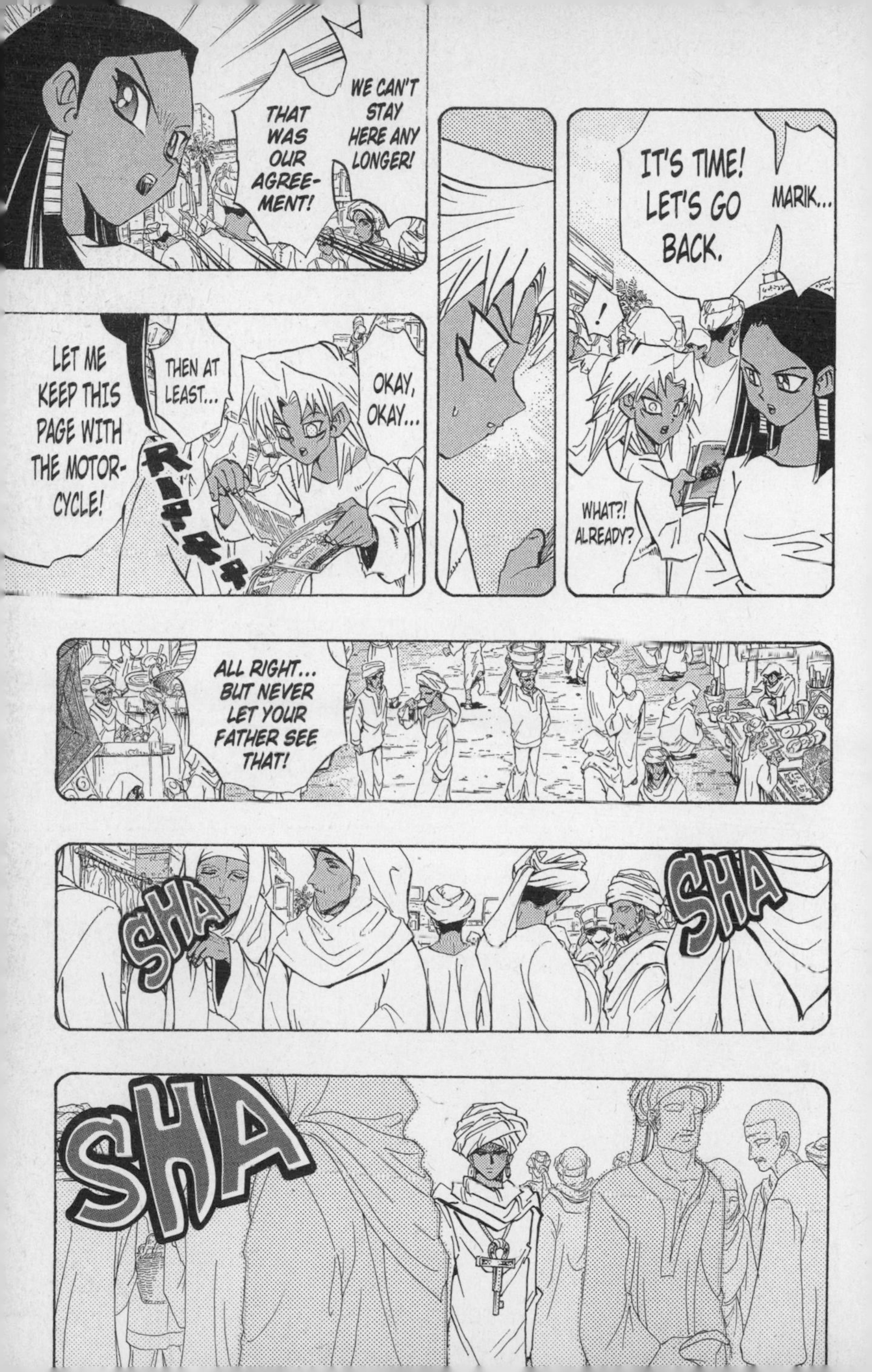
MARIK...
IT'S TIME! LET'S GO BACK.
WHAT?! ALREADY?
!
WE CAN'T STAY HERE ANY LONGER!
THAT WAS OUR AGREEMENT!
OKAY, OKAY...
THEN AT LEAST...
LET ME KEEP THIS PAGE WITH THE MOTORCYCLE!
RIPPP
ALL RIGHT... BUT NEVER LET YOUR FATHER SEE THAT!
SHA
SHA
SHA

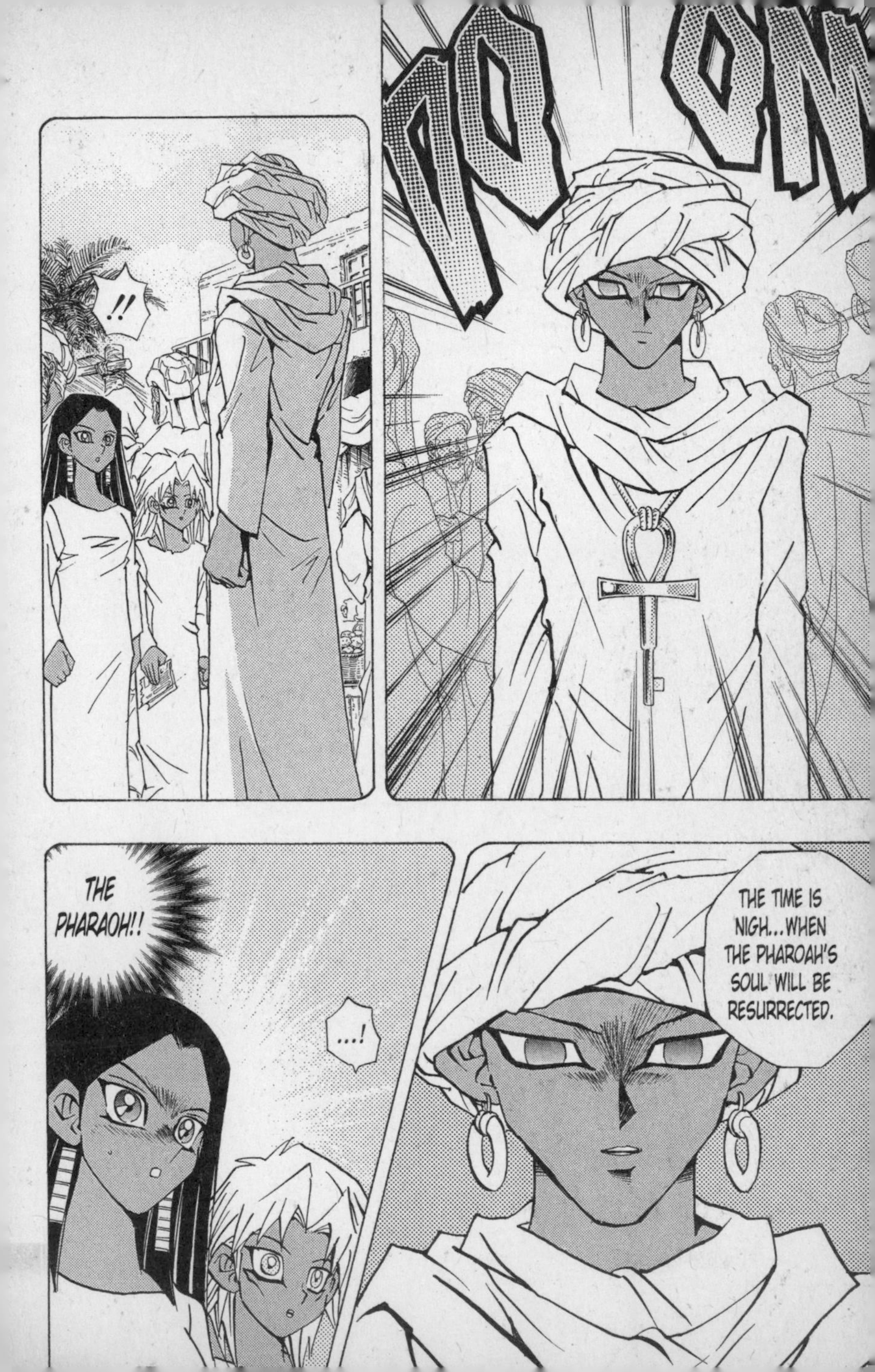
!!
THE TIME IS NIGH...WHEN THE PHAROAH'S SOUL WILL BE RESURRECTED.
THE PHARAOH!!
...!

READ THIS WAY

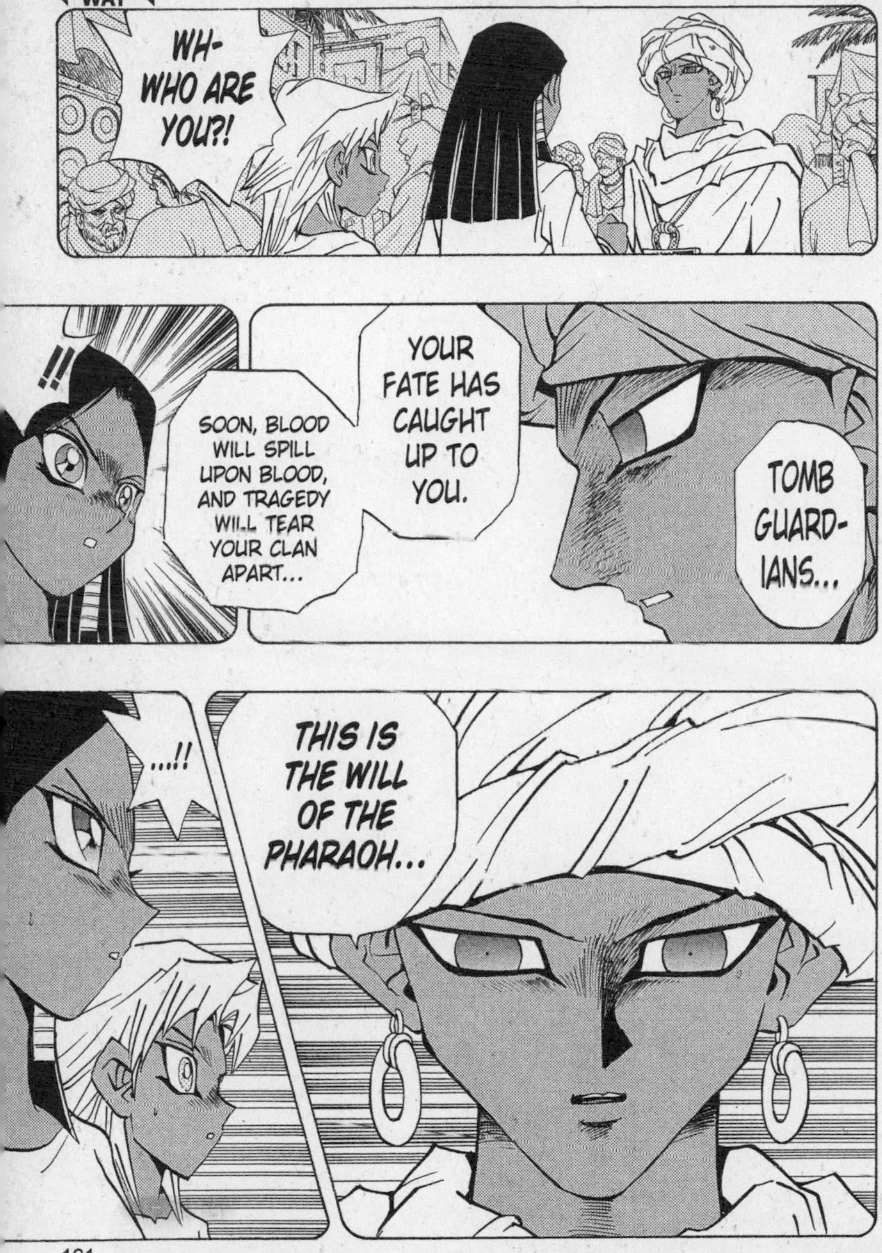
WH- WHO ARE YOU?!
TOMB GUARD- IANS...
YOUR FATE HAS CAUGHT UP TO YOU.
SOON, BLOOD WILL SPILL UPON BLOOD, AND TRAGEDY WILL TEAR YOUR CLAN APART...
!!
THIS IS THE WILL OF THE PHARAOH...
...!!

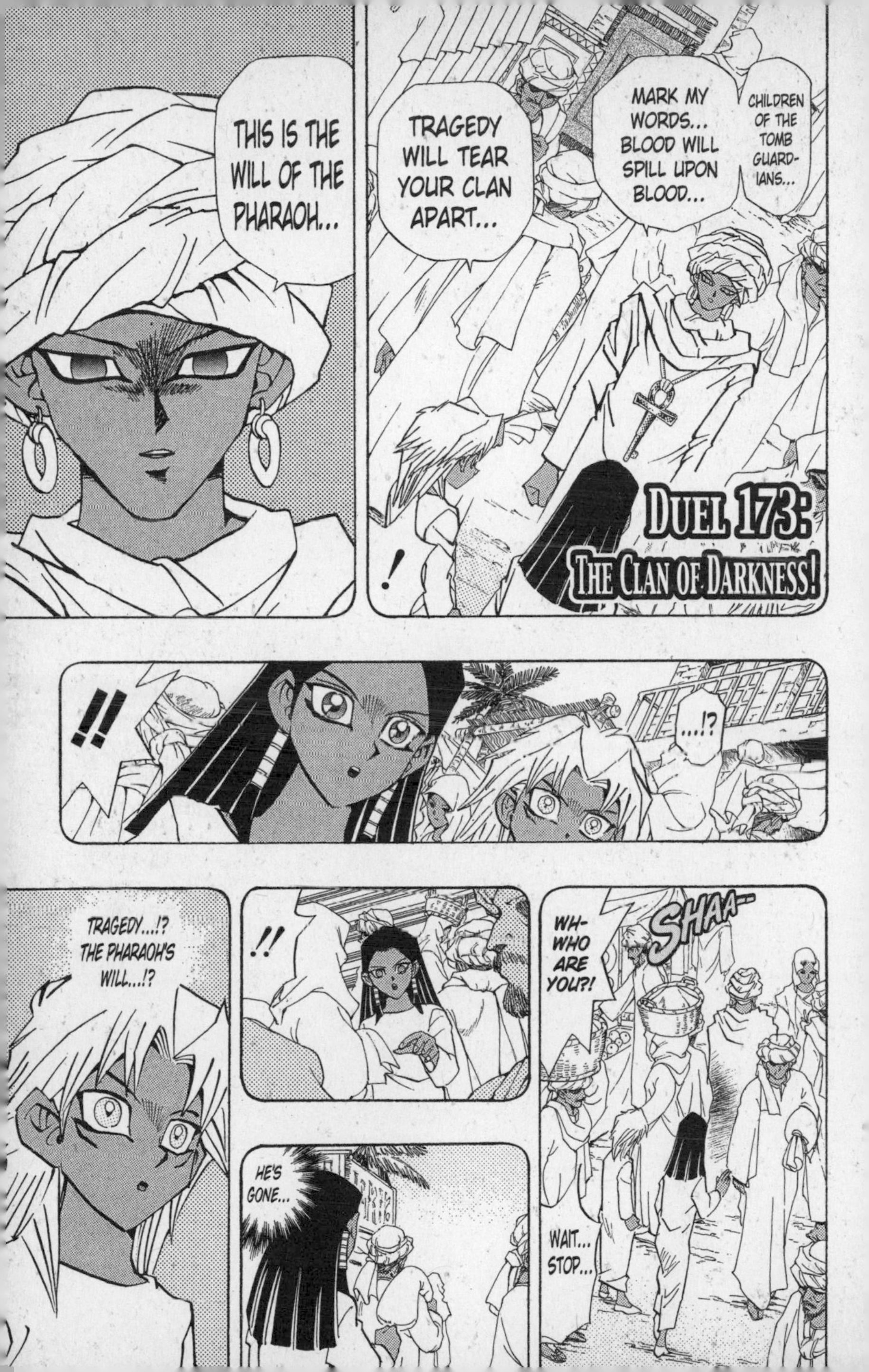
CHILDREN OF THE TOMB GUARD-IANS...
MARK MY WORDS... BLOOD WILL SPILL UPON BLOOD...
TRAGEDY WILL TEAR YOUR CLAN APART...
DUEL 173: THE CLAN OF DARKNESS!
!
THIS IS THE WILL OF THE PHARAOH...
...!?
!!
SHAA-
WH-WHO ARE YOU?!
WAIT... STOP...
!!
HE'S GONE...
TRAGEDY...!? THE PHARAOH'S WILL...!?

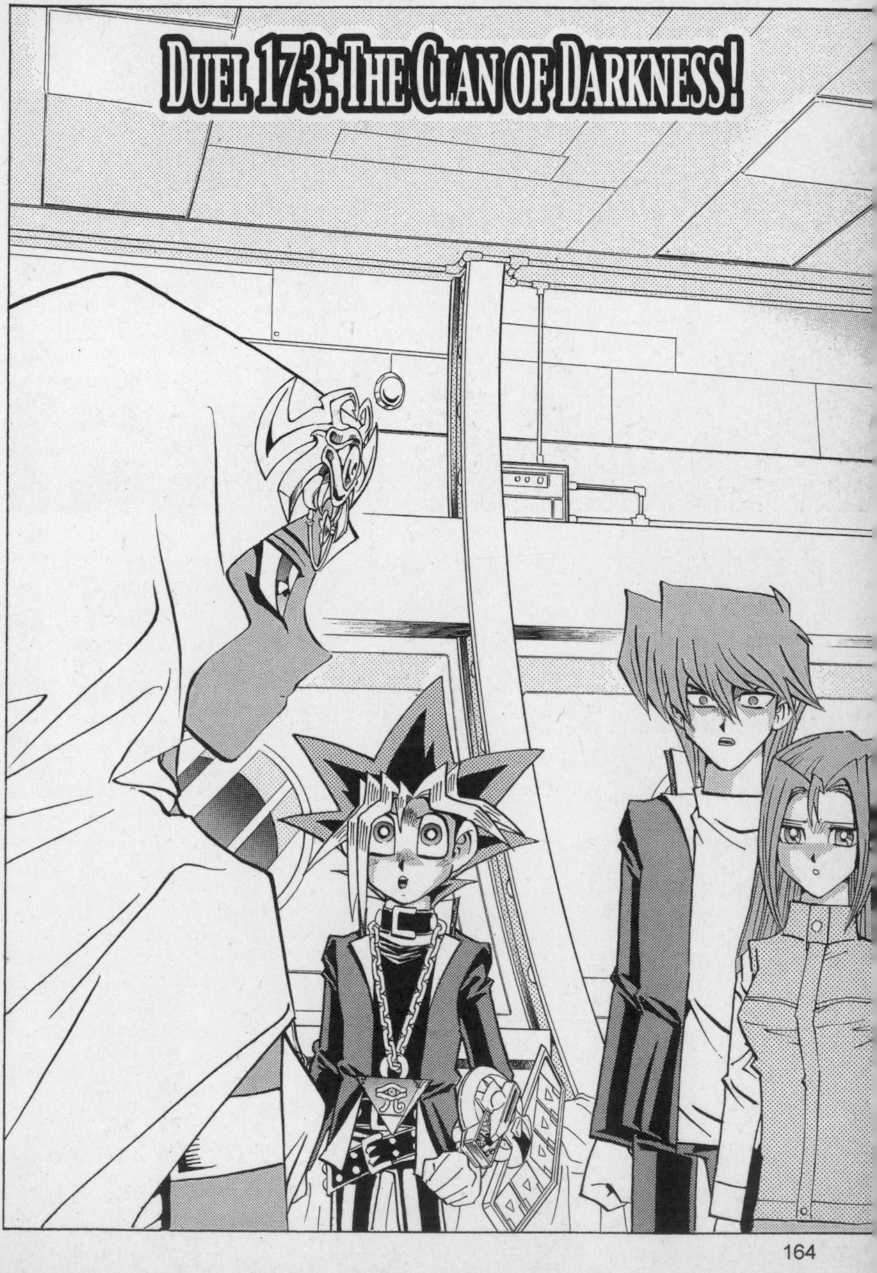
DUEL 173: THE CLAN OF DARKNESS!

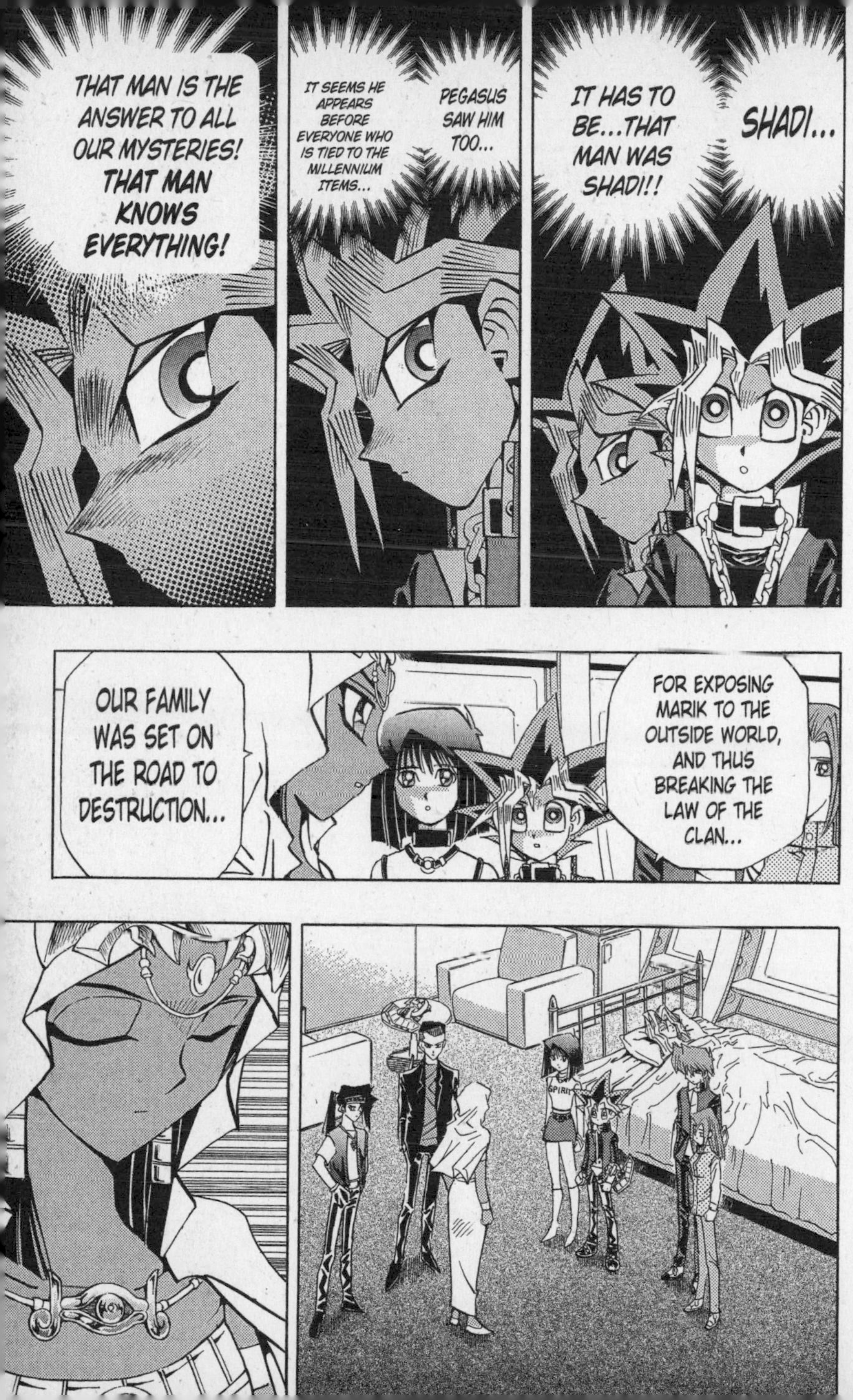
SHADI...
IT HAS TO BE...THAT MAN WAS SHADI!!
PEGASUS SAW HIM TOO...
IT SEEMS HE APPEARS BEFORE EVERYONE WHO IS TIED TO THE MILLENNIUM ITEMS...
THAT MAN IS THE ANSWER TO ALL OUR MYSTERIES! THAT MAN KNOWS EVERYTHING!
FOR EXPOSING MARIK TO THE OUTSIDE WORLD, AND THUS BREAKING THE LAW OF THE CLAN...
OUR FAMILY WAS SET ON THE ROAD TO DESTRUCTION...
SPIRIT

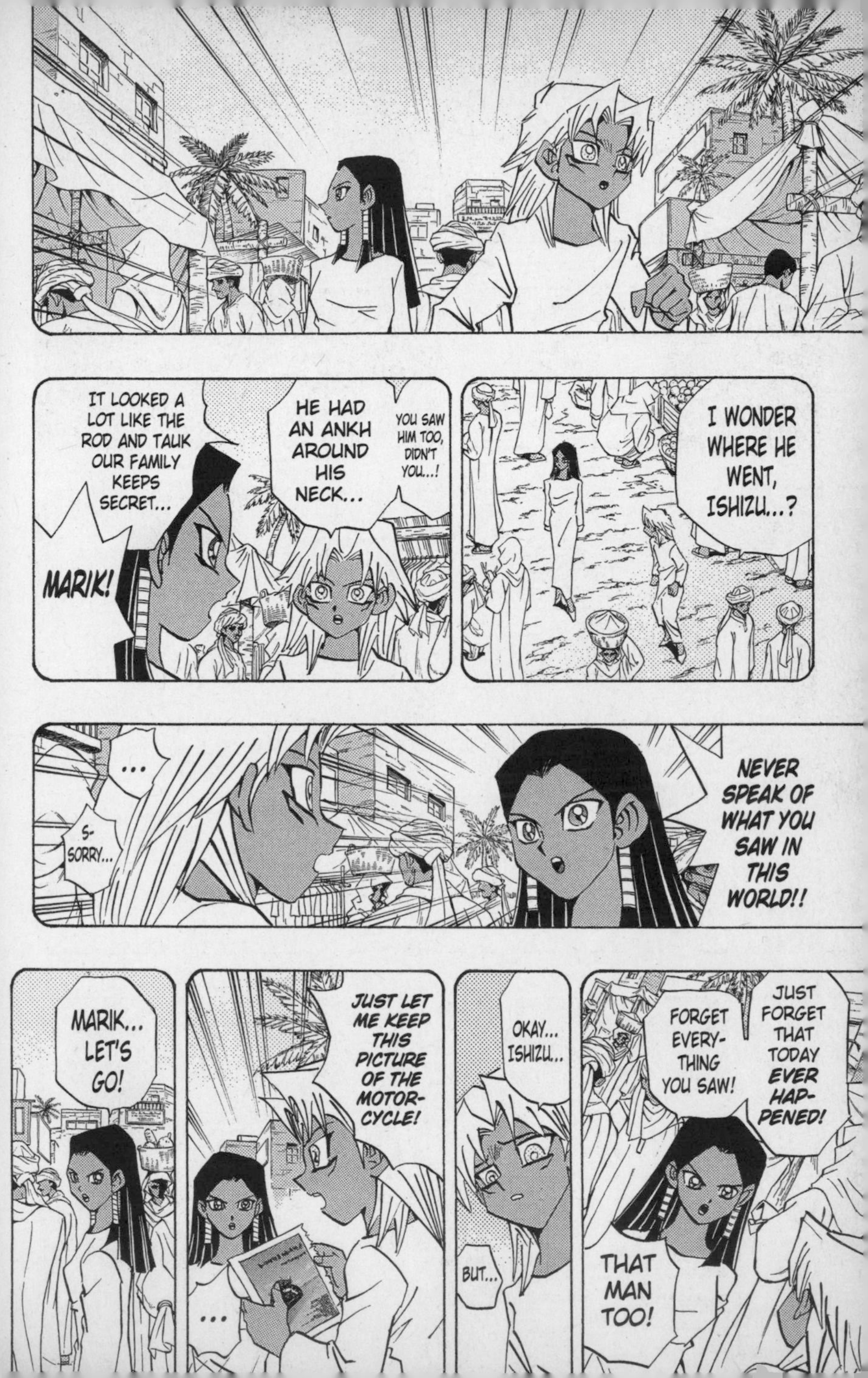
I WONDER WHERE HE WENT, ISHIZU...?
YOU SAW HIM TOO, DIDN'T YOU...!
HE HAD AN ANKH AROUND HIS NECK...
IT LOOKED A LOT LIKE THE ROD AND TAUK OUR FAMILY KEEPS SECRET...
MARIK!
NEVER SPEAK OF WHAT YOU SAW IN THIS WORLD!!
...
S-SORRY...
JUST FORGET THAT TODAY EVER HAPPENED!
FORGET EVERYTHING YOU SAW!
THAT MAN TOO!
OKAY... ISHIZU...
BUT...
JUST LET ME KEEP THIS PICTURE OF THE MOTORCYCLE!
...
MARIK... LET'S GO!

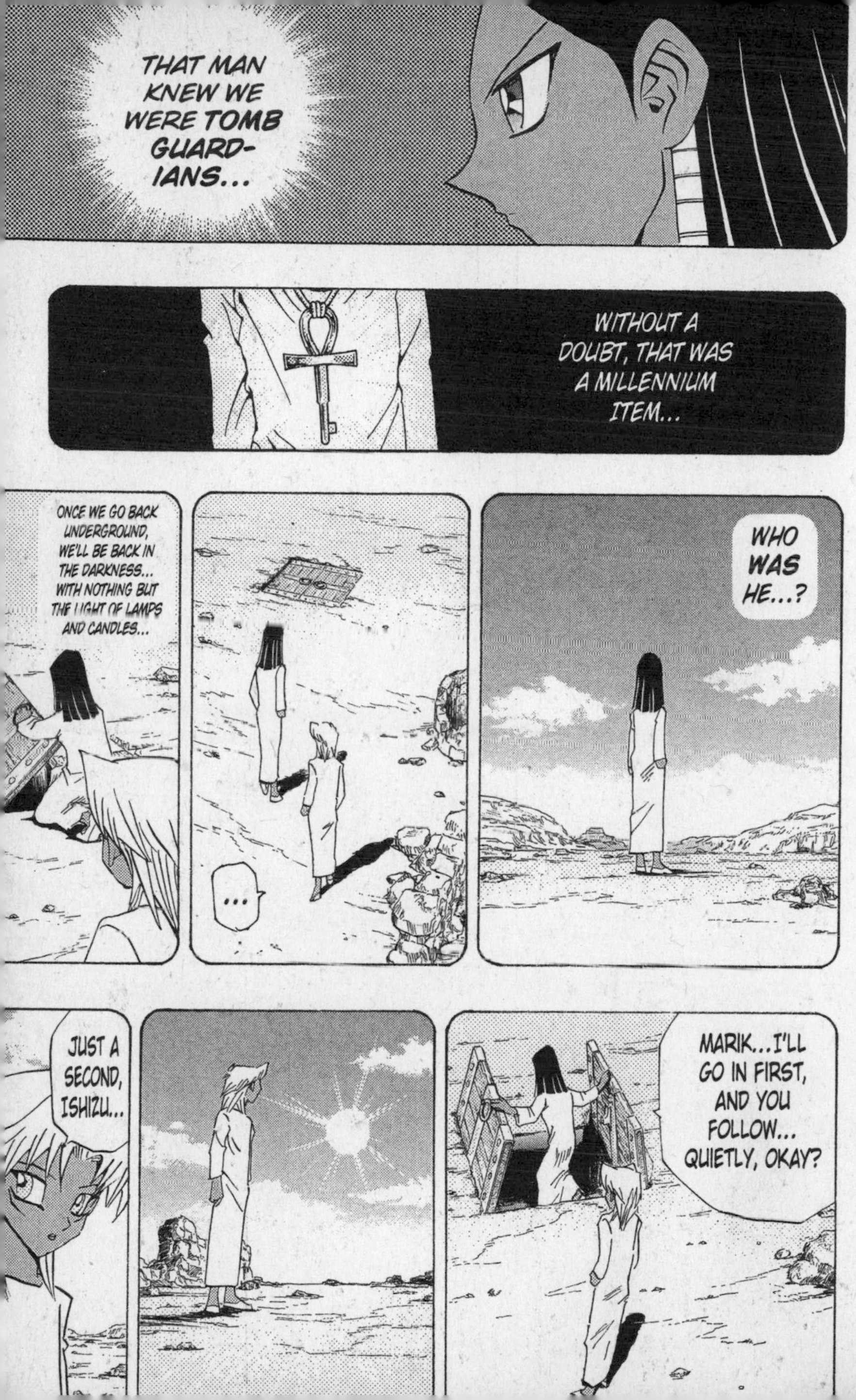
THAT MAN KNEW WE WERE TOMB GUARD-IANS...
WITHOUT A DOUBT, THAT WAS A MILLENNIUM ITEM...
WHO WAS HE...?
...
ONCE WE GO BACK UNDERGROUND, WE'LL BE BACK IN THE DARKNESS... WITH NOTHING BUT THE LIGHT OF LAMPS AND CANDLES...
MARIK...I'LL GO IN FIRST, AND YOU FOLLOW... QUIETLY, OKAY?
JUST A SECOND, ISHIZU...

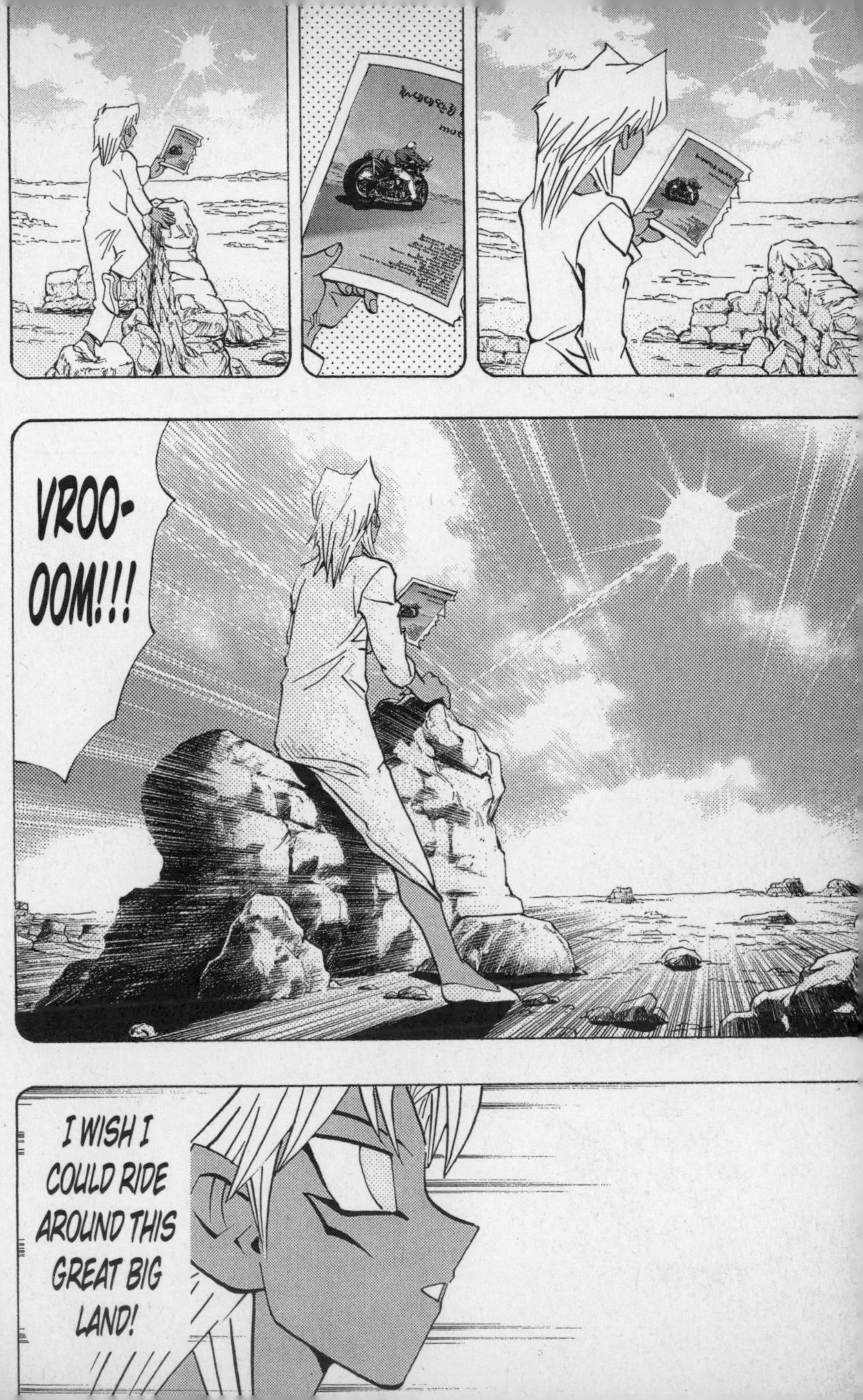
VROO-
OOM!!!
I WISH I COULD RIDE AROUND THIS GREAT BIG LAND!

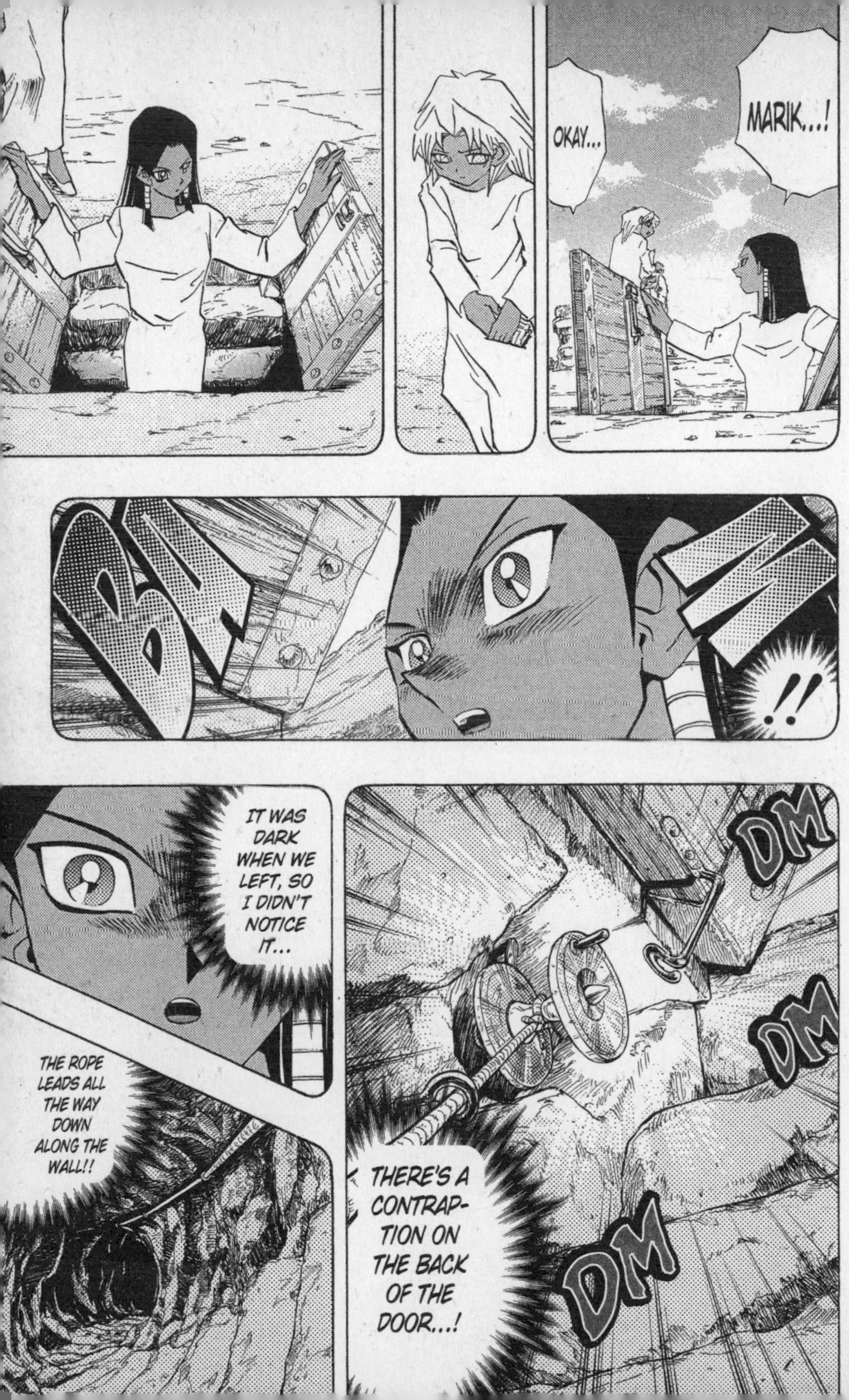
MARIK...!
OKAY...
!!
DM
DM
DM
THERE'S A CONTRAP-TION ON THE BACK OF THE DOOR...!
IT WAS DARK WHEN WE LEFT, SO I DIDN'T NOTICE IT...
THE ROPE LEADS ALL THE WAY DOWN ALONG THE WALL!!

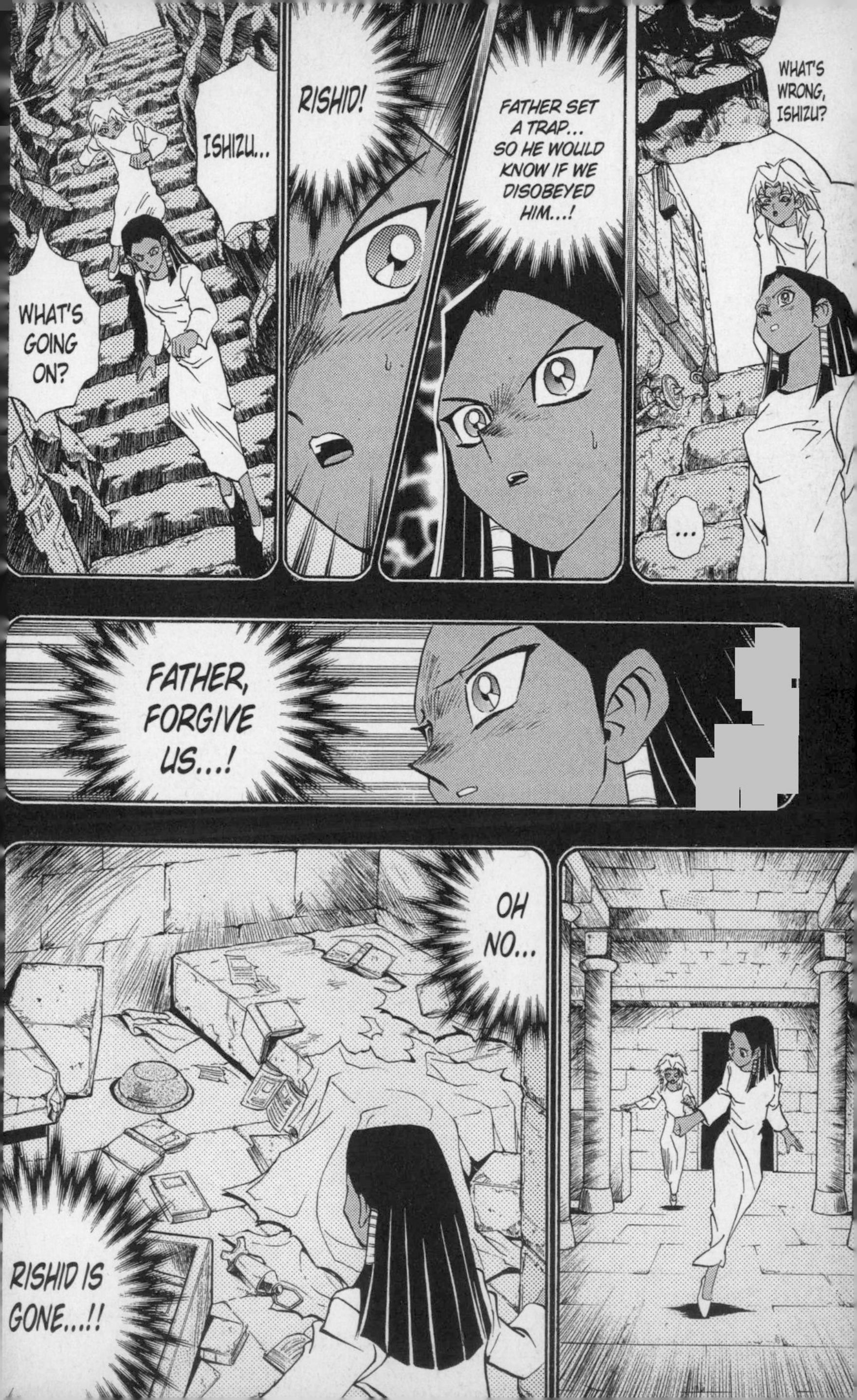
WHAT'S WRONG, ISHIZU?
...
FATHER SET A TRAP... SO HE WOULD KNOW IF WE DISOBEYED HIM...!
RISHID!
ISHIZU...
WHAT'S GOING ON?
FATHER, FORGIVE US...!
OH NO...
RISHID IS GONE...!!

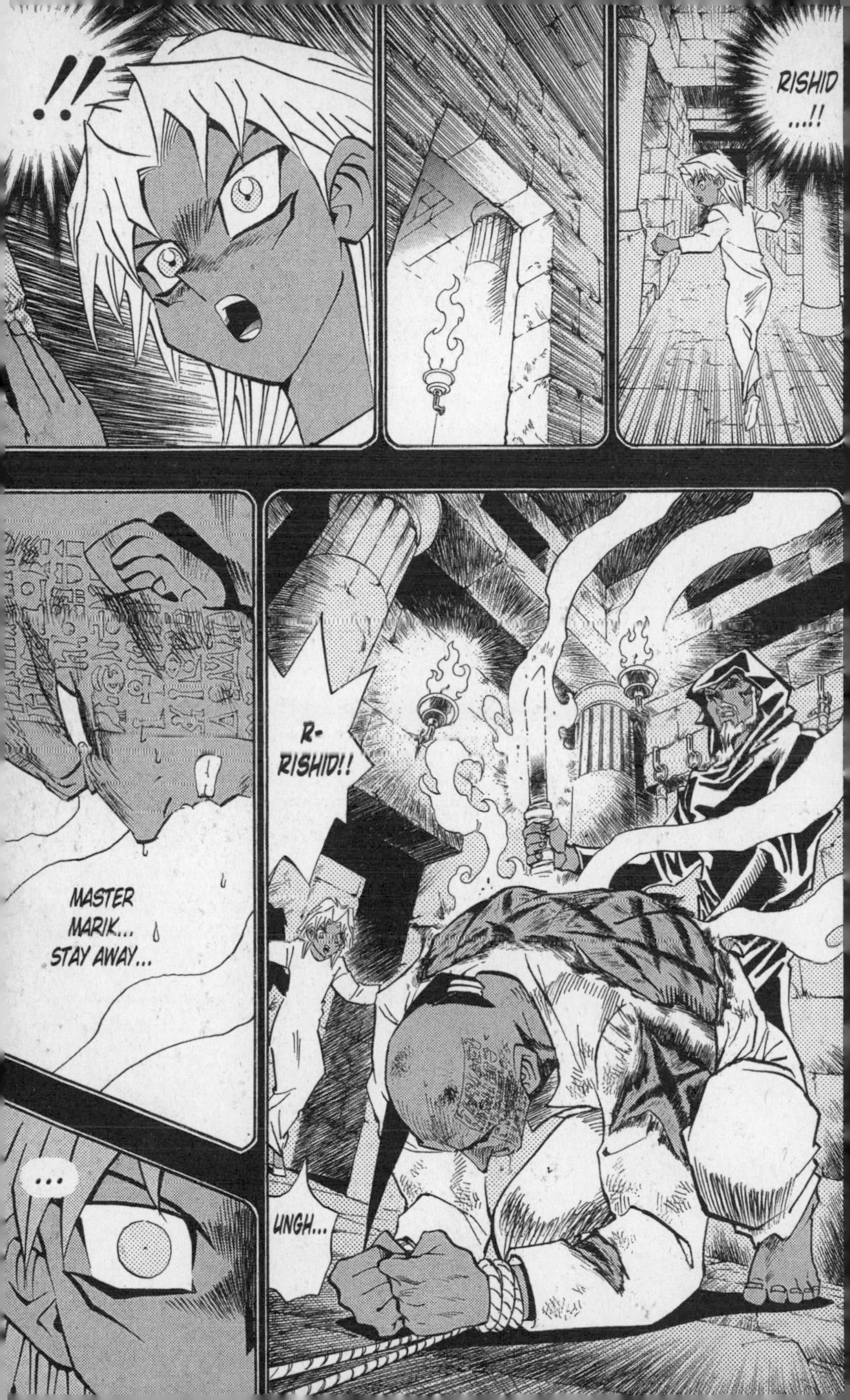
RISHID ...!!
!!
R-RISHID!!
UNGH...
MASTER MARIK... STAY AWAY...
...

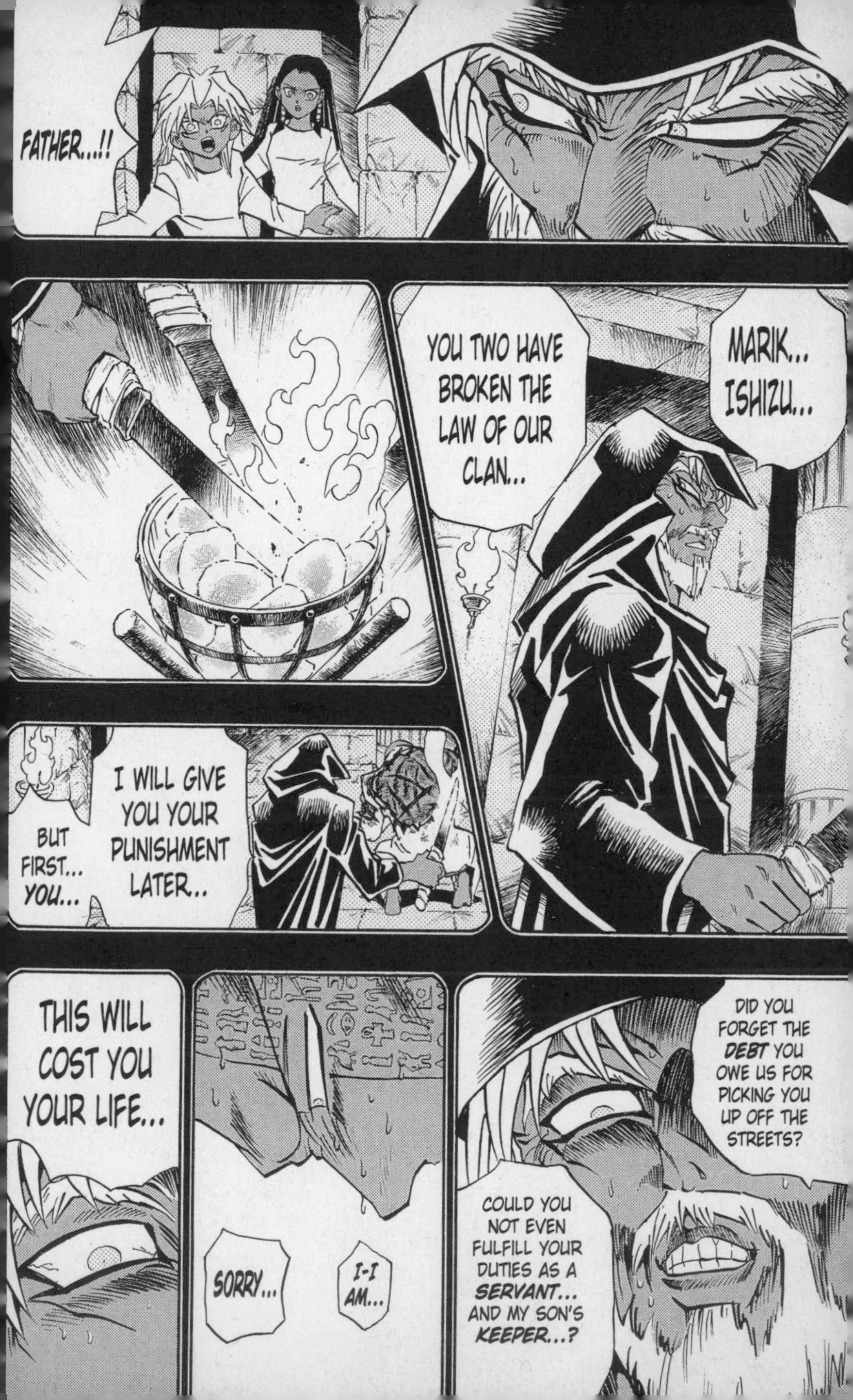
FATHER...!!
MARIK... ISHIZU...
YOU TWO HAVE BROKEN THE LAW OF OUR CLAN...
I WILL GIVE YOU YOUR PUNISHMENT LATER...
BUT FIRST... YOU...
DID YOU FORGET THE DEBT YOU OWE US FOR PICKING YOU UP OFF THE STREETS?
COULD YOU NOT EVEN FULFILL YOUR DUTIES AS A SERVANT... AND MY SON'S KEEPER...?
I-I AM...
SORRY...
THIS WILL COST YOU YOUR LIFE...

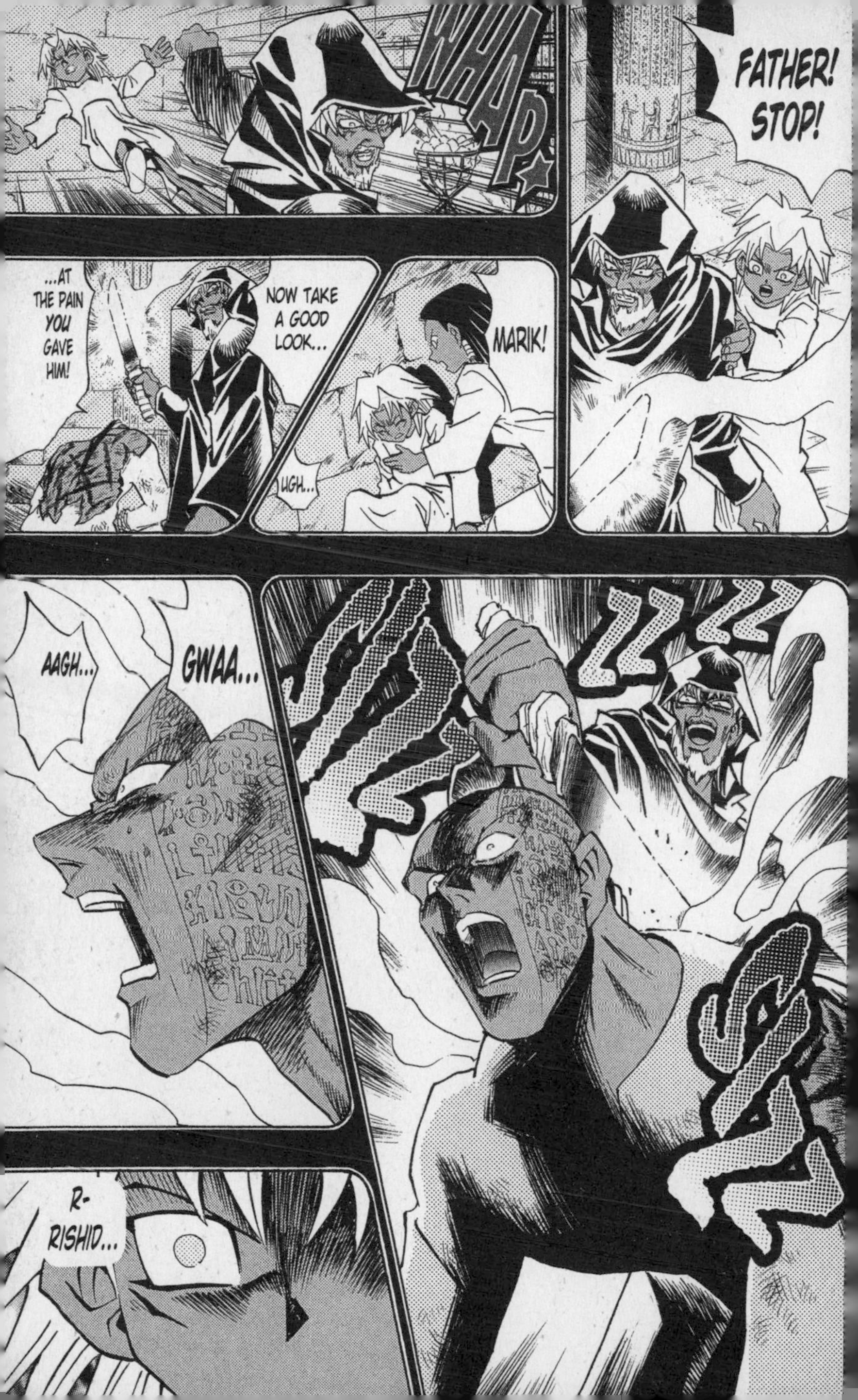
FATHER! STOP!
WHAP
MARIK!
UGH...
NOW TAKE A GOOD LOOK...
...AT THE PAIN YOU GAVE HIM!
ZZZ
GWAA...
AAGH...
R-RISHID...

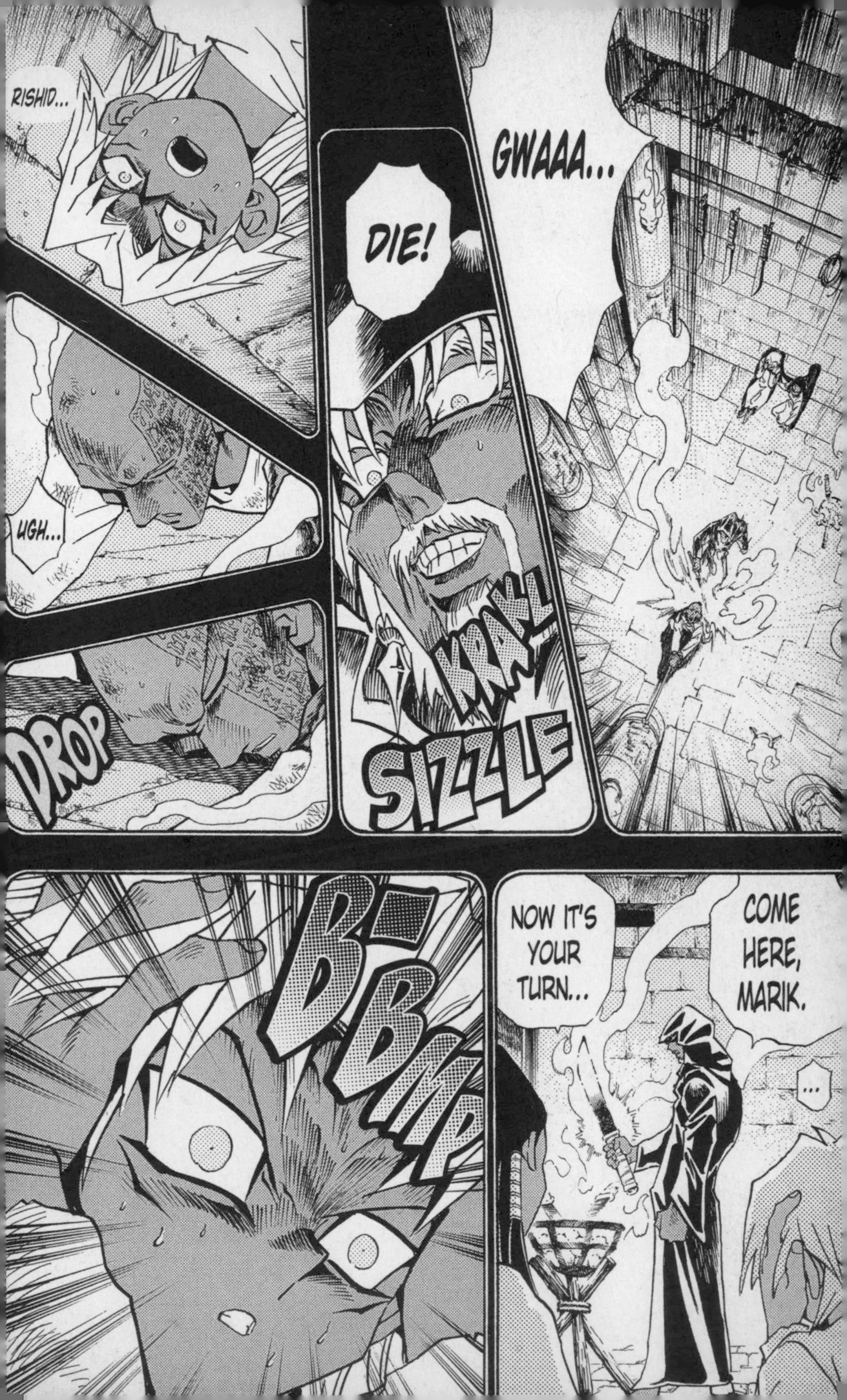
GWAAA...
DIE!
KRAK!
SIZZLE
RISHID...
UGH...
DROP
COME HERE, MARIK.
NOW IT'S YOUR TURN...
...
B-BMP

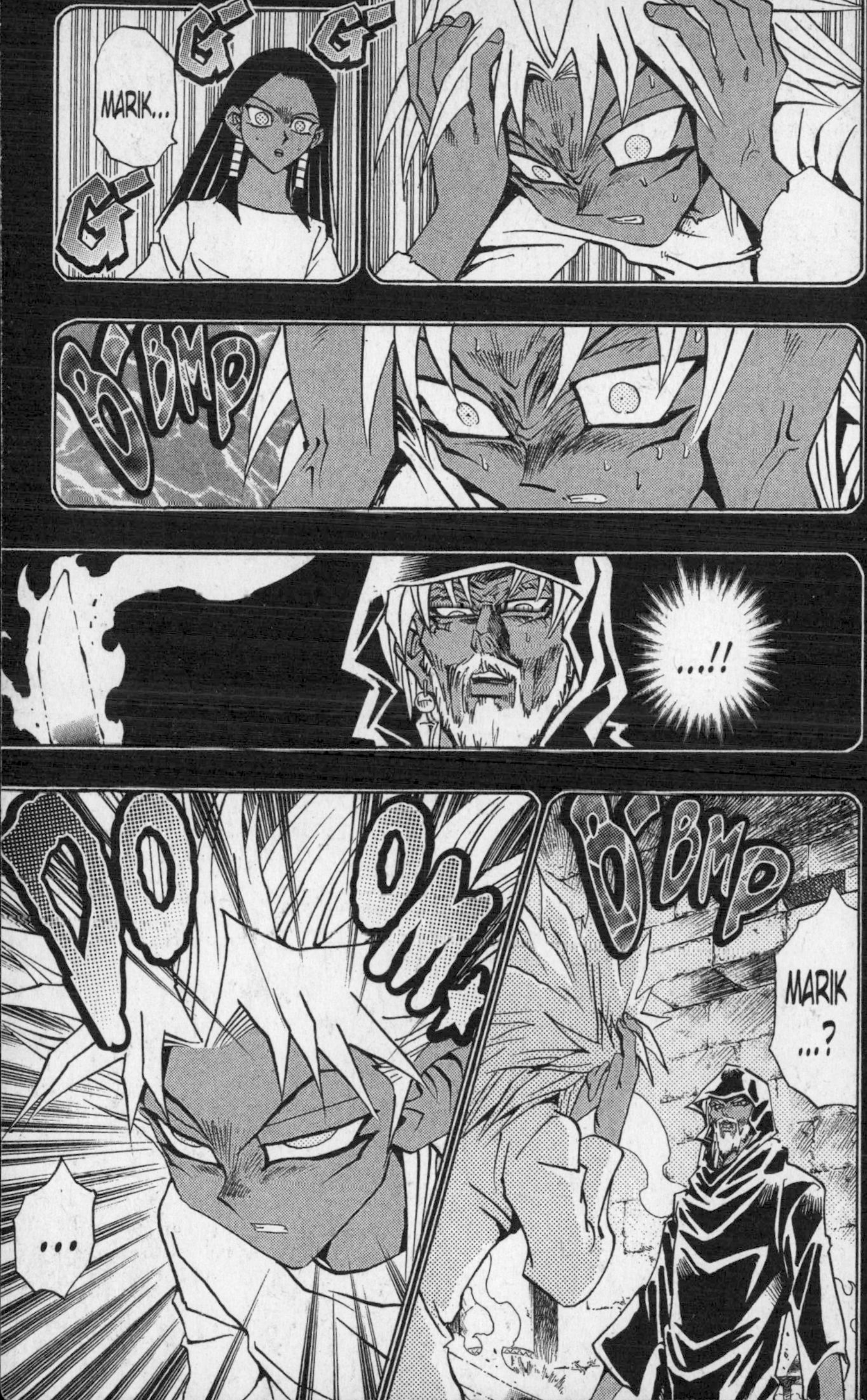
G G G
MARIK...
BDMP
...!!
BDMP
MARIK ...?
DOOM
...

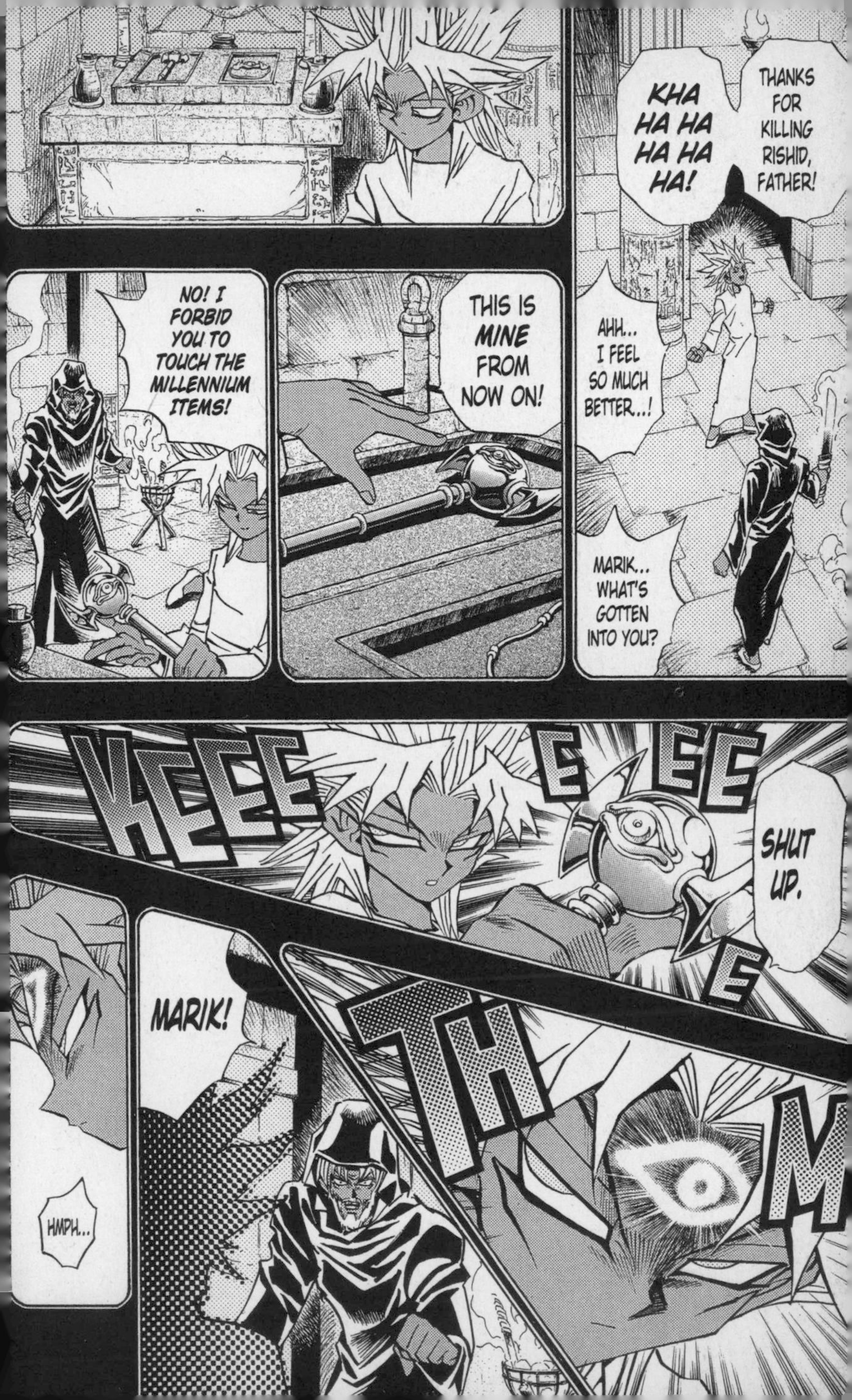
THANKS FOR KILLING RISHID, FATHER!
KHA HA HA HA HA HA!
AHH... I FEEL SO MUCH BETTER...!
MARIK... WHAT'S GOTTEN INTO YOU?
THIS IS MINE FROM NOW ON!
NO! I FORBID YOU TO TOUCH THE MILLENNIUM ITEMS!
KEEE E EE E
SHUT UP.
THM
MARIK!
HMPH...

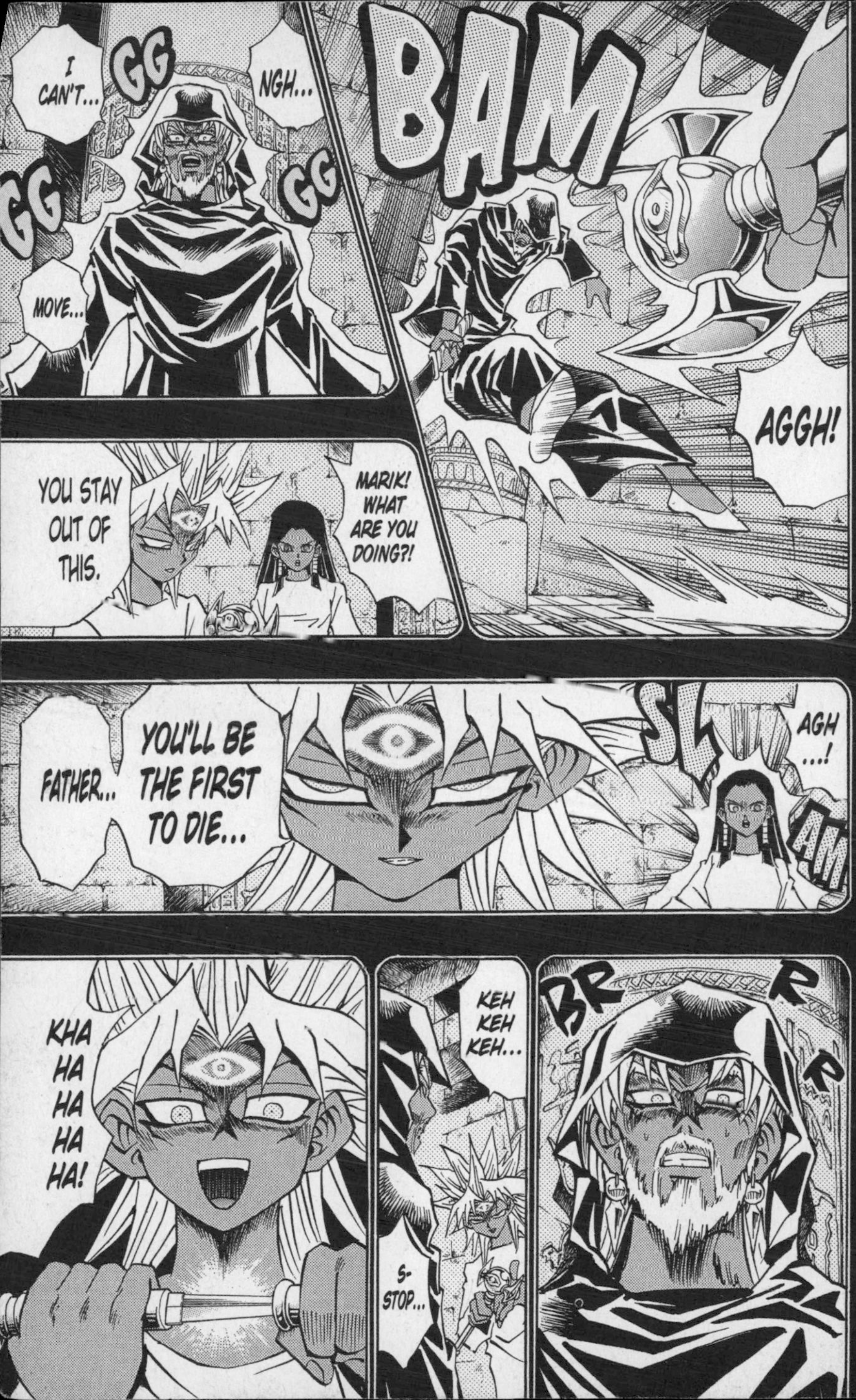
BAM
AGGH!
NGH...
GG
I CAN'T...
GG
GG
MOVE...
MARIK! WHAT ARE YOU DOING?!
YOU STAY OUT OF THIS.
AGH ...!
SL
AM
FATHER... YOU'LL BE THE FIRST TO DIE...
BR R R R
KEH KEH KEH...
S- STOP...
KHA HA HA HA HA HA!

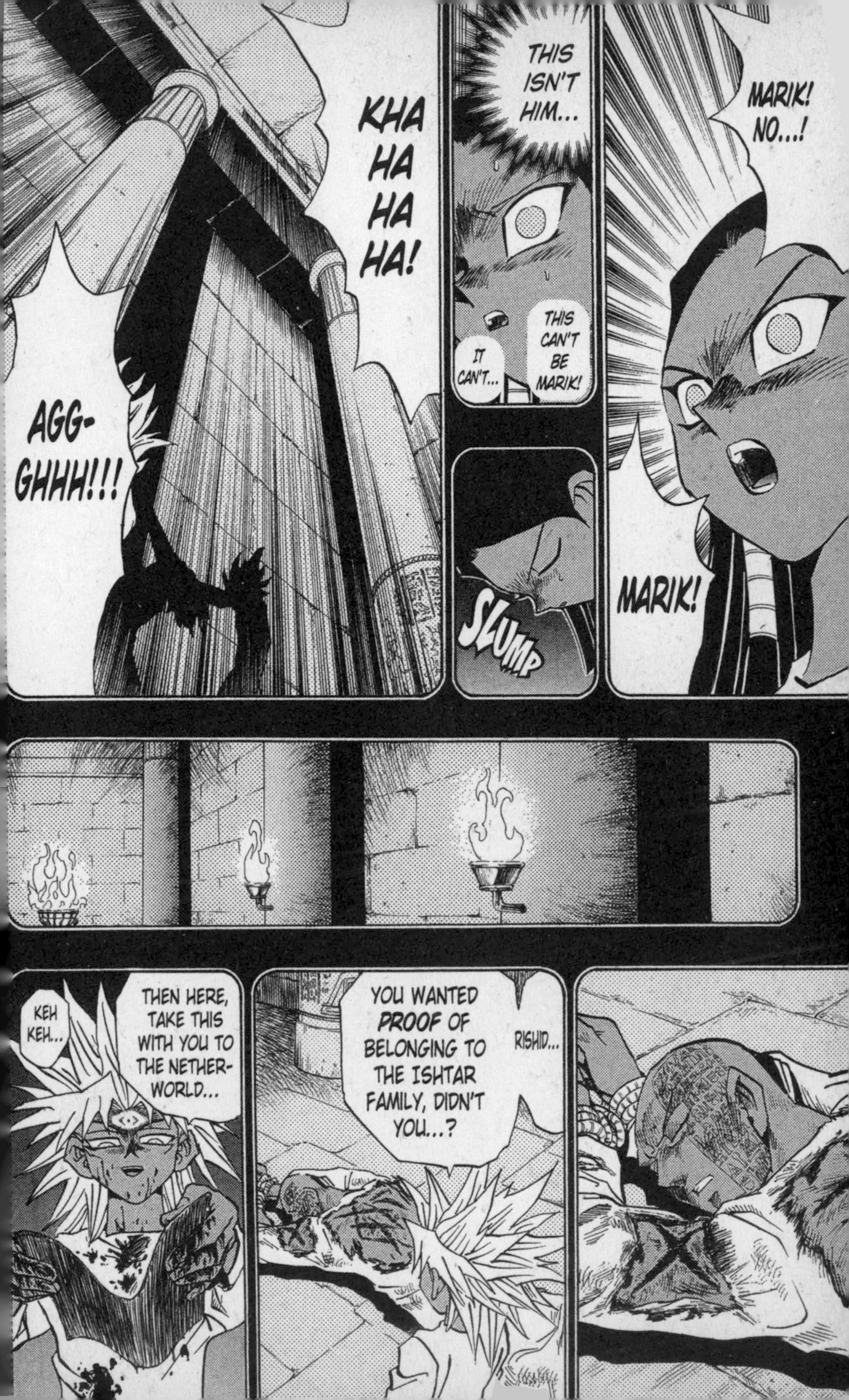
MARIK! NO...!
MARIK!
THIS ISN'T HIM...
THIS CAN'T BE MARIK!
IT CAN'T...
SLUMP
KHA HA HA HA!
AGG-GHHH!!!
RISHID...
YOU WANTED PROOF OF BELONGING TO THE ISHTAR FAMILY, DIDN'T YOU...?
THEN HERE, TAKE THIS WITH YOU TO THE NETHER-WORLD...
KEH KEH...

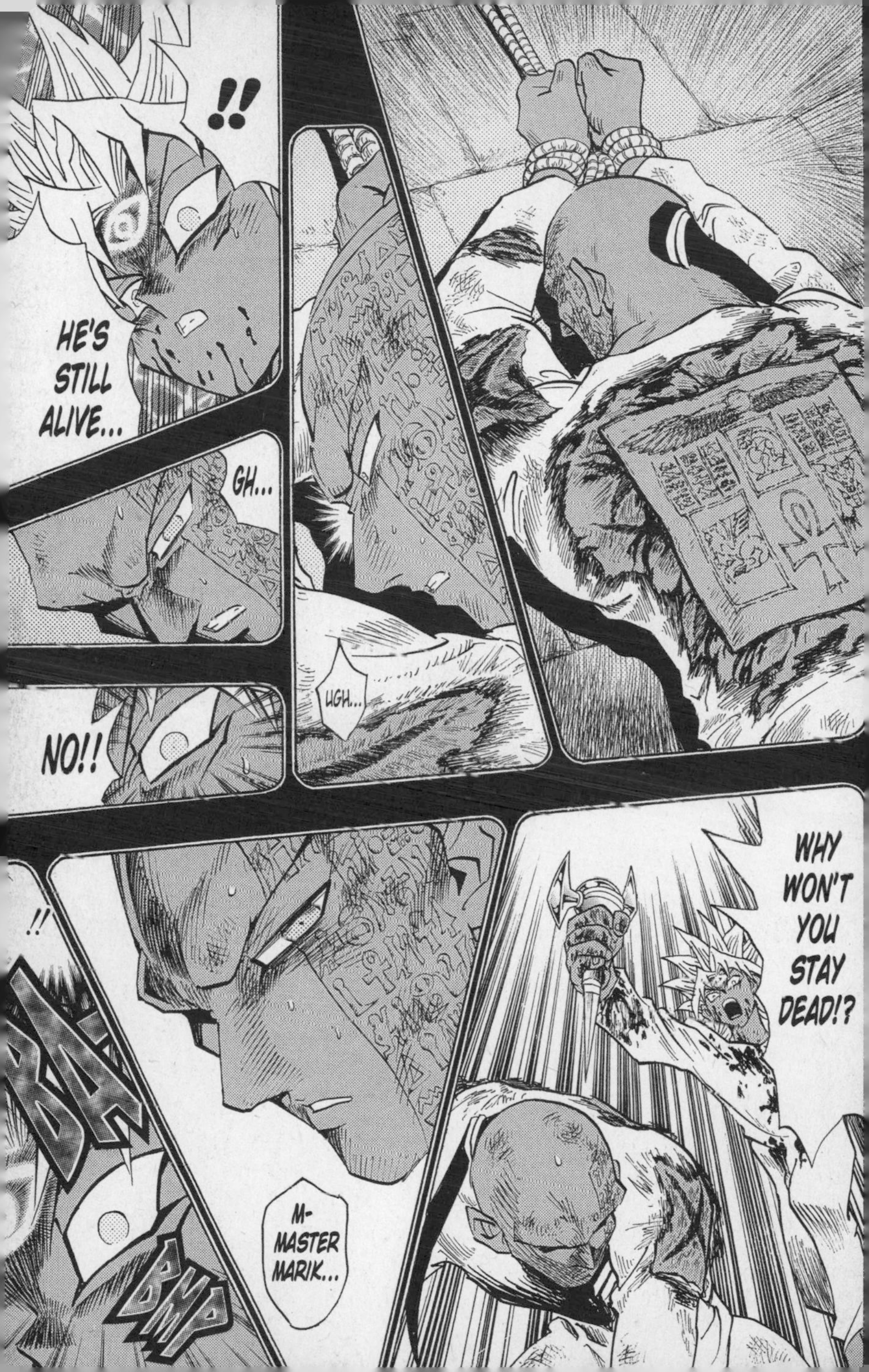
UGH...
!!
HE'S STILL ALIVE...
GH...
NO!!
WHY WON'T YOU STAY DEAD!?
M-MASTER MARIK...
!!
BA
BMP

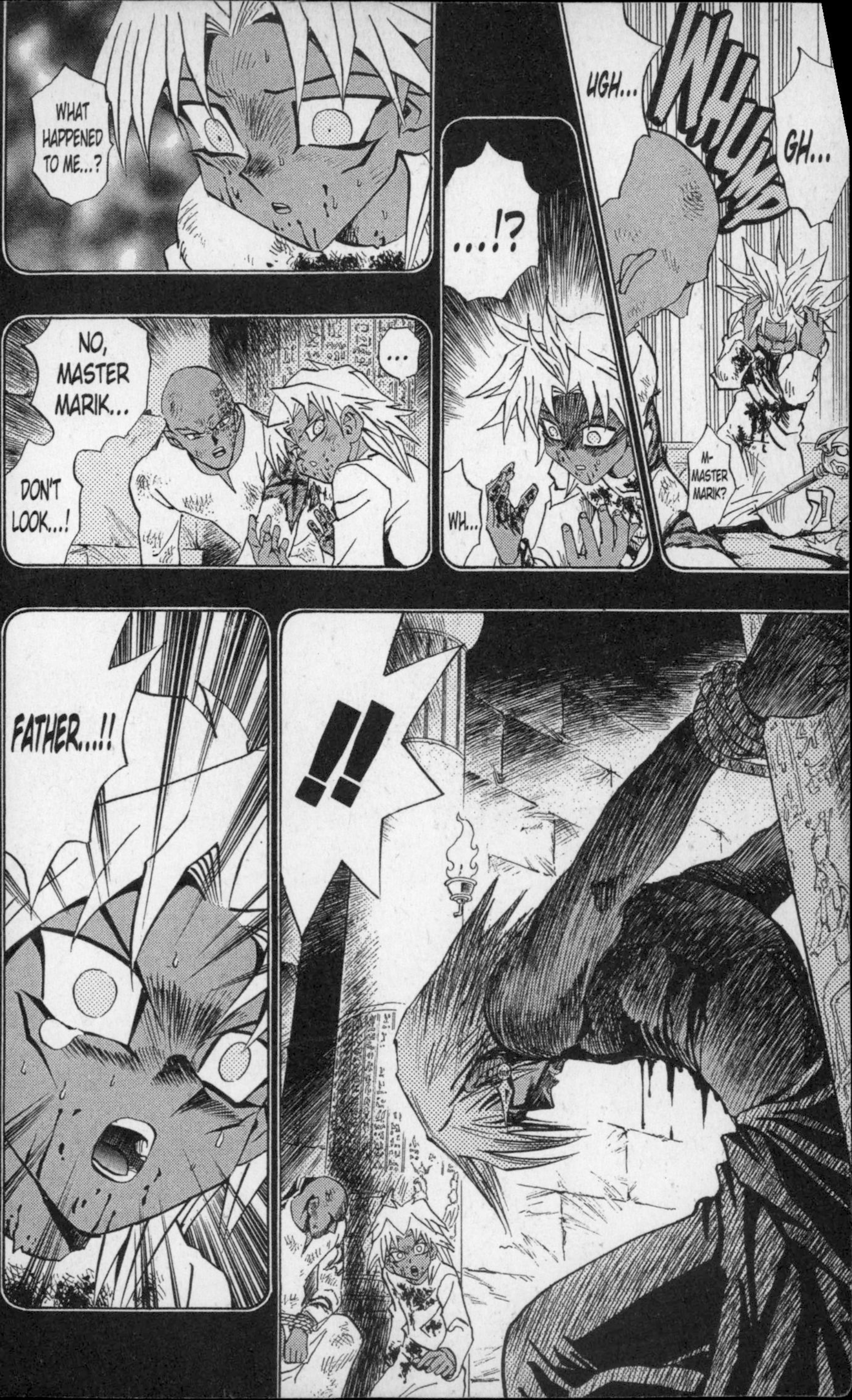
UGH...
WHUMP
GH...
M-MASTER MARIK?
...!?
WH...
WHAT HAPPENED TO ME...?
...
NO, MASTER MARIK...
DON'T LOOK...!
!!
FATHER...!!

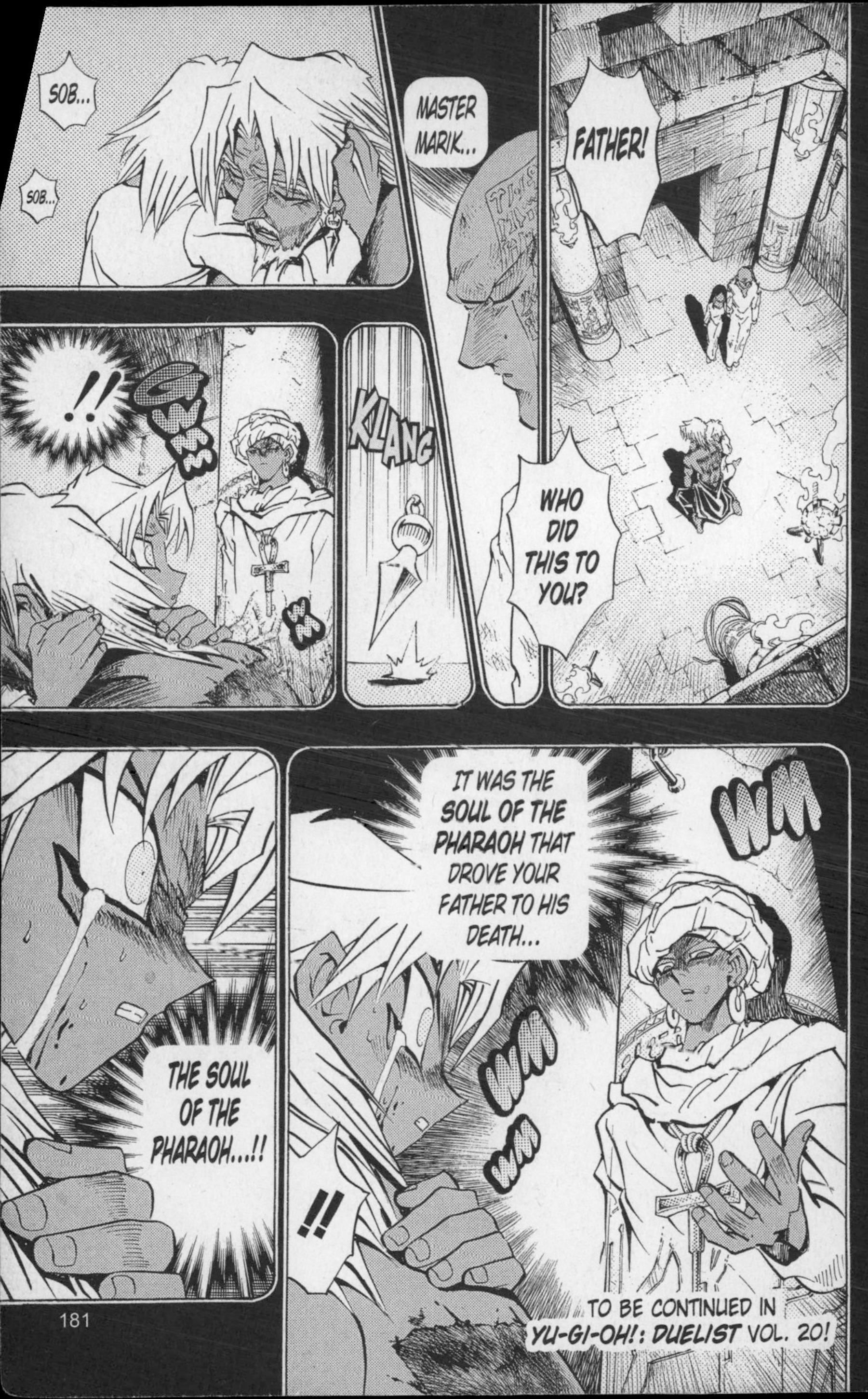
FATHER!
MASTER MARIK...
SOB...
SOB...
WHO DID THIS TO YOU?
KLANG
!!
IT WAS THE SOUL OF THE PHARAOH THAT DROVE YOUR FATHER TO HIS DEATH...
!!
THE SOUL OF THE PHARAOH...!!
TO BE CONTINUED IN YU-GI-OH!: DUELIST VOL. 20!

MASTER OF THE CARDS

The "Duel Monsters" card game first appeared in volume two of the original **Yu-Gi-Oh!** graphic novel series, but it's in **Yu-Gi-Oh!: Duelist** (originally printed in Japan as volumes 8-31 of **Yu-Gi-Oh!**) that it gets really important. As many fans know, some of the card names are different between the English and Japanese versions. In case you play the game, or you're interested in playing, here's a rundown of some of the cards in this graphic novel. Some cards only appear in the **Yu-Gi-Oh!** video games, not in the actual trading card game.

FIRST APPEARANCE IN THIS VOLUME	JAPANESE CARD NAME	ENGLISH CARD NAME
p.7	Ra no Yokushinryū (Ra the Winged God Dragon) (NOTE: The kanji for "sun god" is written beside the kanji for "Ra.")	The Sun Dragon Ra (NOTE: Called "The Winged Dragon of Ra" in the English anime and card game.)
p.8	Cyber Shock	Cyber Shock (NOTE: Not a real game card.)
p.35	Blood Vorse	Vorse Raider
p.37	Keldo	Keldo

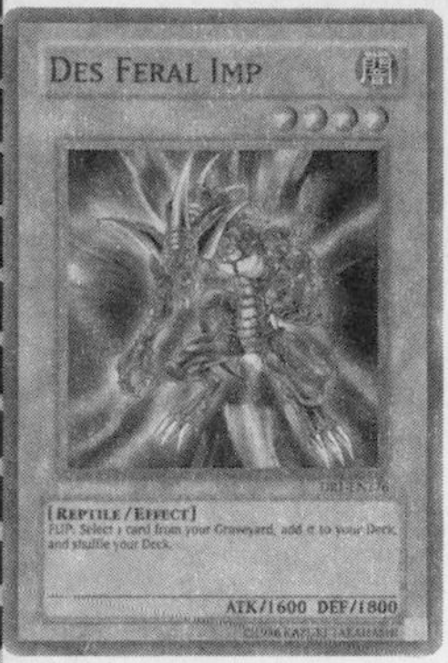
Des Feral Imp
[Reptile/Effect]
ATK/1600 DEF/1800
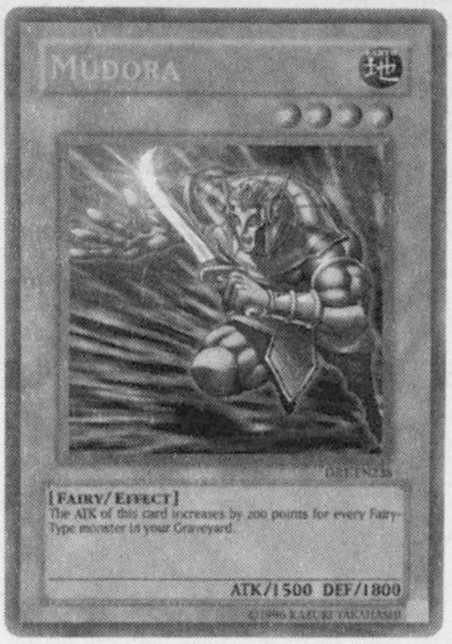
Mudora
[Fairy/Effect]
ATK/1500 DEF/1800
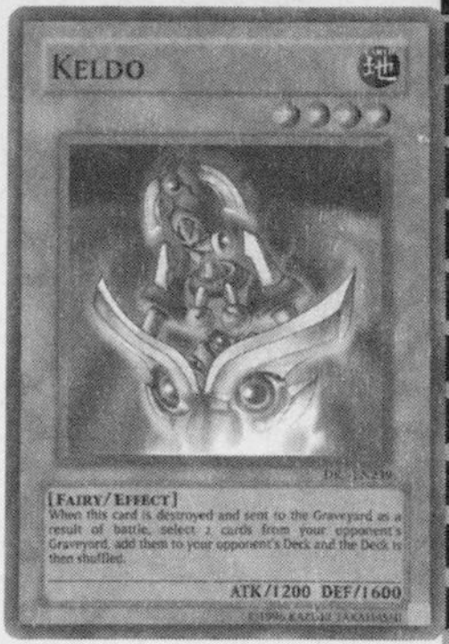
Keldo
[Fairy/Effect]
ATK/1200 DEF/1600

FIRST APPEARANCE IN THIS VOLUME	JAPANESE CARD NAME	ENGLISH CARD NAME
p.37	*Hakaana no Michizure* (Travelling Companion of the Open Grave)	Michizure of Doom
p.38	*Yûgô* (Fusion)	Polymerization
p.38	*Kaiser Glider*	Kaiser Glider
p.39	*Shisha Sosei* (Resurrection of the Dead)	Monster Reborn
p.39	*Mahô Saisei* (Magic Resuscitation)	Revival Magic
p.44	*Shûshuku* (Shrinking)	Shrink
p.44 p.51	*Shi no Deck Hakai* (Deck Destruction of Death)	Crush Card (Note: Called "Deck Devastation Virus" in the English Card game.)

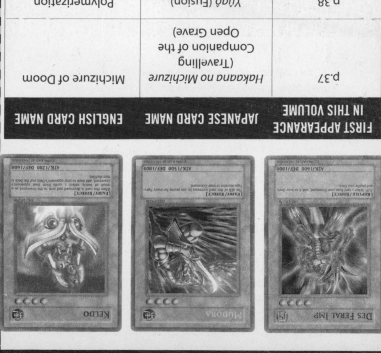

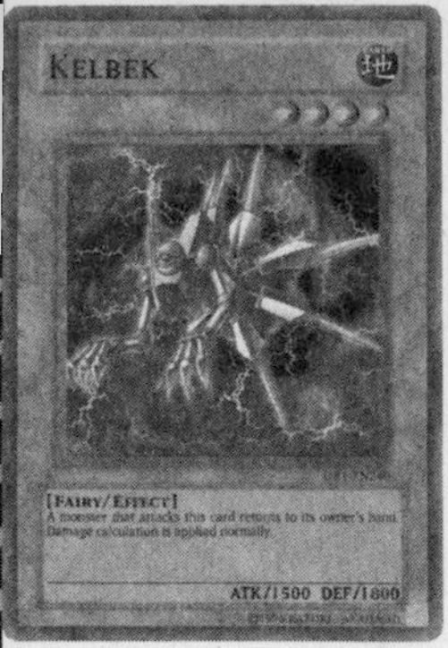
KELBEK
[FAIRY/EFFECT]
ATK/1500 DEF/1800
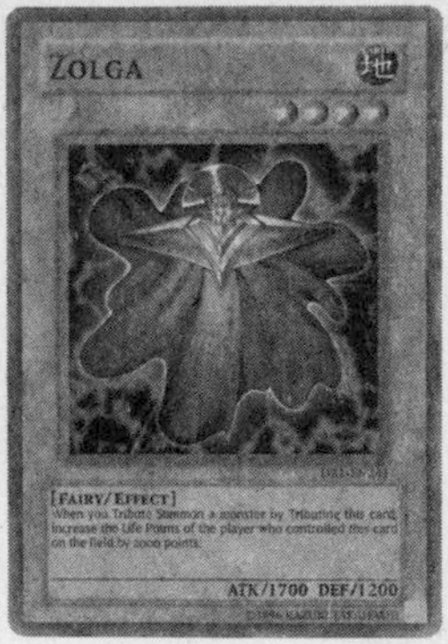
ZOLGA
[FAIRY/EFFECT]
ATK/1700 DEF/1200
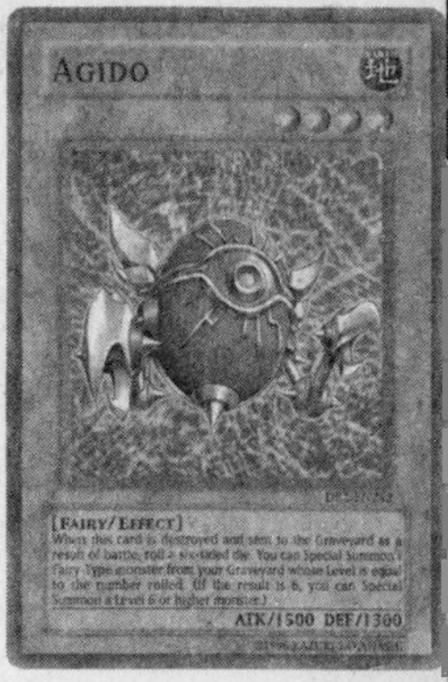
AGIDO
[FAIRY/EFFECT]
ATK/1500 DEF/1300

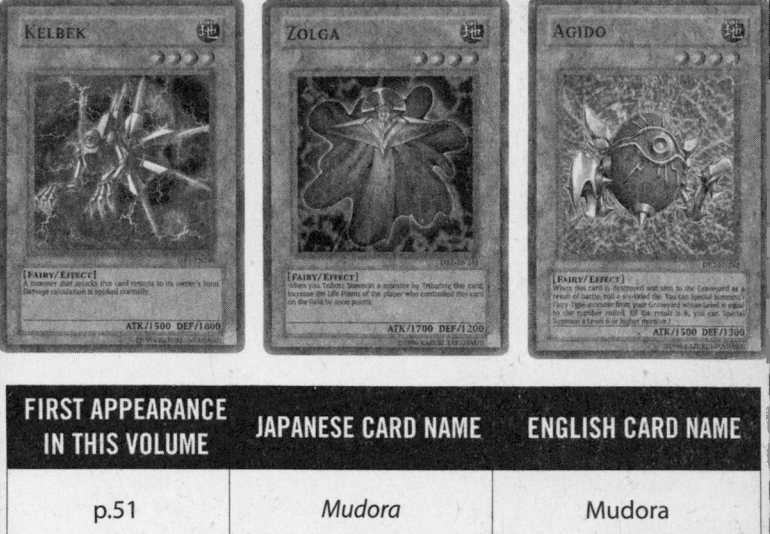

FIRST APPEARANCE IN THIS VOLUME	JAPANESE CARD NAME	ENGLISH CARD NAME
p.51	*Mudora*	Mudora
p.54	*Obelisk no Kyoshinhei* (Obelisk the Giant God Soldier)	The God of the Obelisk (NOTE: Called "Obelisk the Tormentor" in the English anime and card game.)
p.55	*Dagura no Tsurugi* (Sword of Dagura)	Sword of Dogra (NOTE: Not a real game card.)
p.59	*Mahô Jokyo Saikin Heiki* (Magic Eradicating Virus Weapon)	Virus Cannon
p.63	*Death Gremlin*	Des Feral Imp
p.67	*Cross Soul*	Soul Exchange

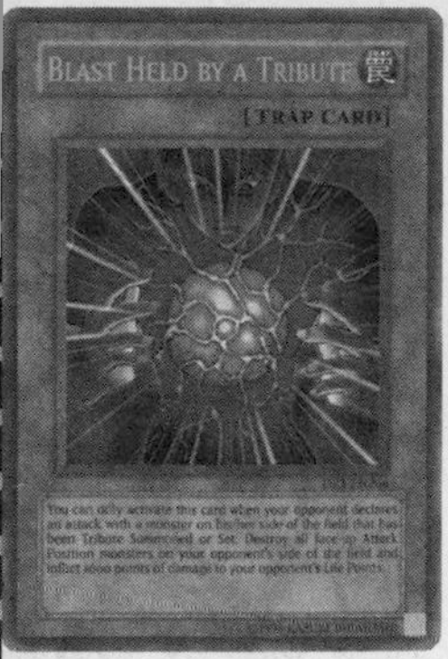
Blast Held by a Tribute
[TRAP CARD]
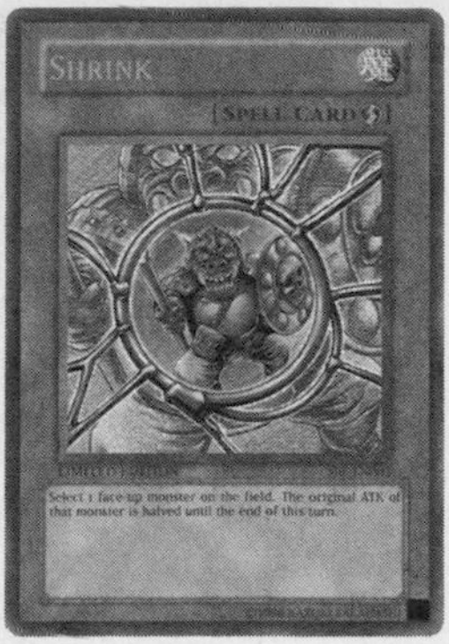
Shrink
[SPELL CARD]
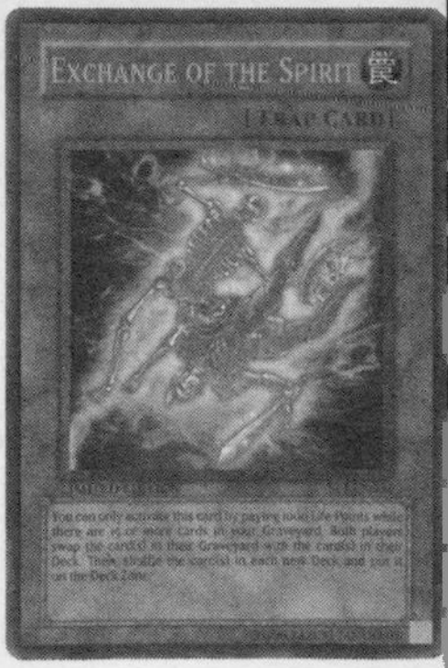
Exchange of the Spirit
[TRAP CARD]

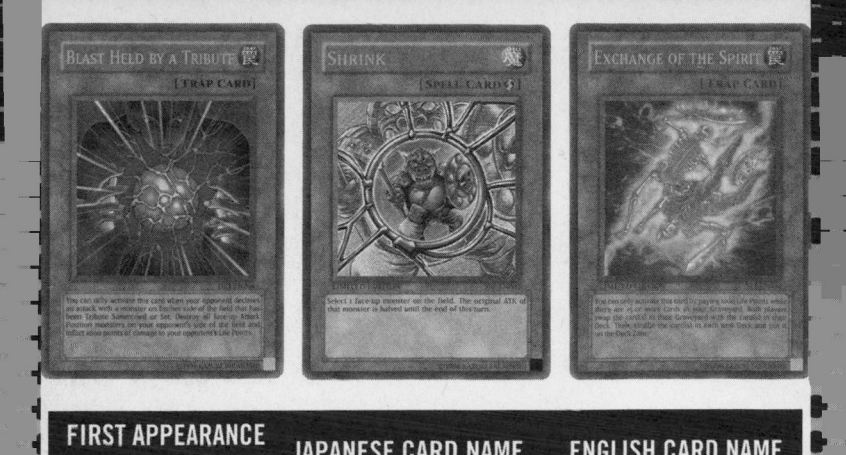

FIRST APPEARANCE IN THIS VOLUME	JAPANESE CARD NAME	ENGLISH CARD NAME
p.75	*Gense to Meikai no Gyakuten* (Reversal of the Living World and the Spirit World)	Exchange of the Spirit
p.79	*Kelbek*	Kelbek
p.80	*Mukô* (Invalidity/Nullity)	Muko (NOTE: Not a real game card.)
p.82	*Zolga*	Zolga
p.96	*Ikenie no Daku Bakudan* (Bomb Held by a Sacrificial Offering)	Blast Held by a Tribute
p.98	*Agido*	Agido
p.109	*Blue-Eyes White Dragon*	Blue-Eyes White Dragon
p.109	*Moku suru Shisha* (The Silent Dead)	Silent Doom

IN THE NEXT VOLUME...

As the airship speeds towards its mysterious destination, Bakura and Marik end their sinister alliance, and fight a vicious duel over the Millennium Rod. But who is Bakura's unexpected ally?! Meanwhile, the four semi-finalists get ready for what could be the last duels of their lives...in the final arena, the Tower of Alcatraz!

AVAILABLE NOW!

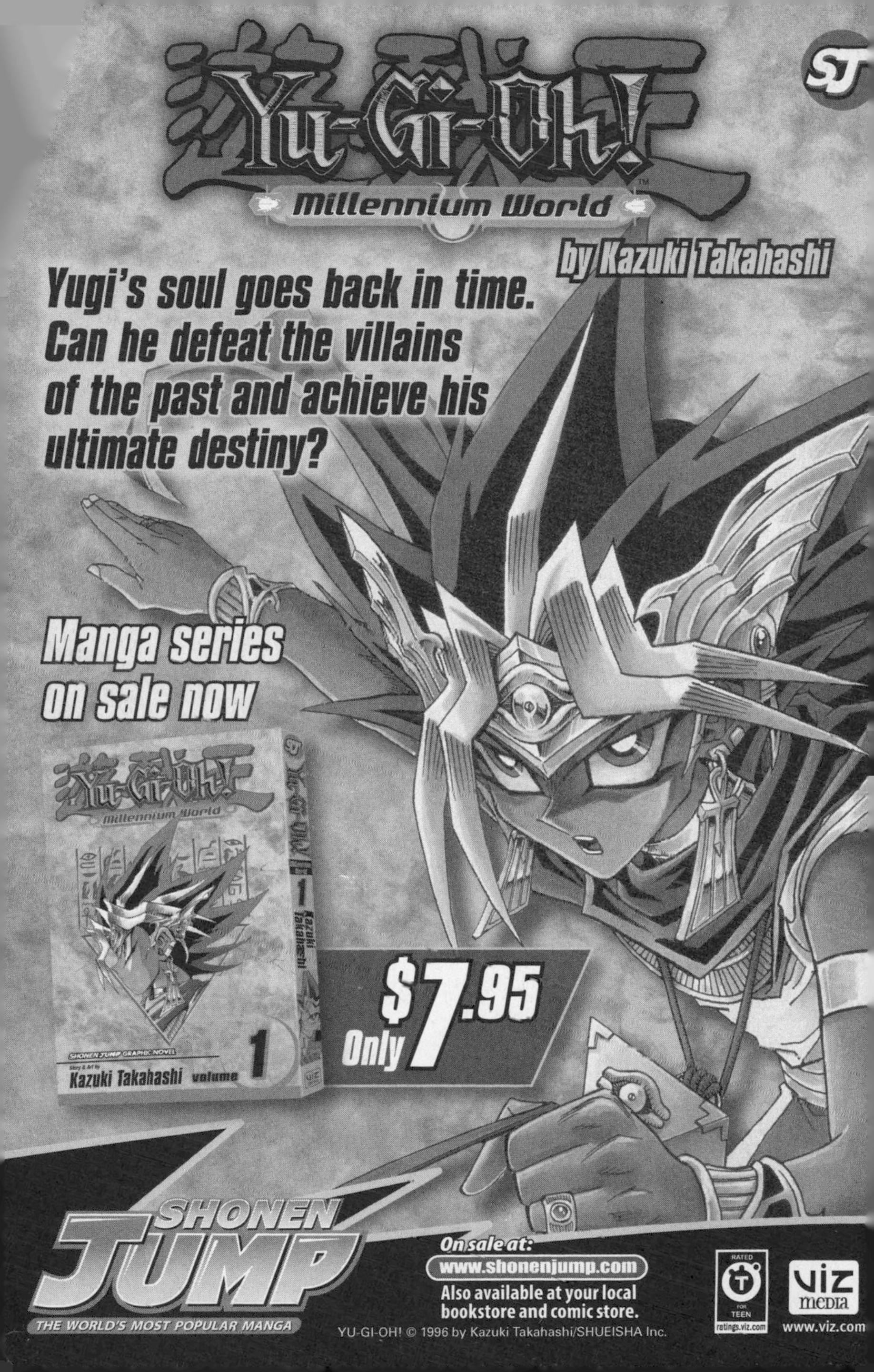

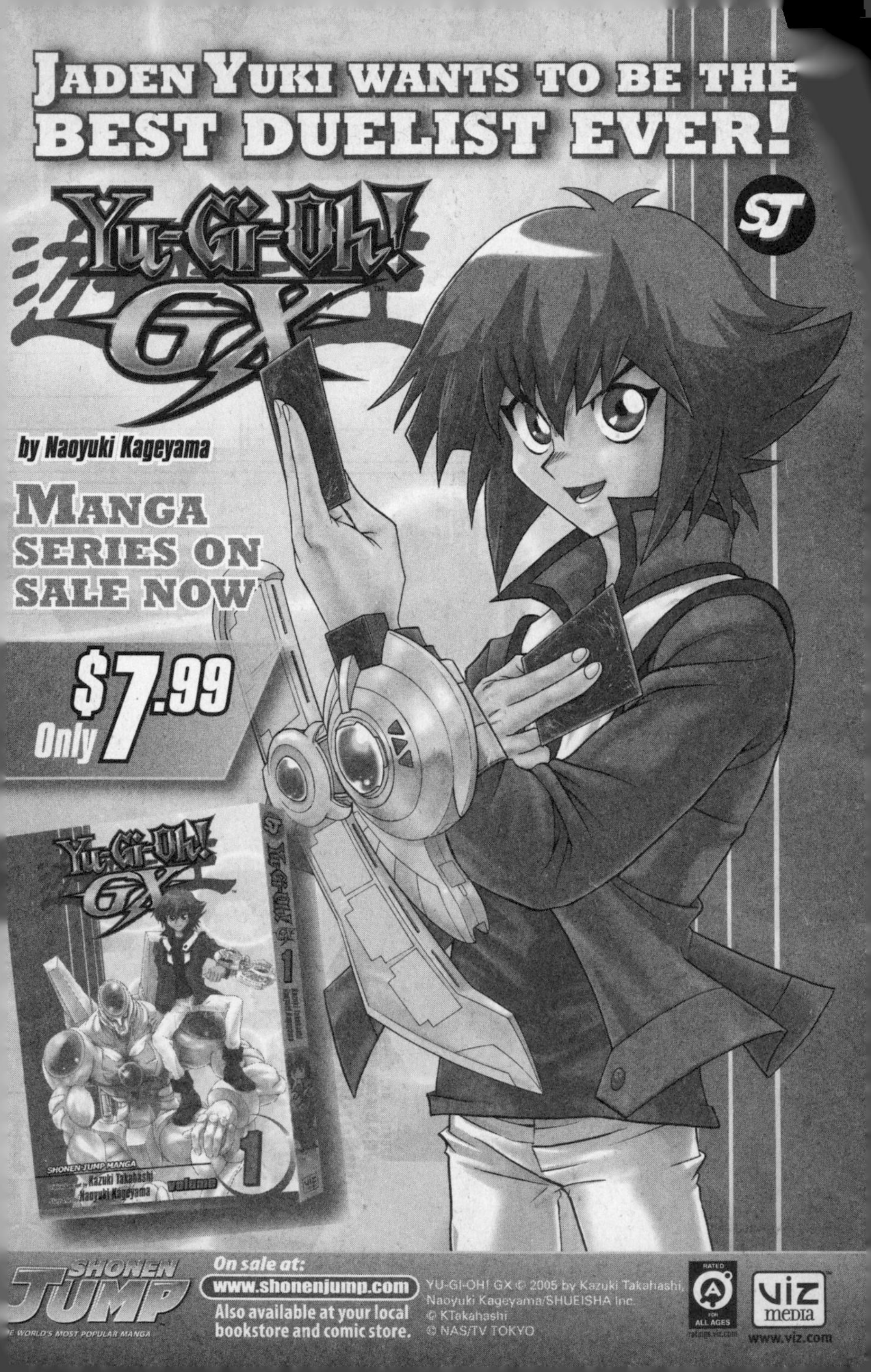

JADEN YUKI WANTS TO BE THE
BEST DUELIST EVER!
SJ
YU-GI-OH! GX
by Naoyuki Kageyama
MANGA
SERIES ON
SALE NOW
Only $7.99
YU-GI-OH! GX
SHONEN JUMP MANGA
Kazuki Takahashi
Naoyuki Kageyama
volume 1
SHONEN JUMP
THE WORLD'S MOST POPULAR MANGA
On sale at:
www.shonenjump.com
Also available at your local
bookstore and comic store.
YU-GI-OH! GX © 2005 by Kazuki Takahashi,
Naoyuki Kageyama/SHUEISHA Inc.
© KTakahashi
© NAS/TV TOKYO
RATED
FOR ALL AGES
VIZ media
www.viz.com